# TWO PRINCES
# AND A KING

## A CONCISE REVIEW OF
### THREE POLITICAL ASSASSINATIONS

C.A.A. SAVASTANO

TWO PRINCES AND A KING
A Concise Review of Three Political Assassinations

ISBN 978-0-9899674-1-9

NEAPOLIS MEDIA GROUP LLC
www.neamg.com

First Edition: January 2016

# Acknowledgements

The author wishes to thank the following individuals:

My wife, family, and friends who offered me support in times of doubt.

The Neapolis Media Group Staff and supporters, all reliable experts, critics, and authors who have contributed verified information to the record.

Your work is appreciated and vital to
discovery of all the original facts.

FOR MY FATHER

# TABLE OF CONTENTS

# MLK

# RFK

*"Hard hitting. fast read...endless facts and references. You cannot, after reading this book, feel anything but strong convictions toward political conspiracy."*

**Dr. Richard Burke**

*"A masterful journey through the three most influential political assassinations of the 1960s. Savastano presents a narrative derived directly from official documents and verifiable testimony...this book is an essential companion for any serious assassination researcher."*

**Rob Clark**
**Researcher and Host of The Lone Gunman Podcast**

*Carmine, in his new book entitled, "Two Princes and a King" has covered the assassinations of three important figures in the turbulent 1960s in the US, namely that of JFK, RFK and MLK. He covers each assassination extremely well and in a very easy to read and digestible manner. Carmine breaks down each assassination into specific and logical subsections, allowing the reader to follow each tragic event by the presentation of the published materials from various investigations. The reader can therefore weigh up the overall evidence in order to make up, in their own mind, who the likely perpetrators were in each of these heinous crimes that forever changed American and world history.*

*I thoroughly enjoyed this fresh approach and it provided me with a basis of continuing my research and reading into various aspects of the cases. What I found interesting were that the same names and organizations came up time and time again in each of the three assassinations. For those of us who have been researching these assassinations, it came as no real surprise. Carmine has presented this vast amount of knowledge and information in a timely and succinct manner.*

*Whether you are a new researcher to these cases or just wanting to read the critical facts, Carmine's book will serve you well. One hopes that in time, the real perpetrators, "the men holding the strings" will be finally ousted and exposed for the horrendous effects that these assassinations have caused, and continue to cause, to the world.*

*A thoroughly well presented, researched and fresh approach, without overwhelming the reader with unnecessary minutia and detail, yet provides and invites the reader to extend the research if so desired. A job well done, Carmine.*

**Dr Antonio Fratini**
**School of Molecular and Biomedical Science**

*In Carmine Savastano's book, "Two Princes and a King" he writes, "Some people collect stamps and art, Hoover collected dangerous secrets." Savastano expounds upon this observation of J. Edgar Hoover by interweaving Hoover's culpability in his role in the investigations of the assassinations of JFK, RFK and Martin Luther King. If you're interested in the many shadings of these three major events in U.S. history, you will appreciate Savastano's approach to covering these events with well-documented facts through his usage of painstaking research and insight into the elements of all three horrific deaths.*

*Savastano offers the reader of "Two Princes and a King" insight into the three most important assassinations in modern American history using logic, research and well-documented sources.*

**Gayle Nix Jackson**
**Author—Orville Nix: The Missing JFK Assassination Film**

"*Carmine has performed a great service by providing a broad view of the potential suspects in the political assassinations of the 1960's, while at the same time dealing with a host of conspiracy related mysteries and urban legends that have actually been resolved over time. In doing so, he makes use of the most contemporary documentary evidence and research, kudos to him for tackling the myths along with the conspiracies.*"

**Larry Hancock**
**Historian and author of Someone Would Have Talked and Nexus: The CIA and Political Assassination**

"*In the new book Two Princes and a King, Carmine Savastano has taken aim at a plethora of myths surrounding the deaths of MLK, RFK, and JFK. What separates this work from many others is the primary source documentation that shatters many of these myths, while bringing forward factually proven truths surrounding the deaths of these three men. Beginning researchers will save themselves a lot of time by starting here, and veteran researchers will love the doors shutting closed tightly on the false mythology of these cases while new doors open for continued research! This is a must read for all of the research community.*"

**Matthew Scheufele**
**Educator and Historian**

# PROLOGUE

For some the word conspiracy holds a near mythological status in America. It became a term for uncomfortable ideas that conspiracy critics and government officials disdain. Crazies, scavengers, government obsessed, liars, and profiteers in tin foil hats. These insults follow some who suggest a modern American plot. Great skepticism is reasonable, yet only a biased view dismisses all contending evidence without some consideration.

Minor conspiracies occur with unfortunate regularity in the United States legal system. Criminal conspiracies are often a part the various charges suspects face. However, these minor conspiracies are not the kind discussed in this book. While they are similar in nature, their scope is usually highly limited and it does not create societal damage of such enduring prominence.

Some books claim to possess every definite answer regarding these events and this book does not. Reviewing every aspect of these historic quandaries has yet to be achieved. No single book, picture, nor expert, without substantial evidence, can offer all the definite answers. This is noteworthy.

Some people will disavow any contending evidence that disturbs their presumptions. They have a disdain for continued inquiry and declassified evidence unavailable to prior investigations. There is no expiration date on new evidence. Reasonable inquiry demands the use of all verified facts, despite what they infer. We must all be willing to refine our views based on proof and retain an open mind but critical eye.

This book reviews three possible "Assassination Conspiracies", defined as the ambush and murder of a political figure to attain profit or advance criminal goals. This includes subsequent unlawful attempts to suppress the truth. These covert acts feasibly profited some involved by damaging the American democratic process. With respectful study and discussion, we can hope to prevent their recurrence.

Modern financial and political conspiracies perpetrated in our time are just the latest. Many in the moment seek to better themselves at the expense of others. Violence is an eternally powerful force within the American experience. Yet if American citizens are willing to pursue it, so is justice.

# JFK

# CHAPTER 1

*"Other sins only speak; murder shrieks out."*

~John Webster
English Playwright

## REASONS FOR THE ASSASSINATION CONSPIRACY

Most inquiries regarding the Kennedy brothers and Martin Luther King Jr. offer a wide range of key figures. Some attempt the entire case of John Fitzgerald Kennedy, Robert Francis Kennedy, or Martin Luther King Jr. Rarely does anyone review all three because of the wide range of evidence and speculation that have nearly merged in some instances. However, it remains possible to verify evidence in these cases.

This review offers strong evidentiary connections to resolve lingering inconsistencies. It uses government reports, declassified official secrets, media, and witness testimony, all inspected with the immeasurable benefit of previous investigations and hindsight. However, it remains daunting to observe the endless pages of information, web resources, interviews, and legal papers. These subjects take years to learn and reasonably understand. Ideally, this book will save you some time and provide the means to observe some important evidence yourself.

An immense body of information exists that is both factual and delusional. Set aside are the famous yet unproven speculations. However, based on the majority of evidence, a handful of men possessed murderous will and intent. Some had motive, means, and opportunity to murder the President of the United States.

Many people discussed within this text have died. A few parties connected still wield power or have faded into obscurity. The truth becomes clearer as the decades have passed. No one could account for the witnesses, television productions, books, laws, and technology available during the Information Age. All were unaware technological advancement would defy the plots feasible creators.

John F. Kennedy was, in my estimation, a victim in the first of three possible modern assassination conspiracies. The President was a target for multiple reasons. President Kennedy attempted to curb industrial and military influences. The Kennedy administration's tax policies and their international programs defied the Military-Industrial Complex. President Dwight Eisenhower, a former general, had previously warned America of this association.[i] These actions resulted in various wealthy powerful men and official leaders despising him.

Kennedy publicly supported the Justice Department's war on the Mafia. For nearly three decades, J. Edgar Hoover denied the Underworld's power and existence. Peace was not profitable to some interests, and the Kennedys changed the American political landscape. When the Kennedy political machine gained power, the possible "Conspirators" political influence and profits suffered.

Greed and fear are relevant possible motives for the death and lies occurring. The alleged Conspirators had an unending desire for greater power, wealth, and control. Among those suspected is the fearful political fringe. Some publicly attacked John F. Kennedy's constitutional belief in the division of church and state.

"I believe no religion should receive political preference nor any money from the Federal government. I believe in the separation of Church and State is absolute. I believe America is neither Catholic, Protestant, nor Jewish".[ii] Some might say this speech was to disarm the public and set aside the fears about a Catholic president.

Admittedly, this might have influenced John F. Kennedy's reasoning. Yet President Kennedy's public agenda displays proof he was no servant of the church, or any other religious movement. His enemies tried to paint him a Godless liberal and later twisted his words. Some critics have additionally attempted to label John F. Kennedy devoid of American values.

Previous modern attacks emerged from defeated presidential candidate Rick Santorum. This evoked a hatred possessed within Santorum's fringe supporters for President Kennedy and his constitutionally protected speech.

It has been generations since any American president has repeated this honest distinction publicly. Most officials ignore the honored American separation of church and state for their religious preference.

John F. Kennedy also supported black Americans' effort to attain civil rights. Whether this action was political or morally inspired remains contended. However, the Kennedys endured the hatred of wealthy prejudiced groups. Fringe associations also launched repeated media attacks targeting them. These media attacks labeled President Kennedy a traitor, liar, and Communist.

Reviewing the major criminal, government, and financial operatives of that period reveals associations. Those who had shared beliefs and interests possibly formed groups. Some individuals greatly benefited from John F. Kennedy's demise. A few had resources, influence, and the desire to kill a President of the United States.

If elected leaders are not safe, the Republic itself cannot be secure. With political murder, the American people and their representatives become irrelevant. Instead of emotional speculation, we must soberly examine the facts. Only making informed decisions, not attacking the Bill of Rights, is freedom and security achieved.

We can avoid the recurrence of history through investigation of all the evidence. Some who claim to have solved this matter are deluded because officially it remains an open homicide. The public was deceived; it must persist in seeking the truth. Some are content to offer mere speculative criticism.

A majority of the presented evidence are official documents. Additional substantiation comes from verified facts, examination of original witness testimony, and media reports. Time provides clearer information and rays of truth have pierced the immense fog of deception blanketing this subject. Speculation remains present within documents supporting and denying the Kennedy assassination conspiracy.

This is a critical review not intended to injure or defame any individual alive or dead. It is merely a reasonable assessment of evidence to answer lingering doubts that remain. These questions have plagued the American conscience and deeply influenced the culture from academic study to entertainment. A fresh review of the facts is essential.

# THE OSWALD QUESTION

Lee Harvey Oswald's final year in the United States Marines was 1959. Among his acquaintances in that year was John Donovan, the officer in command of Oswald's radar crew. Donovan is a former employee of the Federal Bureau of Investigation.[iii] During Commission testimony Donovan stated, "he was not sloppy...I found him competent in all functions...he subscribed to a Russia newspaper...was interested in learning Russian...in some respects he was probably better informed than most people in the Marine Corps, namely, on international affairs." This is not the seeming underachiever many believe Oswald to be. "...I never heard him in any way, shape, or form confess that he was a Communist, or that he ever thought about being a Communist."[iv] Oswald's committed Marxist views are perhaps not as overwhelming as officials imagine.

Oswald subsequently defects to Russia during the fall of 1959; yet the authorities do not revoke his citizenship. Oswald remains a citizen of the United States despite his location. Oswald chooses Helsinki, Finland to begin the process. This is notable because it requires improbable luck or knowledge of intelligence matters from official sources. The Central Intelligence Agency was aware that Finnish authorities were focusing on Soviet, not American or English espionage in the area.[v] He appeared within local Dallas newspapers following his successful defection.

Oswald's wife is the subject of extensive legal wrangling by officials. Officials deny her request for immigration, despite alternate official recommendations for a waiver. The Department of State suggests Marina Oswald be informed to obtain a visa from a different country to circumvent the legal sanction. It took a special pleading by the State Department to convince the Immigration and Naturalization Service to reverse the initial decision.[vi] Subsequently, officials reverse their decisions, despite Marina not qualifying for immigration status according to regular policies.[vii] Mrs. Oswald, the Russian immigrant wife of a defector receives her visa on May 24, 1962, the same day she applied.[viii]

Lee Harvey Oswald, the previous Russian defector returns to America with a new family. The confirmed traitor receives a loan from the American State Department, despite official requirements of "loyalty to the United States Government".[ix] He was not arrested and held various jobs and raised a family. Could the Central Intelligence Agency have been ignorant after they debriefed Oswald when he returned to America?[x]

Federal Bureau of Investigation Agent John Fain interviewed Oswald in August of 1962. Oswald told Fain that he did not enjoy his time in the United States Marines, nor his time in the Soviet Union. Two confidential Bureau informants affirm Oswald has no connection to local Texas Communist groups.[xi] Without any proven link to Communism or Marxist groups, a serious problem exists with the lack of a consistent demonstrable motive.

Consider now that Oswald was disorganized enough to have passed out incriminating photographs of a traceable weapon. Oswald wrote a letter to family, criticized the United States, and made empty threats. Oswald passed out leaflets supporting Cuba publicly, yet he attempted to engage notable anti-Castro groups.

In New Orleans, Lee Harvey Oswald faced arrest for disturbing the peace. His obvious public attempts to label himself a Communist largely succeed. Oswald made radio and television appearances claiming to be a Marxist, and gave a speech regarding Marxism as well. Yet he displays little actual understanding of the political changes in Russia and a seemingly archaic version of Marxism. Authorities ignore Oswald's many unbelievable actions.

These actions were similar to a Federal Bureau of Investigation spy that infiltrated the Communist Party for years. Revealed subsequent to Oswald's death is middle-aged homemaker and undercover Bureau agent Ms. Elsie Piper. She informed the Bureau of Communist activities for over a decade and testified at one hearing of the Subversive Activities Control Board. Ms. Piper was able to convince her family, friends, and the public she was a Communist. She participated and gained a leading position in the Communist Party. This intricate plot was undertaken at the behest of the Bureau.[xii]

If Oswald was a government informant, it made perfect sense to ignore him. Oswald's provocative actions generated public confusion and general anger. Perhaps he infiltrated Communist groups in the Soviet Union. This Communist Oswald presents a thin veneer over the alleged dupe later revealed. Officially, during a November afternoon, Oswald creates a sniper's nest, fires three shots, allegedly doing so without any verifiable firing practice.

Oswald's subsequent capture occurred following the murder of President Kennedy and a Dallas Police officer. Unlike someone with survival instincts, Oswald did not flee. He decided instead to watch a movie and went to a theatre near the crime scenes. Could Oswald arrange these crimes, yet be so foolish?

Alternatively, Lee Harvey Oswald conceivably had orders, resources, and unknown collaborators. President Kennedy's assassination was possibly the work of multiple conspirators. Anything more than a lone gunman and his rifle defines a conspiracy. Other possibilities are far less probable but more widely known and discussed.

The "Grand Conspiracy theory" claiming fifty, one hundred, or more people undertook a presidential assassination remains false. Those convinced the Lone Gunman Theory can discredit all others cite the Grand Conspiracy theory. This idea remains too large to be a single plan accounting for the possible case variations. Some do the facts injustice and claim the possible conspiracy is a huge construct. Too many mistakes are possible. Too many opportunities for later exposure exist.

Perhaps a rogue intelligence, military, and criminal leader utilized a few small redundant groups. These groups are the "Arms of the Conspiracy". Each group possessed its own agenda. Each had limited members known to a select few. Just the alleged Conspirators fully comprehended the plan.

The Arms feasibly delivered faceless orders to clandestine agents who followed them without question. Within military circles, disobeying orders is an eminent failure. This might result in dishonor or death before a military tribunal. In criminal circles, disobedience earns a horrible demise.

Small groups feasibly shared a unified intention. Others involved were under unrelated orders from the Central Intelligence Agency and Federal Bureau of Investigation to suppress evidence. Mafia under-bosses, soldiers, and subordinate members of related groups failed to comprehend the ultimate result. Nearly all involved feasibly served without knowledge of the Conspirators plans.

Historically multiple security threats endangered President Kennedy. One feasible threat may have influenced the Kennedy administration to cancel the President's appearance in Chicago weeks prior to the Dallas trip. This prior threat remains unconsidered within some reviews. This includes the President's (Warren) Commission review.[xiii]

When reviewing past media ridicule concerning most conspiracy statements, honest discussion rarely occurs in public. Disregarded are credible witnesses involved who affirmed a deadly plot. One dismissed aspect refers to mysterious deaths surrounding the event's periphery. However, only a handful of witnesses suffered violent and improbable deaths.

Lives have been lost; decades have passed, and still no honest answers are forthcoming. To discover the truth we can decipher who immensely profited from the outcome. We must address those whose eminence and power resulted from President Kennedy's demise. Despite the facts, some critics refuse to accept modern reviews of evidence.

Some people will hate and degrade later conclusions because they venture from the official story. This review does not claim to possess every definitive answer. It remains unlikely some answers will emerge. This is a result of flaws in memory, the passage of decades, and officially sanctioned obfuscation.

Three historic political murders occurred under nearly all the same American leaders. Each case had a similar absence of investigative procedure, scientific inconsistencies, and government obstruction. All three men died in just over five years. A lone killer shrouded in lies receives blame for each death.

Are countless authority errors merely the results of chance? The official story assumes American government employees are somehow immune to greed, fear, and hatred. Reviewing all the evidence, the official story is largely true and verifies some essential information. However, the story ignores any possible evidence of assassination conspiracy.

Authorities overlooked uncomfortable evidence and testimony. Rather than investigate, some were busy demonizing any Lone Gunman Theory opponents. Officials have long denied a factual series of mistakes and highly suspicious activity. Documented blunders repeatedly appear in the existing record. Certain interests have enjoyed prosperity resulting from a possible conspiracy. To find the answers, distinctions amid fact and speculation are necessary.

## THE ARMS OF THE CONSPIRACY

THE UNDERWORLD ARM:
Mafia leaders using selected criminal associates.

THE OFFICIALS ARM:
Certain elected officials that suppressed relevant evidence in the case.

THE MILITARY INTELLIGENCE ARM:
Agents motivated by enduring feuds, conflicting beliefs, and political agendas.

THE CONSPIRATORS:
Men who possibly sought to murder a United States President and others who concealed the facts.

# CHAPTER 2

*"Two sides of the same coin."*

~Sam Giancana
Regional Mafia leader
*Speaking of the Central Intelligence Agency and Mafia's similarities*

## THE UNDERWORLD ARM

The Central Intelligence Agency, via its agents, allegedly used the Mafia for operations extending back to World War II. However, John and Robert Kennedy's actions defied the Mafia's power and curtailed their profits nationally. Longtime claims about the Mafia aiding in John F. Kennedy's election are speculation. Based on the Mafia's response to the following Kennedy legal prosecutions, they were not friendly.

The Underworld Arm wanted their gaming rights and Casino wealth restored in Cuba. Fidel Castro had seized and nationalized them. Unless President Kennedy invaded Cuba or killed Castro, the Mafia lost millions in yearly profits. This placed financial pressure on the crime syndicate and most invested resources in Cuba were permanently lost. The Mafia's problems had just begun.

Attorney General Robert F. Kennedy crusaded against organized crime by extraditing the Mafia's leaders. Robert Kennedy gave corrupt government agents a choice; resign or pursue his reforms. President Kennedy sanctioned Robert Kennedy to pursue all viable tactics against the Mafia. Throughout the United States, Mafia interests faced legal attack.

The greatest disrespect a gangster could endure is publicly demonstrating their weakness. Disrespect however was secondary to deportation, arrest, and prison. The Kennedy Justice Department used all these methods. This rapidly increased criminal prosecutions and depleted the Mafia's resources. If the Kennedy prosecutions continued, the Mafia conceivably would suffer greater losses in power and influence.

One documentary noted Mafia prosecutions in 1960 amounted to 40 cases. This number rose to 2,300 cases in 1963. Successful prosecutions against Mafia defendants in the same amount of time rose from 35 cases to 160 cases.[xiv] This dramatic increase suggests the Kennedy Justice Department was a lethal threat to the criminal underworld. The Mafia is not renowned for their peaceful diplomacy.

Mafia boss Carlos Marcello controlled many wide-ranging criminal activities in New Orleans. Attorney General Kennedy deported Marcello, who was Italian, to Guatemala. Marcello's false claim using the South American country as his birthplace backfired. Justice Department agents unceremoniously seized Marcello and forcibly exiled him.

Luckily, Marcello was an illegal alien and not provided the protections afforded to American citizens.[xv] When the Federal Bureau of Investigation examined him "...it did not believe Carlos Marcello was a significant organized crime figure..." Prior to the Kennedy administration, a potentially forced ignorance overrides nearly every Bureau investigation into the Mafia. However, Carlos Marcello would not depart without revenge.

Marcello is allegedly the first of three possible Underworld Arm leaders. Marcello possessed the greatest case for vendetta against the Kennedys. The House Select Committee on Assassinations investigated President Kennedy's murder and concluded, "The committee found that Marcello had the motive, means, and opportunity to have President John F. Kennedy assassinated".

Marcello's crime family exhibited feasible motivations to assassinate President Kennedy, according to the Select Committee. It stated, "...Marcello was one of the prime targets of the Justice Department efforts during the Kennedy administration".[xvi] Robert Kennedy additionally broke the power of Jimmy Hoffa and the Teamsters Union. This dramatically affected Mafia profits and sapped influence to defend against Justice Department investigations.

The President's (Warren) Commission failed to discover plausible connections between Marcello and Lee Harvey Oswald. During his legal battles with the United States government, Marcello hired investigators to aid in his legal defense. The House Select Committee on Assassinations corroborated Guy Banister and David Ferrie serving Marcello's cause.[xvii][xviii] [xix] Ferrie served as Lee Harvey Oswald's group leader in the New Orleans Civil Air Patrol. The House Select Committee found credible evidence Oswald and Ferrie associating during August 1963.[xx] David Ferrie's connections to Carlos Marcello further concerned some officials when "substantial deposits were made during November 1963" to Ferrie's bank account. Oswald distributed pro-Cuban leaflets bearing the address of the same building that prior housed a militant group associated with Banister.

Many have prior claimed Guy Banister's connection to the intelligence community. Evidence has revealed he was a Central Intelligence Agency informant. Additionally, his business was considered for use as a "cover mechanism".[xxi] David Ferrie associated with a group attempting to amass military armament for alleged use in paramilitary operations.[xxii] Officials note Banister and Ferrie share documented anti-Communist views and abiding hatred for Castro. These facts infer that officially dismissed associations bear some consideration.

Carlos Marcello associated with Mafia boss Santo Trafficante at least twice yearly, and had previous dealings with Meyer Lansky. Unlike most witnesses, Marcello testified in secret to an Executive Session of the Select Committee on Assassinations. Marcello states he does not know Sam Giancana or Johnny Rosselli. However, at one point Marcello rescinds knowledge of a person he admitted prior to knowing. [xxiii]

After repeated legal clashes with the Kennedy administration, the Select Committee on Assassinations also found Mafia associate Jimmy Hoffa, "had the motive, means, and opportunity for planning an assassination upon the life of President John F. Kennedy." [xxiv] However, the Hoffa theory ignores an important distinction. Regional Mafia bosses were required to sanction the president's assassination. Hoffa did not possess the power, or resources to order the assassination.

Sam Giancana constitutes a second possible related suspect; he was a Regional Mafia leader similar to Marcello. The Senate Select (Church) Committee determined Giancana and other Mafioso previously served the Central Intelligence Agency. The Eisenhower and Kennedy administrations used the Mafia in attempts to kill Fidel Castro.[xxv][xxvi] Using criminals would have had other unforeseen costs.

The American Underworld was a collaborator with the Central Intelligence Agency. However, Federal agencies did not fully understand or respect the power they called upon to serve their agenda. Multiple government assets, who used the Mafia leaders, did not expect their ingenuity or wits. They did not fully appreciate the long memory for vendettas the crime syndicate possessed.

Giancana was a cunning adversary with a shared hatred of Castro. The American government wanted its use of the Mafia. In exchange, the Mafia conceivably used the United States government for money and influence. They provided the Mafia opportunity to infiltrate paramilitary circles. These groups could provide former military assets, tactics, and training.

Giancana was a member of "The Criminal Commission", the Mafia's nationwide ruling body.[xxvii] Most Underworld activity was in the control of men like Giancana, cunning Mafioso. These were deadly, ambitious, and extremely vengeful men. The Central Intelligence Agency understood the Mafia commanded a virtual army of murderers, thugs, and compromised government employees. The Agency wanted to use criminal assassins or scapegoats. Conceivably, Giancana and his alleged fellow Conspirators were able to manipulate the Central Intelligence Agency in return.

Giancana is the first of four murders possibly connected to John F. Kennedy's assassination. Days before a Senate committee schedules Giancana for testimony, he is shot multiple times in the mouth. The timing and manner of Sam Giancana's demise in connection to his scheduled testimony is suspicious. Giancana's violent murder in his secure compound remains unsolved.[xxviii]

Giancana associate Richard Cain is discharged from the US Army in 1950. In 1956, he joined the Chicago Police Department and operated a private investigation business. In 1960, Cain requested a meeting with the Central Intelligence Agency. CIA officials meeting with him note Cain's knowledge of Giancana's prior involvement with the Castro Plots. Giancana used Cain feasibly to advance, "an effort to gain possible leverage with the CIA".[xxix]

Cain offered the Agency information from a meeting with the leader of the Chicago branch of the "Counter Revolutionary Movement in Cuba". "In the summer of 1961- Cain met in Mexico City by a CIA staffer, identity unknown, and purpose unknown." "Cain made an unannounced visit to Agency Officer Winston Scott and (official edit) in Mexico City..." and offered them additional information that concerned some officials.[xxx]

Mexican authorities deport Cain on June 4, 1962, resulting from his possession of illegal weapons and impersonation of a Mexican official. Cain provided additional information to the Central Intelligence Agency contact office in 1963. He was investigating assertions regarding the "Fair Play for Cuba Committee" allegedly collaborating with criminal elements in Chicago to assassinate President Kennedy.[xxxi] Cain had additional meetings with an unnamed Agency officer in the summer of 1963, expressing possible intentions to join the Agency.

Richard Cain reported to the Agency regarding the Directorio Revolucionario Estudiantil (DRE) during August.[xxxii] Cain was "used" by the Agency since September 1963 under a contact clearance, and provided, "eight reports on Cuban activities." The Federal Bureau of Investigation searched one of Richard Cain's criminal associates in September. They discovered a cache of rifles, pistols, handcuff keys, a road map, and various other illegal possessions "in the residence".[xxxiii]

The Agency's Chicago office "was advised to discontinue such association because the FBI was conducting an investigation of Cain because of his alleged relation to the Mafia." The Central Intelligence Agency Domestic Clandestine Service was subsequently destroying related files. A prior Agency memo regarding Richard Cain states, "The 5 June 1967 memorandum enclosed copies of several 1963/1964 documents from the Chicago Field Office's file on CAIN, which ADC/PSD forwarded to the SRS with the comment that "It appears DCS is cleaning out their files re Lee Harvey Oswald, et al."[xxxiv] [xxxv] This memo links Cain with Oswald by the Agency's estimation.

Cain was already a close associate of Sam Giancana. Cain committed murder, and was possibly involved in a Bureau deception related to a failed political assassination plot.[xxxvi] Cain also claimed CHICOMS (Chinese Communists) also controlled the Fair Play for Cuba Committee American operations.[xxxvii] "On November 27, 1963 Cain...gave the Agency some information that Oswald was in Chicago in April 1963 with the Fair Play for Cuba Committee and had purchased the assassination rifle in March 1963."[xxxviii] These claims support a large untenable Communist plot offered by a few leading officials. The Oswald mention is seemingly offered with purpose.

Another possible Conspirator was Santo Trafficante. Trafficante succeeded his father Santo Trafficante Sr. as the Mafia boss of Tampa, Florida. Trafficante ran luxury Cuban businesses in pre-communist Havana. After the loss of all Cuban businesses, the remaining power and fortunes of Marcello, Trafficante, and Meyer Lansky depended on defeating Robert Kennedy's Justice Department. The Kennedy administration is unaware that other government associations with Trafficante were not adversarial.

While Robert Kennedy attempted to investigate and prosecute Mafia leaders, the Central Intelligence Agency worked with Trafficante's agents to murder Fidel Castro.[xxxix] This might have enabled Trafficante access to use intelligence planning and procedures. During the Johnson administration, Mafia prosecutions were no longer the major priority. Like other possible leaders of the Underworld Arm, Trafficante "had the motive, means, and opportunity to assassinate President Kennedy".[xl]

During the early 1960s, Johnny Roselli and Agency operatives decided to contact Trafficante regarding a plot against Cuba. Trafficante affirmed Roselli had contacts with the Agency and Cuban exile leaders. Among those who Trafficante worked is Manuel Antonio Varona de Loredo.[xli] Subsequently, repeated meetings occurred. The topic of the meetings was overthrowing the Castro regime. Trafficante affirms Sam Giancana's participation in the meetings.[xlii]

The Committee compelled Trafficante to admit owning multiple pieces of various Cuban casinos under the Batista regime. Castro, according to him, then forced the casinos to meet unreasonable pay demands. Trafficante was also an acquaintance of Carlos Marcello and Sam Giancana for over two decades. Additionally, Marcello knew he and other Mafia leaders were under Justice Department surveillance..[xliii]

These meetings provide the Mafia with planning insights and greater access to domestic anti-Castro paramilitary leaders. Trafficante possessed the influences and contacts in Cuba to recruit Castro's potential assassins for the Agency.[xliv] Yet the Select Committee reveals official endorsement of a criminal enterprise that was feasibly already underway.[xlv] [xlvi] The Mafia could not force the Kennedy administration to cease the Justice Department investigations. A few powerful criminals realized Cuba was lost to them,[xlvii] and perhaps the plan was changed.

## POSSIBLE ASSASSINS, ADVISERS, AND DISINFORMATION

An individual mentioned within various sources related to possible conspiracy is Johnny Roselli. Roselli had long served Chicago's organized crime syndicate. The United States Senate Select Committee to Study Governmental Operations with respect to Intelligence Activities interviewed Roselli. The Senate (Church) Committee revealed unknown information about the Central Intelligence Agency. They investigated the Agency's Mafia alliances to kill Castro. Roselli's inclusion was not a surprise, having already established a reputation for murder and violence.[xlviii] [xlix] [l]

Roselli stated the Central Intelligence Agency used criminal assassination groups. He affirmed that Agency groups attempted to assassinate Castro repeatedly with his aid.[li] [lii] [liii] Roselli later claimed that Fidel Castro had retaliated and assassinated President Kennedy.[liv] This unproven speculation ignores the strategic flaws in such an act. If Castro were linked by substantial evidence, it provided the excuse needed to crush the Castro regime officials had sought for years. No substantial evidence supports this claim.

Yet Roselli had many associations with the Cuban exile community. The Senate (Church) Committee scheduled Roselli for continued testimony, and then he went missing. Later, Roselli's partially dismembered body is located stuffed into a steel container. His death ranks among the small group of murders associated with the Kennedy assassination conspiracy. Possible key players eventually could have become victims.

Mafia insiders and some officials considered assassin Charles Nicoletti the right hand man of Sam Giancana. Nicoletti is reported to have committed repeated murders for the Mafia. Nicoletti's prior connection with Tampa Mafia leader Santo Trafficante was affirmed in 1964 when the men allied for another criminal enterprise. Years subsequent to the Kennedy assassination, Nicoletti is still considered an important criminal who is reported to lead a "hit squad".[lv][lvi][lvii][lviii][lix] Nicoletti dies prior to his scheduled appearance before the House Select Committee on Assassinations, yet Nicoletti is not the most notable possibly involved.

A final possible suspect is Meyer Lansky. Lansky was a founding member of Murder Incorporated, an infamous Underworld group. Murder Incorporated was a premier gangster association operating during the 1920s until the 1940s. Lansky was its accounting genius, a ruthless investor, and a lethal enemy who collaborated with gangsters Charles "Lucky" Luciano, Benjamin "Bugsy" Siegel, and Santo Trafficante.[lx] Lansky advised Mafia notables in financial ventures for generations and was a talented criminal financier.

Lansky allegedly formulated his plans for Cuba in 1928. While advising notables on the Mafia Commission, Meyer began a campaign in 1933 with Luciano to secure Cuba. This included establishing control of businesses and offering massive bribes to Cuba's President. As the Cuban venture proceeds, Luciano is arrested.[lxi]

Allegations contend that Lansky and Luciano performed operations with the United States Navy to secure American harbors during the 1940s.[lxii] This feasibly happened while Luciano was imprisoned and Lansky was a known criminal powerbroker. This would represent a pattern of officials using the Mafia for their own purposes.

Upon his release for aid to the military, Luciano is freed. Officials deport him to Italy, and Lansky is solely in control of the Cuban venture. A meeting of several of the Mafia's delegates in 1944 included Carlos

Marcello, Santo Trafficante, and their host Meyer Lansky.[lxiii] The Mafia enjoyed a long and profitable venture in the Caribbean paradise, until Fidel Castro's revolution came.

Mafia property and significant resources in Cuba were lost with Castro's military nationalization of businesses. Lansky was allegedly deprived of at least fourteen million dollars after the Cuban Revolution.[lxiv] Cuba reportedly generated one-hundred million dollars for the Mafia yearly.[lxv] Yet not merely vast resources were forfeited, but an enduring dream. In time, officials would verifiably use some of these criminals to undertake failed assassination plots.

In 1960, while the Central Intelligence Agency was "using" Cuban exile leader Manuel "Tony" de Varona, Meyer Lansky used Mafia intermediaries to present Varona overtures as well. Lansky's wish to "educate the American people about Castro…The logical inference to be drawn is that both the Agency, organized crime, and other persons interested in removing the Castro regime, had settled upon Varona, probably independently, as an individual who had the potential of uniting the multitude of exile groups".[lxvi] Similar actions, motives, and methods are instructive. With the United States government decision not to officially invade Cuba with overwhelming force, Cuba was lost to the Mafia.

With Castro beyond his reach, what enemy would suffer for his losses? Meyer Lansky perhaps realized the use of unrevealed operatives for criminal purposes would cast blame toward their official sponsors. While the Agency collaborated with some Mafia leaders, the Kennedy Justice Department sought to imprison them and destroy their criminal empire. How would Lansky advise patient revenge?

Central Intelligence Agency internal documents confirm associations between Meyer Lanksy and related businesses of interest to the Agency, Santo Trafficante, Agency operative Robert Maheu, and Johnny Roselli. They additionally support Lansky and a later Agency operational asset were connected as well.[lxvii lxviii]

Some allege Lansky and Regional Mafia leaders had compromising pictures within their possession. The pictures reportedly contained J. Edgar Hoover and Clyde Tolson having sex.[lxix] No one has ever offered conclusive evidence of these photographs. The claims mistakenly seek to explain what Hoover's ambition and obsession for control sufficiently already has. It may have been in his interest not to pursue the Mafia for other reasons.

# THE ONLY PROVEN ASSASSIN

Jack Ruby is associated with a hundred and fifty Dallas Police Department employees, while owning a popular nightclub.[lxx] Ruby, according to the President's (Warren) Commission told witnesses that fringe elements in Dallas had plotted to kill President Kennedy.[lxxi] Official investigations demonstrated Jack Ruby was acquainted with twenty-five to fifty Dallas uniformed police officers. Legal verification confirmed Ruby had far-reaching official friendships greater than a regular individual did in Dallas.[lxxii]

Ruby had so many friendships within the Dallas Police, one witness suggested impropriety.[lxxiii] One reserve police officer was Ruby's former employee at the Vegas Club. Ruby displayed prior knowledge of Oswald and his former political operations during a press conference.[lxxiv] Ruby had days filled with opportunities to kill Oswald, yet he did not. These are not random actions; Ruby claimed to be enraged, yet used calm and calculated methods. He feasibly wanted to harm no one except Oswald, and this required patience.

Just before Oswald's murder, Ruby's communications and visitations include Mafia associates unspoken to for years. Why suddenly call him? The House Select Committee on Assassinations (HSCA) saw a pattern in Jack Ruby's phone calls before he murdered Oswald. The Select Committee reported the Federal Bureau of Investigation had missed or suppressed the information. Ruby had made calls to Mafia associates of Carlos Marcello and Teamster officers. These facts were unmentioned anywhere in the President's (Warren) Commission Report.[lxxv]

The Federal Bureau of Investigation's Agent in Charge of Houston notified J. Edgar Hoover and the Dallas office about possibly relevant withheld information. Allegedly, Mary Ann McCall was familiar with Jack Ruby, and based on the unnamed Bureau informant's report was a "fixer" and "pay off contact" "between the Dallas Police and Criminal Element." While some regard her related speculations about Oswald's death, in my view the importance rests with her possible criminal connections. If McCall were a connection between the Dallas Police and Mafia, this would further compromise local officials and offer the criminal syndicates blackmail opportunities.[lxxvi]

Unknown to most officials Ruby was a former unproductive informant for the Federal Bureau of Investigation. Lead Counsel Rankin did not reveal this information.[lxxvii] Hoover falsely denied the matter.[lxxviii] Ruby never offered this information to his attorneys.[lxxix] What could prevent a man from using such relevant information in defense of his freedom?

Officials did not question why Ruby failed to use the many various opportunities during prior days to shoot Oswald. Does an enraged man wait to exact his vengeance? The Dallas Police announced Oswald's scheduled transfer was at 10 a.m. Despite knowing this, Ruby got up late, made his breakfast, cleaned up, and decided to stop at the Western Union for an employee since he was already going downtown anyway.

This might have occurred to make Oswald's demise appear spontaneous. Perhaps Ruby learned of the delay with a phone call. Dallas Police Detective Joe Cody stated, "a phone call from Ruby to headquarters was not an uncommon event..."[lxxx] Two detectives who were escorting Oswald to county prison were supposed to meet a waiting car for transfer. The car was late and not in position. Over an hour later, Ruby appears.

Yet a suppressed account from a member of the Dallas Police supports two long held beliefs offered by Commission detractors. Jack Ruby, according to Dallas Police Sgt. Patrick Dean, had stated on November 22, 1963 details about premeditating Oswald's murder. Additionally, Dean stated that he observed Jack Ruby enter the garage just before Oswald's transfer. Commission attorney Burt Griffin "induced" Dean to alter his original statement. Dean affirms Ruby premeditated Oswald's murder and the public transfer provided the opportunity to undertake the deed.[lxxxi]

Without prior notification, Ruby could not foresee the delay. Ruby is over an hour late to kill Oswald. A chaotic mob of reporters and the public had formed to glimpse the alleged murderer. Then four minutes later Oswald suffers a mortal wound fired by Jack Ruby. This pudgy strolling man, present for days, slipped unnoticed to the "secure" basement through an unknowing crowd. Before millions of witnesses, he murdered Lee Harvey Oswald on live television.

Where are the federal agencies that interfered so much when they captured the suspect? Why is Oswald's transfer unsecured? Later Jack Ruby asked if the President's (Warren) Commission would take him safely to Washington. The Chief Justice and President's Commissioner Earl Warren replied if Ruby felt unsafe "... they could stop at any time." In this action, the President's (Warren) Commission might have sentenced Ruby to a meaningless death.

Many authors have subsequently noted the names that appear in Jack Ruby's notebook are significant. This list includes the name Lamar Hunt, son of avid Kennedy detractor H.L. Hunt that some allege was part of the assassination plot. However, little additional information would support a proven connection with Hunt. Yet Ruby's prior statements in the Dallas Police Department attempt to rest blame with outspoken radicals that included the elder Hunt. These actions may infer that Ruby, like Richard Cain, sought to blame local political groups.

The House Select Committee established a prior link between Ruby and Meyer Lansky's brother Jake. Ruby had visited Cuba and resided at Meyer Lansky's hotel the Tropicana.[lxxxii] Another Ruby companion believes Ruby could have been present for meetings that included Santo Trafficante and Sam Giancana.[lxxxiii] Trafficante and Ruby shared a common friend named Lewis McWillie. Ruby companions Joe and Sam Campisi served the Dallas Mafia. Some criminals had various associates located within the Dallas Police force.[lxxxiv lxxxv lxxxvi lxxxvii lxxxviii] Joe Campisi visited Ruby in jail days after he killed Oswald. Based upon some evidence Jack Ruby feasibly premeditated the murder of Lee Harvey Oswald.

One fact most can agree on is Mafia bosses and their criminal armies have killed countless people. Turf wars, betrayal, vendettas, and greed have led to the thousands of deaths. Throughout history, these men have killed to acquire power, profit, and revenge. Ruby's statements and actions support Mafia involvement in the murder of Lee Harvey Oswald.

# CHAPTER 3

*"A real Centaur-part man, part horse's ass.
A rough appraisal, but curiously true."*

~Dean Acheson
United States Secretary of State referring to Lyndon Johnson

## THE OFFICIALS ARM

John F. Kennedy wanted to engage with the Soviet Union in a collaborative scientific effort to conquer space exploration. This could have saved the United States billions of dollars and might have reduced the weapons stockpiling that followed.[lxxxix] It might have allowed the National Aeronautic Space Administration program to continue with greater funding and capabilities. It would have provided fresh insights, and perhaps greater understanding of our former Superpower rival.

This collaboration was unacceptable to the Military-Industrial Complex. The Complex is made of eminent businesses and powerful special interests connected to the American military. They were still profiting from the fear and military actions created about the post-war Soviet Union. Communist paranoia caused the United States to acquire nuclear armaments for generations. To maintain and protect these unused weapons a fortune is spent annually. If both sides use these weapons, it will eradicate most concerned.

Alternative motivations included the first planned American withdrawal of troops from Vietnam.[xc] The entire document states a small, quiet, eventual

United States military withdrawal. This would occur after training the South Vietnamese to assume United States troop duties. Substantiated are President Kennedy's intentions to commence the eventual American withdrawal from Vietnam.

The Vietnam War, a purely impossible military engagement further incited on false information. It would create billions of dollars for the military, technology, defense, and intelligence communities. The Military-Industrial Complex supported accelerating the war in Vietnam, how could it obtain the American people's consent? Less than a year following John F. Kennedy's death, the Gulf of Tonkin incident occurred. The United States reported North Vietnamese forces had attacked its ships.

President Johnson used this as official justification to enact force increases for the Vietnam War. Former Secretary of State Robert McNamara publicly admitted the incident was a government error. He explained both he and senior advisers were "wrong" about the attack.[xci] The incident provided reasoning to pursue goals benefiting a tiny minority at the American people's expense.

More than fifty-eight thousand American men and boys died to make war profits. What did the American people gain from the sacrificed lives of a generation? These interests benefited from the murder of Vietnamese men, women, and children. Did one presidential life matter to the alleged Conspirators?

The question is who most benefited? Suspected are men who lost power and wealth under the Kennedy administration. Each possible man had intricate networks of political, financial, and military influence. Their greatest fear was a Kennedy dynasty. With each Kennedy brother occupying America's most influential posts for at least twenty years.

For John and Robert it was possible, and it was unlikely for Ted Kennedy. However, reality did not matter, revenge and control did. Kennedy had disregarded his generals' demands to offer air support in the Bay of Pigs. He would not launch nuclear missiles against the Russians during the Cuban Missile Crisis. He refused most of the fringe plans of military and Agency leaders. Political hawks viewed Communism as the preeminent threat and disparaged Kennedy's use of diplomacy.

Some men would do anything to stop a prevailing financial and political dynasty like the Kennedys. Especially if they perceived only their concepts of law and order sufficed. They previously engineered political murders and toppled foreign governments. Therefore, it is possible a few employed such tactics on American soil.

# THE SECRET SERVICE

Secret Service failures allegedly began during previous arrangements. Just days prior to a Chicago presidential visit, law enforcement arrested Thomas Arthur Vallee. In Vallee's possession were a high-powered M1 .30-carbine and large amounts of ammunition. Vallee was then arrested, interrogated, and set free. Following Vallee's arrest the Federal Bureau of Investigation receives an informant's message. The informant confides Mafia hit men were awaiting President Kennedy in Chicago.[xcii]

Additionally, the Secret Service destroyed the relevant files concerning presidential security reports from multiple periods in 1963. This occurred long after legal institution of the JFK Records Act to protect these files in the 1990s.[xciii] Thus, Secret Service leaders destroyed evidence despite the law and feasible relevance of the documents. Former Secret Service agent Abraham Bolden asserted Cuban assassins waited in Chicago for President Kennedy during the period contained in the destroyed files.[xciv] A formerly suppressed Agency document states Bolden's ideas were similar to information prior offered by Mafia associate Richard Cain.[xcv]

Bolden affirmed this information was not passed on to authorities in Dallas. Agent Bolden claims fellow Secret Service agents were drinking on duty in Dallas. The Secret Service representative in Washington D.C. stated they "would not have any comment whatsoever about Mr. Bolden's statements."[xcvi] A simple fact long unconsidered was many agents were merely exhausted.

Little sleep would be just as detrimental to agent reactions as drinking. However, other eyewitnesses supported Agent Bolden's assertions of drinking. These statements assert that Secret Service wildly interacted with strippers.[xcvii] They partied until 5 a.m. at the Cellar nightclub on the morning of President Kennedy's visit. Secret Service agents had little sleep, picked up women, and enjoyed afterhours fruit drinks.[xcviii] The President's Commission testimony of Secret Service Chief James Rowley affirms four agents in the subsequent motorcade were previously drinking.[xcix]

Commissioner Warren confirmed the effects feasible exhaustion would have "...even some people in the crowds, saw a man with a rifle up in this building from which the President was shot. Now, don't you think that if a man went to bed reasonably early, and hadn't been drinking the night before, would be more alert to see things as a Secret Service agent, than if they stayed up until 3,4, or 5 o'clock in the morning, going to beatnik joints and doing some drinking along the way?" Chief Rowley responds, "Well; yes; he would be."[c]

Proven agent drinking and exhaustion influenced security actions in Dallas. This explains pained expressions, sluggish reaction time, and poor judgment. Many Secret Service members had been up nearly the entire night before and the morning of the assassination. They could not have slept more than a few hours prior to President Kennedy's arrival in Dallas.

Witness testimony and media reports during the President's assassination note the delayed response of the Secret Service. Two members of the Secret Service were present in the front seat of the presidential limousine. While the first two shots occur, agent James Greer actually slowed the vehicle to a mere crawl. This was merely a possible side effect from disorientation.

President Kennedy's limousine was located in the front of the official cars. Positioned before the presidential vehicle were a front and lead car. Security diminished from six Police motorcycle officers, down to four, and then finally two remained. The remaining motorcycle officers are behind the presidential car. This creates security lapses.

Secret Service agents normally would jog alongside the President or took up positions on the vehicle to deflect gunfire. This did not occur in Dallas. Had the motorcade maintained greater speed it greatly decreases the chance gunfire would successfully hit a vehicle. Despite the contentions of some conspiracy advocates checking every building was not standard Secret Service protocol.[ci] These oversights provided an opening for killing shots to occur in Dealey Plaza.

In media recordings of the presidential motorcade, agent Emory Roberts waves a hand to recall the running Secret Service guards from the presidential limousine. Secret Service agent Henry Rybka pulled off the Kennedy car moments before the shooting appears clearly distressed. You see him waving his arms and shaking his head in response to his removal. Rybka acts confused from the order and it shows.[cii]

Security measures performed by the Secret Service were obviously insufficient.[ciii] Varied unanticipated security problems compounded the situation. Incompetence and inaction, not proven intent affected the Secret Service failures. Some assert the blame for security measures lies with President Kennedy. These people are unaware of the actual power of the Secret Service.

Agents were able to countermand a president's decision legally if the order violated their safety and security. President Harry Truman confirms this policy, "the Secret Service was the only boss the President of the United States really had." So why did the Secret Service commander not account for these security lapses?[civ]

Additional contentious statements regard the shots themselves. Secret Service agent George Hickey followed behind the presidential limousine. Hickey stated hearing two gunshots, nearly simultaneously. Agent Hickey states, "I heard two reports (shots) which I thought were shots that appeared to me completely different in sound from the first...were in such rapid succession that there seemed to be practically no time element between them." Other present officials support Hickey's statement of rapid fire.

Secret Service Agents William McIntyre spoke of "...a shot fired, followed in quick succession by two more". Agent Glen Bennett reported "...a second shot followed immediately..." Agent Warren Taylor said, "In the instant my foot touched the ground, I heard two more bangs..."[cv] It is improbable a single bolt-action rifle can fire so rapidly. Following President's Kennedy's death, the Secret Service interference extended to his body. Secret Service prevented lawful medical procedures at Parkland Hospital forcing doctors to stand aside.

Dallas Police Chief Jesse Curry was the official responsible for coordination of motorcade security between local and national forces.[cvi] Agent Forrest Sorrels noted one of the many local security failures. Sorrels and Jesse Curry rode in the lead car of the motorcade; Sorrels related shots fired indicating the "terrace" area (Grassy Knoll area) and the Texas School Book Depository. Curry directs officers to surround only the Depository.[cvii]

President Kennedy's body, despite jurisdictional law, quickly goes to Bethesda Naval Hospital. Secret Service agents removed his ornate copper coffin to Washington from Parkland Hospital. Lead agents might have suspected possible impropriety. In my estimation, repeated security failures contributed to the death of America's President.

# THE FEDERAL BUREAU OF INVESTIGATION

The Secret Service is not alone in suffering repeated failures. The Federal Bureau of Investigation also committed grave errors. A single man was responsible for the Bureau's adversarial position regarding the Kennedys. He was its leader and founder, J. Edgar Hoover. Hoover secured the Bureau's power with any means necessary.[cviii cix cx cxi]

From the 1920s through the 1950s, Hoover publicly dismissed the existence of powerful organized criminal syndicates. Disorganized local criminal gangs were determined responsible for increased national crime. Bureau field agents lacked active support and resources for associated investigations. Perhaps Hoover did not want the Mafia disturbed.

Subsequently revealed were Hoover's files that detailed hundreds of celebrities, politicians, and many regular Americans private business. The more eminent the citizen, the greater amount of information Hoover acquired. Allegedly, his files included mostly politicians and major celebrities in the United States. Hoover acquired information using illegal wiretapping operations. J. Edgar Hoover had decades to develop a power base expressly created to destroy the lives of those who opposed him.

Being President Johnson's close ally, how many secrets did Hoover let slip for his use and benefit? Johnson made Hoover the only lifelong Bureau leader in executive branch history. The action was no friendly kindness. Johnson owed Hoover, and the future president had many secrets to keep hidden.

J. Edgar Hoover possessed files containing incriminating evidence against thousands of people. This purportedly included Lyndon Johnson. Hoover alluded to holding secrets against nearly every important politician in the United States. One agent described these files as "political cancer". [cxii cxiii cxiv cxv] Some people collect stamps and art, Hoover collected dangerous secrets.

In a text regarding his (the Bureau's) success in prosecuting criminals, Hoover said, "Justice is merely incidental, to law and order".[cxvi] To call justice incidental says much of J. Edgar Hoover's disregard for justice. Hoover forgot without justice, the law becomes tyranny. His actions eventually violated the rights of many American citizens in pursuing Bureau goals.

Hoover created and approved hundreds of illegal wiretapping programs. He sent agents to conduct surveillance and harass American citizens and leaders. The Bureau's creator required higher moral standards in citizens than of himself. It should not surprise Americans some agencies operate as Hoover consistently did.

Following John F. Kennedy's election, J. Edgar Hoover was then answering to a much younger Commander in Chief. Kennedy then appointed his younger brother to command Hoover as well. Having long enjoyed professional independence, this enraged Hoover. The Kennedys would learn he took hatred and revenge to eminent levels.

Hoover's influence and example guided Bureau actions. The Bureau's edited information greatly affected government operations. The President's (Warren) Commission had depended on candid honesty from the Federal Bureau of Investigation. Those conducting the investigation had doomed it to failure. This was no mere coincidence.


## THE BUREAU AND OSWALD

A request from Sam Papich the Bureau liaison to the Central Intelligence Agency sought information regarding Oswald's successful defection. In 1960, Hoover details Oswald being an internal security risk for years prior to the assassination.[cxvii] Bureau special agent James Hosty then appears within related documents. Hosty's previous assignment, the Marina Oswald security case in 1962[cxviii] is largely unknown. Hosty paid multiple visits to the Oswald house in New Orleans attempting to make contact with Lee. He allegedly failed to do so. July 23, 1963 a confidential Bureau informant states Oswald's current address and his rental of a post office box.[cxix]

A prisoner in a New Orleans jail requests a Federal Bureau of Investigation agent in August of 1963. Special Agent John L. Quigley speaks with a man named Lee Harvey Oswald about his arrest.[cxx] Another confidential Bureau informant states that Oswald changed his New Orleans address to receive the Communist publication the Worker.[cxxi] Yet if Oswald was in regular contact with actual Communists, he could have received the Worker secretly via alternate means.[cxxii] This perhaps demonstrates Oswald wanted others to know he was reading the subversive publication, and does not demonstrate any genuine commitment. Additionally unlike Oswald, one Bureau file notes Communists to be "consistent workers".

Mary Bertrucci a secretary at Reilly Coffee Company informs the Bureau of Oswald's employment since May 15, 1963. Subsequently, Alvin Prechter, the Reilly Coffee Company Personnel Manager stated Oswald is terminated in July 19, 1963.[cxxiii] Without regular work, Oswald has no reason to remain in New Orleans. The Oswald family returns to Texas, most outside the Bureau and Agency are unaware.

October 1, 1963 Mrs. Lillian Murret "advised" the Federal Bureau of Investigation regarding her nephew Lee Harvey Oswald's activities.[cxxiv] She gives a description of a woman speaking Russian with Lee and Marina and her knowledge of their activities. Murret's husband Charles is connected to Mafia leader Carlos Marcello. She contacts the Bureau less than two months before the assassination.

Special Agent Hosty attempts multiple times to interview Oswald and encounters Marina and their associate Ruth Paine. Paine is fluent in Russian and allowed Marina and her children to live with her. Hosty learns that Texas School Book Depository employed Oswald. This discovery occurred less than a month before the assassination.

Lee Harvey Oswald allegedly delivers the Bureau a fateful note. Bureau receptionist Nannie Lee Fenner asserts the note states "Let this be a warning. I will blow up the FBI and the Dallas Police Department if you don't stop bothering my wife. Signed-Lee Harvey Oswald." If Fenner is correct, it should have resulted in Oswald's immediate arrest. After showing the note to repeated Bureau staff and agents, she forwards it to Agent James Hosty.[cxxv]

However, Agent James Hosty asserted the note read, "If you have anything you want to learn about me, come talk to me directly. If you don't cease bothering my wife, I will take appropriate action and report this to the proper authorities." The Bureau offered two diverse notes. One message emerged from Fenner and the other from Agent Hosty. Now the reasonable action is to report this possibly dangerous message. Further investigation or questioning should have occurred.

Once reviewing the note's contents, Hosty alleged his supervisor J. Gordon Shanklin ordered him to destroy it. According to Hosty, after trying to throw the note away, he flushed it down a toilet. Yet Hosty's supervisor Gordon Shanklin denied ever ordering this action.[cxxvi] This displays possible quelling of the facts surrounding Oswald prior to President Kennedy's murder. Each version confirms Oswald had prior contact with officials.[cxxvii] Hosty failed to mention the note to the Commission; it was not until a following Congressional investigation he confirmed its existence.[cxxviii]

Bureau Assistant Director William Sullivan testified to the Senate (Church) Committee he and J. Gordon Shanklin "…discussed the Oswald case many times." Sullivan affirmed Shanklin had received "a threatening message from Oswald because the agent was investigating Oswald." When

Shanklin reported he and a superior had dealt with the matter, all superior officers denied knowledge of the note or its destruction.[cxxix] Additionally, Shanklin interviewed Dallas District Attorney Henry Wade regarding Oswald and his asserted informant status.[cxxx] Yet this claim is still unproven. Which official is lying? Could it be more than one?

Associations prior to the Kennedy assassination link Oswald to the Bureau and the Agency. Proving the Bureau knew about Oswald long before the assassination, despite contrary statements.[cxxxi cxxxii cxxxiii cxxxiv cxxxv cxxxvi] They actively sought information about Oswald and his wife. These were not the last questionable actions from the Bureau.

The Federal Bureau of Investigation found no useable prints on the murder weapon following their first examination. The Dallas Police state discovering Oswald's palm print and fingerprints on the Carcano prior. Oswald is without time for sanitizing the rifle completely.[cxxxvii] Should we trust the results of the Bureau or the Dallas Police?

Fingerprints would feasibly have been present in multiple locations. The Bureau found no usable fingerprints. Do we trust the judgment of authorities regarding which test is correct? Publicly unknown is pressure on investigators from Hoover and the Johnson administration.

The Bureau additionally had problematic physical evidence. It related to the paper bag officials allege contained the murder weapon. Similar to the fingerprint tests, two conflicting Bureau determinations exist regarding this item as well. As the President's Commission states about the contended evidence "We are in doubt".[cxxxviii] Questions abound.

Dozens of witnesses disagreed with the final official conclusions. The official mantra of events remains largely unchanged. Authorities supported by some texts still cling to the original conclusions. However, possible questions do not cease with agent concerns. At the highest levels of the American government, disbelief was present. Some affirmed a conspiracy was allegedly under way.

During a phone call to President Johnson on November 23, 1963, Hoover stated, "The case as it stands right now is not strong enough to be able to get a conviction…" (Regarding Oswald) "We have up here the tape and the photograph of the man who was at the Soviet Embassy, using Oswald's name. That picture and the tape do not correspond to this man's voice, nor his appearance. In other words, it appears there is a second person who was at the Soviet Embassy down there".[cxxxix] Publicly undisclosed is a possible imposter at the Soviet Embassy in Mexico City.

Therefore, in Hoover's own words to then President Lyndon Johnson "it appears there is a second person," an "Oswald Imposter". This provides implied evidence of a conspiracy from the lips of the Bureau's leader himself. The conversation was erased by alleged mistake, somehow a transcript survived. Until public attempts to obtain the document years later were successful, it remained unconsidered.

However, evidence subsequently emerged that revealed the Central Intelligence Agency misinformed officials. The House Select Committee highly doubted that Agency employees innocently fueled this mistake. The Oswald Imposter would repeatedly emerge supported by official documents and primary evidence. Over a decade later, nestled within a little known report was the truth.

Yet officials ranging from Hoover to Johnson believed the deception. Despite the inconclusive nature of this hypothesis, officials initially believing it attempted to suppress it. Officials intended to maintain the lone gunman scenario despite any opposing information. Feasibly this includes both contending speculation and evidence.

Hoover and the Agency's primary concern were preserving their reputations. Their primary goals did not include discovering and exposing John F. Kennedy's murderers. They did not publicly consider a conspiracy to kill President Kennedy. The Bureau and Agency denied investigators evidence and gathered unsanctioned intelligence data for years.

Officials instructed Bureau Special Agent Regis Kennedy to withhold any officially gathered information from Prosecutor Jim Garrison while testifying. Kennedy disregarded their prior instructions in court. Attorney General Clark and Hoover were not pleased. This is one of multiple attempts to suppress witness testimony and obstruct investigation. Garrison's New Orleans investigation seems considered a threat to the official findings. The Central Intelligence Agency was disturbed by Garrison's efforts,[cxl] yet feasibly this did not emerge from complicity in the assassination. It may have been Garrison's exposure of many contacts, informants, and assets used by the Agency.[cxli]

Subsequently, the House Select Committee states Bureau files revealed former special agent and later Marcello investigator Guy "Banister also became excessively active in anti-Communist activities after his separation from the FBI... Early in 1961, Banister helped draw up a charter for the Friends of Democratic Cuba, an organization set up as the fundraising arm of Sergio Arcacha Smith's branch of the Cuban Revolutionary Council. The FBI files also indicate (Guy) Banister was performing another service for the Cuban exile group. He ran background investigations on the campus of Louisiana State University on those Cuban students who wished to be members of Arcacha Smith's anti-Castro group... Banister became acquainted with David Ferrie...was also extremely active in Sergio Arcacha

Smith's anti-Castro group."[cxlii] Banister additionally served as a Central Intelligence Agency informant and his business was considered for Agency operational use.

Banister prior served in the Bureau and helped the Agency; he actively participated in holding arms for exile militant group operations as well. "Both Ferrie and Banister were implicated in a raid in late 1961 against a munitions depot in Houma, LA, in which various weapons, grenades and ammunition were stolen. Banister's role may have been limited to storing materiel... Others who participated in the raid, include Andrew Blackmon, a Ferrie associate and former Civil Air Patrol cadet, and Sergio Arcacha Smith." [cxliii]

The Senate (Church) Committee found large flaws in the Federal Bureau of Investigation's tactics. The Bureau inquiry "focused almost exclusively on Lee Harvey Oswald".[cxliv] They reported "Director Hoover, the Justice Department and the White House "exerted pressures" on senior Bureau officials." Pressures applied to quickly conclude the case and determine Oswald the lone assassin.[cxlv] The Bureau did not provide many original reports to the President's (Warren) Commission, "no affidavits were provided from the two New Orleans agents who had the most contact with the Oswald case."[cxlvi]

The Senate (Church) Committee exposed Oswald was the subject of an extensive Bureau security file. It began in 1959. The files allege Oswald was providing "radar secrets" to the Soviets. The Bureau had multiple updates and reports concerning Oswald's return. A Bureau agent interviewed him three weeks following his return to the United States.

The Senate Committee found "There is no indication that any of the FBI agents assigned to the Oswald case were ever warned that an imposter might attempt to assume Oswald's identity." Despite Hoover and other American leaders' foreknowledge of a possible imposter, they did not share this information with the Commission members.[cxlvii] They never bothered to explain it to the American people. Johnson and Hoover constructed repeated deceptions.

The Bureau investigation was a complete failure. J. Edgar Hoover afterwards leveled internal discipline toward Federal Bureau of Investigation agents. Instead of assuming his share of responsibility, Hoover determined others within the Bureau had contributed to the Oswald fiasco. Hoover chastised, "I do not intend to palliate the actions which have resulted in forever destroying the Bureau as the top level investigative organization."[cxlviii]

Hoover asserted Ruby and Oswald had no associations to the government or organized crime, which modern evidence has proven false. It exemplifies why executive branch investigations are not the lone authority in determining truth. Their many documented failures prove executive branch negligence in this matter. The American Congress later addressed certain grievous mistakes.

The Investigation of the Senate (Church) Committee states, "Director Hoover himself perceived the Warren Commission as an adversary. He repeatedly remarked that the Commission, particularly the Chief Justice (Warren) was: "seeking to criticize the FBI" and merely attempting to "find gaps" in the FBI's investigation." When the President's (Warren) Commissioners released their final report to the public, "Director Hoover asked for all derogatory material on Warren Commission members and staff contained in the FBI Files"[cxlix] Why did Hoover want negative information possessed about President's (Warren) Commission members? Most would quickly relent under the attentions of J. Edgar Hoover. His greatest weapons against so many were veiled threats.


## THE DALLAS POLICE DEPARTMENT

Some Dallas Police investigators recorded evidence different from later reports. The first weapon identified in the Texas School Book Depository was a German 7.65 mm Mauser rifle with a scope and three 6.5 mm Carcano shells. Deputy Sheriffs, Eugene Boone, Seymour Weitzman, and Luke Mooney initially stated this.[cl] Dallas District Attorney Henry Wade originally stated the weapon present in the sniper's nest, was a German Mauser.[cli] Possible misidentification feasibly occurred. The close similarity of the weapons should also be considered.[clii]

In all following reports, a Carcano 6.5 mm rifle amends the Mauser description. All in the group of officers initially asserting the rifle was a Mauser states they were mistaken. Considering the substantial mistakes, the disjointed timeline, and other compromised evidence, this is quite reasonable. Deputy Sherriff Roger Craig subsequently insisted the actual murder weapon was a Mauser.[cliii] Yet in a 1967 interview with Mark Lane sent to Jim Garrison regarding investigative areas of interest, Roger Craig does not mention the Mauser.[cliv]

However, most films, photographs, and testimony support a Carcano.[clv clvi clvii clviii clix] A formerly suppressed Central Intelligence Agency document was prior claimed to support a Mauser. Yet only the name appears, all the supporting details listed in the document affirm the Carcano.[clx] The Mauser does not feasibly appear until the Dallas Police misidentification, it has been repeated by some ever since.

The Mauser contention requires most related officers being involved in a large conspiracy without considerable supporting evidence. They would receive orders that require additional complicit superiors who reported to the Conspirators. This hypothesis requires too many people for a tenable plot. A successful conspiracy requires minimizing the number of possible participants to avoid discovery.

The Bureau confirmed the Carcano firing pin is rusty and it required metal shims to properly sight the gun. The sling, used to steady a sniper's grip was a makeshift replacement created from a pistol holster strap. The Carcano stock was prior determined obsolete by the Italian military and were sold abroad. Companies modified, tested, and resold the weapons as surplus rifles. Yet some of these weapons later exploded killing their owners.[clxi] Oswald's Carcano was sufficient at best. It was not defective, nor a quality weapon.

Alleged mistakes included mishandling prisoners and multiple unknown suspects. However, police did not fail to document a group of men detained following the assassination. Among these men are the famous Three Tramps. Many advocates of conspiracy have insisted they remain unidentified. Yet Dallas Police arrest records document the three men as Harold Doyle, John Gedney, and Gus Abrams.[clxii clxiii clxiv] These distractions soon fade because of a second homicide.

Officer J. D. Tippit's murder is the second related killing on that November day. The Dallas Police officer's murder further implies Oswald's guilt. Despite the conflicting speculation about Officer Tippit's demise, Oswald soon faces murder charges. Oswald allegedly killed the president. Additionally he murders a police officer but never flees Dallas.

When Police Officer Tippit died, Dealey Plaza was no longer the sole focus of local authorities. Some Dallas Police proceeded to Oak Cliff; this provides other parties opportunity to escape notice. Tippit's death ruined any chance for Oswald to receive normal treatment from authorities. It covered Oswald in an assumed guilt and cast him a merciless killer. His cries of innocence went ignored.

Oswald is somehow a mastermind and fool. He was unafraid of murdering a police officer in public, although he fled scared twice. Oswald flees the scene yet not the city of Dallas. Instead, he returns to central Dallas where officials apprehend him. He never flees the city.

Some of the current official primary evidence and witness testimony asserts Oswald's guilt in this matter.[clxv clxvi clxvii clxviii clxix clxx] Tippit's murder was a sloppy public act some witnesses confirmed. However, similar to the timeline utilized placing Oswald in the sniper's nest, important discrepancies exist. Primary among them are the contending times of Tippit's death. Officials could not accurately determine the time of Tippit's death.

The hospital record is corrected from 1:09 pm to 1:15 pm, yet neither time supports the Commission. The inconsistent timeline places Tippit being shot and pronounced dead in the hospital at the same time.[clxxi] Some witnesses could not identify Oswald.[clxxii] House Select Committee ballistics analysis could not determine if Oswald's modified revolver fired the shots. [clxxiii] Multiple pieces of primary evidence dispute the official determinations.

Missteps continued in the processing and murder of Oswald. The prisoner lineups conducted to establish Oswald's guilt had largely different suspects. Dallas Police had prisoner's disclose their personal details. All while Lee Harvey Oswald's image began appearing in every media outlet. Two detectives were to transfer Oswald to County lockup days later.

We cannot assume most Dallas Police would participate knowingly in the assassination. Evidence to establish such a massive undertaking does not exist. Not participation but incompetence possibly weakened motorcade security. Police leaders subsequently affirmed outstanding questions remained. The former chief of Dallas Police later offered his own doubts.

Jessie Curry wrote a book detailing his views about the case and maintained a file of evidence. In discussing this possible sniper on the Grassy Knoll, Chief Curry explained: "I'm not saying the shot was not fired from here (referring to the Grassy Knoll) I'm saying we never found anybody that we could connect with it".[clxxiv] Yet the participants could have known or associated with officials controlling the investigation.

## BIG LYNDON'S BOYS

The hatred among Lyndon Johnson and the Kennedys was born long before they decided to run on the same political ticket. On May 10, 1960, Robert Kennedy spoke with friends and Lyndon Johnson's close associate Bobby Baker. Kennedy called Baker "Little Lyndon" and said, "You should ask him why Big Lyndon won't risk running in the primaries against my brother. They're supposed to make 'em tough down in Texas, but Big Lyndon doesn't look so tough to me". [clxxv]

In later personal attacks directed toward John F. Kennedy, Lyndon Johnson described him as the "little scrawny fellow with rickets." Other Johnson allies tried to politicize Kennedy's health. Johnson associated critics referred to John F. Kennedy's Addison's disease stating he "would not be alive today if it were not for cortisone".[clxxvi] Each attack exposes the ruthless tactics of the Johnson political machine.

Despite each political barb, Johnson later receives a vice-presidential offer. This confuses Johnson, his ambition and vanity battled for dominance. Although the position conferred prestige and power, it was in exchange for having to serve a younger Kennedy president. Johnson eventually accepts the offer.

Following the Johnson selection for vice president, it seemed the Kennedys had immediate second thoughts. Robert Kennedy said this was "because Jack thought it would be unpleasant to be associated with him" (Lyndon Johnson). Robert Kennedy decided to visit Lyndon Johnson. Kennedy naively imagined he would convince Johnson to withdrawal his nomination.

The accounts of Robert Kennedy's three visits are mixed and conflicting. However, each visit sowed the seeds of mutual hatred. Lyndon Johnson and the Kennedys soon compromised making him the vice-presidential nominee. Yet as vice-president, he was drawing unwanted legal notice in his third year.

Republican Rules Committee Chief Council Burkett Van Kirk was quietly investigating Johnson regarding claims of previous and ongoing fraud and corruption.[clxxvii] Some assert prior to Johnson becoming president, Republican members of Congress were gathering evidence possibly to impeach him. A White House document might illustrate Lyndon Johnson's true plans.

A draft of National Security Action Memo 273 allegedly existed prior to President Kennedy's assassination. The memo's purpose countermands President Kennedy's plan to reduce military aid in Vietnam. The document indicates planning for Vietnam troop increases under way long before the president was in Dallas. This does not prove Johnson's complicity, but demonstrates each man's future intentions.

While Kennedy traveled, Vice President Johnson and Defense Secretary McNamara constructed the memo's plans.[clxxviii] The final orders release occurred just days following the assassination. Lyndon Baines Johnson's most important action was not his minor role supporting civil rights. The Vietnam War's deadly escalation is Johnson's true historical legacy.

Despite President's Johnson's manipulations, public disbelief regarding the official investigation has increased as evidentiary inconsistencies emerge. Among these problems is the Single Bullet Theory, whose validity many continue to doubt. Critics include President Johnson within released tapes from the United States National Archives. Regarding the Single Bullet Theory Johnson asked,

"What difference does it make which bullet got Connally?" Senator Richard Russell responds to the question: "Well, it don't make much difference...Well, I don't believe it..." President Johnson then replies, "I don't either..." President Johnson and Senator Russell in this point were correct. Oswald's shots as endorsed in the President's (Warren) Commission rely on political not legal standards. Johnson failed to understand the official version allows for only three shots.[clxxix]

A single miss, the second Single bullet, and the head shot. The Single bullet allegedly caused multiple wounds in Governor Connally and President Kennedy. If the bullet did not strike the men exactly as the Commission asserted, a conspiracy possibly occurred. A President's Commissioner and Johnson exchanged private words that offer feasible doubts.

Each leader privately disbelieved the American government's conclusions. With eminent hypocrisy, the Johnson administration publicly denied any criticism to official findings. Despite his own personal beliefs, Johnson concealed what he perceived as true. Senator Russell subsequently commented to public investigators of his views. However, this is not the most contradictory of Johnson's private comments.

The Lyndon Baines Johnson Library released audio tapes of President Johnson alluding to Central Intelligence Agency connections. In a conversation with the Republican leader of the House of Representatives Johnson confides, "I've got to appoint a commission and issue an executive order tonight. On investigation of the assassination of the president, cause this thing is getting pretty serious, and folks are worried about it. It's got some foreign implications, CIA and other things. I'm going try to get the Chief Justice to go on it; he declined earlier in the day..."[clxxx]

Why does he "have to appoint a commission and issue an executive order" immediately, if not to stop other investigations? What were these CIA and other things to which the President refers? Johnson later stated, "I don't think the Warren Commission, or me, or anybody else is absolutely sure of everything that might have motivated Oswald, or others that could have been involved."[clxxxi]

Political rumblings of the Garrison investigation began to trouble officials in 1967. In a Bureau memo from Deputy Assistant Director Cartha DeLoach to Associate Director Clyde Tolson, President Johnson revealed a serious concern. Marvin Watson advisor to Johnson stated "...the President had told him, in an off moment, that he was convinced that there was a plot in connection with the assassination. The President felt the CIA had had (sic) something to do with this plot."[clxxxii]

These men were aware of large problems in the official story. This evidence additionally affirms Johnson deeply suspected CIA involvement in the matter. Johnson and his Commission never revealed these facts in public. However, it was not Lyndon Johnson alone who rose to the White House; he required assistance to get there.

Johnson's political ascendance is due in part to administrator John Connally. Connally was the political lynchpin overseeing Johnson's success for many years. He served as campaign manager, political adviser, and confidant to Lyndon Johnson. His reward under President John F. Kennedy included becoming Secretary of the Navy.

Connally kept the post eleven months. Eclipsed by the Kennedys in Washington D.C., Connally remained hugely popular in Texas and soon returned. Once cementing his own political campaign, Connally became the Governor of Texas. The election occurred shortly after Connally resigned from the Kennedy cabinet.

During the assassination, John Connally sat in front of John F. Kennedy in the Presidential car. He suffered critical injuries during the gunfire and survived. Being in the actual line of fire, John Connally was unaware of the alleged Conspirators plans. Johnson retainers feasibly were not part of any conspiracy. Not a proven domestic murder, but countless deaths in Vietnam rest upon the head of Lyndon Johnson.

Kennedy appointee and later Johnson official Robert McNamara held the position of Secretary of Defense. During the Kennedy administration, McNamara found wide public admiration. During the Johnson administration, McNamara became the Anti-War movement's central enemy. Historical opinions vary widely about McNamara's actions. One description regarding Secretary McNamara's professional character and political tactics stated, "Mr. McNamara has pressured the Joint Chiefs of Staff to sign written statements testifying to Congress that the Administration's defense budget is adequate."

McNamara "...altered statements to Congress by the chiefs of the services and their secretaries. He has downgraded, ignored, bypassed, or overruled the advice of the Joint Chiefs of Staff... It places more and more power over the military-industrial complex in the hands of a few men in the executive branch of the government. The dollar volumes of military contracts amount to more than $20 billion annually; with billions more in backlog orders outstanding. The individual services no longer have the final power to contract... The awarding or cancellation of contracts... is now ultimately controlled by a very few men in the top echelons of the Defense Department".[clxxxiii]

John F. Kennedy formerly offered his intention to withdraw forces in Vietnam by 1965, "I'll become one of the most unpopular Presidents in history. I'll be damned everywhere as a communist appeaser. But I don't care. If I tried to pull out completely now from Vietnam, we would have Joe McCarthy red scare on our hands, but I can do it after I'm re-elected. So we had better make damned sure that I am re-elected".[clxxxiv] [clxxxv] Men with similar beliefs to McNamara's in the Kennedy administration later supported the Vietnam War.

Johnson administration reversals in Vietnam policy rebranded the conflict as "McNamara's War." Like others in "Big Lyndon's Boys", McNamara enjoyed future corporate positions and benefits for his self-destructive military policies. McNamara's actions and political opportunism helped the ascension of executive ambitions. Reflecting about his management of the Vietnam War McNamara commented, "We were wrong, terribly wrong."[clxxxvi] Yet not just bureaucrats were beholden to President Johnson. Murderers and thugs were additionally possible Johnson retainers.

The Boys criminal side feasibly includes Billy Sol Estes. Estes collaborated with Lyndon Johnson purportedly funneling money through reporting fraudulent cotton stores. These actions allegedly gained them lucrative subsidy funding. Prior to a later prosecution, Estes accountant and business partners died. Many were determined suicides after local police investigated. A rampant pattern of violent deaths followed those allegedly within Johnson's sphere of control.[clxxxvii]

Billy Sol Estes later asserted he met with Lyndon Johnson and Malcolm Wallace a Johnson enforcer. They discussed Agriculture official Henry Marshall and his attempts to expose Johnson's alleged business corruption. Marshall's evidence contended Johnson misused funds and manipulated his office for personal benefit. Marshall died before authorities could file charges. He suffered five shots with a bolt-action rifle. Somehow, the original cause of death was officially suicide.

Sol Estes claims Henry Marshall is one of the murders Lyndon Johnson ordered. Johnson allegedly dispatched Malcolm Wallace to kill Henry Marshall with his own rifle according to Billy Sol Estes. Local police gathered no complete forensic evidence. Marshall's body subsequently is exhumed and retested; homicide was the new official cause of death.[clxxxviii]

Some have suggested Malcolm Wallace took part in the Kennedy assassination. Malcolm Wallace had a long prior criminal record, sloppy documented skills, and association with multiple deaths. His notoriety in the Dallas area drew significant notice. These past errors in my view keep Wallace from actively participating in the assassination. In my view, no one directly connected to Lyndon Johnson is a possible assassin suspect.

All these men, from alleged killers to ambitious politicians served the will of Big Lyndon. Johnson ignored legal jurisdiction initially and formed the Commission despite the regular course of law.[clxxxix] This arbitrary blue ribbon group used lesser standards for assigning guilt. In circumventing regular United States law, Johnson acted in the unilateral manner of the dictator he opposed in Cuba.

## THE PRESIDENT'S COMMISSION REPORT

The subsequent wide official support regarding the President's (Warren) Commission developed over time and did not exist initially. Lyndon Johnson and J. Edgar Hoover each strenuously opposed any investigation not led by the Federal Bureau of Investigation. During a phone call, Johnson states his regard for a Presidential Commission "if we have another Commission, hell, you're gonna have people running over each other..." "...now I know some of the lawyers...they thought of the blue ribbon commission first...you see, Katzenbach suggested that (the Commission) and that provoked it...the lawyers and the council hit the ceiling...said, my God Almighty..."

Mr. Joe Alsop responds, "I see... I see... I see that you're right and he (Katzenbach) was wrong...for summing up the result of the FBI inquiry in a way that will completely coherent, detailed, and will carry unchallengeable convictions and this carrying conviction is just as important as carrying on the investigation...in the right way...and I worry about the (Washington) Post (article)." The article suggested the formation of Katzenbach's proposed Commission.[cxc]

President Johnson subsequently contacts J. Edgar Hoover and states "Two things. Apparently, some lawyer in Justice (Department) is lobbying with the Post because that's where the suggestion came from for this Presidential Commission which we think would be very bad and put it right in the White House. Now we can't be checking up on every shooting scrape in the country, but they've gone to the Post now to get them an editorial, and the Post is calling up an saying they're going to run an editorial...if we don't do things. Now we're going to do two things and I wanted you to know about it."

"One: We believe that the way to handle this as we said yesterday--your suggestion--that you put at every facility at your command, making a full report to the Attorney General and then they make it available to the country in whatever form may seem desirable. Second: It's a state matter, two, and the State Attorney General (Waggoner Carr) is young and able and prudent and very cooperative with you (Hoover) – he's going to run a court of inquiry which is provided for by a state law and he's going to have associated with him the most outstanding jurists in the country."

"But he's a good conservative fellow and we don't start invading local jurisdictions that way and he understands what you're doing, and he's for it...Now if you get too many cooks messing with the broth it makes -- mess it up." Hoover responds, "We'll work together on it." Once the American public embraced the suggested Commission, Johnson completely reversed his views. Yet Hoover retained his adversarial stance.[cxci]

J. Edgar Hoover sent a memorandum to Bureau officers relating a phone call with Deputy Attorney General Katzenbach regarding the suggested Commission. "...and advised him that I had just talked with the President who was very much disturbed; that he heard somewhere that the Washington Post had been tipped off by somebody in the Department that a Presidential Commission would be appointed to look into the entire situation down in Dallas; that this is not correct; that he does not intend to have any Presidential Commission, that he wants to have two reports prepared by the Bureau - one on the assassination and one on Oswald."[cxcii]

On November 29, 1963, Lyndon Johnson created the President's Commission on the Assassination of President Kennedy. The group is widely known as the Warren Commission, yet its less known name has meaning. It was indeed the President's Commission. A largely unstated legal fact is Lyndon Johnson disregarded the normal course of law. He first attempted to have the Bureau lead the investigation, after that failed Johnson assented to a commission.

Johnson seemed averse to normal legal procedures of investigation. Normally local authorities conducted the investigation. Yet the Texas Attorney General eventually granted concurrent jurisdiction to federal authorities. This occurred after jurisdictional law was ignored at Parkland hospital.

The Commission was a group of politicians and businesspersons appointed by executive order. Each member conformed to political requirements not investigative ability. Johnson's involvement in the matter is wholly outside concepts of neutrality. Contending internal agendas guided the inquiry since its conception.

While Johnson called for law and order, he acted inconsistently regarding the United States Constitution. The result of Johnson's efforts was the President's (Warren) Commission Report. A document filled with assertions unable to endure the Information Age. Sufficient data has surfaced within declassified government sources that refute significant portions of the official findings.

The President's (Warren) Commission failed to serve as a plausible substitute to judicial process. No trial conducted using the criminal standard of guilt beyond a reasonable doubt occurred. The Commission relied on a varying "preponderance of evidence".[cxciii] Ignored were facts and official evidence deviating from their conclusions.

## MEMBERS OF THE PRESIDENT'S (WARREN) COMMISSION

Johnson tasks seven men with solving the President's murder. No one on the Commission was a medical expert. No person serving was a qualified investigator with police training. Most attempted to conduct the best investigation possible, yet some officials were not motivated to make every evidentiary connection. Some evidence subsequently led to the group one Commissioner had previously directed.

Former Director of the Central Intelligence Agency Allen Dulles is shrouded in notoriety. Yet President Kennedy as some claim did not fire Dulles; he resigned. Letters sent between Dulles and President Kennedy and the award Dulles received for service, contend public hostility.[cxciv] Based on the primary evidence Nicholas Katzenbach and Robert Kennedy suggested Dulles for appointment.[cxcv] These documents support Kennedy insiders supported the Commission's formation and Dulles' membership.

However, Allen Dulles did keep a substantial secret. Allen Dulles was among the handful of Agency leaders who knew of the Castro assassination plots. Internal Agency documents regarding this affirm, "Dulles had approved the entire operation against Castro." Those aware of these plots include "Messers. Dulles, Bissell, Colonel J.C. King, Colonel Sheffield Edwards, William Harvey, and James P. O' Connell...Robert A. Maheu and his attorneys..." [cxcvi] The American public could not rely on the entire Commission to be honest and disclose substantial evidence. Dulles even met with an Agency representative to prepare them for the Commission's probable questions.[cxcvii]

Congressman Hale Boggs was a southern Democrat and opposed repeated Civil Rights bills including Eisenhower executive measures. A segregationist and publicly outspoken against expanded civil rights, Boggs believed in the power of the Old South despite social change. Boggs attended serious private exchanges within the executive sessions of the Commission. He might have observed a possible well-crafted mixture of truth and lies develop.

Being a wise man Boggs came to some reasonable conclusions about the Commission's hidden purpose. Boggs tried to retain his integrity and disputed some of the Commission's final judgments. He was notable for his objections to Oswald as the lone sniper. Commissioner Boggs' possible ideas and mine differ, yet we each doubted what officials claim transpired.

The Commissioners were men in a horrible political conundrum. Years before later congressional investigations were underway, Congressman Boggs was publicly critical of the Commission. Some have speculated Boggs' following demise in a plane crash is a conspiracy. The claim is unsubstantiated speculation without verified proof.

Johnson appointed Kentucky Senator John Sherman Cooper for his reasonable disposition and international political experience. He was a Republican who supported Democratic Party led civil rights legislation. Cooper had formerly denounced Senator Joseph McCarthy and his actions during the Red Scare. Cooper was among those who disagreed with key findings of the Commission.

"Yes, there were disagreements. I think the most serious one…" regarded the Single Bullet theory. "I heard Governor Connally testify he was not struck by the same bullet…I could not convince myself the same bullet struck both of them (Connally and Kennedy)…I was not convinced by it, neither was Senator Russell."[cxcviii] Cooper later opposed the unnecessary use of American forces abroad. He was a brave man who served admirably.

Most in the American Government are decent people, doing the utmost to make a laborious and corrupt system function. Unfortunately, fear, self-interest, and professional survival can render the bravest person silent. We cannot reasonably hold the entire American government responsible for John F. Kennedy's death. Not the regular people in the American government but a fringe minority sought to alter history. A Kennedy Assassination Conspiracy was conceivably a small collection of people.

Critics are correct; no sweeping government tyranny undertook the Kennedy assassination. It was more likely a cadre of cowards responsible for using official distortions. Unfortunately, the idea of assassination conspiracy remains taboo in public study. The Commissioners who observed these factual instances still publicly supported the incorrect findings. Assorted Single Bullet theorists additionally seek to recast history in the flawed image of every Commission determination.

Gerald Ford joined the President's (Warren) Commission while serving in the American Congress and later was the nation's president. He reported President's (Warren) Commission members who doubted Chief Justice Earl Warren's decisions to the Federal Bureau of Investigation. Ford informed Lyndon Johnson about President's (Warren) Commissioners who doubted the official timetable.[cxcix]

Gerald Ford was chosen as one of the seven "wise men" Johnson appointed to the President's (Warren) Commission. Johnson had commented to advisers' previously of Ford's intelligence, "He can't fart and chew gum at the same time".[cc] Why appoint someone you perceive to be a fool to the Commission? How would this affect the investigation?

Commissioner John J. McCloy had longtime associations with the Military-Industrial Complex. McCloy served as lawyer, the United States assistant Secretary of War, and held important positions in the financial sector. Johnson appointed McCloy from ideas Robert Kennedy and Nicholas Katzenbach offered. Despite the origins, how is this bureaucrat suddenly a qualified investigator?

Unfortunately, Kennedy loyalists did not realize Johnson feasibly wanted attorneys not detectives involved. Johnson did not realize McCloy's insight, or his contempt regarding some government agencies. President Johnson definitely never believed McCloy's words could eventually reach the public.[cci] Not just McCloy expressed disgust toward other groups involved with the Commission.

A friend and mentor of once upcoming Texas legislator Lyndon Johnson was Senator Richard Russell Jr. He aided in political victories including Johnson's appointment as Majority Leader of the Senate. Russell strongly opposed his appointment to the Commission in private with Lyndon Johnson. After his tenure Russell stated, "I think someone else was involved with Lee Harvey Oswald."[ccii] He also maintained his dissent to any Single Bullet Theory. Senator Russell affirmed "so much possible evidence was beyond the reach of the (President's Commission)…"[cciii] The senator's words are remarkable and true.

Similar to Commissioner Hale Boggs, Richard Russell had great reservations, yet Russell was not just any other member. Having been Johnson's enduring ally, Russell knew his tactics intimately. Senator Russell was aware the Federal Bureau of Investigation and Central Intelligence Agency were unable or unwilling to offer necessary information. Johnson's own longtime allies had reservations about the Commission's findings. Once reviewing all the facts how can some not question the Commission's results?

President Johnson selected a final key member. Appointed to lead the Commission is the United States Chief Justice Earl Warren. The Chief Justice was another suggestion from Nicholas Katzenbach and Robert Kennedy. Yet Warren is a sharp intellect who might have realized the executive branch was possibly manipulating the law. Speaking to the Commission's staff, he confesses as much.

"...the Chief Justice discussed the circumstances under which he had accepted the chairmanship of the Commission. When the position had first been offered to him he declined it, on the principle that Supreme Court justices should not take this kind of role. His associate justices concurred in this decision." Warren and the entire Supreme Court understood he should not be involved. President Johnson then convinced Warren stating dire international rumors and shadows of war.

Primary among the rumors were those "...attributing the assassination to a faction within the government wishing to see the Presidency assumed by President Johnson. Others, if not quenched, could conceivably lead the country into a war which could cost 40 million lives. No one could refuse to do something which might help to prevent such a possibility. The President convinced him that this was an occasion on which actual conditions had to override general principles."[cciv] Yet these concerns were not fact but rumor, Johnson disregarded principal for politics. Warren's appointment created multiple unforeseen consequences.

It offered the appearance of two branches in the American government supporting the Commission's recommendations. This prevented the Chief Justice from later reviewing the Commission's actions, and left the Supreme Court marginalized. Would the other Justices attempt to impeach the Chief Justice's decisions? These consequences would blunt legal opposition to the Commission's findings.

Warren required total agreement in the Commission's final decisions. Despite the many witnesses and experts who dispute their contentions. The Chief Justice retired from the Supreme Court six years later. His appointment leant credibility to superseding the natural course of legal events. This prevented American Congressional authorities from launching legal investigations for years.

From its creation the President's (Warren) Commission suffered various procedural delays. Adding to the problems was the Commission's failure to include many witness statements. The entire Commission observing a witness interview rarely occurs. Most had other duties often preventing their attendance to statements. Those who credit the Commission with a complete investigation ignore the myths surrounding it.

Supposed President's (Warren) Commission independence was one such myth. Representative Gerald Ford seemed to infer an unseen influence, "The more we disassociate ourselves, as I understand our mission, from the White House the better it is for all of us, and I should think the President (Johnson) would want it that way himself".[ccv] Commissioner Ford has mentioned a mission, not an investigation. This admission implies set goals and conclusions; perhaps it was a poor choice of words.

However, the only reason to disassociate from the White House would be to conceal Lyndon Johnson's influence. Gerald Ford mentioned, "The better it is for all of us" which could imply a threat hung in the air. What Johnson wanted is of little interest to actual investigators. Why appoint a Commission if Johnson was making the decisions?

Commissioner John J. McCloy uttered the most blatant confession of the President's Commission being under Johnson's control. McCloy in referencing their inquiries said "...I don't think any door is closed to us, unless the President closes it to us..." Therefore, if Lyndon Johnson wants an issue suppressed, the President's Commission ignores the subject. How can a full investigation occur if Johnson can conceal any evidence he wished?

Additionally problematic was the President's (Warren) Commission reliance on certain organizations to conduct a full investigation. Some Commissioner's did not expect honesty in these associations. Allen Dulles insisted the Central Intelligence Agency should analyze Commission evidence. In response, Richard Russell stated, "I think you've got more faith in them than I have. I think they'll doctor anything they hand to us".[ccvi]

The President's (Warren) Commission additionally claimed subpoena powers. So why did the Commissioners initially never subpoena any witness to testify? Perhaps because of largely unmentioned American Congressional objections. Commissioner Russell affirmed, "That the Commission, not having been established by Congress with a deliberate legislative purpose, the subpoena power just isn't there. I don't think there is an exception to it, but you can make one." [ccvii] Weeks later Congress made the necessary exception.[ccviii]

President Lyndon Johnson displayed the ambitions of executive power openly. Chief Justice Warren knew federal authorities had initially bypassed the legal jurisdiction of Texas officials. However, the legality of Commission powers was not the only thing in question. Some

Commissioners doubted the Federal Bureau of Investigation and presented medical evidence.

Commissioner McCloy suggested "...let's find out about these wounds, it is just as confusing as could be. It left my mind muddy as to what really did happen...why didn't they turn the body over, who turned the body over, who were the people up there, why did the FBI report come out with something which isn't consistent with the autopsy?"[ccix] Many experts and witnesses share the Commissioner's doubts.

McCloy wished to ask J. Edgar Hoover and the Bureau "What is all this talk about you having no liaison with the Secret Service? You did have an interview or at least you located this man (Oswald) two or three weeks before the assassination. Didn't you pass this on to the Secret Service? Why didn't you if you didn't..." [ccx]

The Commission pondered if Lee Harvey Oswald was an undercover agent serving the Federal Bureau of Investigation. Commissioner Dulles stated the Bureau would conceal anything to protect itself. Dulles was "...confident that the FBI would never admit it, and I presume their records will never show it, or if their records do show anything, I would think their records would show some kind of numbers that could be assigned to a dozen different people according to how they wanted to describe them".[ccxi] Other Commissioners were more concerned.

An insight about the Federal Bureau of Investigation's behavior emerged from Commissioner Russell: "If Oswald never had assassinated the President or at least been charged with assassinating the President and had been in the employ of the FBI and somebody had gone to the FBI they would have denied he was an agent?" Allen Dulles responds "Oh, yes." Senator Russell continues, "They would be the first to deny it. Your agents would have done exactly the same thing." Allen Dulles, former Director of the Central Intelligence responds "Exactly." Dulles clearly affirms the Bureau and Agency willingness to deceive any official group to secure their interests.

A phone book obtained after Oswald's arrest supports the Bureau's possible employment of Oswald. The phone book contained various contacts officials used to assert Oswald's guilt. Yet the Bureau did not include a single name in many reports. Bureau Agent James P. Hosty's name and phone number appeared in the suspect's phone book.[ccxii] Classified Bureau statements reveal legitimate substantial legal flaws.

Concerning Lee Harvey Oswald and his treatment by officials J. Edgar Hoover privately commented, "Oswald having been killed today after our warnings to the Dallas Police Department was inexcusable. It will allow, I am afraid a lot of civil rights people to raise a lot of hell because he was handcuffed and had no weapon. There are bound to be some elements of our society who will holler their heads off that his civil rights were violated--(official edit) which they were."[ccxiii] Officials declassify the document after Hoover's death. Hoover's words refute official claims of propriety regarding Oswald.

Lead Counsel Rankin asserts of the Bureau "I just don't think they are going to come out and say they fabricated this, if it is a fabrication. It is too serious for that"[ccxiv] Some Commissioners had to rely on the Bureau for honest information while believing it might have connections to the president's death. This represents the critical flaws and political dysfunction within the entire President's Commission inquiry.

The Commission feared information beyond their reach, and possible Bureau collusion with Oswald. The signs of a plot upset Commissioner Ford. Regarding these fears he stated "...the Chief Justice and I were just briefly reflecting on this we said if that was true and if it ever came out and could be established, then you would have people think that there was a conspiracy to accomplish this assassination that nothing the Commission or anybody could dissipate".[ccxv] These fears became reality with each public mention of conspiracy.

Despite what critics have claimed, serious doubt existed among the Commissioners. Some leaders in the President's (Warren) Commission were blind to evidence not furthering Johnson's mission. Multiple reasonable theories existed including among government officials. In discussing this Bureau theory, the Commission exposed a conceivably evolving plot.

Allen Dulles said to Lead Counsel "Lee (Rankin), if this were true (the Federal Bureau of Investigation was not conducting a full investigation regarding suspects other than Lee Harvey Oswald) why would it be particularly in their interest --- to say he is clearly the only guilty one? I mean I don't see that argument that you raise particularly shows an interest." Commissioner Hale Boggs responded, "I can immediately --- (official edit) "They would like to have us fold up and quit...".

"This closes the case, you see. Don't you see?" Boggs declares. Allen Dulles responded to Boggs "Yes I see that".[ccxvi] Those who doubt all conspiracy should refer to multiple Commissioners' words regarding that exact idea. Official and independent sources alleged Oswald possessed official ties.

When Allen Dulles requested the destruction of all notes from the meeting, his desire to suppress information becomes clear. Allen Dulles claimed Lee

Harvey Oswald was too irresponsible to be a Federal Bureau of Investigation agent. In response, a separate man present tells a story. Commissioner John McCloy had sincere opinions about certain government employees.

McCloy, having associated with them many times in his life commented, "Well I can't say that I have run into a fellow comparable to Oswald but I have run into some very limited mentalities both in the CIA and the FBI (Laughter)." The Commissioners were quite amused in these once private observations. However, McCloy is not alone in his contempt. Half the Commission commented while the others laughed.

Chairman Earl Warren added, "Under agents, the regular agents, I think that would be right, but they and all other agencies do employ undercover men who are of terrible character." Senator Russell completed the verbal smashing with "Limited intelligence, even the city police departments do it…"[ccxvii] This exchange supports corruption and incompetence in some American government agencies was enduring.

The Commission pondered if Oswald received aid in his Mexican travels. It came provided from the Central Intelligence Agency, yet in their report they assert otherwise: "…it is possible he talked to people about such plans, and had collaborators concerning them in Mexico City… He tried to get a visa at the Cuban embassy, and he tried to get a visa at the Soviet Embassy…" [ccxviii] A later House Select Committee inquiry focusing on Mexico City failed to identify any collaborators. The verified evidence does not support the Agency's speculations.

In time, multiple individuals would emerge to fuel the ideas of Oswald collaborators and imposters. Evidence was twisted and still fuels speculations that cloud the matter. Other Commissioners waited to comment about irregularities. Some delayed until after their deaths.

Within "A Presidential Legacy and the Warren Commission," President Gerald Ford noted the Central Intelligence Agency had committed illegal actions. The Agency interfered with the Kennedy investigation and hid facts about the assassination. President Ford commented of the Agency's concern over "certain classified and potentially damaging operations in danger of being exposed".[ccxix] The Agency began to destroy evidence without the approval of higher authorities.

Ford noted the Central Intelligence Agency's intentions were to "hide or destroy some information, which can easily be misinterpreted as collusion in John F. Kennedy's assassination."[ccxx] If the Agency had nothing relevant to conceal, why destroy the files? They launched a suppression campaign to hide former illegal actions. How could the Agency not expect public backlash?

The Federal Bureau of Investigation "...informed the White House and Acting Attorney General Katzenbach that the Commission's report is seriously inaccurate insofar as its treatment of the FBI is concerned".[ccxxi] Hoover's letter displays the Bureau's image not actual conduct was ever the primary concern. Experts, authorities, and researchers contend sections of the President's (Warren) Commission Report. The Commission had to rely on a few biased and unreliable officials.

President's (Warren) Commission Lead Counsel J. Lee Rankin, offered later classified testimony before the House Select Committee on Assassinations. The Agency did not provide relevant documents, photographs, and some evidence. Only the Agency's mistaken release of information to third parties provided some evidence to the Commission. Rankin states the pattern of inaccurate evidence was "...quite incompetent or deliberate."

To verify Oswald was not an operative of the Central Intelligence Agency or Federal Bureau of Investigation, the Commission needed to examine internal Bureau and Agency files. J. Edgar Hoover objected to such necessary measures and the Commission instead agreed to accept Hoover's statement that Oswald had no connection. The Commission allowed Agency Director John McCone to forgo evidentiary inspection with a personal statement. Their assurances do not serve as reasonable inquiry.

Rankin admits to the Select Committee "It is obvious in light of what has happened that you could not rely on those assurances. I don't know about Mr. McCone, whether there is anything in the record that would show he misrepresented anything...but certainly it is evident you could not rely on Mr. Hoover's word." Rankin offers Hoover's deceitful tendencies damaged the President's (Warren) Commission investigation.[ccxxii]

## OTHER RELATED OFFICIALS

Dallas Mayor Earle Cabell helped orchestrate the presidential visit and could influence the minimal local security measures present during the trip. In the aftermath of President Kennedy's murder, Earle Cabell spoke to the public in a television broadcast. "This is not a time to point the finger at anyone but for personal reflection".[ccxxiii] Cabell additionally ignored Dallas Police officer protests for enhanced measures to secure Oswald's transfer. Subsequent to serving as Mayor of Dallas, Cabell became a Congressional Representative. He recommended to Attorney General Katzenbach the President's original "handsome casket…in keeping with the best interests of the country, be destroyed."[ccxxiv]

A longtime Kennedy political enemy, Richard Nixon, was earlier defeated in a presidential race against John F. Kennedy. He remained a staunch lifelong political rival. However, Richard Nixon's history might be more complex than imagined. Nixon was associated with many publicly suspected men including Lyndon Johnson and J. Edgar Hoover. Yet Nixon remained an outsider among his political allies.

History has revealed most of Nixon's "Watergate Plumbers" had mixed loyalties. They were alleged and confirmed Agency employees past and present. These agents included Eugenio Martinez (CIA), Bernard Baker (CIA), James McCord (CIA and FBI), and E. Howard Hunt (CIA). Hunt admitted to sending information to the CIA during his employment by the Nixon administration.[ccxxv]

Nixon attempted repeatedly to force the Central Intelligence Agency to provide all classified information of interest. Included were files about John F. Kennedy's assassination. The Agency never invited those outside its organization to peruse secret files. They also did not want President Nixon running his own espionage group. Perhaps the Agency decided to end Richard Nixon's curiosity and career.

As the Watergate scandal closed in, Nixon attempted in vain to force the Central Intelligence Agency to protect him. Nixon believed the Agency would serve him, having no idea they might be later responsible for destroying his presidency. The Agency could have used assets high in the Nixon administration. Richard Nixon said in a later interview with David Frost, "…they gave me a sword, and I fell on it".[ccxxvi]

A post-Watergate discussion of payoffs appears on the Nixon Presidential Library tapes. It contained a conversation about E. Howard Hunt demanding money for legal fees and not exposing his executive branch ties. Hunt was a confirmed asset loyal to the Agency and its chosen plots. Hunt possibly served as the asset who intentionally compromised the

Watergate burglary. Nixon's amateur raid on the Democratic National Convention offices was feasibly destined to fail. Perhaps a few officials decided that some knowledge was not for American presidents. Yet Nixon was among many officials with serious doubts.

Nixon as well might have suspected a former assassination conspiracy. He wanted power over the forces that could topple a president, which is exactly what the Agency represents. A subordinate organization beyond presidential control was reprehensible to Nixon. He could have felt the Agency must be controlled and humbled. Nixon failed to comprehend the allegiances of those surrounding him and did not realize the price of these actions.

The Nixon administration ordered Richard Helms to pay hush money to E. Howard Hunt. Nixon then renewed demands to surrender all files and information regarding subjects of his interest. Central Intelligence Agency Director Richard Helms refused the orders, and President Nixon fired him. Nixon's political fate was sealed.

James Schlesinger became the next Agency leader. Schlesinger commented, "The clandestine service was Helms's Praetorian Guard. It had too much influence in the Agency and was too powerful within the government. I am going to cut it down to size." Director Schlesinger over the next three months slashed nearly ten percent of Central Intelligence Agency officers from the ranks.[ccxxvii][ccxxviii] These wide reaching actions created shockwaves throughout the Agency.

Schlesinger later issued a command to all Central Intelligence Agency employees: "… report to me immediately on any activities now going on, or might have gone on in the past, which might be considered to be outside the legislative charter of this Agency. I hereby direct every person presently employed by Central Intelligence Agency to report to me on any such activities… Anyone who has such information should call my secretary and say that he wishes to talk to me about activities outside the Central Intelligence Agency's charter".[ccxxix]

The Richard M. Nixon Presidential Library over time has also released many controversial tapes regarding the former president. They reveal Nixon and his close aides were not averse to crime in achieving their goals. Nixon's paranoia was allegedly correct; forces indeed were rising against him. Nixon ended his presidency chasing political ghosts and hiring feasible Agency spies to discover them.

Richard Nixon was possibly set up for his eventual fall. If a beloved President could die from attack, Nixon might have realized so could he.

Would any lament the increasingly unpopular Richard Nixon? Nevertheless, assassination was not the only weapon Nixon's possible enemies possessed.

Nixon theoretically wanted information to leverage against his enemies, hide any links of illegality to him, and for peace of mind. Once the Nixon administration's actions triggered Watergate, Nixon's Chief of Staff H.R. Haldeman began a cover up. It was unsuccessful to say the least. Nixon's demands to the Central Intelligence Agency might have ensured his political demise.

Despite various plots, Richard Nixon actually might have believed he was protecting his country, party, and himself. However, conspiratorial actions denied him the adoration and respect he so desperately sought. Richard Nixon has become a parodied figure in American history. The Nixon legacy is a cautionary tale to others in government.

Similar to President Nixon, President Johnson's greatest fears were more realistic than he imagined. The idea of being a pretender to the American presidency haunted Johnson's entire life. Not Johnson's reforms but his sweeping ambition ensures this historical curse. His actions repeatedly denied the law its due course. Beyond Johnson's power was the ability to cease repeated public questioning of his intentions.

Nixon and Johnson were attempting to redefine the American Executive's constitutional powers. Nixon attempted to deny the American Congress and legal authorities' documents and tapes that eventually proved his guilt. Nixon tried justifying these claims as executive privilege. This privilege can potentially conceal grave miscalculations, lies, and current unknown illegal actions.

These American leaders designed policy to increase executive authority at the cost of congressional power. Lyndon Johnson began seizing power as most in the country mourned. Richard Nixon attempted to assert executives powers beyond those in the American Constitution. This ambition has passed to most following Presidents of the Unites States. It has allowed the ascension of the current Military-Industrial Complex.

# CHAPTER 4

*"But who is to guard the guards themselves?"*

~Juvenal
Roman Satirist

## THE MILITARY INTELLIGENCE ARM

The diplomatic path John F. Kennedy used concerning Soviet foreign policy infuriated some. Among them was Chairman of the United States Joint Chiefs of Staff, General Lyman Lemnitzer. Lemnitzer disregarded reasonable limits on military power in his tenure. He advised President Kennedy to launch an attack on Cuba to topple Fidel Castro. Kennedy refused Lemnitzer's repeated attempts to involve the American military in unnecessary foreign wars and domestic illegality.

Lemnitzer presented a plan calling for a surprise nuclear attack on the Soviet Union without provocation. His ideas disturbed President Kennedy.[ccxxx] Lemnitzer soon presented Secretary Dean Rusk with a new top-secret plan. He created a reprehensible treason to stir American public sentiment for the invasion of Cuba. The operation was codenamed NORTHWOODS.

NORTHWOODS would use planned attacks on the United States by its own military. The justification given was to incite anti-Cuban sentiment and create opportunity for military action. This included attacks on American cities, military installations and other domestic targets. NORTHWOODS could have caused nuclear war with the Soviet Union. Brash ignorance has incited many American foreign policy disasters.[ccxxxi]

When Lemnitzer met with President Kennedy in 1962, Kennedy immediately shut down operation NORTHWOODS.[ccxxxii] Eventually President Kennedy reassigned Lyman Lemnitzer. This effectively banished Lemnitzer from the Joint Chiefs with foreign duties to occupy him. Under Lyndon Johnson, Lemnitzer's fortunes reversed and he eventually became Supreme Commander of Allied Forces. The Johnson administration made repeated military errors; this includes Lemnitzer's subsequent appointment.

The Gulf of Tonkin event accelerated the War in Vietnam based on lies. So what possible lies have led to current wars? The ghostly threat of weapons of mass destruction still costs monthly in American deaths, casualties, and two trillion dollars spent in just Iraq so far.[ccxxxiii] What future lies will provide wealth and power for those who act in the name of national security?

## THE INDUSTRIALISTS AND FANATICS

Southern business interests aligned opposing the Kennedys based on their political and social agendas. John F. Kennedy's full commitment did not lay in the Vietnam War; some deemed him soft on Communism. For seeking unprofitable peace in the world, men hated John F. Kennedy. The success of America's Nuclear Test Ban Treaty additionally incited wealthy Kennedy detractors.

President Kennedy reduced nuclear threats using diplomacy to engage the Soviet Union. Hard line forces present inside Washington D.C. had spent their entire careers fighting Communism. The president's opponents despised logical international restrictions on nuclear arms and testing. This strategic action cemented fringe groups opposing Kennedy policies.

One dominant Kennedy detractor was Clint Murchison. His wealth resulted from oil profits and many varied businesses. Among them, Murchison held a business interest located in California, the Hotel Del Charro. This hotel was a lavishly appointed environment catering to his powerful clients desires. Murchison had guests such as Richard Nixon, J. Edgar Hoover, and Clyde Tolson frequenting this seemingly idyllic destination.[ccxxxiv]

The hotel was complimentary for Murchison's special guests, conceivably this was a form of acceptable bribery. Ironically, Hoover had a lifelong friendship with the hotel's later owner. Allegedly, the new owner was a Mafia associate with a considerable Bureau file and criminal history.[ccxxxv] For Hoover, brazen conflicts of interest were secondary to luxury accommodations.

Murchison's brand of politics was far right of conservative. He appears as the original mold of later fringe partisans. He funded the campaigns of Joe McCarthy, the senator who fiercely incited the Red Scare. He was a major financial supporter of Lyndon Johnson and had strong influence in Texas politics. Murchison was unfortunately not alone in his beliefs.

Joseph Milteer was a similar wealthy Kennedy political enemy. Milteer had spoken at length to an undercover police informant William Somerset about President Kennedy's hypothetical assassination. He said it would probably be from an office building with a high-powered rifle. Milteer also notes a fellow militant named Brown who sought to assassinate Martin Luther King. Milteer additionally states "they will pick up somebody within hours afterwards, if anything like that would happen just to throw the public off."[ccxxxvi] Milteer was a notable member of the militant National States Rights party as well.

The House Select Committee on Assassinations noted the similarity of possible assassins in Chicago (Vallee) and Dallas (Oswald). These two events are similar to the ideas of a rifle and sniper Milteer had mentioned. Authorities did not offer these "Significant threats" in Chicago and Miami to the Secret Service constructing security in Dallas.[ccxxxvii] These security lapses would soon prove fatal.

Among the loudest anti-Kennedy political coalitions was the John Birch Society. The Birchers were a fringe group who opposed civil rights initiatives. Among their propaganda was their founder Robert Welch's pamphlet "The Time has come," a fictional Communist civil rights strategy. Welch's pamphlet contends integration was creating a "Negro Soviet Republic".[ccxxxviii] Other Birchers sought to impeach Chief Justice of the United States Earl Warren for legally enforcing American school desegregation.

Unsurprisingly, the John Birch Society still exists today. Although its public image has changed, its political roots speak for themselves. The John Birch Society previously accused Communists of launching repeated conspiracies. Their repeated unsubstantiated Communist "plots"[ccxxxix ccxl] reduced the credibility of others exposing genuine political conspiracy supported with evidence. Yet informed observers can discover the truth.

Among the same group's membership was General Edwin Walker. Walker used his military office to aid his own political interests. He publicly handed out John Birch Society literature to American troops. His propaganda labeled President John F. Kennedy and some of his appointees as Communist sympathizers. This was an attempt to associate John F. Kennedy with Soviet ideals and programs.

Following a generous offer of reassignment, Walker resigned his commission to pursue his political goals. After a failed campaign for Texas Governor, Walker publicly took up the causes of the John Birch Society. Walker's political activities included publicly speaking out against federal troops trying to enforce the law.[ccxli] Walker's own statement's reveal his commitment to cultural segregation despite the American government.

"I am in Mississippi beside Gov. Ross Barnett. I call for a national protest against the conspiracy from within. Rally to the cause of freedom in righteous indignation, violent vocal protest, and bitter silence under the flag of Mississippi at the use of Federal troops. This today is a disgrace to the nation in 'dire peril,' a disgrace beyond the capacity of anyone except its enemies. This is the conspiracy of the crucifixion by anti-Christ conspirators of the Supreme Court in their denial of prayer and their betrayal of a nation".[ccxlii]

Due in part to Walker's actions, the angry pro-segregation gathering became a riot. The violence killed two men and twenty state marshals required medical assistance. Edwin Walker faced charges of Insurrection against the United States.[ccxliii] Despite Walker's incendiary speech, all charges were dropped. Edwin Walker's vanity earned him honorary citizenship in the City of Dallas. Presiding was Mayor Earle Cabell.[ccxliv]

Officially, Edwin Walker and President Kennedy had a common enemy in Lee Harvey Oswald. Oswald publicly spoke out against Walker, his military career and political associations. Oswald shot at Walker later according to the official record. Authorities initially identified the bullet as likely fired with a Carcano.

Oswald had allegedly ordered a Carcano under an alias previously and he was determined responsible. This was because Oswald had former sharpshooter designation. A government labeled sharpshooter failed to kill his target. The man Oswald supposedly decried and despised was unharmed because Oswald waited and missed a simple shot. If he was firing, he could not kill Edwin Walker.

Walker is not sitting in a moving vehicle, he possessed no security, and this was not a brief time in which to fire. Based on the official account, Oswald failed in successfully completing this simple plot. How more unlikely is the chance Oswald alone could undertake the entire Assassination Conspiracy? Later reports affirm Lee Harvey Oswald possibly did not commit the Walker attack.

Among the problems with the scenario is every witness. One stated that two men were observed days prior outside the Walker home "peeking in windows".[ccxlv] [ccxlvi] The other witness states that two men left the area in separate cars after the shooting. No witness identified Lee Harvey Oswald.[ccxlvii]

However, Marina Oswald claimed Oswald buried the Carcano before and after the attack.[ccxlviii] This action increases the chance of the weapon being discovered and requires Oswald to return near the scene. He is never observed doing any of these actions. The witnesses the Commission did rely upon often did not prove their assertions.

Both Marina and Robert Oswald gave conflicting witness assertions that lack proof. Each supported that Oswald planned to attack Richard Nixon; officials found neither claim substantial.[ccxlix] [ccl] Marina additionally claimed that Oswald while in New Orleans planned to hijack a plane to Cuba. She asserts Oswald eventually decided she would aid his armed takeover.[ccli] The Commission also remarked Marina was dishonest regarding identification of the Carcano and had destroyed possible related evidence.[cclii] Beyond Marina's claims, there is nothing but pictures of Walker's home connecting Lee Harvey Oswald to these unlikely plots.

The Walker note regarded by the Commission as evidence of Oswald's guilt has substantial deficiencies. This includes a lack of fingerprints from Lee and Marina, yet unidentified prints were on the letter. How could Oswald write the letter and Marina read it without leaving fingerprints?[ccliii] [ccliv] To whom do the other prints belong? Some may doubt fingerprints can endure for months, yet they can for years in some cases,[cclv] hence the unidentified prints. Additionally the Walker note has no date; it does not specifically mention Walker, nor any plot.

A Federal Bureau of Investigation report supports that Edwin Walker allegedly stated to foreign press that Lee Harvey Oswald fired at him. This statement would not be controversial if it had not occurred days before officials found the related evidence. Thus, Edwin Walker's offered rumor could feasibly taint public ideas and the jury pool. A second Bureau report is titled "German Press and extensive factual and editorial of killing of Oswald".[cclvi]

Though the Commission and Bureau were aware, they did not mention this report.[cclvii] Perhaps Walker's claims of a worldwide Communist conspiracy including leading American officials were relevant to his credibility.[cclviii] A prior ordered mental review is additionally worth mentioning.[cclix] Walker is not the reliable witness the Commission believed. His subsequent claims of a Communist cell operative in Dallas were additionally unproven.[cclx] Walker's many claims offer a pattern of paranoia coupled with his overt political actions, he is not the picture of reliability.

Lieutenant J.C. Day of the Dallas Police "took the bullet to the City-County Criminal Investigation Laboratory, Parkland Memorial Hospital." After analyzing the evidence, "the Laboratory could not identify the gun which fired the bullet because of the battered condition of the bullet."[cclxi] Bureau ballistics identification expert Robert Frazier was "unable to reach a conclusion" regarding the bullet retrieved from Walker's home. Experts could not match the bullet to Oswald's Carcano. [cclxii]

These additional inconsistencies were among those contending official presumptions. Officials ignored their own inconclusive expert statements. A further problem includes the alloys of the Walker and Kennedy bullets did not match.[cclxiii] It too challenges the official findings.

According to the President's Warren Commission experts, the bullet "could not be identified as having been fired" by Oswald's rifle.[cclxiv] Significant evidence infers no identified weapon and at least one other person in the area. Most could not designate Oswald's rifle being responsible for the shot. He possessed the single Carcano according to officials. The question becomes who shot at Edwin Walker, and who gained from the action?

Conceivably, it would support Oswald's later "subversive" credentials. It provides Walker and his associates international attention and credibility to their cause. If Oswald was the Communist assassin some claimed, he was a poor shot. This man could likely not fire the shots in Dealey Plaza based on failing to kill an easier target. Yet authorities did not consider these ideas.

If Oswald fired the shot at Walker, he did so with a second rifle and missed. If he did not, then we have further attempts to entrap Oswald. This offers possibilities implying multiple participants are necessary. Some have speculated the John Birch Society allied with Texas millionaires to murder John F. Kennedy. Yet conclusive evidence is less forthcoming.

Harold Lafayette Hunt was a fourth outspoken Kennedy detractor. He controlled oil and refining businesses that suffered under Kennedy tax policies. Hunt funded radio stations featuring his radical political views. He developed fringe domestic opinions and helped set-up a political network.

Harold Hunt used these radio stations to support anti-communist rhetoric. Using media campaigns, he accrued large political contributions for Lyndon B. Johnson. Hunt's actions included full-page newspaper ads claiming President Kennedy committed treason with baseless accusations. The President's (Warren) Commission discussed this matter without result.

A strong opponent of Fidel Castro, Hunt allegedly helped to fund the Cuban Revolutionary Council. This group aided the Central Intelligence Agency in several covert efforts to diminish and defeat Fidel Castro.[cclxv]

Harold Hunt was a close friend of General Edwin Walker, associate of Clint Murchison, and each man was anti-civil rights. Each of them hated Communists; all were members of the John Birch Society. [cclxvi] Every man is a political enemy of the Kennedys.

These men sought to achieve a dominant political agenda. Similar attitudes and organizations exemplify a mentality that still exists. Inflexible political beliefs and hyperbole became weapons against those not supporting their cause. Instead of sober assessment, partisan opinions were dominant.

Lead Counsel Rankin of the President's Commission Report exhibited a deeper understanding regarding these fringe groups. Rankin stated, "...communities can be like people, and if you let those forces work long enough it will have an effect upon their approach to many problems, and it may be something that the country should be well aware of".[cclxvii] He refers to possible far-left and right-wing conspiracies. This insight reflects the modern political truth.

These men were the most dangerous kind of religious and political fanatic, wealthy ones. Behold the handful of rich men and corporations who have influenced the last American presidential election. Have limitless funds supporting political candidates improved the state of the American Republic? Perhaps they are financing its end. Do wealthy fanatics aid or marginalize smaller citizen funded organizations?

Men such as these continually fund self-destructive politics. What they supported grew more pervasive as the years passed. Untenable modern partisanship becomes the legacy of those failing to deal in beneficial compromise. As future United States citizens shall pay for modern political inaction, whose bankrupt partisanship do current Americans now pay for?

Whether these men influenced a murderous plot, or were just distraction to muddle the facts remains open to debate. However, now we can observe influential men were seriously discussing violent attacks on President Kennedy. One discussed the possible financing and murder of John F. Kennedy. Men with related official and public associations were overlooked.

Other authors contend some of the men previously listed financed and helped aid the President's assassination. However, without aid from criminals and officials these men could never succeed. The alleged concealment of activities following John F. Kennedy's death was far beyond their abilities. Someone with official power would be necessary to provide security lapses.

Associations establish multiple groups were motivated to murder the president. These were not strangers; they helped finance the political careers of prominent men. These men were powerful financial interests but a conspiracy required men with greater legal influence. It requires President Kennedy perhaps to have lethal enemies among his own executive branch.

These men had already drawn sufficient public attention with their anti-Kennedy exploits. For them to directly aid the Assassination Conspiracy in my view is beyond the proven evidence. They possessed resources and influence, not total control over American leaders. These men alone lacked the power and expertise required.

They were absent the Mafia's disregard for murder and the Central Intelligence Agency assassination training. None possessed the Bureau's secrets and army of informants. Although possessing the motive and means they did not possess opportunity without official aid.


## THE CENTRAL INTELLIGENCE AGENCY

John F. Kennedy had mixed views of the Central Intelligence Agency. He fired well-connected intelligence leaders, and once purportedly vowed to destroy the Agency. However, President Kennedy praised the Central Intelligence Agency for successful operations. Kennedy used them repeatedly for secret activities. The relationship was impossible to maintain because of the egos involved.

President Kennedy's problem did not rest with the whole Central Intelligence Agency. The problem was a few men in leadership positions who displayed overt ambition and disregard for the law. President Kennedy realized he must reform, not destroy the Agency. Yet he might have been unaware his enemies retained important positions in the Agency's ranks.

Among the most dangerous of President Kennedy's political opponents was spymaster Allen Dulles. Dulles was a prominent member of the Office of Strategic Services a former American intelligence agency. While in this organization, he trained and developed his Intelligence credentials. Dulles later joined the Central Intelligence Agency rising to its highest position Director of Central Intelligence.

Dulles' actions still deeply affect current American foreign policy. In the 1950s, the Iranian government previously nationalized their countries oil reserves. Some interests would have lost a fortune if the legal decision stood. Multiple officials from the United States and British governments formed a plan to ensure their political and financial interests. They toppled the last democratic government in Iran exchanging it for a puppet regime.

The Central Intelligence Agency under Allen Dulles assisted the dictatorial Shah's Iranian government takeover. The coup was successful in part to Agency participation, funding, and United States military aid.[cclxviii] The newly crowned Shah led Iran on a heinous and torture filled reign of terror. The United States helped fund these actions without concern to the future consequences.

Repeatedly similar flawed operations have cost America billions of dollars, thousands of lives, with no useful long-term return. The Agency's Iranian allies later fell with the Shah's overthrow; hundreds of millions in business investments were lost as well. The American people have endured Iran and its government as enemies since. America suffers because of Allen Dulles and the Agency's repressive operations. All these failed policies have made the United States less secure.

Following John F. Kennedy's assassination, Lyndon Johnson chose Allen Dulles for the President's (Warren) Commission. The Commission investigation reviewed possible criminal actions by the Central Intelligence Agency. How can the man who led the Agency for over a decade now be an impartial judge? Dulles influenced many aspects of Commission business.

Some Agency leaders attempted to use official powers to suit personal agendas. As Hoover dismissed his superiors' authority, so too did Allen Dulles conduct his organization despite ethics. These men for decades were key figures in the United States establishment. Each disregarded the law when convenient. Despite these actions, subordinates respected and defended Hoover and Dulles. Their repeated breaches of law and sworn oath were unknown to most underlings.

Despite the retirement of Dulles, the Agency continued in his image. Its actions have long continued to violate the Agency's founding Charter. Section 202 within the National Security Act of 1947 contains an important restriction. It states, "...the Agency shall have no policy, subpoena law enforcement powers, or internal security functions..." These provisions were included to prevent what some termed an "American Gestapo".[cclxix] Some Agency members acted wholly outside the law.

William Harvey was a former Special Agent of the Federal Bureau of Investigation. He later became a long serving Agency intelligence officer. Harvey assumed control of the Castro assassination plots in April 1962; he advanced the ZRRIFLE assassination plot with the authorization of Richard Helms.[cclxx][cclxxi] Harvey and Mafia notable Johnny Roselli met frequently over the years.[cclxxii][cclxxiii][cclxxiv][cclxxv][cclxxvi]

Agency and military officer Sheffield Edwards also met with Johnny Roselli concerning a strange encounter with alleged Bureau agents.[cclxxvii] Walter Osborn, the Agency Director of Security, eventually did "not trust" Harvey's motivations.[cclxxviii] Despite his alleged status of master spy, he was "allowed" to retire due to alcoholism.[cclxxix]

Among the intelligence officers directly involved with the assassination case is James Angleton. He worked in the Office of Strategic Services previously with Allen Dulles. After joining the Central Intelligence Agency, Dulles and Angleton soon developed a mutual agenda. Allen Dulles charged Angleton with leading the Agency's Counter Intelligence section. A post Angleton occupied devoutly for twenty years.

Nixon administration Chief of Staff H.R. Haldeman states, "After Kennedy was killed, the CIA launched a fantastic cover up. The CIA literally erased any connection between Kennedy's assassination and the CIA... in fact, Counterintelligence Chief James Angleton of the CIA called Bill Sullivan of the Federal Bureau of Investigation and rehearsed the questions and answers they would give to the Warren Commission investigators".[cclxxx] Why rehearse the truth?

Angleton was subsequently disturbed to learn of Agency officer William Harvey and criminal Johnny Roselli's long-term friendship from Bureau Agent Sam Papich. Papich had advised Harvey to discontinue these associations, and had Bureau surveillance of Roselli canceled.[cclxxxi] Angleton states he learned of the Castro assassination plots involving Roselli and Harvey after the Commission had concluded.

Regarding the deficiencies of the Commission investigation James Angleton stated, "I personally believe that the United States intelligence services did not have the capabilities to ever come to adjudication. I don't think the capabilities were there." Angleton previously discussed the President's (Warren) Commission findings with Commissioner Allen Dulles. Angleton stated, "I told him (Dulles) personally I believed there should not be a finality to the report. In other words, the door ought to be left open." [cclxxxii] Angleton's formerly classified statements reveal the many problems surrounding the investigation. He reasonably states the finality and presumption of officials was misleading and precipitous. Angleton had prior influenced the Agency's investigation.

Richard Helms first tasked Agent John Scelso with the assassination investigation. Scelso affirmed the Bureau did not provide critical evidence and kept most at the Agency "...busy tracing the names and researching it, and so on; but these vital things had never been communicated to me. Maybe they were communicated to Angleton, but not to me." When Agency superiors ordered Scelso to investigate James

Angleton's counterintelligence operations he feared for his life. "I used to go in fingering my insurance policy, notifying my next of kin. This happened many times over the years." This assessment speaks much of Angleton's tactics.[cclxxxiii]

James Angleton repeatedly defied orders from Agency leadership and influenced the Kennedy case to support Communist origins. Angleton was often in communication with Allen Dulles regarding the investigation and the Commission's views. When Agent Scelso demanded Richard Helms force Angleton to follow orders, Helms responded "...you go tell him." "None of the senior officials at the Agency were ever able to cope with him. He had enormously influential contacts with J. Edgar Hoover..." Additionally Angleton had "ties to the Director (McCone)."[cclxxxiv]

Agent Scelso stated Angleton has operational ties to organized crime. Angleton vetoed at least one Agency operation that targeted the Mafia's financial interests. Scelso discussed these ties with Colonel Joseph Caldwell King, Chief of the Western Hemisphere Division. King allegedly stated, "The real reason is that Angleton himself has ties to the Mafia and he would not want to double cross them, or something like that." These claims receive backing from Angleton later supporting assassination plans against Fidel Castro using the Mafia.[cclxxxv]

James Angleton had prior dealings with Mafia penetration agent Mario Brod. Brod supported a Bureau investigation regarding Jimmy Hoffa in 1963, yet Angleton recruited him in 1944. Brod represents a prior Mafia association with Angleton years before the Agency existed. Angleton neglected to mention this in a timely fashion to his Agency superiors.[cclxxxvi]

Eventually Angleton received total control over the assassination investigation; it predictably was subject to Angleton's delusion regarding a worldwide Communist Conspiracy. Scelso affirms this assessment, "...I think that after Angleton took it over, that (the possible Soviet connection) was the case, yes." "I find Mr. Angleton's appreciation of intelligence situation to be colored by a sense of dread of foreign conspiracies, and an over-suspiciousness."[cclxxxvii] One Agency member sent a report three days after the assassination that supports prior intelligence interest regarding Lee Harvey Oswald. Additionally the memo suggests Marina Oswald was considered in relation with repeated prior instances of Soviet women marrying, leaving their husbands, and resettling as possible Soviet intelligence assets.[cclxxxviii]

Agency operative Thomas Casasin privately admitted "1. It makes little difference now, but...had at one time an interest in Oswald...sometime in the Summer of 1960...the laying on of interview(s) through... or other suitable channels. At the moment I don't recall if this was discussed while Oswald and his family were en route to our country or after their arrival." "2. I remember Oswald's unusual behavior in the USSR had struck me from the moment I read the first STATE (dispatch on him) and I told my subordinates something amounting to "Don't push too hard to get the information we need, because the individual looks odd. We were particularly interested in the info Oswald might provide on the Minsk factory...certain sections of the city itself...and of course we sought the usual biographic information that might help develop foreign personality dossiers."

"3. I was phasing into my next cover assignment...at the time. Thus, I would have left our country shortly after Oswald's arrival. I do not know what action developed thereafter." "4. As an afterthought...we had discovered in the course of our bio and research work...the number of Soviet women marrying foreigners, being permitted to leave the USSR, then eventually divorcing their spouses and settling down abroad without returning "home". The... case was among the first of these, and we eventually turned up something like two dozen similar cases." The memo officially confirms someone in the Agency prior contemplated using Oswald for intelligence purposes.[cclxxxix]

Richard Bissell is a related Intelligence commander that served in both the Office of Strategic Services and the Agency. Subsequently in 1960, Bissell "approached Colonel Sheffield Edwards to determine if the Office of Security had assets that may assist in a sensitive mission requiring gangster-type action. The mission target is Fidel Castro." The official who formulated the Castro assassination plots was Richard Bissell. "Robert A. Maheu was contacted" and proceeded to speak to his social acquaintance Johnny Roselli of the Chicago Mafia.[ccxc]

Allen Dulles promotes Bissell to Agency Deputy Director for Plans, his directorate conducted varied illicit projects. These plots included utilizing theft, fraud, drugs, poisons, biological attacks, bribery, torture, and murder. The plans contain political deception, propaganda to overthrow elected governments, and financing wars abroad. They included the infiltration of governments, ignoring United States Congressional oversight, and the deception of American Presidents. Some in the Agency concealed much of what they knew from the President's (Warren) Commission and the American public.[ccxci]

Repeated failed attempts to kill Fidel Castro led to a futile military invasion of Cuba. Bissell formed paramilitary groups using suggested methods from past successful Agency operations. This culminated in the Bay of Pigs failure. In hindsight, Richard Bissell seemed to reconsider his motivations.

"So emotionally involved was I that I may have let my desire to proceed override my good judgment on several matters. Each new restraint or restriction or cutback was disturbing, but I [like the direct commander Jack Hawkins] was deeply committed to the plan and eager to have a go at it. I think I retained too much confidence in the whole operation up to the end, more than was rational-but that is the way it was" (Richard Bissell referring to the actions of the Central Intelligence Agency during the Bay of Pigs).[ccxcii] This is among the Agency's eminent failures.

The Agency's blindness to American law would continue undeterred from past failures. The Central Intelligence Agency used the Mafia during the Eisenhower and Kennedy administrations. Unknown to the higher officials outside the Agency, Mafia agents collaborated with Agency officials in assassination plots.[ccxciii] The Kennedys were unaware of the Mafia's access to paramilitary forces and its ability to turn them to advantage. Conceivably the reins of power could have slipped from official hands into the Conspirators' waiting grasp.

Agency statements portray Oswald as the only person involved. Official documents place guilt before an investigation had occurred. Without laws such as the Freedom of Information Act, no available evidence could disprove later government statements. Yet the demise of America's leader pales to the Agency's history of inhumanity.

MK-ULTRA was among the Central Intelligence Agency schemes later scrutinized by investigators. The MK-ULTRA trials used psychoactive drugs, hypnosis, dangerous chemical injections, and physical abuse to simulate mind control. The Agency conducted illegal tests using willing and unwilling participants. They manipulated the constitutional rights of Americans for their own goals; these human trials illustrate the lengths the Agency would use to succeed.[ccxciv ccxcv]

The Agency's programs extended as it gained political power and hidden finances. Among documents released from Central Intelligence Agency files was a guide for assassination. These documents instruct how to assassinate enemy leaders effectively. The assassination proposals specify the most preferred weapons, circumstances, and victims.[ccxcvi]

The Agency assisted toppling multiple foreign governments during the 1950s. Subsequently, the Agency created a guidebook displaying how to murder political targets. Was it so unbelievable a few rogue agents might attempt to utilize these tactics domestically? Perhaps criminals or rogue Agency members again worked together.[ccxcvii]

Former Agency accountant James Wilcott states, "CIA people killed Kennedy. Either it was an outright project of Headquarters with the approval of McCone or it was done outside; perhaps under the direction of Dulles and Bissell. It was done in retaliation to Kennedy's renegging (sic) on a secret agreement with Dulles to support the invasion of Cuba." "It was believed unless Cuba was seized by military force all of Latin America would eventually go communist and the US would fall to the communists soon after. Elaborate preparations had been made to firmly put the blame on Castro, and an immediate attack on Cuba would follow. But something had gone wrong. The attack was called off at the last moment."

"Prior to the election, the Eisenhower administration was in complete agreement with the CIA, that Cuba must be invaded. (Richard) Bissell had been assigned the task of directing the operation. The original plan called for an extensive spy network throughout Cuba that would be of great support to the invasion (Bay of Pigs)...Nixon's support of all this was a certainty, had he won." "Kennedy was a disaster to the Bissell 'brain child' as the invasion came to be called. Even before the inauguration, much effort was directed to influence and pressure Kennedy, especially through the military."

"By the time of the secret agreement meeting in November of 1960 some softening up had been achieved, but he was, by no means, ready to buy (the Bay of Pigs plan). The accomplishments of the project to date were behind schedule and Kennedy knew it. The spy network was far from established. Evidence of popular support against Castro was lacking. Reports and analysis lacked substance. Rumors of bad planning, air drop failure, poor morale and difficulty with the exiles leaked out. More serious, however, was the charge of falsified reports of the popular sentiment fabricated by the CIA."

"As Bissell pressured his top lieutenants, they in turn pressured the case officers, intelligence officers and project officers who in turn pressured field agents to turn in reports that the Cuba Desk wanted to hear. This was not simply a question of poor management. It was a contrived plot to secure a minimum basis to claim support after it was realized that truly valid minimum support could not be had. The original plans were then changed to call for an all out attack by the US military. Kennedy was not to know of this change and it was not discussed at the November 1960 meeting of the invasion briefing."

"One such plan was to somehow get Castro to attack Guantanamo by making him believe that rebels were attacking from there. Another was to interpose a ship in a rebel attack and get it blown up." This plan considered utilizing similar false attacks suggested within the proposed Operation NORTHWOODS. "This was...discarded when the ONI (Office of Naval

Intelligence) got wind of it and became very angry, and perhaps was the source of some of the snitching on the Cuba foul ups to Kennedy."[ccxcviii]

Further problems with the operation resulted from a "lack of Spanish speaking staff with the proper knowledge and clearance. More difficult was the conflict between the pro-Batista and the anti-Batista exiles. Pro-Batista exiles received better training, lodgings, meals, and gear. These were the exiles offered as representative, yet many anti-Batista exiles faced less generous circumstances. Additionally, the plan called anti-Batista exiles to fill the front lines. The heaviest casualties would be inflicted on this group."

"Word somehow got back to the anti-Batista faction, making them very angry, and they informed to Castro agents just prior to the invasion." "From the November 1960 meeting right up to April 15, 1961...events deteriorated from bad to worse. It was said that this was due to 'sabotage' by Kennedy." President Kennedy realized the ineffectual and deficient operation should not be launched. Dulles operated as if "...it was a responsibility; a higher duty, to exceed the limitation of the CIA charter, or even the congress and the president to 'preserve democracy, keep the world free for investment and meet the communist threat."[ccxcix]

"Oswald was recruited from the military for the express purpose of becoming a double agent assignment in the USSR. It was said they had some kine (sic) of special "handle" on him. Perhaps went the speculation, they had discovered he had murdered someone or committed some other serious crime, during a routine lie detector test. In any case it was a very risky assignment. CIA taught him Russian and it was said that he had been to the farm (CIA's agent training camp, Camp Peary, Va.) although probably not in one of the regular training programs. He may not have even known that he had been there. (That was often done with very special cases. They would be put to sleep and wake up in a strange place and be told that it was some other place than the farm)".[ccc] Wilcott's controversial allegations were classified and not available for public consideration until the 1990s.[ccci]

The account is by no means definitive. Wilcott does not identify all his sources for questioning. Yet his assessment of the nature of the Agency, its practices, and the pervasive fear and hatred of Communism is quite accurate. Wilcott does not lay blame on the entire Agency. Yet some of its leaders' repeated operations are consistent with these allegations.

Richard Helms was involved in Agency operations since the group's inception in the late 1940s. Helms subsequently told the House Select Committee on Assassinations "... the only assassination that had any even semblance or substance to it was one involving a couple of Mafia chieftains and which were supposed to have taken place before the Bay of Pigs invasion." This uncharacteristically frank admission from Helms confirms officials authoring a murderous plot. The plot could be redirected from targeting one head of state to another.

Concerning Allen Dulles' prior knowledge of such plots, Helms affirms "He (Dulles) certainly knew about the Mafia one that I mentioned. I think there is abundant evidence that he did know it. I do not have that firsthand, because that particular operation was being handled by Mr. (Richard) Bissell and Colonel Edwards with Mr. Dulles and General Cabell and I was not brought in on it."[cccii] Official assassination operations using the Mafia existed years prior to President Kennedy's murder.

Deputy Director of Plans Richard Helms made additional statements conceivably to keep President Kennedy's murder unsolved forever. Helms faced questioning before the President's (Warren) Commission, "...after the Commission completed its report you would keep the matter open if there was anything new that developed in the future that could be properly presented to the authorities?" Helms replied, "Yes I would assume the case will never be closed".[ccciii] If the case remains unsolved, it conceals the Agency and Bureau's surrounding actions forever.

Disregard for outside authority eventually led to internal Central Intelligence Agency corruption. Richard Helms withheld critical evidence from the President's (Warren) Commission investigation. Helms' offered vague testimony regarding these events to the Senate (Church) Committee. Senator Morgan of the Senate Committee affirmed "... (In 1963) you were not...just an employee of the CIA. You were in the top echelon, the management level, were you not?" Helms affirmed the fact.[cocciv]

The senator then questioned Helms about involvement in lethal plots against Fidel Castro. Helms then responded, "I was aware that there had been efforts made to get rid of him by these means". Senator Morgan then inquired "...you, charged with furnishing the Warren Commission information from the CIA, information that you thought was relevant?" Richard Helms then commences to respond evasively.

"No sir. I was instructed to reply to inquiries from the Warren Commission for information from the Agency. I was not asked to initiate any particular thing." Senator Morgan then replies "...in other words if you weren't asked for it, you didn't give it." Director Helms finally decides to give a straightforward answer, "That's right, sir".[cccv] Richard Helms testimony and actions display a clear disregard for relevant evidence. Helms would initiate multiple nefarious activities in his tenure.

"The very thought of Helms entrusting (William) Harvey to hire a criminal to have the capacity to kill somebody violates every operational precept, every bit of operational experience, every ethical consideration. And the fact that he chose Harvey -- Harvey could keep a secret, you see. Harvey could keep a secret. This was one way to make sure nobody ever found out about it."[cccvi]

Agent John Scelso admitted in classified House Select Committee on Assassinations testimony that Agency officer William Harvey was a criminal. Harvey retained at least one assassin using Agency funds according to official documents. Scelso attempts to distinguish between Agency operations from Harvey's alleged ones. Scelso disapproves of the Agency "...engaging in assassinations as distinguished from guerilla warfare or coup d'états, and so on, setting out by stealth and surprise to kill an important foreign person was abhorrent to the standards of the clandestine service and the fact that the way--you know, what the response was in the (Patrice) Lumumba case. They (agents in Africa) refused to carry out the order, but they were guilty of conspiracy to commit homicide."[cccvii]

Scelso added "...the very thought of using a former criminal for anything, let alone to assassinate people or to be on a standby basis to assassinate people--here Helms cannot turn around, you see, after establishing standards and training officers...and so on, he cannot turn around, just because he is the DCI (Director of Central Intelligence), and appoint a thug like Harvey to hire some criminal to commit assassinations." When questioned about Harvey's asserted involvement in the Kennedy assassination Scelso replies ominously. "He was too young to have assassinated McKinley or Lincoln. It could have been anything."[cccviii]

The FBI did not share with the Agency pre-assassination material of importance. Material that might have allowed their Oswald related cables to trigger security protocols. The Bureau failed to mention details regarding the Walker shooting, Oswald's political activities, and specific biographical information to the Agency. A preliminary Agency report created two days subsequent to the assassination decided Oswald was the lone gunman. Even Scelso's later report was in his view "...more comprehensive, but was obviously, completely irrelevant in view of all of this Bureau information." Official channels failed to support a complete investigation again.[cccix]

Two weeks before President Kennedy's death, J. Edgar Hoover sent Richard Helms a document with various official files on Lee Harvey Oswald. Hoover states, "For your information, I am enclosing communications which may be of interest to you."[cccx] Helms later attempted to destroy all related documents via orders in 1973. Director Helms was committed to protecting the Agency despite legal concerns. The Senate (Church) Committee later obtained the witnesses and surviving documentation. Congress later finds Richard Helms guilty of perjury, for denying his knowledge of past Agency coup operations.

The truth remained hidden for decades. The Central Intelligence Agency developed the following plan to influence public opinion. This document's existence shows active manipulation under then Director of Central Intelligence Richard Helms. Its purpose was to enforce the President's (Warren) Commission findings.

> **"CIA Document #1035-960, RE: Concerning Criticism of the Warren Report:**
>
> **1. Our Concern. From the day of President Kennedy's assassination on, there has been speculation about the responsibility for his murder. Although this was stemmed for a time by the Warren Commission report, (which appeared at the end of September 1964), various writers have now had time to scan the Commission's published report and documents for new pretexts for questioning, and there has been a new wave of books and articles criticizing the Commission's findings. In most cases the critics have speculated as to the existence of some kind of conspiracy, and often they have implied that the Commission itself was involved. Presumably as a result of the increasing challenge to the Warren Commission's report, a public opinion poll recently indicated that 46% of the American public did not think that Oswald acted alone, while more than half of those polled thought that the Commission had left some questions unresolved. Doubtless polls abroad would show similar or possibly more adverse results."**

Why did the Agency care about further inquiries if they had faith in the Commission's findings? This document violates the Agency Charter by influencing domestic policy. The report was intentional disinformation. Its purpose was to support the official conclusions despite the evidence.

> **"2. This trend of opinion is a matter of concern to the U.S. government, including our organization. The members of the Warren Commission were naturally chosen for their integrity, experience and prominence. They represented both major parties, and they and their staff were deliberately drawn from all sections of the country. Just because of the standing of the Commissioners, efforts to impugn their rectitude and wisdom tend to cast doubt on the whole leadership of American society. Moreover, there seems to be an increasing tendency to hint that President Johnson himself, as**

the one person who might be said to have benefited, was in some way responsible for the assassination."

Only in hindsight do Agency leaders' true motivations become observable. They did not care about people "casting doubt on the whole leadership of American society." During the Kennedy administration, some Intelligence Arm members attempted to obstruct and deceive the leaders of American society. Key members of the Agency have often valued its determined interests first.

> "Innuendo of such seriousness affects not only the individual concerned, but also the whole reputation of the American government. Our organization itself is directly involved: among other facts, we contributed information to the investigation. Conspiracy theories have frequently thrown suspicion on our organization, for example by falsely alleging that Lee Harvey Oswald worked for us. The aim of this dispatch is to provide material countering and discrediting the claims of the conspiracy theorists, so as to inhibit the circulation of such claims in other countries. Background information is supplied in a classified section and in a number of unclassified attachments.

> 3. Action. We do not recommend that discussion of the assassination question be initiated where it is not already taking place. Where discussion is active [business] addresses are requested:

> a. To discuss the publicity problem with [?] and friendly elite contacts (especially politicians and editors), pointing out that the Warren Commission made as thorough an investigation as humanly possible, that the charges of the critics are without serious foundation, and that further speculative discussion only plays into the hands of the opposition. Point out also that parts of the conspiracy talk appear to be deliberately generated by Communist propagandists. Urge them to use their influence to discourage unfounded and irresponsible speculation.

> b. To employ propaganda assets to [negate] and refute the attacks of the critics. Book reviews and feature articles are particularly appropriate for this purpose. The unclassified attachments to this guidance should provide useful background material for passing to assets. Our ploy should point out, as applicable, that the critics are (I) wedded to theories adopted before the evidence was in, (II) politically interested, (III) financially interested, (IV) hasty and inaccurate in their research, or (V) infatuated with their own theories. In the course of discussions of the whole phenomenon of criticism, a useful strategy may be to single out Epstein's theory for attack, using the attached Fletcher [?] article and Spectator piece

**for background. (Although Mark Lane's book is much less convincing that Epstein's and comes off badly where confronted by knowledgeable critics, it is also much more difficult to answer as a whole, as one becomes lost in a morass of unrelated details.)"**

"...employ Propaganda assets..." the Agency's own words betray its intent. The Agency desired the public to embrace the official findings. It wanted to construct a domestic campaign to undermine anyone who questioned the Commission. It was conspiring against those it was responsible for protecting.

**"4. In private to media discussions not directed at any particular writer, or in attacking publications which may be yet forthcoming, the following arguments should be useful:"**

This highlights the delusional and dismissive attitude of Agency leaders regarding free thought and communication. The Agency was not seeking honest discourse but its preconceived talking points. Citizens needed to be supportive or discredited. Officials expected public support and targeted some who publicly disagreed.

**"a. No significant new evidence has emerged which the Commission did not consider. The assassination is sometimes compared (e.g., by Joachim Joesten and Bertrand Russell) with the Dreyfus case; however, unlike that case, the attack on the Warren Commission have produced no new evidence, no new culprits have been convincingly identified, and there is no agreement among the critics.**

**(A better parallel, though an imperfect one, might be with the Reichstag fire of 1933, which some competent historians (Fritz Tobias, A.J.P. Taylor, D.C. Watt) now believe was set by Vander Lubbe on his own initiative, without acting for either Nazis or Communists; the Nazis tried to pin the blame on the Communists, but the latter have been more successful in convincing the world that the Nazis were to blame.)**

**b. Critics usually overvalue particular items and ignore others. They tend to place more emphasis on the recollections of individual witnesses (which are less reliable and more divergent--and hence offer more hand-holds for criticism) and less on ballistics, autopsy, and photographic evidence. A close examination of the Commission's records will usually show that the conflicting eyewitness accounts are quoted out of context, or were discarded by the Commission for good and sufficient reason.**

**c. Conspiracy on the large scale often suggested would be impossible to conceal in the United States, esp. since informants could expect to receive large royalties, etc. Note that Robert**

Kennedy, Attorney General at the time and John F. Kennedy's brother, would be the last man to overlook or conceal any conspiracy. And as one reviewer pointed out, Congressman Gerald R. Ford would hardly have held his tongue for the sake of the Democratic administration, and Senator Russell would have had every political interest in exposing any misdeeds on the part of Chief Justice Warren. A conspirator moreover would hardly choose a location for a shooting where so much depended on conditions beyond his control: the route, the speed of the cars, the moving target, the risk that the assassin would be discovered. A group of wealthy conspirators could have arranged much more secure conditions.

d. Critics have often been enticed by a form of intellectual pride: they light on some theory and fall in love with it; they also scoff at the Commission because it did not always answer every question with a flat decision one way or the other. Actually, the make-up of the Commission and its staff was an excellent safeguard against over-commitment to any one theory, or against the illicit transformation of probabilities into certainties.

e. Oswald would not have been any sensible person's choice for a co-conspirator. He was a "loner," mixed up, of questionable reliability and an unknown quantity to any professional intelligence service.

f. As to charges that the Commission's report was a rush job, it emerged three months after the deadline originally set. But to the degree that the Commission tried to speed up its reporting, this was largely due to the pressure of irresponsible speculation already appearing, in some cases coming from the same critics who, refusing to admit their errors, are now putting out new criticisms.

g. Such vague accusations as that "more than ten people have died mysteriously" can always be explained in some natural way e.g.: the individuals concerned have for the most part died of natural causes; the Commission staff questioned 418 witnesses (the FBI interviewed far more people, conduction 25,000 interviews and re interviews), and in such a large group, a certain number of deaths are to be expected. (When Penn Jones, one of the originators of the "ten mysterious deaths" line, appeared on television, it emerged that two of the deaths on his list were from heart attacks, one from cancer, one was from a head-on collision on a bridge, and one occurred when a driver drifted into a bridge abutment.)

5. Where possible, counter speculation by encouraging reference to the Commission's Report itself. Open-minded foreign readers

**should still be impressed by the care, thoroughness, objectivity and speed with which the Commission worked. Reviewers of other books might be encouraged to add to their account the idea that, checking back with the report itself, they found it far superior to the work of its critics."[cccxi]**

The Agency neglects to mention that speed and thoroughness are not often associated. They sought to deceive, and intimidate American citizens. All seeking to conceal uncomfortable truths the Agency wanted forgotten. Allegedly, the Central Intelligence Agency had agents in most administrations with and without presidential knowledge. Sometimes they served many causes with conflicting loyalties.

The Agency's express purpose is to serve the American government's executive branch. They were to procure information unavailable internationally using normal channels. The original intent of the Central Intelligence Agency was to benefit American society. Instead, non-compliance with the law has occurred repeatedly. Competition among the Agency and other government organizations would lead to future deadly failures.

The Agency continued to breach local jurisdiction in dealing with those it determined to be threats. Since its founding, Agency leaders and employees undertook many domestic operations. They have created unsanctioned secret bases inside the United States. On a few occasions, Agency assets disregarded the laws justifying their existence.

Some Agency secrets were greater than most, such as its functioning Moscow station. Agency leaders compartmentalized this foreign holding and its activities from the most in the Agency. Operatives of the Central Intelligence Agency were active in Moscow during Oswald's visits. "But there were...a number of operations in the clandestine services that neither the DDO (Deputy Director of Operations) or ADDO (Assistant DDO) knew." Additionally some at the Agency would purge personnel files in some manner.[cccxii]

The most contentious of the relevant files purged are within Oswald's 201 file and its connected volumes.[cccxiii] The 201 files contain most relevant material the Agency collected about the subject in question. Oswald's 201 file, unlike many others, has dozens of volumes of information. Even the subsequent House Select Committee on Assassinations who was granted "full" access feasibly did not review them all.[cccxiv]

The Chief of the Agency's Information Management Staff William Larson commented on the discrepancies in Oswald's files. Larson affirms documents connecting the 201 file to the Agency could be absent. Internal Agency documents affirm 37 items are missing.[cccxv] This would defeat the complicated Agency filing system and render the connection inaccessible to normal inquiry.[cccxvi]

Larson additionally stated Oswald's possible cryptonym would conceal internal conversations about him. Another document missing but included in the 201 file index is a psychological report conducted by the Agency from gathered evidence and witnesses. These details would correspond to procedure regarding the target of Agency operations, an informant, or possible operative status.[cccxvii] In prior classified testimony Bernard Tovar, the Chief of Agency Counterintelligence Staff offered additional insights. Reviewing Oswald's 201 file Tovar indicated Oswald was of interest to the US Army. Oswald's psychological testing possibly was undertaken to assess him for intelligence operations.[cccxviii]

Research and Analysis Agent Melbourne Hartmann affirmed the Agency was monitoring Oswald's mail for extended durations. This was based upon notations in Oswald's 201 file. Hartmann reveals substantive material about Oswald regarding the Agency HTLINGUAL communications intercept program was not in Oswald's 201 file. Compartmentalization methods of the Agency concealed this information until the House Select Committee investigation. Hartmann testified previously requesting any Oswald files for investigative research, the Agency Security Research Section replied that it possessed no files regarding Oswald. Hartmann "really was shocked" their claim was proven false.[cccxix] [cccxx]

A former notorious Central Intelligence Agency holding was J. M. Wave, a secret local base. Operating in the 1960s, J. M. Wave employed hundreds of agents and was located in Miami, Florida. This base was the headquarters to many past Central Intelligence Agency Black Ops. This was Agency slang for illegal acts called Black Operations, including assassinations. Located domestically, J.M. Wave's existence may violate the Central Intelligence Agency's founding charter.

Some have alleged the base was not involved in any matter concerning the assassination. Yet the findings of the Senate (Church) Committee refute these claims. "The CIA JMWAVE Chief of Station in Florida...", "The JMWAVE station passed along any information its intelligence network collected on the assassination".[cccxxi] It becomes apparent some Agency leaders had no respect for the Constitution and United States law. It is doubtful they respected the power of American Presidents who opposed Agency operations.

The Committee affirmed, "...the CIA inquiry was deficient on the specific question of the significance of Oswald's contacts". The Senate (Church) Committee additionally found, "This evidence indicates that the investigation of the assassination was deficient and that the facts which might have substantially affected the course of the investigation were not provided to the Warren Commission"[cccxxii] These conceivably included pro and anti-Castro Cubans, the Mafia, Intelligence community assets, and former American military.

## REVOLUTIONARY EXILES

Fidel Castro was a difficult man to murder. Among the many situations that feasibly should have killed him was an unplanned escape at sea. Castro was among militants launching a failed revolutionary coup against the government of Raphael Trujillo, the dictator of the Dominican Republic. The coup was cancelled just prior to its appointed time and some were too eager for retreat. When the coup failed among those captured was Castro and Rolando Masferrer, a mercenary leader and Cuban official with little regard for the law.

Castro and Masferrer's interests prior aligned to remove Trujillo. With the mission aborted, he resumed his place among Masferrer's enemies. Castro faces arrest and sat aboard an official vessel bound for prison and feasibly death at the hands of Masferrer and his minions. Castro instead jumped into the sea nine miles off the coast of Cuba. He swam to safety and was lucky not to encounter sharks.[cccxxiii] Seeking Fidel Castro's death by any means eventually consumed many, including the Central Intelligence Agency. The Kennedy administration supported the efforts but was not fully aware of the lengths the Agency would employ to achieve success. Among their subsequent allies is Masferrer.

The Central Intelligence Agency funded a variety of militant groups, it created the Cuban Democratic Revolutionary Front (Frente Revolucionario Democratico) or FRD in 1960. With seasoned revolutionary Antonio Varona at the helm, the Front was a "political action, propaganda, and military unit. Initial actions consisted of extensive radio and printed propaganda, demonstrations, and trips throughout the Hemisphere to gain support for the fight against Castro. The FRD also functioned as the front organization for recruiting the members of the Bay of Pigs invasion force and carried out a massive program of social assistance to Brigade 2506 members in training camps and their families. Although FRD headquarters was based in Miami, delegates were assigned to other areas which included New Orleans, Louisiana, Tampa, Florida, and Mexico City... Members of the Front also had direct access to President Kennedy and top White House aides...a large number of (official edit) and (CIA) Headquarters were directly involved with both the FRD and CRC" (Cuban Revolutionary

Council)[cccxxiv] The FRD attempted to bring most Exile groups into a manageable political hierarchy and Varona tried leading the Exile Executive Committee. Rivalry between the various factions prevented this from occurring.

The CRC delegate in New Orleans Sergio Arcacha Smith sought large amounts of weapons, ammunition, vehicles, and medical supplies for anti-Castro efforts. According to a Bureau informant, Smith met with Marcello investigator David Ferrie and others at his residence. Additionally Smith was in repeated contact with the New Orleans Federal Bureau of Investigation office regarding his group's activities.[cccxxv]

One related episode demonstrates Smith's loyalty to Ferrie. "Ferrie had gained entrance to the New Orleans Detention Center to visit one runaway boy by signing himself in as a doctor...As a result, Ferrie was arrested on August 8, 1961 for contributing to the delinquency of a juvenile. Cuban exile leader Arcacha Smith intervened on Ferrie's behalf by telling police the boy would be returned to his parents if they did not press charges against Ferrie. But Ferrie was arrested again on August 11, 1961, for crime against nature on 15 year old boy and indecent behavior with three others." The two men were verifiably often associated.[cccxxvi]

A few with enough funding and influence could utilize these networks of dangerous men. It feasibly could allow someone in the Agency, Bureau, or Mafia to manipulate a few among these groups. "An FBI report of April 1961 indicated (Carlos) Marcello offered (Sergio) Arcacha Smith a deal whereby Marcello would make a substantial donation to the movement in return for concession in Cuba after Castro's overthrow."[cccxxvii]

A connection between militant groups and the Agency is Carlos Bringuier. Bringuier was a delegate of the New Orleans chapter of the Cuban Student Directorate (Directorio Revolucionario Estudiantil) or DRE, and met Oswald on August 5, 1963. Oswald wanted to "join the organization and to help train Cubans to fight against Castro. Bringuier considered him either an FBI informant or a Communist penetration agent and rejected his offer." Subsequently, local news carried photographs of Oswald's activities. He and Bringuier had a public altercation some officials believe was staged based upon their later scheduled radio debate.

During the Commission investigation, Bringuier outlined a book proposal to discredit the Commission findings by implying a connection between Oswald and Castro. He asserts consultant Norman Redlich is part of a Communist conspiracy to hide the facts. He surely realizes none of this is true and offers no substantial evidence.[cccxxviii] Notably the Revolutionary Student Directorate was not just a mere political club.

The Central Intelligence Agency covertly funded this group. House Select Committee segregated files reveal that in fall 1962, the Agency "rolled up" their project. The Agency provided nominal financial support until September 1966.[cccxxix] Bringuier is the delegate of an organization that included militant anti-Castro Cubans and receives Agency funding. Other different Agency employees prior associated with Santo Trafficante and Sam Giancana in order to train criminals to assassinate Castro. David Ferrie helped train anti-Castro Cubans and associated with Carlos Marcello. Guy Bannister helped form a group himself and served Marcello as well. Prior ideas refined by additional evidence offer greater credibility to a few long contentions of some conspiracy advocates.

The Agency further sought to utilize internal Cuban assassination plots. Rolando Cubela Secades known by the Agency cryptonym AMLASH-1 was "a rather celebrated Cuban national and operational contact of the DDO (Deputy Director of Operations) mentioned throughout both of the Senate Select Committee assassination reports."[cccxxx] Secades was an inside agent who reported Castro's activities to the Agency and aided in the efforts to depose him. "On October 1963, Desmond Fitzgerald met AMLASH/1 outside the United States. At this meeting the CIA maintained that Fitzgerald rejected AMLASH's request for an assassination weapon: specifically, a high-powered rifle with a telescopic lens."[cccxxxi] Secades was upset the Agency had provided weapons to many other Cuban exiles without such hesitation.

He allegedly pondered associations with terrorists to complete his mission.[cccxxxii] The Agency subsequently demanded Secades undertake a polygraph; he refused. Officials were suspicious that he was a double agent. The possibility AMLASH-1 or those connected may undertake independent plots deeply concerned some in the Agency.[cccxxxiii]

Manuel Francisco Artime Buesa was another anti-Castro group leader. "40 or 50 men... mostly Artime followers" received paramilitary training at Fort Sherman in Panama for two or three months. When additional forces were required, the group expanded to become Agency Brigade 2506. "...the group was split, with some going to Guatemala and others to the New Orleans area." After the Bay of Pigs failure, group leaders were released and met President Kennedy in Palm Beach according to the Agency document. Some gained membership and training in the United States Army for six months to a year in early 1963 at Fort Benning, Georgia.[cccxxxiv]

Official documents further revealed Artime served as an Agency operative from "1959-1963."[cccxxxv] Carlos Hernandez joined Artime in Mexico City to serve as a bodyguard. "Hernandez returned to the United States in

March or April of 1960 and almost immediately went into guerilla training in Guatemala." Hernandez received continued training on "an island around New Orleans". He then moves to Miami and performs various tasks, training, and purchases weapons from the DRE.[cccxxxvi]

The Senate Select Committee reproached the Agency stating, "Senior CIA officials also should have realized their agency was not utilizing its full capability to investigate Oswald's pro-Castro and anti-Castro connections. They should have realized that CIA operations...particularly operations involving the assassination of Castro, needed to be considered in the investigation".[cccxxxvii] The Agency's intentions went uninspected for more than a decade.

To secure the fall of the Cuban government the Central Intelligence Agency employed not just the Mafia but militant anti-Castro exile groups. The officially sanctioned militants armed, trained, and dispatched to harry and end the Castro regime. Their existence violated and endangered international treaties and created threats which might endanger their former official sponsors. These are just a few of the dozens of exile leaders aided by officials.

## THE IMPOSTERS IN MEXICO

Some call the most noted example the Mexico City Man, Saul, and a host of other names. Often this man was the basis of conspiracy theory. He is one of nearly a dozen unknown white males photographed near the time of Oswald's visits.[cccxxxviii] However to understand the matter we must deconstruct the misinformation and deceptions. The most often cited possible imposter has created serious problems.

The imposter photograph is President's (Warren) Commission exhibit 237 and is supported by witness testimony[cccxxxix cccxl] He then appears in over a dozen related official documents. Agency, Bureau, State Department, and White house documents imply he impersonated Lee Harvey Oswald multiple times. Yet these documents are wrong.

The first message establishes this possible imposter's existence. It describes the Imposter as "... male who spoke broken Russian said his name was Lee Oswald..." he in fact was not. Described from Agency photographs he is a "Male... American, Apparent Age 35, Athletic Build, Circa 6 Feet, Receding Hairline, Balding Top. Wore Khakis and Sport Shirt"[cccxli] Clearly, this was not the much younger, wiry, shorter, Lee Harvey Oswald.

Similar classified Agency memos allege interactions and interference. In a separate document, another "Lee Oswald" is making a phone call. He called the Soviet Embassy speaking broken Russian. This "Oswald" seems interested about information he should already possess. He asks questions Lee Harvey Oswald would not require answers to.

"Soviet (Embassy Worker) "What else do you want", (North American): "I was just now at your embassy and they took my address." Soviet: "I know that," North American: "I did not know it then..." Why does Oswald not remember his address? Why does this man not possess basic information about himself? "(North American) "...I went to the Cuban Embassy to ask them for my address because they have it..."[cccxlii] This is feasibly again not Lee Harvey Oswald. He knows Oswald's activities, he is aware Oswald had traveled recently, yet he does not recall Oswald's address.

Additionally within the document a call occurs, "Oswald" states he was at the Soviet Embassy a week ago. He states making a former visit and cannot remember the person's name he talked with. This call happens October 1, the same day the Agency photographs the Oswald Imposter at the Soviet embassy. However, the House Select Committee staff determined the photograph attributed occurred the day after the memo of his first appearance. Thus, October 2 does not conform to the many documents offered.[cccxliii] There is no conclusive proof Oswald made attributed phone calls to the Soviet and Cuban diplomatic headquarters.[cccxliv]

Problems include Oswald could not speak Spanish as one caller did. This taped evidence is uncorroborated by later investigations because they were erased. Standard operating procedure for the Agency's Mexico City Station erased all irrelevant messages after two weeks. The first telephone call attributed to Oswald is erased four days later.[cccxlv] The House Select Committee confirmed a call during October 3 likely was not Oswald.[cccxlvi]

Tapes possibly containing Oswald's voice existed until 1970 in Agency possession.[cccxlvii] Agency officials claimed they destroyed the tapes years earlier. This denied full examination of the evidence for verification. Neither tape presently exists, only the flawed transcripts filled with misinformation are left. Officials ignored the caller's lack of political knowledge and basic information to obtain a visa. Oswald had prior knowledge of these requirements; the Agency speculated Oswald was the first caller.

These actions ignore the reminder written on a related document by Chief of Mexico City station Winston Scott. Scott notes "By the context of other conversations by Oswald and the fact that this called (sic) spoke in broken Spanish and English rather than Russian which he used previously, it is probable that this caller is not Oswald."[cccxlviii] A local server officials interviewed corroborates Chief Scott. She noted Oswald was unable to converse sufficiently and had problems ordering meals.[cccxlix] Again disregarding the facts, Agency officers had a Mexico City chronology complied. It repeats that October 1, 1963 an imposter visited ("Apparent age 35, athletic build, circa 6 feet, receding hairline...") the Soviet Embassy.

The asserted Oswald visits to the Cuban and Soviet diplomatic headquarters were partially based upon rumors emerging from Mexican radio broadcasts. The Agency had no conclusive evidence Oswald contacted Communist officials in the Soviet Embassy.[cccl] Identification of Oswald additionally relied upon the caller identifying himself as Oswald. Regarding the matter Agent John Scelso affirms, "Of course any of the people who went-in and out (of the Soviet Embassy) could have been impersonating Oswald, not just the man in that photograph."[cccli] On November 22, Agents posted in the Mexico City station learned of Oswald's apprehension in less than two hours. These agents produced speculative "Oswald" cables minutes after the assassination as reliable information to other agencies.[ccclii]

The most famous asserted imposter appears once more in another Agency document mistakenly sent to the Secret Service. J. Lee Rankin lead counsel of the President's Commission subsequently requests the document. It details an unknown man who visited the Cuban and Soviet embassies who "...might be identical with Lee Harvey Oswald".[cccliii cccliv] Agency spy cameras were located outside the Soviet and Cuban Embassies to capture those entering and exiting. In another memo the Agency states after President Kennedy's assassination they recalled the October 1 report about Oswald. "It turned up pictures of a man believed to be Oswald entering the Soviet and Cuban embassies on various days including 1 October, 1963."[ccclv]

The CIA completely reviewed of all their photographic evidence of Oswald's alleged visits to the Soviet and Cuban Embassies. "Complete Recheck Photos all visitors to Cuban EMB August thru first half NOV against good press photos shows no evidence Oswald visit. Similar blank against all SOVEMB photos from 1 Sept. Note only visit we know he made was Cuban Embassy 28 Sept, Saturday on which Emb closed and we have not had coverage...Check manifests all planes arriving Mexi Central Airport from US fails show Oswald arrival under any likely variant his name."[ccclvi] "At no time during his stay in Mexico City did the CIA acquire a photo of Oswald...It is, therefore, firm that there was no

CIA photo coverage of Oswald at any time during his Mexico trip or stay in Mexico City."[ccclvii]

The Agency has no pictures of Oswald in Mexico City. Agency officer David Atlee Phillips feasibly supports Oswald did not appear at the Soviet Embassy affirming the Agency possessed no conclusive proof of a visit. He states his initial assignment in Mexico was disseminating propaganda. Phillips reaffirms the Agency was not honest with the Warren Commission.[ccclviii]

Agency cameras photographed many unidentified, possibly American males, yet Lee Harvey Oswald is not among them. Photographic confirmation did not support Lee Harvey Oswald's visits.[ccclix] A dispatch from the Agency's Mexico City Chief of Station confirms the alleged Imposter appeared on October 1, 4, and 15.[ccclx] However, it was October 2 he was photographed. Yet evidence and photographs actually credit possible imposters with more confirmed visits than Oswald to the Soviet Embassy.

Subsequently, the Agency reversed its efforts and the Commission removed the Soviet Embassy from the photograph. They cited motives unrelated to the Assassination of President Kennedy.[ccclxi] It would seem the Agency placed some importance on this unrelated operation and possible asset. The Agency Director states, "Our present plan in passing info to the Warren Commission is to eliminate the mention of telephone taps, in order to protect your continuing Ops (operations)"[ccclxii]

Perhaps someone in the Agency knew of him. A letter from Winston Scott to Joseph Caldwell King may clarify this fact. "Dear J.C.: Reference is made to our conversation in which I requested permission to give the Legal Attaché copies of photographs of a certain person known to you..." On the page is handwritten "WH (Western Hemisphere) Division of transmittal of photos which were thought to be of Oswald." Mr. Scott and Mr. King, the Agency Chief of Western Hemisphere Division, both knew the asserted imposter's identity.[ccclxiii]

J. C. King and the Agency Western Hemisphere Division provided material and financial support to anti-Castro groups in Miami. King was noted to conduct "all sorts of personal operations." "Nothing is too farfetched for him to have done." King allegedly went personally to meet a militant anti-Communist leader in South America. The guerilla leader King met was allegedly "murdering people right and left when he (King) was Division Chief."[ccclxiv]

Why did Agency officers collaborate in these repeated deceptions? Who were the false imposters? How many appearances or phone calls did officials assign to Lee Harvey Oswald? The imposters appearances fueled the later public speculations of guilt repeated about Oswald. A few key figures in the Agency knew about Lee Harvey Oswald before the assassination and remained silent.[ccclxv]

Central Intelligence Agency Mexico City station employee Anne Goodpasture learned all twelve original photographs associated with the false Imposter were destroyed.[ccclxvi] [ccclxvii] [ccclxviii] The most recent official mention of the unproven Imposter occurs during the 1995 testimony of Goodpasture. During questioning Mr. T. Jeremy Gunn asks, "Do you know whether there were any other conversations specific tapes that had been made that had Oswald or the Oswald substitute on them?" Goodpasture states, "No, I don't know." [ccclxix] Yet we can make a few determinations using the verified evidence.

The Agency repeatedly deceived and suppressed evidence from most official investigations; this includes the President's (Warren) Commission.[ccclxx] The Agency suppressed a handful of relevant files that suggest Colonel Yuri Ivanovich Moskalev; officer of the KGB was the imposter.[ccclxxi] Yet employees of the Agency have provided multiple pieces of corroborating false evidence. Not conspiracy advocates but the Central Intelligence Agency is responsible for the most famous asserted imposter.


## A Single Friend

The unlikely infrequent companion of Lee Harvey Oswald was George de Mohrenschildt. De Mohrenschildt despite some claims was not an Agency operative, yet he was considered for Agency use in 1942 until the Agency believed he might be a Nazi infiltration agent. His business trips in 1957 generated new Agency interest, de Mohrenschildt's frequent social acquaintance J. Walton Moore served the Agency's Domestic Contacts Division (DCD aka Domestic Contacts Section, DCS) .[ccclxxii] The Agency granted George informant clearance August 13, 1958.[ccclxxiii] Allegedly, Moore had prior discussed Oswald with de Mohrenschildt in 1962, and subsequently asserted far less associations with de Mohrenschildt than evidence supports.[ccclxxiv]

George intervened in the domestic problems of the Oswalds. De Mohrenschildt asked Gary Taylor and his wife to provide Marina living arrangements. He advised Oswald to live at the local Young Men's Christian Association. "Either de Mohrenschildt or his friend George Boure, paid Oswald's bill at the YMCA." Taylor stated to the Bureau "De

Mohrenschildt took a great interest in Oswald...Oswald would do anything that De Mohrenschildt told him to do."[ccclxxv]

De Mohrenschildt based on Agency documents was in repeated contact with a commercial asset regarding his business in Haiti during May of 1963. De Mohrenschildt asserts someone was entering his home and changing his book manuscript. He asked the Bureau if they were responsible and they denied it. In 1964, the Central Intelligence Agency was monitoring de Mohrenschildt's communications.[ccclxxvi] During the President's Commission, he affirms being in prior contact with J. Walton Moore. [ccclxxvii] One day before his scheduled testimony to the House Select Committee, de Mohrenschildt kills himself.

George de Mohrenschildt's demise was among the few in which the timing is highly suspicious. Why did he die just prior to his scheduled testimony? How could grief unfelt for years suddenly overcome him? De Mohrenschildt was also releasing a book about Oswald titled "I am a Patsy!"[ccclxxviii] Other interests might not wish his ideas to reach the public.

Unfortunately, de Mohrenschildt had no extensive recorded testimony and his death hurt later inquiry. Yet his alleged knowledge of ties between Lee Harvey Oswald and the Intelligence community might have incited certain interests. De Mohrenschildt's wife later gave the House Select Committee a copy of the famous backyard Oswald assassin photograph. However, the photo, like other non-essential information, has become a distraction.

Various arguments exist about the Oswald photograph and its origins remain contended. No matter who created the photograph, it cannot prove Oswald's innocence or guilt. It displays either Oswald's trusted de Mohrenschildt or de Mohrenschildt aided further covering actions regarding Oswald. The photograph is an iconic distraction that has appeared infinitely more than any important photographic evidence.

## THE OFFICIAL ASSASSIN

Cast as lone assassin by some, Lee Harvey Oswald was possibly a mere dupe. In Oswald's youth, he idolized Herbert Phillbrick, a Federal Bureau of Investigation double agent. Phillbrick over the years convinced friends and family he was a Communist. Phillbrick infiltrated Communist groups and then exposed them to the House Committee on Un-American Activities.[ccclxxix] Phillbrick's exploits were the plot of a popular television series. Oswald was an avid fan.

Oswald in some opinions was later emulating his hero Phillbrick when he tried to join the Socialist Party Youth League. After building a childish "Socialist" cover, he trained in the New Orleans Civil Air Patrol. Oswald later joined the Marines despite his political views. He received training in marksmanship and qualified as sharpshooter during his duration in the United States Marines. Yet prior to leaving the Marines his skill deteriorated and he qualified as a Marksman.[ccclxxx] Marksman is the minimum required firing score.[ccclxxxi]

Oswald's became a Radar Controller and served at the Atsugi Air Base in Japan. The base was a Central Intelligence Agency operating center used for training. Oswald quickly conflicted with his commanders and faced a second court martial.[ccclxxxii] Oswald's first court martial had resulted from possessing a handgun and accidentally shooting himself. Soon Oswald redoubles his Marxist views and his alleged double life as a possible unofficial asset.

Many allege the Federal Bureau of Investigation or Central Intelligence Agency employed Oswald.[ccclxxxiii] This might explain why the Agency-Naval Base previously admitted this vocally committed Marxist. Oswald had attempted to revoke his United States citizenship and counted public agitation in his skill set to prove his Russian devotion. If Oswald were the Agency's operative he would be "...in a contractual obligation of some kind. This is a myth, of course, because there is not any contract, really, but there is an agreement. There are certain types of high-level agents who are staff agents who have staff status, but they are not employees."[ccclxxxiv]

A Central Intelligence internal memo relayed Bureau liaison Sam Papich's request for any information about "this ex-Marine who recently defected in the USSR."[ccclxxxv] Yet Oswald never lost his citizenship but takes a Russian wife and finds a job. However, the KGB (Russian Intelligence) eventually determined Oswald to be untrustworthy. Supposedly believing he is part of an important spying assignment, Oswald became suicidal when the Soviet authorities told him to return to America. He attempted suicide because he feasibly wanted to continue his dangerous gambit.

Was Lee Harvey Oswald an intelligence asset? A media source contacted more than thirty Agency operatives who affirmed Oswald's debriefing after his return from the Soviet Union.[ccclxxxvi] The debriefing was not standard operating procedure; of the one hundred and seventeen returning defectors, only 10 were fully debriefed. Robert Edward Webster defected and returned at the same time Oswald did. The Agency debriefed Webster for two weeks in Virginia.[ccclxxxvii]

During House Select Committee executive sessions, Agent John Scelso recalls prior alleged Oswald connections to Agency personnel.[ccclxxxviii]

Agent James Hosty previously destroyed one message from Oswald to the Bureau. While in custody, Oswald had previously requested Bureau agents. The Agency and the Bureau observed Oswald for years.

Exactly how many government agents have to associate with Lee Harvey Oswald until connections become possible? This could imply authorities ignored Oswald intentionally. Why did the President's (Warren) Commission not consider these interactions? Officially, enforced ignorance links just Lee Harvey Oswald to President Kennedy's death.

In October 1962, Oswald returned to Dallas. This previous defector and possible Soviet agent brought his Russian family to America. Oswald had no large savings and Marina was pregnant with their second child. The Oswald family was only able to return to America with funds courtesy of the American State Department.[ccclxxxix]

The United States government does not often hand out money without a reason. Offering to fund a traitor is quite strange. Some domestic agency or group was conceivably using Oswald. This supports what some President's Commission members themselves proposed. Oswald was far more than he appeared.

Lee Oswald could have remained unknown prior to his alleged attack on the presidential motorcade. Instead, he made public appearances supporting Marxist ideology. Some often attempt to assign Oswald legitimate Communist status without sufficient proof. Oswald claimed membership in the Fair Play for Cuba Committee. However, according to Bureau files the group held all meetings in New York. The Committee acknowledged no chapter or members in New Orleans.

The Bureau and Agency subsequently asserted A.J. Hidell was Oswald's created alias, not an officer of the Fair Play for Cuba Committee. Oswald did send letters to the Committee. Yet Oswald just exchanged letters with this group, they did not include him as a member. Nor did they feasibly influence his actions.

Following his public fight over Communist politics, police arrest Oswald. Oswald requests a Bureau agent while in jail. Bureau agent John Quigley asked several questions about Oswald's possible association with the Fair Play for Cuba Committee, Oswald offered few specifics.[cccxc] According to Bureau files, Oswald stated A.J. Hidell sent his Fair Play for Cuba membership card. Oswald claimed also to be a member of the national committee of this organization and received a monthly flyer. Oswald could not recall the name of it.[cccxci]

Quigley states Oswald was "probably making self-serving statements..." and being deceptive. It also supports he had no actual knowledge about the group to offer. Consider the Commission states "...Oswald's use of a nonexistent Hidell to serve as the president of the so-called New Orleans Chapter of the Fair Play for Cuba Committee." "Marina Oswald testified 'I knew there was no such organization'" and this supports a false connection to a pro-Castro group.[cccxcii]

In my view, Oswald sought to associate with these groups to strengthen his Communist veneer. His repeated statements and some associations would imply that he was a loyal follower of Marxism. What purpose does Oswald serve by frequently mentioning the benefits of Marxism? Despite these actions, Oswald does not pursue the actual agenda of a Marxist. Oswald's actions merely damaged the causes he professed being important to him.

Many of his actions would imply he was a Communist, yet Oswald never joined the Communist Party in Russia, nor attended official meetings.[cccxciii] Oswald according to the Commission believed "Communist Party officials in the Soviet Union were opportunists who were betraying their positions for personal gain."[cccxciv] Oswald is reported as stating they (Russia) had "fat stinking politicians over there just like we (America) have over here."

Yet provocateurs do make public appearances to enrage the public against the enemy of the day. These agents receive clandestine orders from government agencies. They might receive a "loan" to cover necessary expenses or travel documentation that included quick processing. Decades of the Bureau and Agency denying foreknowledge of Oswald were nothing less than deception. They knew most details about Oswald and they said nothing to the American public.

J. Edgar Hoover later admitted to foreknowledge of Oswald in a message to the President's (Warren) Commission General Counsel J. Lee Rankin. The interaction was from years preceding the assassination of President Kennedy.[cccxcv] Days before the assassination Hoover receives information from a confidential informant regarding Lee Harvey Oswald. The message asserts Oswald has visited the Soviet Embassy and planned to go to Cuba.[cccxcvi] The Bureau attributes prior mention of Oswald being a Bureau informant is part of a Communist plot.[cccxcvii] A plot officials stated did not exist.

The Bureau often privately tracked and speculated about Oswald's actions. Despite the Federal Bureau of Investigation being aware of Oswald's repeated activities, it consistently suppressed knowledge of them. The Bureau feasibly remained silent regarding many Oswald's implications and suspicious actions. It did not consider all the contending evidence in relation to Oswald.

Consider Oswald feasibly had no practice with the Carcano.[cccxcviii] He dry-fired and operated the bolt in New Orleans, yet he never practiced firing the rifle. In the time before the assassination, some officials and witnesses claimed Oswald practiced. A handful of contending witnesses asserted Oswald had practiced at the local firing range.[cccxcix cd]

One example of Oswald allegedly practicing is attributed in part to the Wood family. Dr. Homer Wood and his son Sterling were present at the SportDome, a Dallas rifle range. They and others assert Oswald was present on November 16, 1963. Dr. Wood first connected the man at the rifle range with Oswald after the picture "flashed on the television screen at home several times".[cdi]

Wood's son Sterling had also viewed the television and told his parents Oswald was the same man he encountered. The young man states the gun was an Italian carbine and related this to his father. "It was scratched and it was a surplus gun. It was probably-you can tell it was probably used in the war" (WWII).[cdii] The Woods support Oswald's appearance with an off brand rifle that Dr. Wood is afraid might explode. This does not resemble the Carcano in evidence.

Another problem with the account is the asserted accuracy of the person the Woods observed. Oswald had no practice according to most official evidence.[cdiii cdiv cdv cdvi cdvii] How could he fire such impressive shots without practice? Contending witnesses are the sources for these claims of training.

Sterling noticed the man collected all shells after firing and placed them in his pocket. He noticed the rifle had a sawed off barrel and fire exploded out of the rifle during each shot. Sterling testifies Oswald left in a newer model car with another man driving. Officials never identify this other person. Their reasoning in this specific matter refreshingly accounts for the many witness discrepancies the Wood testimony exemplifies. The Commission found "there was other evidence which prevented the Commission from reaching the conclusion that Lee Harvey Oswald the person these witnesses saw."[cdviii] Thus, Oswald has no confirmed firing practice with the Carcano.

How could Lee Harvey Oswald undertake all preparations necessary and somehow forget to practice regularly? Regular practice would be the minimum requirement for success.[cdix] Perhaps authorities imagine Oswald was so qualified he required no practice. Oswald may have failed to repeatedly practice because he possibly never fired a shot in Dealey Plaza.

Ruth Paine eventually tells Oswald of a job at the Texas School Book Depository in October.[cdx] He cannot foresee the motorcade route and has no idea Kennedy will pass the building. Oswald cannot learn of the motorcade route passing the Depository until November 19 in the local media[cdxi], not if he is acting alone. This drastically constrains the prior asserted official timeline.

It allows less than seventy-two hours for Oswald to develop a realistic motive, plan, perform all preparation unseen, and make no mistakes. Now consider he worked each day, he slept, and went to bed early the night before the assassination. He was tired from playing with his daughter in the yard and dining with the Paine family. Oswald did not practice the night before.[cdxii] Reasonable doubt is created by no clearly discernible motive, nor prior known intent to kill President Kennedy.

Oswald feasibly has no more than twenty-four to forty-eight hours to do all these things, once time from other activities is subtracted. This limited duration possibly infers he did not prior seek flight to Cuba because of the assassination but for other reasons. He could not meet with KGB members to plot without prior knowledge. Oswald did not have months to prepare for something he could not know, unless someone aided him. If that occurred, so too did a conspiracy.

Official's state he worked the morning of November 22, 1963. Oswald does not decide to cancel work, rest, and find a more advantageous firing point with less obstruction. Instead, he decides to work, firing if he obtains the chance, since others had access to the area. Ponder now some other timeline problems.

The President's (Warren) Commission never constructed a full timeline based on most witness statements about Lee Harvey Oswald's location. Some witnesses place him on different floors of the Depository in the moments before the shots began. A few have claimed that Oswald is present in various media outside the building. Yet Oswald in a media interview places himself inside the building.

Instead of addressing conflicting testimony, the President's Commission just ignores these problems. The official timeline jumps to 12:30 p.m. placing Oswald in the sniper's nest. The final report regarding Oswald's position and actions relies on incomplete testimony and circumstantial evidence.[cdxiii] Oswald then allegedly creates a sniper's nest using boxes and fires three times.

He supposedly acts with no proven escape plan. There is no easy way to dispose of the weapon that bears his fingerprints. He allegedly leaves the shells and has no decent false alibi. Lee Harvey Oswald was not afforded his legal rights, and has no lawyer. Jack Ruby murders Oswald days later.

# CHAPTER 5

*"Our little bit of grandeur is gone"*

~Anonymous Dublin, Ireland bus rider
Shortly after the reported assassination of John F. Kennedy
*"Dictionary of Quotations"*

## THE ASSASSINATION CONSPIRACY

Gunfire commences from the School Book Depository. Witnesses report shots from the Grassy Knoll area as well. A possible assassin quickly conceals their weapon and fades into the chaotic scene. The Knoll was subject to public use and alteration following the assassination. Most Dallas Police were initially busy elsewhere.

The official timeline states Oswald kills the president, and dashes away. However people a floor below watching the motorcade do not hear him. Somehow, witnesses did hear the bullet casings fall to the floor. Why do they not hear the loud movements associated with running or hiding the weapon? Oswald then officially deposits the rifle between some boxes where Dallas Police discover the Carcano. Oswald races down four flights of stairs, and past anyone near a doorway. He is unheard by any individuals in the building and approaches the second floor lunchroom.

Following his long dash, Oswald does not leave the building and flee to freedom. Less than two minutes after the shots cease Dallas Police Officer Marion Baker and the Depository manager allegedly see Oswald. He was calm and standing in the second floor lunchroom.

While Officer Baker and Manager Truly at the second floor question Oswald, other movement appears in photographic evidence of the sixth floor sniper's nest. The stack of boxes in the snipers' nest changes as witnesses photograph the School Book Depository. This occurs in the minutes following the last shot. From the photographic evidence, the House Select Committee concluded, "There is an apparent rearranging of boxes within 2 minutes after the last shot was fired at President Kennedy."[cdxiv]

This conclusion additionally contends the Lone Gunman Theory. Oswald was four floors down and unable to alter the sniper's nest, if the official timeline is correct. Someone else was possibly changing the crime scene. This individual might have altered ballistic evidence, and it was not Lee Harvey Oswald.

The boxes in the area offer additional questions in the form of unknown fingerprints present. Bureau agents required another round of tests in order to rule out all Depository employees. When they make the request to Depository Manager Roy Truly he "strongly objected" and wished to limit the scope of such fingerprinting. The Bureau decides to limit themselves to twelve employees that were considered "who would have had occasion" to touch the boxes. None of them matches the unknown prints.[cdxv]

According to Roy Truly and Dallas D.A. Henry Wade, Oswald was the only Depository employee unaccounted for after the shooting. However, a Dallas police officer at the scene affirms, "there were people going in and out". The Texas School Book Depository's front entrance is unsecured for three to ten minutes. A Secret Service agent noted the rear Depository entrance was unsecured twenty minutes later.[cdxvi] Where is this regard for any other individual absent from the Texas School Book Depository? Authorities seemed to predetermine Oswald's guilt.

Oswald eventually left the Texas School Book Depository past the crowds for his rooming house before authorities secured the building. He again has escaped! Why does he not flee the city? Oswald does not depart to easily accessible trains, bus stations, and encounters no initial roadblocks. The way remains clear. Why did Oswald not flee to the nearby Communist aligned embassies in Mexico?

CBS News Report with Walter Cronkite just following President Kennedy's assassination stated "...after that shooting incident of course, pandemonium broke out." Other unknown initial suspects were reported "...the man the officers were looking for or one of them has been taken from the building (School Book Depository), now I see Police officers running back to the Texas School Book Depository building.." Who was this man? A few witnesses reported Dallas Police arrested a second man. Despite the initial report, Oswald is the sole focus of authorities.[cdxvii]

Officially, Lee Harvey Oswald departs on a bus and then proceeds by cab to an area past his rooming house. Once he retrieves a handgun, Oswald prepares to commit his second alleged murder of the day.[cdxviii][cdxix] Oswald's conduct preceding his capture varies between cold-blooded assassin and desperate criminal. Diverse behavior may imply that different suspects were possibly responsible for each crime.

The second victim attributed to Oswald is Dallas Police officer J.D Tippit. Tippit's murder was unlike the previous distant shots Oswald supposedly fired. This act was direct and vicious. Oswald never committed murder until the day of the assassination. He kills the president and is calm minutes later. Oswald then officially executes a police officer in daylight at close range, and goes to a movie.

Lee Oswald had been so emotional he attempted suicide in Russia. Now he reverts to emotionless killer, committing murder twice in a few hours. He does not flee Dallas as a lone criminal might. He officially flees on foot eventually going to a movie theatre. Oswald failed to spend less than a dollar for a ticket. A cold-blooded assassin would not make this emotional mistake.

What happened to the mastermind giving a flawless performance? He calmly spoke with Officer Tippit prior to allegedly murdering him.[cdxx] Then he flees petrified. Oswald did not act casually at the theatre as he did when allegedly killing the president. Oswald's apparent illegal entrance causes witnesses to summon the Dallas Police.

Did Oswald hear the description from the radio and realize the net was closing? In this last action, Oswald seemingly attempts to meet someone. Perhaps he wanted authorities to capture him. Why intentionally force your own surrender? Yet Oswald resisted arrest and officials claim he attempted to use his gun when surrounded.

Following his capture Oswald then endures repeated interrogation. Officials charged him for the murder of President Kennedy and J.D. Tippit. Dallas Police were too busy questioning Oswald to provide him with full judicial process. They might understand they possessed no evidence to keep him indefinitely. No Patriot Act existed at that time.

Despite claims that Dallas Police could not anticipate Oswald's murder, they were given an official warning from the Federal Bureau of Investigation. J. Edgar Hoover stated, "Last night we received a call in our Dallas office from a man talking in a calm voice and saying he was a member of a committee organized to kill Oswald. We at once notified the Chief of Police and he assured us Oswald would be given sufficient protection."

"This morning we called the Chief of Police again warning of the possibility of some effort against Oswald and he again assured us adequate protection would be given. However, this was not done."[cdxxi] Police Chief Jesse Curry informed the news media of Oswald's transfer despite the recent death threats.[cdxxii] The crowd offered a distraction that Jack Ruby used to conceal himself. Why did Dallas Police proceed without a secure transfer? Officially, none of these repeated security lapses had any connection; unofficially patterns of deception were forming.

## OFFICIAL FACTS SUPPORTING A CONSPIRACY

Officials allege Oswald brought a disassembled rifle to the Depository and told witness Buell Frazier it was "curtain rods" in a long paper bag. Yet his description of the bag Oswald carried was "a grocery store" paper sack. The bag was "roughly around two feet". Frazier informed the Commission he "did not pay much attention to the package..."[cdxxiii] In his prior statement Frazier stated "27 inches" as the bag's length, the problem is neither size could accommodate the disassembled rifle.[cdxxiv]

When the Bureau laboratory assessed the package, it was determined not to match the Depository paper supply. In a supplementary report, they reversed this to state the paper did match. The Commission replied, "we are in doubt".[cdxxv] This was another evidentiary problem due to incompetent methods or possible suppression of evidence. The alleged reconstruction of the weapon additionally consumes precious unobserved time before the assassination that Oswald requires.

It is possible Oswald did bring a disassembled rifle to work that day. Yet the matter is contended because witnesses cannot place a sufficiently large paper sack in Oswald's hands. He had no tools and little time to reassemble the weapon. The Commission failed to demonstrate this occurred with consistent evidence. It remains possible Lee Harvey Oswald did not transport the official murder weapon.

The official suspect used a surplus gun nearly two decades old with a rusty firing pin. The Carcano had a "two stage pull"; this mechanism does allow for more accuracy if time allows the ability to preset the trigger for each shot. However, Oswald according to authorities missed the first shot. Yet the disadvantages of the two-trigger pull are critical as well. The mechanisms were a safety feature in military rifles, and they require more time and pressure to fire accurately. [cdxxvi] Oswald's failure to familiarize himself with firing the weapon is significant and consumes more time.[cdxxvii]

Ronald Simmons was Chief of the Infantry Weapons Evaluation Branch of Ballistics Laboratory of the Department of the Army. Simmons testified, "I think with the opportunity to use the weapon and get familiar with it, we could probably have the results reproduced by more than one firer." [cdxxviii] Most of these professionals made the shots quickly, yet only a single person was able to hit all the necessary areas. A group of experts under advantageous test conditions, with more recent practice, could not consistently recreate the improbable shots more than once. According to the Commission Oswald is in the sniper's nest and fires, hides the weapon, and dashes four floors down. He allegedly encounters Roy Truly and Officer Baker; descends a floor, and casually exits the Depository in approximately three minutes at 12:33pm. [cdxxix]

With these supporting facts and witness details in mind, we can inspect the essence of the President's (Warren) Commission case. Did Oswald fire the shots? Authorities insist Oswald aimed and missed the first shot. Even practiced military experts could only recreate the shots once in a related test.

The subsequent assassination trajectory simulations conducted by FBI and Secret Service agents had a few significant problems. The Presidential limousine was not used in the tests. Agents used a Secret Service follow up car "similar in design." The Commission states, "Any differences were taken into account." Two Bureau Agents sat in the limousine in the "same relative positions as President Kennedy and Governor Connally." [cdxxx] This was not an exacting scientific study.

Within the simulation's report is the admission of feasible inaccuracy, "the same bullet probably passed through both men", "...the precise distance cannot be ascertained," between Governor Connally and President Kennedy. "The alinement (sic) of the points of entry was only indicative and not conclusive that one bullet hit both men." Thus, in the Commission's own determinations, the Single Bullet Theory is not "conclusive", it was "indicative" of the evidence and witnesses they chose to regard.

The Army Wound Ballistics Branch conducted additional tests. They found that the same bullet "probably" struck Kennedy and Connally. However, "Dr. Frederick W. Light Junior, the third of the wound ballistics experts...testified that the anatomical findings were insufficient to formulate a firm opinion..." [cdxxxi] The simulations relied on the Bethesda medical evidence that was subject to destruction, suppression, and presumptions. [cdxxxii]

While the later Select Committee ballistics studies assert the Commission was correct about the Single Bullet, their source material relies upon the Commission's problematic hypotheses. It is possible the Single Bullet Theory occurred based on some testimony and evidence. Yet repeated credible evidence reasonably contends this hypothesis. All but a single official previously handling the original bullet fail to confirm it was the same one.[cdxxxiii] The Single Bullet Theory is famous not conclusive.

Some modern television programs, edited programs, have claimed to have recreated and solved all ballistic questions. Having reviewed many of these claims, I must utterly disagree. The premise of many programs is inaccurate and unproven claims support portions of their conclusions. Consider that subsequent modern tests did not even use the actual sniper's nest in the Texas Schoolbook Depository. Many tests claim to have ended all reasonable debate. All have failed to do so.

Some tests perhaps rely on standards of marketing, not standards of science. Most have not addressed the important questions remaining. Despite how famous their celebrity participants are, some remain poorly contrived inspections. Others seek to generate ratings not reasonable conversation and independent review.

Just because a show or book uses scientific terms and speaks with authority or style, does not validate its results. Verifiable facts validate results. Many critics attempt to use these shows as incontrovertible proof. Additionally some conspiracy advocates dabble in this television black magic to prove unsubstantiated theories.

All people have a right to personal views. Yet no celebrity without most facts can ever determine the truth. Most fail to consider opposing viewpoints. Scientific testing is for independent experts under proper conditions. Science is not for creating a visual spectacle to impress television audiences.

The Federal Bureau of Investigation conducted a series of tests using three trained forensic analysts. They found no usable fingerprints on the Carcano. According to the first Bureau report, "No latent prints of any value were found on the inner parts of the rifle". The President's (Warren) Commission Report contains the original Federal Bureau of Investigation conclusions.

Sebastian F. Latona worked in the Latent Fingerprint Section within the Federal Bureau of Investigation's Identification Division. This was one of the best labs in America and had several experienced technicians available. Supervisor Latona affirmed: "...the formations, the ridge formations and characteristics, were insufficient for purposes of either effecting identification or a determination that the print was not identical with the prints of people. Accordingly, my opinion simply was that the latent prints which were there were of no value".[cdxxxiv]

No fingerprints proving the assassin's identity are present. A finger and palm print later emerge. Dallas Police assert they "lifted" them with alternative means prior. The President's (Warren) Commission deemed the Dallas Police test superior to the Bureau's laboratory assessment.

So which investigators do we trust? The Federal Bureau of Investigation Lab had not found them. Yet the Dallas Police also may have finally done something timely. Some disputes remain.

The official timeline concludes Oswald died shortly following his arrival at Parkland Hospital. Lee Harvey Oswald died without ever giving a confession, possessing representation, or receiving a full trial. Everyone deserves the presumption of legal innocence, contrary to modern executive branch declarations of power. Overlooked is all consideration of other possible assassins.

However, a different sniper might have possessed time and practice. Possible snipers would require great natural ability, extensive training, and use modern weapons. They would have to be ready in a moment notice, and disappear just as swiftly. It would necessitate express directions and planning.

"Consequently, the decision to employ this technique (assassination) must nearly always be reached in the field, at the area where the act will take place. Decisions and instructions should be confined to an absolute minimum of persons. Ideally only one person will be involved. No report may be made, but usually the act will be properly covered by normal news services…"[cdxxxv]

"Killing a political leader whose burgeoning career is a clear and present danger to the cause of freedom may be held necessary. But assassinations can seldom be employed with a clear conscience. Persons who are morally squeamish should not attempt it". [cdxxxvi] The Central Intelligence Agency sought a loyal murderer who did not possess empathy or a conscience.

"Techniques will vary according to whether the subject is unaware of his danger…If the assassin is to die with the subject, the act will be called "lost." If the assassin is to escape…If such concealment is desirable the operation will be called 'secret'…while if the assassination requires publicity to be effective it will be termed 'terroristic'.[cdxxxvii] Except in terroristic assassinations it is desirable the assassin be transient in the area. He should have an absolute minimum of contact with the rest of the organization and his instructions should be given orally by one person only…"

"It is preferable that the person issuing instructions also conduct any withdrawal or covering action which may be necessary… In lost assassination, the assassin must be a fanatic of some sort. Politics, religion, and revenge are about the only feasible motives. Since a fanatic is unstable psychologically, he must be handled with extreme care. He must not know the identities of the other members of the organization, for although it is intended that he die in the act, something may go wrong." [cdxxxviii]

"When the decision to assassinate has been reached, the tactics of the operation must be planned, based upon an estimate of the situation similar to that used in military operations...When all necessary data has been collected, and effective tactical plan can be prepared. All planning must be mental; no papers should ever contain evidence of the operation." [cdxxxix] The need for plausible deniability was paramount.

"The essential point of the assassination is the death of the subject...The specific technique employed will depend upon a large number of variables, but should be constant in one point: Death must be absolutely certain. The attempt on Hitler's life failed because the conspiracy did not give this matter proper attention." [cdxl] Agency operations can include the assassin's escape or demise.

The assassin should have a "minimum contact" with "the rest of the organization" or the conspirators. If this was a "secret terroristic assassination", the true assassin could escape. The "terrorist" dupe bears the guilt. Those who remain might have conducted "...any withdrawal or covering action which may be necessary".

"However there are many cases in which firearms are probably more efficient than any other means. These cases usually involve distance between the assassin...The precision rifle...a good hunting or target rifle, should always be considered a possibility. Absolute reliability can nearly always be achieved at a distance of one hundred yards." "In ideal circumstances, the range may be extended to 250 yards." [cdxli]

"The rifle should be a well made bolt or falling block action". "...Public figures or guarded officials may be killed with great reliability and some safety if a firing point can be established prior to an official occasion. The propaganda value of this system may be very high..." [cdxlii] President Kennedy dies less than ten years after the creation of this guide.

The assumed lone assassin was feasibly Lee Harvey Oswald. Concealed were all links to other members in the possible operation. These assassins could use the efficiency of a well-made bolt-action rifle. The "absolute reliability" kill zone was one hundred yards or under. President Kennedy is between fifty-eight and eighty-eight yards from the sniper's nest during the shots.

Oswald feasibly was the "terroristic" assassin. A possible sniper elsewhere was the "secret" assassin. Many remain unaware witnesses and original evidence feasibly indicates a separate firing location. The Grassy Knoll ranks among the most discussed locations at the crime scene that some claim was a firing location.

The Grassy Knoll area is comprised of the Knoll proper, the Bryan pergola, and immediately adjacent train yard and parking lot sections. The Grassy Knoll firing line was less than ninety yards from the President. Repeated eyewitnesses stated observing smoke and figures near the Knoll. Some identified a police officer and unknown officials behind the divider fence on this area.

Complicating the situation is the infamous Badge Man, one of the many alleged figures present in photographic evidence of Dealey Plaza. Multiple people have claimed or are claimed to be the Badge Man. Among them are James Files, Roscoe White, and J.D. Tippit. No verified official evidence supports these men being responsible.

A few witnesses observe fake officials in the rioting crowd. Critics have declared this occurrence was unlikely. Yet an outside party impersonated Assistant Director of the Federal Bureau of Investigation William Sullivan at least once prior to November 4, 1963. Bureau officials reprimand but do not prosecute this officially unnamed person.[cdxliii] The Bureau's affable treatment of this impersonation is peculiar.

Thus, it was possible that another party could have impersonated federal officials in Dealey Plaza. Evidence from the scene, some witnesses' credibility, and opportunities to capture those responsible were lost. Many people have spent countless years concentrating on the periphery figures and unproven speculation. Instead, we can focus on the evidentiary record.

This assassination unfolded just as the former cited Agency guide had recommended. The House Select Committee on Assassinations determined through scientific testing, two snipers likely fired at President Kennedy. The gunman on the Grassy Knoll according to Select Committee experts fired one missed shot, "The area behind a picket fence atop the grassy knoll, since there was considerable witness testimony suggesting shots were fired from there".[cdxliv cdxlv]

The complete body of evidence placing Oswald in the sniper's nest was not beyond a reasonable doubt.[cdxlvi] Most complete versions of the evidence do not obviously point to a lone gunman as officially repeated. The legal standards the Commission used had certain requirements. In my view, the Commission ignored them when convenient.

# ORIGINAL EVIDENCE AND MEDICAL FINDINGS

Instead of allegedly modified subsequent versions of medical witness statements, we review the original documents and testimony. When the events were crisp and fresh, and no chance for historical alteration was possible. These are the medical conclusions of President Kennedy's wounds prior to any revision by later authorities. Some reviews ignore these vital observations doctors and medical staff at Parkland Hospital offered.

Critics and official sources deny President Kennedy suffered a throat wound of entrance. Dr. Paul Peters instead confirmed, "We saw the wound of entry in the throat".[cdxlvii] Dr. Charles Carrico "...observed a small wound in the anterior (front) lower third of the neck".[cdxlviii] Authorities determined this to be an exit wound, contrary to the original reports of medical professionals and experts. Dr. Peters testified: "...Dr. Perry and Dr. Baxter were present and they were working on his (President Kennedy) throat." Dr. Peters noted, "Well as I mentioned, the neck wound had already been interfered with by the tracheotomy..."[cdxlix]

Dr. Robert McClelland said referring to the throat wound "The incision had obliterated it, essentially the skin portion, that is".[cdl] Dr. Malcolm Perry was the resident surgeon at Parkland hospital, he testified the throat wound was "...roughly spherical to oval in shape, not a punched out wound".[cdli] Dr. Ronald Jones testified, "As we saw him (President Kennedy), we noticed a small wound...no greater than a quarter inch in greatest diameter".[cdlii] A large exit wound was not present. Based on original medical evidence it was an entrance wound. Doctors note the wound prior to a tracheotomy occurring.

Most attending doctors originally report President Kennedy possessed a throat wound of entry. A throat wound "obliterated" from the doctors endeavoring to revive him. The wound in the President's throat was "not punched out". Parkland doctors said, "We saw a wound of entry." This requires a second gunman, weapon, and point of fire.

Being a possible entrance wound, it struck John F. Kennedy in the front. The wound may indicate a shot from a second location. However, the most lethal wound was to President Kennedy's head, it had similar conflicting implications. Conceivably, it was a second frontal entrance wound according to original medical evidence.

A bullet wound of entrance appears small; it expands becoming a larger exit wound. When the bullet expands, it does greater damage piercing all obstructing tissue. Fragmentation of the bullet additionally damages the victim. The back of President Kennedy's head received extensive damage verified from originally released medical reports. These facts are from official testimony and surviving original evidence.

Parkland Hospital Nurse Diana Bowron observed damage to the president's head upon arrival. She explained the "the back of his head...Well, it was very bad...I just saw one large hole". Nurse Pat Hutton stated, "Pressure bandage was no use...because of the massive opening on the back of the head."[cdliii] Some qualified eyewitnesses spoke from direct interaction with the damaged area.

The original head wound description is far different from later medical reports. Dr. Marion Jenkins description stated, "There was a great laceration on the right side of the head (temporal and occipital), causing a great defect in the skull plate so that there was herniation and laceration of great areas of the brain, even to the extent that the cerebellum had protruded from the wound. There were also fragmented sections of brain on the drapes of the emergency room cart. With the institution of adequate cardiac compression, there was a great flow of blood from the cranial cavity, indicating that there was much vascular damage as well as brain tissue damage".[cdliv]

The human skull's temporal and occipital regions are located in the rear base and side of the skull. The original description submitted to authorities was Kennedy's exit wound had indeed been in the back right side of his skull. This would denote a large exit wound entering from the front. Dr. Carrico reported "...the scalp and skull was fragmented and bleeding cerebral and cerebellar tissue." The President's (Warren) Commission ignored these implications.[cdlv]

Dr. William Clark testified to the Commission, "I then examined the wound in the back of the president's head. This was a large, gaping wound in the right posterior part with cerebral and cerebellar tissue being damaged and exposed".[cdlvi] Dr. Malcolm Perry agreed stating "A large wound of the right posterior cranium".[cdlvii] Dr. Don Curtis stated he "...went around to the right side of the patient and saw the head wound". Dr. Curtis continues "fragments of bone and a gross injury to the cranial contents".[cdlviii]

Describing the area Dr. Paul Peters affirmed, "It seemed to me that in the right occipital parietal area that there was a large defect. There appeared to be bone loss and brain loss in the area".[cdlix] Dr. Gene Akin added his observation "The back of the right occipital parietal portion of his head was shattered, with brain substance extruding."[cdlx] Dr. Kenneth Salyer "...noted that his major wound seemed to be in the right temporal area...-nothing other than he did have a gaping scalp wound-cranial wound."[cdlxi]

The testimony of Dr. Charles Baxter referred to the damage stating "…in a word – literally the right side of his head had been blown off".[cdlxii] Dr. Ronald Jones testified the head wound "…appeared to be an exit wound in the posterior portion of the skull".[cdlxiii] Nurse Audrey Bell observed a posterior wound in the occipital area of the President's skull.[cdlxiv] All these eyewitnesses reaffirmed the original wound locations.

In later autopsy photographs, a ragged incision within the president's throat officially transforms into a rear exit wound. Parkland Hospital doctors reported medical procedure not exiting bullet damage was responsible. Repeated medical experts' testify an exit wound was in the rear of President Kennedy's skull. These were frontal entrance wounds according to reports of varied Parkland first responders.

These statements feasibly infer shots from the front. Lee Harvey Oswald could not have fired these shots. Regarding injuries to Governor Connally and the problematic Single Bullet Theory, Dr. Robert Shaw commented, "I feel that there would be some difficulty in explaining all of the wounds as being inflicted by bullet Exhibit 399 without causing more in the way of loss of substance to the bullet or deformation of the bullet." "I thought I knew just how the Governor (Connally) was wounded until I saw the pictures today, and it becomes a little harder to explain." Dr. Shaw tells the Commission "I have no firm opinion" regarding the Single Bullet Theory.[cdlxv]

Regarding a single bullet causing all the wounds attributed Dr. Charles Gregory who operated on Governor Connally states, "I would have to concede that would be possible." Yet it was not probable according to most related medical experts. "I believe one would have to concede the possibility, but I believe firmly that the probability is much diminished…I think that to pass through the soft tissues of the President would certainly have decelerated the missile to some extent. Having then struck the Governor and shattered a rib, it is further decelerated, yet it has presumably retained sufficient energy to smash a radius (bone). Moreover, it escaped the forearm to penetrate at least the skin and fascia of the thigh, and I am not persuaded that this is very probable". Dr. Gregory's opinion stands with the majority of related medical experts.[cdlxvi]

Remember, no immediate consequences occurred from stating medical truth. Did all doctors and medical staff at Parkland Hospital lie to investigators? They gained no benefit and did not present varied testimony. If they were trusted in all other cases, why doubt them now? Before normal medical procedures are complete, Secret Service agents forcibly remove the president's body to Bethesda Hospital. This illegal seizure feasibly taints subsequent medical evidence.

# BETHESDA NAVAL HOSPITAL

President Johnson would not depart Parkland Hospital without Mrs. Kennedy, and she would not leave without the President's body. Admiral George Burkley explained the "need" to expedite procedures. A questionable transfer of Kennedy's body occurs despite the refusal of the Parkland Medical Examiner, doctors, and staff. Mrs. Kennedy selected Bethesda Naval Hospital to honor President' Kennedy's former Navy service. Yet the reasons are insufficient and do not warrant ignoring the law. Despite the feelings or emotions of attending officials, Parkland Hospital should have conducted the autopsy.

Federal authorities could have overseen the entire procedure in Texas. This may have prevented several discrepancies and possible mischaracterization of the medical evidence. Despite the later grant of federal jurisdiction, this brash disregard of basic legal responsibility occurred.[cdlxvii] J. Edgar Hoover when subsequently interviewed told author William Manchester the "FBI immediately entered the case, despite non-jurisdiction..."[cdlxviii]

Three medical pathologists conducted a majority of the Bethesda autopsy, Dr. J. Thornton Boswell, Pierre Finck, and James Humes. Dr. Humes was the ranking officer, yet only Dr. Finck was a forensic pathologist with an extensive background in gunshot wounds. Now consider that Secret Service agents, Federal Bureau of Investigation agents, non-essential military officers, and civilians were present. This created a chaotic environment unsuitable for accurate and undisturbed medical inquiry during portions of the autopsy.[cdlxix cdlxx cdlxxi]

"There were Admirals, and when you are a lieutenant -colonel in the Army you just follow orders..." According to Finck, Dr. Humes stated aloud in the autopsy room, "Who is in charge here?" An unidentified General replied, "I am". Finck explains this statement. "You must understand that in those circumstances, there were law enforcement officers, military people with various ranks, and you have to co-ordinate the operation according to directions."[cdlxxii]

Dr. Finck is not present when officials conduct x-rays of the President's head, and removal of the brain. Finck is unaware of the number of photographs and x-rays taken, nor their sequence.[cdlxxiii] Finck reported Dr. Humes collected all notes present; Dr. Finck's notes vanish. During testimony to the Assassination Records Review Board Finck testifies certain necessary procedures were not undertaken. "The removal of the organs of the neck. In my training we were trained to remove the organs of the neck. And in this particular case they were not removed."[cdlxxiv]

Among the standard procedures additionally disregarded was complete notation of vital weights and measurements. They did not initially speak to doctors at Parkland hospital, and neglected to inspect the President's clothing. Nor was access granted to any films of the assassination. The Bethesda doctors were under the false impression that President Kennedy fell forward.[cdlxxv] This further may have influenced their medical judgments.

Mr. T. Jeremy Gunn counsel of the Assassination Records Review Board asked, "Does that mean that Dr. Humes, Dr. Boswell and you yourself were not free to perform a complete medical/legal autopsy on President Kennedy? Dr. Finck replies, "That's right."[cdlxxvi] Based on the instructions of Admiral Burkley, the autopsy had a set duration and limited scope. Finck asserts it was the Kennedy family's wishes. Subsequently, Mr. Gunn presents Finck with an interview of Dr. Humes stating the ballistics angles used in testimony were a "guesstimate".[cdlxxvii]

Dr. Finck's original testimony to the President's Commission confirms serious public doubts. When questioned by the President's (Warren) Commission, Finck disputes a single bullet causing the many wounds in Kennedy and Connally. Commission counsel Arlen Specter inquired if Exhibit 399, the Single Bullet, could have inflicted the wounds attributed by officials. When Specter asks, could the bullet have remained intact Dr. Finck replies "Definitely not." Specter replies "... could it have been the bullet which inflicted the wound on Governor Connally's right wrist?" Dr. Finck affirms "No; for the reason that there are too many fragments described in the wrist."[cdlxxviii] This Commission medical expert fails to vindicate their determinations.

Dr. James Humes burned his original autopsy draft report and notes. He asserted this was due to President Kennedy's blood being present on them.[cdlxxix] When defending his actions during testimony Humes referred to this as "splitting hairs..."[cdlxxx] However, a noticeable problem exists with Humes' explanation. Among the papers Humes previously returned was a bloodstained page of Dr. Boswell's notes. Humes asserts he would not destroy other people's notes, despite the reasoning for destroying his.[cdlxxxi]

Humes subsequently makes further objections to "splitting hairs", Mr. Gunn affirms while the handwritten notes may have blood on them, the draft report Humes burnt did not. Humes then begins a deficient explanation about this action. "Well, it may have had errors in spelling or I don't know what was the matter with it, or whether I even ever did that. I don't know. I can't recall. I absolutely can't recall, and I apologize for that. But that's the way the cookie crumbles."

Humes then shifts from his seemingly apologetic stance to justify his actions with an egotistical claim. "I didn't want anything to remain that some squirrel would grab on and make whatever use that they might. Now whether you felt that was reasonable or not, I don't know. But it doesn't make any difference because that was my decision and mine alone. Nobody else's"[cdlxxxii] Thus, Humes cannot recall or he did it intentionally.

Humes did not contact Parkland Hospital to discuss the original state of the wounds until the autopsy was complete.[cdlxxxiii cdlxxxiv] This would have given the Bethesda medical team the insight of Parkland doctors. Humes did not check the President's clothing to corroborate wounds. No log initially recorded the autopsy photographs, x-rays, or the procedures occurring.

However, Dr. Humes sheds possible light on the presence of the unknown general Dr. Finck mentioned prior. The general in charge of the military district of Washington D.C. is feasibly who Humes asked, "Who is in charge" to have someone control a photographer complicating the autopsy scene.[cdlxxxv] This explanation is reasonable and in my view sufficient.

The General who feasibly claimed this based on Humes' description is Major General Philip Wehle. Wehle commanded the Washington DC Military District.[cdlxxxvi] He was reasonably able to assert some control over military staff. Thus, the statement does not signify anyone but Dr. Humes controlled the autopsy. Many other inconsistencies occur without requiring speculation to explain them.

Yet Humes neglected medical procedures regarding a gunshot wound, and rushed to complete the autopsy report in "36 to 48 hours." Admiral Burkley had given a timeline for the autopsy to be complete.[cdlxxxvii] Dr. Humes additionally reveals despite the previous reports of the President's wound it may have been larger. Humes states, "I'm not going to debate it. I mean, it would depend on how you were measuring it, because it wasn't a-- like this room is 25 by 35. Its got walls and extreme--this was irregular, so you make any kind of measurement you want..."[cdlxxxviii]

Humes' reply offers interpretation was necessary, and the many distractions and various contending notes, statements, and confusion impeded this. Humes additionally cannot recall where he cut the skull to remove the President's brain. "...it was a real problem because it was all falling apart, the skull. And I can't recall the details of exactly how we managed to maneuver that, because it was a problem."[cdlxxxix] Humes noted a specific photograph absent from the National Archives collection. "One was inside the occipital region, which we interpreted as the wound of entrance, for obvious reasons, and one that never came--whatever happened to it. I was very disturbed by it."

As his testimony wore on Humes again complained, "we're doing a lot of nitpicking here that I'm having difficulty with, you know. It doesn't lend itself to what you're trying to have me do."[cdxc] Humes states doctors proceeded to "...dissect the lungs, heart, and abdominal contents and so forth". Yet they neglected to fully dissect the bullet wound area and organs of the President's throat.

Humes notes a few autopsy pictures he recalled were not present in the evidence.[cdxci] Dr. Humes did not perform standard procedures to determine the conclusive origin of President Kennedy's wounds. Dr. Humes states Admiral Galloway suggested they insert the word "presumably" into the report. Humes states, "...because they were presumptions. We didn't know who shot who or anything about, you know. But our conclusions were that this was probably the entrance wound, this was probably the exit wound." [cdxcii]

The autopsy protocol itself is vague regarding any contending medical opinions and evidence. Dr. Humes records that Dr. Perry of Parkland Hospital noted a wound in the President's head.[cdxciii] Yet Humes does not reveal Perry's head wound placement "A large wound in the right posterior (rear) cranium". Humes' does not list the throat wound as possibly of entrance based on Dr. Perry's official description.

Subsequent to Humes' command of the President's autopsy, he received a written order to reaffirm previous verbal orders. "You are reminded that you are under verbal orders of the Surgeon General, United States Navy, to discuss with no one events connected with your official duties on the evening of 22 November - 23 November 1963." "This letter constitutes official notification of those verbal orders. You are warned that infraction of these orders makes you liable to Court Martial proceedings under appropriate articles of the Uniform Code of Military Justice."[cdxciv]

When testifying before the President's (Warren) Commission Dr. Humes states the improbability of the Single Bullet theory. Arlen Specter asks Humes "Now looking at that bullet, Exhibit 399, Doctor Humes, could that bullet have gone through or been any part of the fragment passing through President Kennedy's head in Exhibit No. 388?" Humes replies, "I do not believe so, sir." Specter states "And could that missile have made the wound on Governor Connally's right wrist?", "I think that is most unlikely."[cdxcv]

Dr. Humes adds, "The X-rays made of the wound in the head of the late President showed fragmentation of the missile..." "The reason I believe it is most unlikely that this missile could have inflicted either of these wounds is that this missile is basically intact; its jacket appears to me to be intact, and I do not understand how it could possibly have left fragments in either of these locations."[cdxcvi] Thus, two of three officially supported medical experts dispute the Single Bullet theory.

In 1996, Dr. J. Thorton Boswell offered confirmation of initial orders that would prevent full medical procedures. Boswell noted, "I never saw Admiral Burkley in the morgue. But at some point Jim (James Humes) understood we were to do a limited autopsy to find-- I think the initial thing they told us was that we were to find the bullets, that they had captured the assailant, and that was all they needed."[cdxcvii] Dr. Humes denied this request according to Dr. Boswell. "...And Jim (Humes) argued and said that that was--you know, we couldn't do that kind of autopsy." These military doctors were subject to official attempts to suppress evidence.[cdxcviii]

Boswell additionally states the President's clothing was uninspected for weeks to corroborate wound locations. Boswell then describes the neck wound. Parkland doctors found this to be a wound of entry before the tracheotomy occurred. Boswell states "And then we had difficulty in interpreting the wound in his anterior neck."[cdxcix] This is wholly understandable with the reduced information possessed during the autopsy.

Bethesda physicians had to "interpret" the wounds. Based upon a rear wound that was "distorted" they concluded it was a wound of entrance. However, Boswell confirmed the dissection of the President's throat to determine the bullet path was incomplete. Mr. Gunn asks "With there being a bullet wound transiting the neck, would it not be standard autopsy procedure to remove all of the organs of the neck?" Boswell replies, "Normally it would. The trachea, larynx, and everything."

Mr. Gunn then asks, "Do you know whether the trachea, larynx, and thyroid were removed?" Boswell answers "I'm almost sure we did not remove the trachea and larynx...Normally you would take all the neck organs out with the thoracic organs." Yet they never did. Despite Boswell's claims that no rushed procedures occurred he subsequently states "...but on the other hand, Jim (Humes) was anxious to get all the material down to the Admiral...Because we were expediting things so rapidly and getting everything down there..."[d] Boswell affirmed Dr. Humes collected all notes to compose an autopsy report.[di] Boswell further confirmed unlogged staff handled autopsy evidence.

During subsequent testimony, Mr. Gunn presents a handwritten document Dr. Humes and Boswell signed. The document corroborates a rear "exit wound" in President Kennedy's head. Characteristics noted on the document such as "the beveling of the bone characteristic of a wound of exit."[dii] This contends the official story and confuses Dr. Boswell.

Boswell cannot identify portions of the autopsy material in question and admits non-hospital staff participated in the autopsy inventory. He believes this is due to a "terrible" photograph, and confirms at least one additional photograph he recalls of the President's throat is missing. Some members of the autopsy team undertake a subsequent exam where some of the current autopsy photographs emerge. Doctor Boswell further states discrepancies exist in some official photographs that were not present the night of the autopsy.[diii]

Dr. Boswell's details a jaunt to conduct damage control after Dr. Finck's public testimony during the Garrison inquiry. Acting Assistant Attorney General Carl Eardley from the Justice Department enlisted Boswell to visit New Orleans. Eardley states "J, we got to get someone in New Orleans quick. Pierre is testifying, and he's really lousing everything up." Boswell boards a plane to New Orleans the same day. Officials covered his airfare and accommodations, and had Boswell meet unnamed agents.

These men provided Boswell with Finck's testimony, which he studied for the evening. The details of the unknown Army general in the autopsy room troubled some present. However, no one identified this man and Boswell was unneeded.[div] A few important questions are now possible. Why did the Justice Department attempt to interfere with an ongoing trial?

Boswell describes the matter stating "And the government won their case." Mr. T. Jeremy Gunn, the Review Board's Counsel responds, "Actually, the government was the district attorney (Jim Garrison)." Thus, the United States government was obstructing the case. Gunn then asks Boswell "What was the United States Department of Justice doing in relationship to a case between the District Attorney of New Orleans and a resident of New Orleans?" Boswell responds "...I don't know who he was representing. But, obviously, the federal attorney was on the side of Clay Shaw against the District Attorney." Boswell could not recall the names of these men; however, he recounts the purpose of his visit. "All I know is that they-he (Finck) was answering in very strange ways their questions, and, yes, they sent me down and talked to me and tried to get me to agree he was strange and that I could do a better job or something."

Authorities were attempting to discredit their own expert if the need arose. Government employees were influencing cases outside their legal jurisdiction. They prepared to discredit a witness used to support official conclusions. Yet when the public offers such allegations and claims, they face ridicule and attack.

Dr. Boswell affirms official hypocrisy and disregard for honest inquiry. The subtle hidden message is clear, act against the officially determined conclusions and unfortunate things might occur. Despite serving the official agenda, some were politically expendable. The evidence of such practices is repeatedly part of the official record.[dv] Dr. Boswell received the same order as Dr. Humes not to discuss the autopsy.[dvi] United States authorities subsequently attempted to enlist Dr. Boswell to conduct Martin Luther King's autopsy, he refused and suggested a different physician.

Mr. John Stringer conducted most of the original photography of the President's autopsy based on the attending physicians' instructions. When asked the number of photographs taken during the autopsy, Mr. Stringer replies, "I haven't the slightest idea."[dvii] Stringer confirms no attempt was made to record the number of photographs taken. The Secret Service had collected the photographs; rolls of film, and instead of regular procedures, officials send the photographs to the Anacostia Naval Center for processing. Stringer explained, "They said they want to keep everything secret, and they had the facilities over there to do it." Stringer disputes but signs a subsequent official affirmation of the autopsy photographic inventory. Humes, Boswell, and Ebersole agree to an inventory of dozens of pictures having reviewed them twice, years after the autopsy concluded.[dviii dix]

Stringer confirms only Dr. Humes, Boswell, a corpsman to assist, and he attended a supplementary autopsy exam. The second examination of the evidence lasted approximately sixty minutes. Mr. Gunn inquires regarding this inconsistent processing of the evidence; Stringer explains "...they were in a hurry and said, "Let's get it over with." When Stringer was asked if some people would object to these practices, Stringer replied, "Yeah, they do. But they don't last long."[dx]

Dr. Humes did not order magnified photographs of the President's gunshot wounds. This might have revealed the size of the bullet and clearly displayed the wounds. It would clarify tissue abrasion to mark the bullet's angle of entrance. These important factors might have supported the official case. Stringer explains, "It would, again, depend upon the doctor and what they wanted to show."[dxi]

When presented with his statement from a visit to the National Archives in 1966, Mr. Stringer is surprised. He notes other photographs taken were not in the National Archives. Stringer confirmed multiple autopsy photographs were missing. Stringer cannot explain why Dr. Humes, Boswell, and he signed a statement confirming the incomplete photographic inventory. He additionally contends the President's brain photography is not accurate.[dxii] Stringer had also prior received orders to remain silent about the Bethesda autopsy.[dxiii]

Dr. John Ebersole was responsible for the President's x-rays as the Acting Chief of Radiology. Dr. Ebersole confirms a back wound of entry, yet massive damage to the rear of President Kennedy's head. "The back of the head was missing and the regular messy wound."[dxiv] This contends the other Bethesda doctors, yet it would affirm the Parkland head wound descriptions. Ebersole then states a communication with Parkland hospital established they surgically repaired the throat.[dxv]

Not a single person at Parkland hospital ever claimed this occurred in original evidence. No officials or civilians at Bethesda hospital confirm this claim. Parkland evidence reports a wound of entrance in the throat before the tracheotomy. No public documents report a wound of exit or any surgical repair undertaken. Ebersole's speculation possibly fueled public suspicions.

Dr. Ebersole then states the portable x-ray equipment used was not the best available in Bethesda. Instead of going to the X-Ray Department for "exquisite" detail, the doctors agreed the portable x-ray machine was adequate. Yet Ebersole supports corrections are necessary because of the distortion created by the portable x-ray unit.[dxvi] Ebersole never adequately explains why the best equipment for the autopsy goes unused. These factors compound mounting deficiencies in method and inquiry.

Additionally present were two Federal Bureau of Investigation agents, the President's (Warren) Commission calls neither person to testify. J. Edgar Hoover instructed Agent Francis O'Neill to stay with the President's body. Agent O'Neill confirms the lack of legal clarity or jurisdiction; agencies were seemingly competing to obtain control of situation. "Bear in mind now, nobody knew who had jurisdiction over what at that particular time." [dxvii] The subsequent legal release of jurisdiction to Federal authorities occurred after the autopsy. Legal jurisdiction belonged to the Texas authorities during the autopsy.

According to Agent O'Neill, "... the Bureau, from our way of thinking, had the investigative jurisdiction..." yet legally the Bureau did not. In testimony O'Neill confirms the statements of Parkland doctors and Dr. Ebersole, "...you could not miss the wound in the head." Mr. Gunn replies, "Again, you're pointing to the back of your head?" Agent O Neill responds, "Yes, it was a massive wound."[dxviii] This clearly is not the wound recorded in the final autopsy protocol.

After reviewing relevant photography, O'Neill states a few did not reflect the wounds he witnessed at the autopsy. He states one photograph of the President's alleged rear head wound was "This looks like it's been doctored in some way/ let me rephrase that, when I say 'doctored'. Like the stuff (brain matter and bone fragments) has been pushed back in, and it looks like more towards the end (of the autopsy) then at the beginning. All you have to do was put the flap back over here, and the rest of the stuff (the gaping wound) is all covered up."[dxix]

O'Neill additionally does not confirm official photographs of the President's brain. He states, "It appears to be too much" in the photograph. O'Neill confirms that brain was present on the clothing of Secret Service Agents in the Presidential vehicle, and at Parkland hospital. This is in addition to any lost at the scene or during multiple transports of the body. After reviewing photographs of the brain presented in the official files, O'Neill states "...I can't say that it looks like the brain I saw...I did not recall it being that large."[dxx] The brain's original weight is unconfirmed in official documents during the autopsy and supplementary review.

Unlike Dr. Finck, the Bureau agents were present before the autopsy began. Agent James Siebert of the Bureau described the wound is originally blood-soaked and hair was matted. He describes a "big cavity" of bone was "literally blown out of the skull" from the back of the President's head.[dxxi] The Bureau agents confirmed a large wound in the rear of the President's head.

When viewing one of the Kennedy autopsy photographs of the head wound Siebert comments "Well, I don't have a recollection of it being that intact, as compared with these other pictures. I don't remember seeing anything that was like this photo."[dxxii] " The hair looks like it's been straightened out and cleaned up more that what it was when we left the autopsy." "Well, the wound was more pronounced. And it looks like it could have been reconstructed..."

Agent Siebert confirms he took extensive notes during the autopsy, Mr. Gunn subsequently offers Siebert a Commission file written by Arlen Specter. The memorandum states "Specials Agent Siebert advised that he made no notes during the autopsy." Gunn asks, "Is that correct?" Sibert responds, "That is absolutely false. There would be no way in the world I'd make a statement that I made no notes during the autopsy."[dxxiii] The Bureau's prior highly detailed surveillance files support Siebert's testimony.

The Bureau as regular practice often made notes and compiled them for the official files. To imagine J. Edgar Hoover sent agents to observe the autopsy without keeping written documentation is highly unfeasible. The Bureau's power relied upon documenting information, including their previously illegal actions. This disputes the claims of Arlen Specter and ideas of no Bureau documentation. Similar to Dr. Finck, leading officials may again have sought to marginalize these contending witnesses.

Floyd Riebe assisted John Stringer in photography the autopsy of President Kennedy. Riebe claimed taking photographs and submitting them to Stringer for approval. Riebe testified, "The right side in the back was gone. Just a big gaping hole with fragments of scalp and bone." "The occipital...." and he remarks the second wound to the head was the temporal (side) flap. Riebe is subject to the same non-disclosure notice Captain Stover previously dispatched to Humes and Boswell.[dxxiv] [dxxv]

Riebe later reverses his testimony and based on the photographs decides his memory was incorrect about the rear head wound. Yet despite the reversal, he states he did not take some of the black and white photographs in the National Archives. Riebe states the President's scalp was pulled back into place during some photographs; this possibly may explain later discrepancies in Riebe's memory and the evidence. Yet other present Bethesda military staff members did not agree with Riebe's changing assessment. Dennis David stated reviewing a film of the autopsy photographs and a "gaping wound in the back of the President's head", official threats of court martial to anyone who spoke out silenced David.[dxxvi] James Jenkins stated a "big hole" in the rear of the President's head was present in the area where doctors presumed a rear "entry" wound.[dxxvii]

Saundra Spencer is the official who developed one set of the autopsy photographs. She appeared before the Assassination Records Review Board and confirmed previous evidentiary problems. Spencer identified repeated photographs in the National Archives she did not process. [dxxviii] Missing from these photographs was a large wound on the back of the President's head. She affirms some color photographs were not among the original prints during the autopsy. Identifying paper traits used in processing did not match the originals, and the President's wounds appeared too pristine.[dxxix]

Mistakes, assumptions, and manipulation of evidence occurred. Over twenty people were present at times during the autopsy. Some were having multiple discussions, some making phone calls, entering and exiting, taking notes, and conducting medical procedures. Competing agencies were attempting to deliver evidence to solve the case. All these factors with the human element and under a rushed examination allowed for serious evidentiary problems.

Some medical experts were unmindful of standard procedures. Most Bethesda autopsy witnesses confirmed the x-rays lacked clarity and orientation of medical evidence was difficult. At various portions of the autopsy, physicians replace bone fragments to reconstruct the possible wounds of entrance and exit.[dxxx] They adjust President's scalp for some photographs. This does not conclusively prove nefarious action. Yet the Bethesda autopsy contained inconsistencies, contending views of major events, and challenged previous official determinations.

Dr. Finck, Humes, and Boswell "presumed" wounds of entrance and exit. Many photographs in the National Archives support them. It is largely upon these men the Bethesda inquiry relied. However, Dr. Finck did not arrive until after initial procedures began and some photography had occurred. Dr. Humes, Finck, and Boswell noted a full dissection of wounded organs did not occur. Each confessed a few officials were attempting to influence the autopsy's duration.

Agents O'Neill and Siebert confirm a request for expedited conclusions. Subsequent requests by superior officers feasibly cause this to occur despite the initial refusals. Dr. Humes incinerates the original autopsy report draft. Humes and Finck dispute the Single Bullet theory. Witnesses supporting and contending official conclusions affirmed the rushed medical process in a crowded room. Despite the wound location inconsistencies, a majority dispute the official current medical and ballistics evidence.

Most official medical experts refute one bullet caused most wounds to President Kennedy and Governor Connally. Why are these people experts when confirming the official story yet dismissed when contending it? Consider the authorities involved who additionally disputed the current exhibits and the wound placement. Divided credible primary witnesses are the basis of the United States government's case.

Dr. Ebersole, Special Agents O'Neill and Siebert, Mrs. Spencer, Mr. David, and Mr. Jenkins all place a large gaping wound in the rear of the President's head. Dr. Ebersole used a portable x-ray unit subject to distortions for the autopsy. Three x-ray or photographic experts, Ebersole, Spencer, and Stringer, dispute the National Archives collection. O'Neill and Siebert confirm the President's Commission disregarded their previously offered report. Bureau agents state the brain and wounds in official exhibits did not reflect the original wounds present.

Multiple autopsy witnesses noted photographs are missing or not genuine. Dr. Humes, Boswell, Ebersole, Agents O'Neill and Siebert, Mr. Stringer, Riebe, Dennis, Jenkins, and Mrs. Spencer, all support this. Many witnesses viewing the original evidence support a large rear head wound at Parkland and Bethesda hospitals. A majority of the Bethesda witnesses recount evidentiary deficiencies. Based on the repeated testimony of medical experts, the expedited conclusions were feasibly inconclusive presumptions.

President Johnson and Acting Attorney General Ramsey Clark were aware of the autopsy's photographic inconsistencies. The matter was briefly discussed, Clark offers "I think we have three pathologists (Humes, Finck, Boswell) and the photographer (Stringer) signed up now on the autopsy review and their conclusion is that the autopsy photos and x-rays conclusively support the autopsy report rendered by them to the Warren Commission..." it is then Clark's definite statement crumbles bearing the weight of facts. Clark states "...though we were not able to tie down the question of the missing photo entirely but we feel much better about it and we have three of the four sign to an affidavit that says these are all the photos they took and they do not believe anybody else took any others."

This statement is a blatant falsehood. Within the very document that claims no photographs were missing is verification of a missing photograph. Expert witnesses support missing and additional photographs that feasibly taint the National Archives collection. Clark additionally states, "There is the unfortunate reference in the Warren Commission report by Dr. Humes to a picture that just does not exist as far as we know...." [dxxxi]

No original count of photographs and Secret Service confiscation broke the chain of evidence. The supplementary autopsy exam of medical evidence provided additional opportunities. This was not the complete second autopsy claimed by some. Yet Bethesda Hospital, the Whitehouse, and Anacostia Naval Center all had access to photographic materials. This allowed changes to medical exhibits following the original autopsy.

The unofficial trip to conduct damage control at Dr. Finck's expense in New Orleans verifies ongoing federal manipulations. The possibly missing and altered exhibits in the National Archives collection imply feasible evidence tampering. In comparing the two inquires, I believe that each medical unit had problems and were plagued by interference and confusion.

Subsequently rescinded were previous military non-disclosure orders to Bethesda medical personnel. This allowed relevant testimony during the House Select Committee on Assassinations. Unfortunately, the President's (Warren) Commission had ended nearly twenty years prior with a finding of probable guilt. Yet a majority of medical witnesses support an exit wound in the rear of his skull. Nearly all medical experts involved dispute the Single Bullet theory.

The President's brain was unavailable for full analysis during some official investigations. Perhaps the most important piece of forensic evidence was later misplaced or taken for burial. Some attributed this action to Robert Kennedy. However, this was a glaring occurrence in a long series of vanishing exhibits and changing statements. [dxxxii]

Former Justice Department Head of the General Crimes Section Carl Belcher was among those to authenticate the photographic evidence of the President's autopsy. Mr. Belcher stated he never observed the final signed inventory until decades later. Officials assert he composed the final inventory, yet Belcher does not recall doing this. Nor could he remember visiting Bethesda Hospital to obtain the signatures on the document.[dxxxiii] Thus, Belcher additionally supports possibly fabricated evidence.

Various questionable materials influenced the later House Select Committee on Assassinations review as well. However, by that time, the evidence was "unaccounted for"[dxxxiv] The Select Committee attempted to authenticate the photographs taken at Bethesda Naval Hospital. Unfortunately, the Department of Defense could not find the camera for verification.

House Select Committee Chief Counsel Robert Blakey sent a letter to Secretary of Defense Harold Brown. The letter read, "After examining the camera and comparing its features with characteristics noted on the autopsy photographic experts have determined that this camera, or at least the particular lens and shutter attached to it, could not have been used to take the autopsy pictures".[dxxxv] Congressional investigators had received additional tainted evidence.

Members of the House Select Committee on Assassinations believed the camera authentic. The second camera in question was unaccounted for when memo's writer attempted to relocate it. This implies the camera was a fake or some of the original Bethesda images from the National Archives could be.[dxxxvi] Multiple evidentiary discrepancies exist because of repeated security failures.

Drawings not actual medical images subsequently replaced evidence. Drawings having the incorrect wound position replaced original evidence to the House Select Committee on Assassinations. Some official photographs indicate possible modification based on original reports. The President's (Warren) Commission did not inspect President Kennedy's x-rays.

The Commission valued Kennedy family privacy concerns over the investigation. These actions obstructed the Commission's ability to examine critical evidence. The Commission decided further inaction was appropriate. Important evidence remained withheld until the next decade from investigators.

Additional opportunities to alter the medical evidence occurred during the House Select Committee on Assassinations investigation. Information and Privacy Coordinator George Owens responded to a particular conundrum.

The Agency Security Escort to the Select Committee staff handled "...the notebook containing photographs of the autopsy of President John F. Kennedy. He did this on at least two occasions when the notebook was left unsecured in the reading room of the HSCA, where he had been sent to control Agency classified material.

The investigation has established that this officer acted on his own out of curiosity, not at the direction of anyone else. Certainly his actions did constitute a serious indiscretion, although they should not be described as 'rifling' HSCA files. Immediately after the occurrence of this incident, the Agency asked for, and received the officer's resignation."[dxxxvii] This was another curious associated episode.

The Agency had a reasonable need to "sanitize" (redact) certain extraneous information offered to investigators. However, a "memo of understanding" between the Agency and the Select Committee Counsel and Staff reveals "For their part the HSCA has agreed to take no documents or notes from the building, and will write their report in the building and submit it for review and censorship prior to taking it from the bldg."[dxxxviii] These measures feasibly do not just prevent unintentional security breaches, but could allow the censorship of possible evidence.

A constant string of unfortunate circumstances seemed to follow this case, and two others. Related medical experts offered consistently overlooked information. Most Commission members ignored conflicting official determinations. The investigation was many things, but complete is not among them.

The American government has maintained hundreds of millions of files with functional accuracy. Yet the Justice Department, executive branch investigators, and the National Archives failed to keep the evidence of one murder in order. A series of destroyed files, ignored evidence, and failing memories plagued this inquiry. Further evidence, witnesses, and documents began to slip away. A "covering action" might have begun.[dxxxix]


## THE CONSPIRACY

It became apparent legal authorities were discussing launching investigations in late 1963. The public remained unaware President Johnson "...wanted to get by..." on just the Federal Bureau of Investigation report, it was the only way to prevent the "rash of investigations".[dxl] [dxli] Director of Central Intelligence John McCone offered the Justice Department recommendations of conducting an independent investigation. McCone later writes, "President Johnson rejected this idea".[dxlii] [dxliii] Johnson wanted to stop any non-presidential controlled inquiry.[dxliv] Subsequently President Lyndon Johnson formed the President's (Warren) Commission.

"Legally, the assassination of President Kennedy and the subsequent murder of Lee Harvey Oswald were within the jurisdiction of Texas State Authorities".[dxlv] Unfortunately, the Texas State authorities later consented to federal oversight. Yet interference plagued the President's (Warren) Commission. The Johnson administration perceived oversight as manipulation of the investigation.

The Senate (Church) Committee references an official letter from Deputy Attorney General Nicholas Katzenbach to Johnson Presidential Assistant Bill Moyers, "1. The public must be satisfied that Oswald was the assassin; that he did not have confederates who are still at large; and that the evidence was such that he would have been convicted at trial." In other words, the public must be compelled to believe these statements. "2. Speculation about Oswald's motivation ought to be cut off, and we should have some basis for rebutting thought that this was a Communist conspiracy or…a right wing conspiracy to blame it on the Communists." [dxlvi] [dxlvii]

Why did they undertake these efforts if no plot existed? For what reason did all speculation and questions about "Oswald's motivation need to be cut off?" Who benefited from these orders? [dxlviii] Obviously, it was not the American public. How could Katzenbach reasonably determine Oswald's guilt two days after the President's death? Such presumptions compromised the official inquiry.

The Central Intelligence Agency sought to suppress the false Imposter while alleging Oswald's unproven appearances.[dxlix] Internal Agency documents reveal a lack of evidence that Oswald repeatedly visited foreign diplomatic buildings. "From all evidence on hand, we deduce that Oswald visited the Cuban Consulate…There is not evidence that he visited more often than once in the days mentioned… We believe that Oswald both telephoned to the Soviet Embassy or Consulate, and was interviewed by officials there."[dl] The Agency places Oswald in Mexico City and disregards all the contending evidence.

To remove the supposed Imposter from consideration, the Agency requested the President's (Warren) Commission suppress and alter Exhibit 237. They stated the photograph would compromise ongoing intelligence operations. "Since 23 July 1964 we have been on the record with the Commission opposing the publication of this picture, on the grounds that it would jeopardize a sensitive operation and could be embarrassing to the individual involved…" They also state in a separate document, "not only retouch the background in photos but also retouch face to degree obviously not identifiable with Ruby but also not with actual subject of photo."[dli dlii] Attempts to conceal the subject of this deception remain in several existing Agency related documents.

Despite foreknowledge of a mixture of fact and fiction, the Agency does not mention him. Following the President's death, Agency employees created memos suggesting Oswald had contacts with Soviet agents. This implies a foreign conspiracy that no government investigations support. The Federal Bureau of Investigation received these memos; Hoover unlike the public knew the truth. Hoover joined the Agency's efforts.

Hoover allegedly ordered a memo leaked suggesting "An exhaustive FBI report now nearly ready for the White House will indicate Lee Harvey Oswald was the lone and unaided assassin of President Kennedy, Government sources said today." This report soon appeared in the media nationwide. The later convened Senate (Church) Committee offers J. Edgar Hoover's statement regarding investigative efforts, "...so far as the FBI is concerned, the case will be considered in an open classification for all time".[dliii] The Bureau required no conclusion. They disliked public scrutiny interfering with their efforts just as the Agency did. Certain authorities had preordained the results.

## THE KNOWN UNKNOWNS

Some authors have proposed the Daltex building was a sniper location citing a triangulation of fire theory. Although it seems reasonable to some, based on substantiated evidence it remains speculation. No large group of witnesses at the Daltex building reported sounds of gunfire. Large groups of corroborating witnesses confirm gunfire at the Grassy Knoll and Texas School Book Depository.

Likewise, among the most famous photographs of that day were possible distractions. Many pictures appear featuring the "Three Tramps" in related inquires of the Kennedy Assassination. When you examine the entire possible Kennedy assassination conspiracy, the Tramps were an effective channeling of public attention. They might unintentionally have provided experienced agents time to fade away.

The identities of the Tramps based on subsequently released Dallas Police records are decided. Yet some ignore this evidence and speculate on possible alternate people. These speculations deny the actual evidence and promote misinformation. Some disregard opposing evidence, just as officials did.

The Senate (Church) Committee explained possible alteration of witness reports by government agents. "The Committee has on many occasions noted that witnesses have no recollection of the events described in documents which they either prepared or in which they were mentioned".[dliv] Witnesses confirm alterations occurred when their statements disputed the official story. The President's (Warren) Commission repeatedly endured interference by outside influences.

The Commission spoke of additional manipulation in their private executive sessions. Gerald Ford referred to government officials manipulating public opinion. "In my judgment, somebody somewhere is planting or leaking these stories. And I must go back, if I might, to a letter you received". Ford continued "...Mr. Katzenbach (the Johnson Attorney General) wrote ...if the Commission would release a statement to the effect that there was no foreign involvement, there was no conspiracy, or in the alternative that we would authorize the Department of Justice to make such a release"[dlv]

Again observable were attempts to push the Commissioners to make statements of fact prior to investigation. Before the Commission undertook any significant review, the Johnson administration wanted results. How could the Commission have operated independently? They could not prevent the executive branch from pursuing its goals using the Commission's legitimacy. Commissioner Ford continues:

"I think the Commission used good judgment in denying both requests. But I happen to know that subsequent to that meeting...both Associated Press and the United Press, on the same day, with the same dateline, had the stories that in effect are the same stories that now appearing". Ford continues "...there is no doubt that it was a leaked story by a government official" "And ever since that time, and in growing intensity, and in growing volume... there is this kind of newspaper propaganda with the same intent in mind...it disturbs me".[dlvi] It should disturb all who learn of these attempts to conceal the truth.

Commissioner John McCloy commented on public speculations this propaganda was reinforcing. "I don't know how many times I have been stopped in New York and people saying "I see, Jack, what your Commission is going to come out with. The report has already been written for you, hasn't it?"[dlvii] The average individual spoke to Commissioners of the obvious propaganda in the newspapers.

Additionally disturbing the Commissioners and Counsel Rankin was the Bureau's predisposition to Oswald as the lone assassin before a full investigation occurred. Rankin states, "Part of our difficulty in regard to is that they have no problem (with official discrepancies). They have decided that it is Oswald who committed the assassination, they have decided no one else was involved, they have decided--". Commissioner Russell affirms, "They (the Bureau) tried the case and reached a verdict on every aspect." Commissioner Boggs supports this appraisal replying, "You have put your finger on it." Commissioner McCloy notes, "They (the Bureau) are a little less certain in the (report) supplementals..."[dlviii]

Johnson supporter and Congressman George R. Brown authored a few relevant letters to the Department of Justice. The letters reveal criticism of the President's (Warren) Commission. Brown similar to Commissioner Russell was a supporter of President Johnson. Yet he firmly supported a new investigation after noting the previous Commission's deficiencies.[dlix] Senator B. Everett Jordan inquired why the Zapruder original film was sold to *Life Magazine* thus preventing duplication under copyright law. Officials responded, "...no purpose was seen in taking and paying for the copyright since the availability of the print in the National Archives serves the interest of the Government and the public in a complete investigation of the assassination."[dlx]

Congressman Graham Purcell of Texas inquired about "ascertaining that a true picture of the circumstances behind the assassination of President Kennedy has been derived."[dlxi] Congressional representatives Tom Railsback and John Byrnes had doubts as well[dlxii,dlxiii] Most requests emerged from Congressional leaders seeking to answer their constituents' related questions.[dlxiv,dlxv,dlxvi,dlxvii,dlxviii,dlxix,dlxx,dlxxi,dlxxii,dlxxiii,dlxxiv,dlxxv,dlxxvi,dlxxvii,dlxxviii,dlxxix,dlxxx] The deficient executive branch responses did not dissuade most doubts.

Citizens believed the Johnson administration was merely using the Commission as a mouthpiece. What once was speculation now comes into focus as truth. Revealing contrary to most critical opinions, the Commissioners are divided and troubled. Not every Commissioner was the loyalist or fool desired.

The American public received a possible cover up story. Despite the contrary evidence, Oswald becomes the lone gunman. If the Commissioners had decided against the Johnson administration's suggestions, Johnson could simply have rescinded his executive order. It would be as if the President's (Warren) Commission never existed.

# The Assassins

Claims of their exact identity remain unverified speculation. Unless official documents and new credible witnesses emerge, use of available facts becomes necessary. These compiled facts can render the most reasonable deductions. Some possible assassins offered too many chances for identification or failure. The best trained, most successful, and least recognizable men available are necessary for success. My proposal alleges two snipers attacked John F. Kennedy.

Following the shots in Dealey Plaza a Motorcycle officer charged the Grassy Knoll. Running crowds and screaming filled the plaza creating a near riot. Anger, grief, and fear gripped many spectators causing further confusion in Dealey Plaza. The crowds surged toward a man and woman perceiving them as suspects. The mob surrounded the couple near the Grassy Knoll.[dlxxxi] This rampant confusion might secure a separate assassin's escape.

Possible assassins would have committed previous murders and had the skill to avoid detection. More importantly, they had strong verified connections to an Arm of the Conspiracy. The assassin's are designated as Sniper A and B. These snipers conceivably operated for the possible Conspirators. Instead of a lone assassin, unknown men spotted by witnesses and evidence at the scene conceivably suggest accomplices.

# Sniper A

This individual feasibly is located at an unknown location ahead of the motorcade. They require a concealed location where they could remain undisturbed and the crowd was not present. The details appear in both the President's (Warren) Commission report and the House Select Committee on Assassinations' findings. In my estimation, a military trained sniper awaited the motorcade. Yet this location based on substantial evidence and expert assessment was not the Grassy Knoll.

Criminals, Mercenaries, or rogue members of Military Intelligence community purportedly hired the snipers. Utilizing significant training and superior position, this person allegedly fired the shots killing President Kennedy.

# Sniper B

A second individual feasibly was located in the Texas School Book Depository. In my estimation, a paramilitary sniper lay in wait for President Kennedy's motorcade. Allegedly, in this firing position shots hit Kennedy, Connally, and debris strikes Tague. To concede the improbable hypothesis of Lee Harvey Oswald firing, he in my view could not have killed President Kennedy alone based on the substantial contending evidence.

The Texas School Book Depository employed other white males that like Oswald resembled some attributes officials recorded of the sniper. Yet none faced initial questioning. At least two other Depository employees feasibly could have been possible suspects. However, the President's Commission only focused on one man and ignored the opposing evidence.

People came and left in the confusion. If Oswald could simply enter and later escape, so could a possible assassin. Dozens of people quickly exited the building, and some were unaccounted for with Oswald. Subsequent to the president's death, many employees left the Depository. This person could have escaped the building into the crowds of Dealey Plaza.

The Possible Assassins:
Mercenaries, Intelligence assets, or foreign exiles

The Alleged Assassin:
Lee Harvey Oswald

They conceivably spent months in training and were armed with rifles easily concealed or disassembled. They had planned for security holes and possible escape routes to avoid capture. Each Sniper worked in tandem firing on orders received from the Arms of the Assassination Conspiracy. The Assassins could fire and fade away into the chaos they created.

The evidence and the affirmed results of congressional investigations state two assassins fired four possible shots. They allegedly killed the president in front of thousands in Dealey Plaza. Authorities initially held no proper legal investigation. Cooperation between local and federal authorities did not happen. Suppression of the facts had begun.

# CHAPTER 6

*"Discovering witnesses is just as important as catching criminals."*

~Simon Wiesenthal
Austrian Activist, and Author
*"The Sunflower"*

## EXPERTS, WITNESSES, AND POSSIBLE DISINFORMATION

Unrecognized by many are those who have spent time, money, and put themselves in the largely unfavorable limelight. From their tireless, thankless, and often attacked work, an extensive amount of evidence is available. Many believe in assassination conspiracy, fewer set out to prove it. It necessitates a certain dedication to do so in the face of character assassination and derision.

Jim Garrison served as New Orleans District Attorney and as Louisiana State Appeals judge. Garrison faced years of internal government harassment and intimidation. He endured character assassination throughout the American media. In death, Garrison continually suffers attacks by critics and government officials.

Since initially realizing a feasible conspiracy in the mid-1960s, criticism has not ceased against him. It is doubtful many understood the barrage of constant threats, stress, and pressures Garrison faced daily. He repeatedly faced nationwide derision for undertaking a prosecution to hold someone beyond Oswald responsible for President Kennedy's death. Garrison's conclusions imply traces of a larger intrigue.

Some of Garrison's suspicions were quite reasonable and some were not. Subsequent to the Clay Shaw trial, former Secret Service Agent Bolden offered the Chicago assassination plot assertion to Jim Garrison. Unknown to Garrison, the legal official conducting the trial, members of the Department of Justice were secretly interfering. These officials provided all the files regarding Bolden to defendant Clay Shaw's attorneys. Under normal circumstances, they would provide files to Garrison the official with jurisdiction.[dlxxxii]

Although personally disagreeing with many of his ideas, I respect his dedication and intentions. Most importantly, Garrison deduces a possible conspiracy under way. It was more than any lone American prosecutor undertook to hold officials accountable. It still is.

Mary Ferrell was a legal secretary in Texas prior to President Kennedy's murder. Ferrell unlike most government agencies immediately began to collect a handwritten and typed database of credible information. It included records detailing thousands of witnesses, officials, and references to the case. Some of Ferrell's organized information is integral to provide insights to the public.

Many witnesses did not appear before the President's (Warren) Commission, officials ignored certain testimony. Using official and media sources dozens of witnesses reported shots emerged from the Grassy Knoll.[dlxxxiii] A larger minority of witnesses' affirm the shots emerged from the School Book Depository, a handful asserted each location. Multiple interviewed witnesses cannot determine the origin of the gunfire.[dlxxxiv] Hundreds of people were present and many depart without giving official statements.

The Commission decided testimony from witnesses such as Howard L. Brennan reliable. Brennan reversed his testimony three times and finally settled on Oswald being in the window. Two different chapters in the Report include Brennan's eyewitness statements. The Commission Report later attests its findings do not rely on Brennan's testimony.

Then why not interview a relevant disregarded expert or eyewitness? Instead, the Commission accepts lengthy testimony from Brennan who is not influencing their decision.[dlxxxv] Why include his testimony over qualified eyewitnesses that are certain of what they observed? Why do so many official pages contain unimportant information?

Why mention Brennan's location and that he "was in an excellent position to observe anyone in the window" if he remains inconsistent? Brennan's position was not as excellent as the Commission imagined due to his testimonial reversals. The Commission was unsure if learning Oswald's description from the media affected Brennan's statements. Nor did Oswald resemble the "closest" line up suspect to the man Brennan saw in the Texas School Book Depository.

Brennan later identified Oswald to Federal Bureau of Investigation agents. Then he reversed back to his "earlier inability to make a positive identification". Brennan states if a Communist conspiracy was under way, identification of Oswald could put his family or himself in danger.[dlxxxvi] Finally, Brennan decides to support his original claims of Oswald. Why did officials consider such impeachable testimony so relevant?

The only eyewitness the Commission has to identify Oswald in the sniper's nest, cannot consistently identify Oswald. Brennan refers to a Communist plot the President's (Warren) Commission and the CIA evidence supports did not exist. The President's Commission Report lacks the actual proof necessary to support many of their findings.

Yet evidence offered by corroborating witnesses possibly supports a different person than Oswald carrying a feasible weapon and firing it. Official witness Howard Brennan was puzzled how Oswald wore a brown shirt in comparison to the man with the rifle. He originally described the man in light colored attire and possibly a jacket.[dlxxxvii] Brennan's description of the sniper's size and weight however were highly speculative, consider Brennan also incorrectly believed the person to be standing. Tippit shooting witness Domingo Benevides stated Oswald wore a light colored jacket but a dark shirt and pants. [dlxxxviii] Oswald had changed at his rooming house prior. [dlxxxix dxc dxci dxcii dxciii]

However, Philip Hathaway worked at the nearby Texaco building. As he was walking with a fellow employee he noticed a man he describes as "...approx 6´6...over 250 pounds...in his 30s, dirty blonde hair worn in a crew cut...wearing a grey colored business suit with white dress shirt." The man was carrying a rifle case according to Hathaway that contained a weapon.[dxciv] Witness Ronald Fischer reported the sniper had a "light colored open neck shirt which could have been a sports shirt or t-shirt" Based on Fischer's statements he observed a "light headed" "brown haired man" in his mid twenties.[dxcv] Some may consider this color dirty blonde. Similar to Howard Brennan, Fischer's perspective of the man does not conclusively determine the sniper's height or size.[dxcvi] Oswald's shirt was not a definite match, the fibers on the Carcano "could have" matched, such methods are subjective.[dxcvii dxcviii]

Despite further assumptions about the sniper's size and height from six stories down, Robert Edwards states the person in the window revealed a person he thought, "had light-brown hair". Edwards further noted the sniper was clothed in "a sport shirt, it was light colored, it was yellow or white, something to that effect, and his hair was rather short; I thought he might be something around twenty-six".[dxcix] Edwards's description of the sniper's hair, clothing, and relative age match Brennan, Fischer, and Hathaway's descriptions. Each description feasibly corroborates these similar witness statements.

Affirming the deposition of Philip Hathaway was his work companion John Lawrence. Lawrence states he did not view the rifle or case described by Hathaway due to crowds obstructing his view. However, Lawrence did view the alleged man carrying the case. Lawrence states the man was 6'5 "maybe a little taller...maybe 250 pounds or more, but no fat...he had dirty blonde hair and a was a short crew cut...he was approximately in his 30's (sic)".[dc] Five witnesses identify an armed man that possessed largely different characteristics and clothing from Oswald. This possible alternate sniper never appears in the Commission's report.

James Tague was an injured bystander to the Kennedy assassination. Standing near the triple underpass shrapnel hit Tague from a fired shot. Tague's injury reduced the bullet count for all other victims. Officially two bullets remain. The final shot to President Kennedy made the remaining count one. A single bullet had to account for every other wound.

Government advocates created the Single Bullet Theory to hold the official story together. Tague's injury forced authorities to defend the scientifically indefensible. Although some have claimed jump seats in the limousine account for ballistic discrepancies, these statements remain without repeated verified independent testing. Additionally, this still does not explain shots occurring from the front.

Buell Frazier, who gave Oswald a ride to work explained, "...from where I was standing it sounded like it was coming from down the railroad tracks there." Eyewitness William Newman testified, "the shot had come from the garden directly behind me, that was on an elevation from where I was...right on the curb." [dci dcii] Witness Orchus Campbell stated the shots emerged from "a point near the railroad tracks..." Roy Truly, Manager of the Texas School Book Depository stated "I thought the shots came from the vicinity of the railroad or the WPA project (the concrete structure), behind the WPA project west of the building."[dciii dciv]

Sheriff's Deputy Harry Weatherford noted hearing three shots that emerge from the railway yards near the Grassy Knoll.[dcv] Witness Austin Miller stated viewing "smoke or steam coming from a group of trees" from possible shots.[dcvi] Witness Edgar Smith heard shots near the railroad tracks and small concrete structure.[dcvii] Many witnesses affirm the Grassy Knoll and surrounding area being the source of feasible gunfire.

Eyewitness Frank Reilly states hearing shots emerge from "...where all the shrubs is up there-it's to the North of Elm Street--up the slope." Dallas Deputy Sheriff Harold Elkins states, "I immediately ran to the area from which it sounded like the shots had been fired. This is an area between the railroads and the Texas School Book Depository which is east of the railroads."[dcviii] [dcix] Many agreed the Depository was not the source of the shots.

Eyewitness James Simons affirmed to authorities it "Sounded like the shots came from a wooden fence on the embankment," (the Grassy Knoll). He witnessed smoke visible and footprints in the mud and on the fence railing. Simons is among those never called before the President's (Warren) Commission. When questioned why Simons believed the Commissioners had not called him to testify he replied, "I thought that's the way they did business."[dcx]

Eyewitness, S.M. Holland noted he saw the fourth shot come from behind the picket fence on the Grassy Knoll. He reported smoke and sounds of possible gunfire. S.M. Holland's testimony further substantiates a second sniper.[dcxi] Dozens of witnesses repeatedly indicate shots from the Knoll.

Some witnesses had seen men running from the Knoll following the shooting. The Commission did not call every witness for testimony.[dcxii] Eyewitness Richard Dodd stood with three fellow railroad workers including S.M. Holland. Dodd commented about the scene, "...the smoke came from behind the hedge (referring to the Grassy Knoll) on the north side of the plaza."

Dodd further offered, "A motorcycle policeman dropped his motorcycle in the street, his gun in his hand and run the embankment to the hedge." After checking the Knoll, Dodd found shoeprints in the area. This statement offers physical signs of someone at the Knoll. Some witnesses detect smoke, and others hear feasible gunfire. [dcxiii]

Two railroad workers Thomas Murphy and Walter Winborn observed smoke around the Knoll. They indicated the shots emerged from the Grassy Knoll. The President's (Warren) Commission Report failed to include these observations in its final report.[dcxiv] Who altered witness testimony?

Regarding the shots eyewitness Danny Arce stated, "Yeah, I thought they came from the railroad tracks to the west of the Texas School Book Depository."[dcxv]. Witness Billy Lovelady stated hearing shots from "...around that concrete deal on that knoll."[dcxvi] This affirms the many witnesses prior stating the Knoll as the origin of gunfire. Dallas Sheriff Luke Mooney described after hearing the shots "I was running at full speed...Across Elm, up the embankment, which is a high terrace there, across-there is a concrete building there, more or less a little park. Jumped over the fence and went in to the railroad yards...Well, that was--from the echo of the shots, we thought they came from that direction." [dcxvii]

Sheriff Eugene Boone stated "And we raced across the street...We went west and then cut across the grass out there behind the large cement works there...So there was some city officer...was running up the embankment (Grassy Knoll) to get over a little retaining wall that separates the freight yards there. He went over the wall first, and I was right behind him..." Boone similar to Sheriff Mooney ran to the Knoll believing it the source of gunfire. [dcxviii]

Virginia Baker confirmed the shots emerged from "Immediately behind Dealey Plaza away from Elm Street..." from the rail yard adjoining the Grassy Knoll. [dcxix] Eyewitness Ronald Fischer thought shots appeared to come from "...just west of the School Book Depository Building. There were some railroad tracks and there were some and there were some railroad cars back in there." [dcxx] Ms. Dorothy Garner was employed at the Depository, she reported hearing gunfire emerge "...from a point west of the building" near the Grassy Knoll. [dcxxi]

Orville Nix stated the shots "...came from a fence...between the book depository and the railroad track." [dcxxii] This would further indicate repeated witness agreement upon the origin of at least one shot. Mrs. Roberta Parker states the shot came from "...a cement memorial building (pergola) to the north of the Texas Schoolbook Depository on Elm Street." [dcxxiii] Officer Joe M. Smith determined "I heard the shots and thought they were coming from the bushes of the overpass." [dcxxiv] Secret Service Agent Forrest Sorrels observes feasible shots from "...up on the terrace there". [dcxxv]

James Tague observed gunshots from around "...whatever you call the monument... (pergola near the Grassy Knoll)" [dcxxvi] Steven Wilson placed the shots origin "...from the colonnade located on Elm Street across from the west end..."(Grassy Knoll Area). [dcxxvii] The exact number of witnesses identifying the Grassy Knoll is contended based upon the interpretation of some unspecific statements. Yet dozens of witnesses clearly identified the Knoll and the adjoining area being a possible source of distractionary gunfire.

Some witnesses gave partial descriptions and others stated a sniper was present on the Depository's Fifth floor. Authorities, experts, and authors ruled out this speculation. The Commission had accepted fact mixed with the partial testimony of chosen witnesses. The Commissioners based Oswald's guilt upon evidence that was circumstantial and incomplete. These large operational flaws discredit some official assumptions.

Dozens of witnesses, officially and independently state the Grassy Knoll Area being a source of gunfire. These people were located in view of the Grassy Knoll and Texas Schoolbook Depository. One was in a Depository window. Repeated witnesses affirm shots from other portions of Dealey Plaza.

How many witnesses do officials ignore until the possibility of a repeated claim being true is considered? Can we consider these witnesses credible? Critics ought to because most emerge from the official reports. Logic necessitates regarding the testimony of all credible witnesses. To discover the entire truth we must consider the entire record.

Yet significant ballistic and medical evidence, in addition to many experts, precludes a killing shot from the Grassy Knoll. The trajectory, wound locations, and evidence feasibly indicate a distractionary or missed shot. Indeed substantial evidence and experts suggest gunfire outside the Depository; however, the shots killing John F. Kennedy likely emerged from elsewhere.

Without any serious consideration of a feasible second gunman, Oswald's guilt is decided. Critical misrepresentation has clouded this fact. The repeated testimony infers at least one shot emerged from elsewhere in Dealey Plaza. Once reviewing the evidence, the House Select Committee would conclude two gunmen possibly fired four bullets.

The President's (Warren) Commission had assumed no suspect apprehended, equated to no other shots fired. One has nothing to do with the other. It would have taken a few seconds to vanish into the mass of running people in Dealey Plaza. It would take moments to disappear within the train yards nearby. When police and investigators later arrived, the possible snipers were gone.

Varied eyewitnesses confirm the same details of a shot fired outside the Depository. A feasible second gunman disputes vital assumptions of the President's (Warren) Commission. As Hoover once privately stated to President Johnson, officials had no solid case. They ignored testimony and implied facts, never addressing why many witnesses would alter the truth.

Witness testimony in some cases was at risk to themselves. Why endure threats and character assassinations if not for the truth? Critics might state fame, but in some cases infamy results from honest discussion. Some endure lifelong ridicule and harassment for speaking the uncomfortable facts. While most connected with the Assassination or Lee Harvey Oswald did not wish to publicize their association, some did. One person in particular was privately eager to have their story heard.

# FRIEND AND ADVISER

Ruth Paine is often referred to as a generous, benevolent, and charitable figure. She met the Oswalds at a prior dinner party at which Marina and Ruth became acquainted. When Lee Harvey Oswald left for New Orleans in 1963, Paine invited Marina and their baby to stay with her. Ruth Paine drove Marina and June Oswald to meet Lee in New Orleans and provided transportation when the pregnant mother and daughter returned.

Those who affirm Mrs. Paine's intentions offer there is no evidence that Ruth Paine had any connection to any official group. However, Ruth Paine's father William Avery Hyde was prior considered for covert use by the Central Intelligence Agency in the Vietnam War.[dcxxviii] William and Carol Hyde were Ruth's parents who associated prior socially with Agency employees.

Paine's sister Sylvia Ludlow Hoke was a former employee of the Department of Defense, her husband worked for the American government's National Aid for Undeveloped Countries organization.[dcxxix] Sylvia Hoke was of Agency interest because of associations with her mother in law, a member of the Communist Party. Sylvia Hoke was also a CIA employee.[dcxxx] Ruth's brother Carl Hyde was a peace activist. Michael Paine's family has other connections as well. Lyman and Frances Paine were members of a militant political organization.[dcxxxi]

Those who support the Paine's and their families overlooked valid associations. Namely, Lee Harvey Oswald only had to leave New Orleans for Dallas due to Marina being at the Paine's home at Ruth's invitation. Ruth Paine is also the person who told Oswald that a job was available at the Texas School Book Depository.[dcxxxii] While these facts do not infer Ruth Paine's complicity, they do offer more than just Oswald influenced his actions.

It also feasibly demonstrates that as of October 1963, he had no definite plan to kill the President. Without Ruth Paine, he would not have applied for the job. The definite motorcade route had not yet finalized and publically announced. Thus, he could not know before his employment of the route. This precludes most reasonable planning; it does not infer Oswald planned much, if at all. This alleged assassin operating by instinct is seemingly improbable and not supported by substantial evidence.

Ruth Paine subsequently informed Sylvia Hoke she intended "to sell her story to 'Life' magazine but this apparently did not pan out." Mrs. Hoke said her sister would probably look after Marina's welfare, at least for the present, since Marina had only Ruth to assist her". Paine's "connection" and commitment to Marina seemed far more than mere property owner and tenant. Was it genuine friendship, the obsessive need for companionship, or an unexplained intelligence purpose connecting these women for a time? The Oswalds, Paines, Hokes, and Hydes were all the subject of repeated Bureau and Agency investigations.

In 1962, another geologist Declan Ford befriended Marina Oswald. Ford eventually served as Marina's personal adviser. Ford's prior occupations include serving in the United States Navy, the Internal Revenue Service, the Federal Power Commission, and two different oil companies. Mr. Ford was a world traveler, member of several geological organizations, and civic groups. Ford later served in multiple official capacities.[dcxxxiii]

Mrs. Ford was born in Russia and served as Marina Oswald's interpreter following the Kennedy assassination. Both the Fords testified before the President's (Warren) Commission and gave additional official statements.[dcxxxiv] Declan Ford is yet another officially connected person surrounding the Oswalds. He is Marina's de Mohrenschildt, the friend with a feasibly questionable background and loyalties.

## SPECULATION AND THE LOVE STORY

News reports broadcast the Dallas Police rushing toward a couple near the Grassy Knoll. They also speculate police might have a possible assassin in custody.[dcxxxv] This demonstrates the inaccurate and ever speculative atmosphere surrounding the events. Multiple assassins were not just possible, but initially suspected by some leaders and media organizations.

Walter Cronkite later reports "…he (President Kennedy) was being greeted lavishly by the crowd in a very warm Texas welcome, when the bullet fired out of the crowd." Cronkite did not say from high above the crowd but "fired out of the crowd." Although highly unlikely, it displays the widespread confusion of facts. "Some of the Secret Service agents thought the gunfire however was from an automatic weapon fired from the right rear of the Chief Executives car possibly from a Grassy Knoll, that's the Knoll where motorcycle policeman were seen racing, where the huddled figures of a man and woman were seen on the ground with the crowd surrounding them".[dcxxxvi]

Where did the automatic shots come from, could multiple rifles firing explain this description? Possibilities are varied the result is the same. The official story is largely deficient. You can fire a Carcano, three times in the allotted time. However, you must aim, fire, and reload. It additionally requires the firing practice necessary to make the shots.

Another popular claim that relies on hearsay and speculation is the claim of Oswald being a paid Federal Bureau of Investigation informant. Former Bureau agent and Dallas District Attorney Henry Wade prior discussed an alleged Bureau payment voucher given to Oswald, yet no voucher was ever produced. The assertions included Oswald was known at Bureau headquarters as their informant. "Mr. Wade added that Mr. Storey indicated that the Central Intelligence Agency had informants that no one knew about except the Central Intelligence Agency Agent and that the informant might have an informant."[dcxxxvii] There is no proof that supports Oswald was considered for Bureau informant status as he prior was for the Central Intelligence Agency.[dcxxxviii]

Many officials have speculated or simply dismissed any idea of any larger plot. No matter the basis of these actions, a few officials acted not in national interest but self-interest. They used the events surrounding the death of President Kennedy to enrich their political and financial power. Others fearful of possible peripheral implication suppressed repeated evidence.

Many official errors and denials are not the only possible myths. Random clearly mythical conspiracies have cropped up over the years. For each well-developed inspection of the president's assassination, twenty ridiculous theories exist. Unfortunately, unlikely claims have gained support from the uninformed.

James Files claims to be the Grassy Knoll sniper from prison. Files said he was in Dallas with Charles Nicoletti and they killed President Kennedy. Whatever the reason, Files has attempted to pursue infamy from prison. His story does not stand up to intense scrutiny.[dcxxxix]

Files was likely not the sniper or near the Grassy Knoll based on inconsistencies which impeach his story. One such discrepancy occurred when he alleged a mistaken assumption regarding the motorcade route. Files said he received advanced notification of a secret motorcade route change.[dcxl] Files claimed security changes that did not occur.

The Dallas Morning News printed the official motorcade route prior to John F. Kennedy's arrival in Dallas. The route was unchanged, contrary to Files' declared beliefs. Multiple diagrams appeared the day before and the day of President Kennedy's assassination. Some diagrams are more detailed than others were. The Dallas Morning News and its front page did not include a fully detailed route.[dcxli]

However, a map within the Dallas Times Herald included Elm Street, and the infamous turn was indeed on the original route. James Files declared he was privy to a "secret" alteration that never happened. Files potentially added this detail to his story after reading a book or seeing the Dallas Morning News. However, the Dallas Times Herald had the full route on its front page and this proves no change occurred.[dcxlii] Files statements do not account for the Secret Service control of the route when his first claims emerged. This requires not just proven incompetence but improbable massive official complicity.

Files previous speculations additionally misinformed some of the American public. This modern confession mixes huge amounts of speculation with some truth. The claim does not provide verifiable evidence. Varying claims do not feasibly support Files was involved.

A second problematic case is the story of Judyth Vary Baker. Baker claims she had a romantic relationship with Lee Harvey Oswald. Baker claimed they possessed cover jobs at the Reilly Coffee Company and simultaneously worked on covert medical research. In my estimation, portions of Baker's story are highly suspect.

Baker claims Oswald was her "bodyguard" and he worked for the Central Intelligence Agency and the Federal Bureau of Investigation. She offers an unconvincing aggregate of spy novel and love story without sufficient proof of its occurrence. As Baker led a "Strange True Tours" event, she claimed one tryst in New Orleans "was paid for by a kingpin among the assassination conspirators..."(Carlos Marcello)[dcxliii] Can verified past employees' of the Montleone hotel be contacted to confirm or deny her claims?

If you love someone deeply as Baker claims Oswald regarded her, why did they never take verified pictures together? If Oswald was indeed busy with "multiple missions" as Baker attested, why suddenly decide to share his innermost secrets with Judyth Baker? Would officials waste an asset to guard someone using a makeshift lab? Would Oswald risk exposure of a conspiracy to Baker, despite that he would later maintain his innocence until death?

Baker additionally claims Oswald's wife Marina was a cover.[dcxliv] No other woman after Oswald returned from the Soviet Union besides Marina Oswald appears in most verified evidence. Oswald's children would feasibly again render Baker's claim of Marina being a cover story untenable. Why did neither possess a picture of them together? It is improbable to assume Oswald would care so much about Baker and never mention her to anyone.

Baker is not the person who Oswald verifiably loved or romanced based on notations in his diary. Oswald notes an affair with Nell Korobka and prior dating other Russian women. Ella German is Oswald's first Russian love.

Oswald's devotion is exhibited by his diary entries. Oswald attributes his marriage to Marina as means to hurt Ella as a consequence of her prior refusal of marriage.[dcxlv dcxlvi]

Yet Oswald states he did love Marina. He never mentions Judyth Baker. A similar claim is given that preceded Baker's story by decades; the unlikely tale claimed that Oswald was dating pop singer Connie Francis in New Orleans.[dcxlvii] Baker later asserted interactions with Oswald transpired in New Orleans, yet no substantial evidence supports either claim.

When first offering her Oswald assertions Baker stated having intentionally constructing a semi-fictional series of stories. They were embellished to generate publisher interest. Baker when seemingly appropriate would later release the "actual" information. Yet how can we distinguish truth and fiction based on the mixture of Baker's various accounts?[dcxlviii] Her name has not appeared in the original evidence.

Baker claims to have known or met Oswald, David Ferrie, Carlos Marcello, Jack Ruby, and Clay Shaw. Yet none of them mentioned her or ever corroborated her ideas. Baker additionally claims Oswald had extensive ties with the Marcello criminal organization. Much like James Files, her claims are divergent and contradictory. Her name never appears in any of the original evidence. Baker could easily confirm her assertions with substantial evidence, rather than unverified claims.


## THE ASSERTED LOST WITNESS

Some assert that Gordon Novel, a witness in the Garrison investigation was of great importance. Some claim his failure to appear following a second subpoena was proof of his complicity. Gordon Novel was an electronics salesperson, and bartender. He approached Jim Garrison with claims of working for the Central Intelligence Agency.

Among his ominous references was an operation "Double-Chek". Some mistakenly attributed this to a Bay of Pigs military program. Double-Chek was instead a scheme providing money to a widower's fund supporting the participants' families. According to internal Agency files Novel had no association and was feasibly used by the NBC network to generate viewers for its upcoming program "expected to bury" Jim Garrison. Novel states he infiltrated the Garrison camp and provided information to NBC reporter Walter Sheridan.[dcxlix]

Some Agency officials state Novel and those he associated with are not connected to the Agency. Evidence reveals this as not reliable. Yet if the

Agency wished to dispel the Novel exaggerations, they might reveal others associated with Novel. The possibility of Novel being an Agency operative remains unproven. It is possible but substantial evidence does not support this idea. Yet the Agency does admit that by funding the anti-Castro Cuban groups it may have provided funds to those associated with Novel.

Novel's activities include a telegram to Richard Helms containing an amateurish overuse of cryptonyms and pseudonyms (coded names and false names). His many claims within the message do not affirm its credibility. "Attn UNCLE Hdqrs Good Guy Div. Regarding Garrison conspiracy case; code reference Jackass. Dear Richard. Today according to the jolly green giant (Mr. Garrison) 'You are paying my legal fees in Louisiana and Ohio. Since my attorneys are crying and pressing me because of not being paid for my various...Instead of a no comment S.O.P. reply, how about a public ha-ha..."[dcl]

Agency cryptonyms serve to protect and mask identities, not reveal them, or use obvious code. If the message were coded "jolly green giant" to indicate Garrison, the next sentence would not require Novel to specify who the next pseudonym was. He would likely use a cryptonym for Richard Helms or at least his official title. Perhaps Novel's design was to misinform and discredit Garrison, if so he succeeded in some respects. Novel in my view is a distraction from more important figures. Novel, Baker, and Files each have made vast assertions that remain unproven.

Some credible witnesses speak out despite the danger, yet unverified claims have emerged as well. If they are proven credible we owe them due respect, if not due exposure. We owe ourselves the truth and must have it. Without the truth no clear definition of choice exists, only ignorance and gossip. Informed society cannot function properly without the uncomfortable truth existing. Occasionally truth must dispel official and public deceptions.

No freedom exists without truth. You live by the leave of accepted lies, subject to the information others allow you. If the deception continues to be spoon fed to American citizens, they will forget. They will forgive the wrongs done and believe future manufactured truths. This will be the fall of critical thought and popular speculation shall reign.

# CHAPTER 7

*"Rather than love, than money, than fame, give me truth."*

~Henry David Thoreau
American Poet
*"Walden"*

## FINDINGS AND CONCLUSIONS

In 1979, the final Report of the House Select Committee on Assassinations was complete. The Report concluded a high probability of conspiracy existed in President Kennedy's assassination. The House Select Committee still believed Lee Harvey Oswald fired all but one of the shots. They determined an unknown sniper was responsible for the fourth shot.[dcli] These official decisions have faced repeated critical attacks.

The Select Committee decided "the FBI's investigation into a conspiracy was deficient in the areas that the committee decided most worthy of suspicion —organized crime, pro- and anti- Castro Cubans, and the possible associations of individuals from these areas with Lee Harvey Oswald and Jack Ruby."[dclii] Yet still no serious recent official investigation has occurred. This is not coincidence. After this last investigation, the government's case nearly unraveled.

The Committee's review displayed two nearly simultaneous shots that had to come from two different guns. The official investigation yielded a fourth shot after continued study. Those who support the United States government's Lone Gunman Theory have denied this evidence as tampered with, fabricated, or disproven. Only evidence admitted to the President's (Warren) Commission Report seems worthy of their recognition.

Since then many studies were performed which support and refute the determinations of the House Select Committee on Assassinations. However, no credible official panel has retested these findings using independent experts. Unfortunately, some of the worst President's (Warren) Commission findings remain on the record unchallenged.

Once reviewing the President's (Warren) Commission and their efforts, the House Select Committee determined they had been thorough and reasonable. Yet the Select Committee determined they had failed to accept any notion of conspiracy.[dcliii] Consider most original evidence, testimony, and standing official reports. Now ask yourself a question, is assassination conspiracy a reasonable inference?

# A HANDFUL OF MYSTERIOUS DEATHS

Greatly overestimated by some advocates and utterly denied by critics are related deaths to the President's assassination. Speculation has long accompanied those conceivably killed in association with a conspiracy. Some authors have put the number above fifty, which is nearly impossible. More people than ten would cause huge notice. Merely a handful of key witnesses and related pawns might have died to prevent their later testimony. Considering historical criminal and intelligence practices, these are realistic concerns.[dcliv]

Deaths possibly related to the assassination of John F. Kennedy number five, George de Mohrenschildt, Sam Giancana, Johnny Roselli, Richard Cain, and Charles Nicoletti. All of these five people died under improbable circumstances. De Mohrenschildt is the lone suicide whereas Giancana, Roselli, Cain, and Nicoletti were apparent homicides.

George de Mohrenschildt was an unpaid occasional informant to the Central Intelligence Agency, and Oswald's friend. Prior to de Mohrenschildt's scheduled testimony for the House Select Committee, he decides to kill himself. George de Mohrenschildt died prior to completing a book about Lee Harvey Oswald. He died the same day following an official investigator's attempt to contact him. The suicide denies officials related testimony about Oswald.[dclv]

Sam Giancana schedules testimony before the Senate Select (Church) Committee. Someone murders Giancana less than a week before his planned appearance. Some allege Santo Trafficante silenced his possible talkative former ally.[dclvi] The timing of Giancana's demise is highly dubious. Giancana's primary knowledge of illegal official activities posed a threat to varied interests. His death severed feasible Mafia connections to a plot and prior collaboration with the Central Intelligence Agency.

Johnny Roselli had extensive Mafia connections including Sam Giancana and Santo Trafficante. He often associated with anti-Castro Cuban groups, and collaborated with the Agency. In Roselli's earlier official testimony, he named three Cubans involved in illegal plots. Roselli scheduled additional testimony before the Senate Select Committee; unknown parties subsequently dismember him. The Dade County Police inquired with the Agency to obtain the identities of these Cuban individuals in connection with Roselli's murder. The Agency initially refused to provide the identities of these individuals because of the "principal of the protection of sources and methods of the Agency clandestine operations." The Agency had many unanswered questions related to Roselli's death.[delvii]

Evidence links Richard Cain to the Agency, Bureau, anti-Castro Cuban groups, and the Mafia. He was privy to related information based upon his access to these groups and his attempt to implicate the Fair Play for Cuba Committee for the Kennedy assassination is notable. This may have taken attention from the true feasible Conspirators. Masked gunmen murder Richard Cain publicly in 1973. Cain was the reportedly enduring companion and fixer of Sam Giancana, his knowledge of events feasibly necessitated his death.

Charles Nicoletti was a Mafia assassin credited with more than a dozen brutal murders. Nicoletti like, Giancana, Roselli, and de Mohrenschildt had a scheduled appearance before a congressional committee. The House Select Committee on Assassinations had called Nicoletti to testify; just prior to his appearance, he was murdered. Mafia hit man and FBI informant Charles Crimaldi believed Nicoletti's association with the Central Intelligence Agency led to his death. Crimaldi had no knowledge of any connection to President Kennedy's assassination. Yet again, the timing and manner of death are reasonably suspicious.[delviii]

In my view, claims of a relationship between Nicoletti and possible improbable assassins are without substantiation. These additional claims are unproven and unnecessary to consider. Ultimately, it is up to the reader to determine if they agree. Although not endorsing the huge number of deaths others suggest, stating no proof exists for any suspicious death is self-deception.

Evidence and legal documents support prior officially sanctioned murders. Until recently, the United States government had the decency to deny such beliefs and actions. Modern American executive ambition is largely in the open. Critics might consider these obvious realities.

# WHO WERE THE CONSPIRATORS?

Most people feasibly involved were akin to Lee Harvey Oswald. They were disposable, used to distract investigators, and undertake operations. If heightened security had been present in Dealey Plaza, the assassination may never have occurred. Condemned is a dupe who could not obtain a job or housing without help. Instead of a lone man, these were possibly the men behind it all.

Some held nearly unassailable positions of power in American society. They had access to immense untraceable resources. Others possessed the greed, fear, and hatred to see the Assassination Conspiracy completed. Allegedly, some men feasibly killed a president and others concealed the truth.

## POSSIBLE ASSASSINATION SUSPECTS:

### THE UNDERWORLD SCENARIO:
Meyer Lansky, Carlos Marcello, Johnny Roselli, Richard Cain, Sniper A and B

### THE MINUTE PLOT SCENARIO:
Unknown Conspirator, Lee Harvey Oswald, Sniper A and B

### THE ROGUE INTELLIGENCE SCENARIO:
J.C. King, William Harvey, Sniper A and B

### THE CONGLOMERATE SCENARIO:
Meyer Lansky, Antonio Varona, Johnny Roselli, William Harvey, Sniper A and B

### THE LEADERS OF THE CONSPIRACY
Those men who based on their actions and statements feasibly oversaw the official suppression of events in the following years:

### THE OFFICIALS ARM:
Lyndon B. Johnson, J. Edgar Hoover

### THE MILITARY INTELLIGENCE ARM:
Allen Dulles, John McCone, Richard Helms, James Angleton

Sufficient facts and testimony exist to demonstrate means, opportunity, and the intent of some to murder John F. Kennedy. Others spent years recasting the actual events to implicate Lee Harvey Oswald as the lone gunman. The reasoning could have been revenge, to avoid a greater national scandal, or perhaps threats of nuclear war. Despite the intent, the results secured political and financial power for some. No ends could justify the potential means.

Bureau Director Hoover and subsequent Director of Central Intelligence Helms expected the case to be open forever. Some critics allege the evidence and inspections supporting a conspiracy have endured not because of the truth. Critics instead contend theories endure because they are more interesting than actual truth. Yet the truth is always more interesting because it is never easy to discern.

The full truth is a mixture of all reasonable supporting testimony and evidence. Declassified evidence provides new sections of the truth. Continued official investigations have changed past truths into the current sanctioned truth. The truth is clearer with the passage of time. Yet those who state they have a singular grasp of the truth beyond question are ridiculous. Only full public disclosure with a rational legal inquiry will reveal the entirety of the matter.

## DID THE ASSASSINATION CONSPIRACY OCCUR?

The last official investigation decided two snipers likely fired. The majority of original medical evidence from Parkland and Bethesda affirmed possible frontal shots. Many verified facts and experts dispute the Lone Gunman Theory. Based on a majority of evidence reviewed, allegedly at least one shot killing John F. Kennedy came from the front.

It feasibly emerged from the areas outside the Depository and was beyond Oswald's power. Present official claims ignore the feasible alteration of medical evidence. Compounding this was alleged official deception and revisions of testimony. Some authorities contented themselves by destroying evidence and obstructing justice.

Did the Central Intelligence Agency believe its own mistaken information? Were all these associated undertakings at concealment just innocent oversights? Did officials transform misinformation into disinformation? A deceit willingly offered to confound the best official investigators.

After consideration of all the evidence, President Kennedy feasibly died resulting from a premeditated assassination conspiracy. The final official conclusion supports a reasonable probability of multiple assassins. All the relevant evidence, supporting facts, and most witness testimony should enjoy consideration. In my view, they provide Lee Harvey Oswald with reasonable doubt.

Yet we cannot overlook the evidence which supports Oswald possibly murdered J.D. Tippit. However, officials recorded contending facts as well. Yet guilt in Tippit's death would not affirm Oswald being the single assassin officials' claim. Oswald has feasible associations to a greater conspiracy. Consider his lack of practice, the particular weapon's deficiencies, and repeated evidence that does not support a lone gunman scenario. Consider the lack of time he possessed to complete a successful plot, and his many mistakes in all other alleged undertakings.

Congressional and the independent research of some associated experts in time offered new evidence. The information revealed supports actions beyond Oswald's ability occurred. Authorities denied and obliterated contending evidence. A small group of officials was attempting to conceal the truth.

# MLK

# CHAPTER 8

*"And then I got into Memphis. And some began to say the threats, or talk about the threats that were out, or what would happen to me from some of our sick white brothers."*

~Dr. Martin Luther King Jr.
American Civil Rights Movement leader
*"I have been to the Mountaintop" speech*

## REASONS FOR THE ASSASSINATION CONSPIRACY

Controversy surrounds Martin Luther King Jr's death in part due to the many similarities between the assassinations of Dr. King, and John F. Kennedy. Similar intent possibly exists in the gratuitous incompetence of a second official investigation. Conflicting witness testimony and familiar influences become apparent. Repeated official mistakes litter a second assassination's files.

Dr. King and those comprising his inner circle were under long-term surveillance by the Federal Bureau of Investigation and Central Intelligence Agency. Civil Rights Movement heroes now honored were formerly radicals and enemies of American society. This was King's classification according to most American legal authorities. As peaceful civilian protest began affecting the national conscience, other interests targeted Dr. King and his cadre.

Southern officials railed against the social changes President Kennedy undertook with integration. This continued under Lyndon Johnson's adoption of earlier legislation. President Johnson's long private negative views regarding black Americans remained unnoticed. However, Johnson was more politician than prejudiced.

Johnson was a man leading an increasingly unpopular war with a past full of alleged misdeeds. He was feasibly more pliable than sincerely prejudiced Deep South authorities were. Johnson had thoughts of political survival and financial gain, not ignorant practices better left to the past. Southern interests however did not have the real fears of Lyndon Johnson. They instead had a deep multi-generational hatred for what Dr. King represented and of the man himself.

These small groups might have believed following President Kennedy's demise, any rival figure's murder was possible. Authorities estimate James Earl Ray was alone in the plot, although he lacked the skills necessary to explain his later escape and travels. Ray officially somehow executed a one shot assassination and escaped without help of any sort. We have a second Lone Gunman Theory.

Unlike Oswald however, James Earl Ray is a less qualified candidate. Ray was a proven unsuccessful criminal offender possessing intelligence but minor criminal prowess. James Earl Ray joined the Army near the end of World War II. However, Ray had no possible intelligence connections like Oswald.

Noted are Ray's consistent mistakes regarding Dr. King's murder. Errors the mastermind of a successful conspiracy would not make. After reviewing much of the official record and independent research, many questions remain. Martin Luther King's death was possibly beyond the power of James Earl Ray alone.

King was fighting for civil rights in the recently post Jim Crow South and using non-violence to do so. Unlike Martin Luther King's political opponents, he invited all people to join his protests. This included Bayard Rustin, a successful human rights protester. However, Rustin was a former Communist party leader. Senator Strom Thurmond spoke out against Rustin's involvement in constructing legislation calling him "…communist, draft dodger, and homosexual".[dclix] A Central Intelligence Agency file offers similar assessments.[dclx]

Based on the many public attacks on Dr. King and his associates, they clearly had enemies. Many adversaries were dominant federal officials in Washington. Alleged intrigues were born of vile cultural ignorance, and futile acts to prevent American citizens from legal equality. Unknown to Dr. King was the level of fear and hatred his agenda evoked.

Dr. King died four years following John F. Kennedy and less than three months before Robert Kennedy. His murder benefited similar political leaders, financial interests, government agencies, and criminal associations. The assassination occurred during the tenure of the same powerful men.

King knew of the great danger to his life. He did not know powerful forces might attempt to publicly murder him then erase the truth from American history. These possible Conspirators never realized the shifting tidal forces of American society. They never imagined massive public support would recognize Dr. King as hero and martyr.

Now Martin Luther King has a personal official holiday, thousands of cities have named public areas bearing King's name. Dr. King's likeness appears on a large statue in the American Capitol and wide variety of public media. If any involved in the possible conspiracy are still living, they must despise Martin Luther King Jr. Day. Weeks later, they can enjoy Black History Month.

The legacy and legend of Martin Luther King shall exist centuries following any conspirator's demise. Possible conspirators insured Dr. King's place in history. For sacrificing his life for citizen freedom, King was enshrined in American history. Let us not forget the terrible price this American martyr paid for human rights. It dishonors Martin Luther King's sacrifice to remain silent.

## THE HANDS OF THE CONSPIRACY

These associations refer to the "Hands" to differentiate them from the larger encompassing "Arms" of the previous Kennedy assassination conspiracy.

### THE CRIMINAL HAND
Men with long standing anti civil rights ties including criminal figures conceivably involved in the conspiracy.

### THE OFFICIALS HAND
A mixture of local, state, and national officials with shared motives or interests in the death of the Civil Rights Movement and its leader.

### THE MILITARY INTELLIGENCE HAND
Consisting of personnel ordered to conduct surveillance and possibly aiding in the assassination of Dr. King.

### THE CONSPIRATORS
Those who allegedly planned and executed the assassination, some later might have conspired to conceal the truth.

# CHAPTER 9

*"...that hatred is acquired just as much by means of good actions as by bad ones ..."*

~Niccolo Machiavelli
*"The Prince"*

## THE CRIMINAL HAND

Those possibly responsible for the death of Martin Luther King Jr. perhaps used criminals to undertake their plans. King was a religious man who embraced non-violence and community unification. These criminals were possible minions of interests opposing King; men who despised him for skin color. King's peaceful message and political accomplishments further incited his detractors.

Public hatred regarding Dr. King was greater than for President Kennedy. Some authorities had long ago judged King a revolutionary, Communist, and national threat. Wealthy prejudiced men formerly dominated America's political structure. In my estimation influential men attempted futilely to control the evolving American society.

Within the suggested assassination conspiracy of John F. Kennedy, the organized Underworld Arm had recognizable motives. The Underworld Arm now becomes the Criminal Hand, because the Mafia likely did not participate in this operation according to verified evidence. Though speculation exists, conclusive proof has been less forthcoming. Instead, these Conspirators would feasibly require at least the assassin and the expendable dupe.


## THE OFFICIAL ASSASSIN

In the death of President Kennedy, the conspiracy and innocence of the official assassin have a possible link. Oswald's possible innocence emerges from his being deprived his civil rights and contending evidence. Ray conversely was an escaped prisoner; this does not imply his innocence. Unlike Oswald, James Earl Ray did plead guilty to the charge of King's murder.

Unlike Oswald, Ray actually had counsel, despite the many deficiencies of his earlier representation. Using facts and the President's (Warren) Commission timeline, doubt exists for Lee Harvey Oswald. Whereas Ray cooperated, confessed, and initially accepted his guilt. James Earl Ray's plea of guilt is verifiable. Yet did Ray have assistance beyond his means?

James Earl Ray's purported handler according to his testimony was the unknown Raul. In official and independent research, Raul is still publicly unidentified. James Earl Ray is seemingly not the self-reliant expert some critics have claimed. He failed to undertake major decisions and met with his brothers to plan large crimes. The alleged individual giving Ray orders is his "Contact". Whether it was Ray's brother, Raul, or an unnamed intelligence asset remains contended.

James Earl Ray rented a room in Memphis near the Lorraine Motel. For most of the period before the King assassination, Ray does little more than his possible Contact's errands. How can Ray be a qualified sniper and not bring the equipment he required? Instead, Ray bought items piecemeal locally, similar to someone who failed to devise a plan.[dclxi]

James Earl Ray purchased infrared binoculars, new clothes, and a car. Ray used money to undertake living expenses, a locksmith class, dancing lessons, and multiple new rifles. All purchased without explained access to funds. The last being the official murder weapon. If Ray was a qualified sniper who executed King, why did he later have to switch rifles?

Not included in Ray's many activities was practice with rifles anytime near the murder of Dr. King. Unlike Oswald who had previous firearm qualifications, Ray was an unimpressive shooter without practice. From the Brewer's Boarding house restroom atop Jim's Grill, officially Ray would make the shot killing Dr. King. The shot itself implies a practiced sniper. Despite his lack of qualifications, Ray officially becomes the second lone gunman.

Unfortunately, no ballistics information was available for years to the public. These circumstances account for wide public skepticism. A single witness purportedly saw Ray running from the official sniper's nest. No one, like in the case of Oswald, saw him fire the shot. Officially, Ray eludes authorities; he then deposits a box of incriminating evidence on Main Street. Yet he was intelligent enough to develop multiple identities.

One alias used was a Canadian citizen named Eric S. Galt. Galt lived in Toronto and broadly resembled James Earl Ray. When interviewed Ray's brother Jerry stated the alias emerged from a past Canadian trip. Having returned from Canada, Ray alluded to smuggling unknown materials across the northern American border. Ray did this for his Contact; this marks the first mention of Raul. When James Ray later met Jerry Ray, he stated, "from now on I'll be known as Eric S. Galt".

Ray used this name to obtain a vehicle, Alabama driver's license, and plastic surgery before the assassination of Dr. King.[dclxii] While later escaping, Ray used false documents to deceive border authorities in the United States, Canada, and Europe. Ray often used aliases that were actually a real person's identity. He obtained the documents using deception at the Kennedy Travel Bureau in Canada.[dclxiii dclxiv] Upon Ray's arrest a different alias is discovered, Ramon George Sneyd. This alias was a Canadian citizen and Toronto police member.[dclxv dclxvi] Ray additionally used the names John Willard, Harvey Lowmeyer, and Paul Bridgeman.

Yet how did James Earl Ray interact successfully in foreign countries, having never traveled in Europe? He spoke no other language. The combined Federal Bureau of Investigation and International police agencies could not catch Ray for months. He like Oswald appears simultaneously as genius and fool. These inconsistencies are problematic for official judgments.

"I've never understood how a bumbling petty crook like Ray could singlehandedly evade a police dragnet in Memphis....get out of the country as far as Portugal before finally being apprehended in London. He had to have help... It most likely came from white racist groups, not the FBI or CIA..."[dclxvii] Following his capture, Ray's first attorney was Arthur Hanes Sr. a noted anti-integration figure.

As Mayor of Birmingham, Hanes publicly opposed Dr. King and his protests in Alabama. Hanes was also a former Federal Bureau of Investigation agent. This compromised independent treatment for Ray in my view.[dclxviii] Appointment of this stark anti-civil rights figure was already sealing James Earl Ray's legal fate. Hanes' connection to J. Edgar Hoover did not offer Ray neutral representation.

Then just two days prior to James Earl Ray's trial, he fires Arthur Hanes over a financial dispute. The parting of ways emerged from a book deal gone awry. In this deal, Hanes received compensation and author William Bradford Huie obtained exclusive rights to Ray's story. Financial wrangling amid trial preparation is a conflict of interest. Hanes, instead of creating Ray's defense, brokers a book deal to enrich himself. All Hanes' rights to the book deal ceased with his dismissal.[dclxix]

James Earl Ray then retained attorney Percy Foreman. Foreman's actions would be just as questionable as Ray's prior attorney. Percy Foreman similarly might have attempted to profit from his client's misfortune. On February 3, James Earl Ray having no funds assigned all portions of various book deals to Percy Foreman. Again, Ray's legal counsel considered financial benefits instead of fully preparing a defense.[dclxx]

A relevant letter to James Earl Ray from Percy Foreman included further evidence of theoretical impropriety: "This will shorten the trial considerably. In consideration of the time it will save me, I am willing to make the following adjustment of my fee arrangement with you: If the (guilty) plea is entered and the sentence is accepted and no embarrassing circumstances take place in the court room". "...I am willing to assign to any bank, trust company, or individual selected by you all my receipts under the above agreement in excess of 165,000.00".[dclxxi]

Why did Ray's attorney offer financial incentive for the guilty plea? Percy Foreman additionally did not consult every file and lead of Arthur Hanes to prepare Ray's defense.[dclxxii] Foreman later referred to James Earl Ray's possible innocence. If Foreman believed his client innocent, why did he subsequently not pursue all evidence of interest?

We cannot allow our leaders to implicate a man without the required legal process. Legal representation must not act counter to their client's interests. If justice is the aim of these officials, they cannot just ignore the law when sentiment dictates. Can America be a just nation if authorities deviate from law whenever politically advantageous?

## THE SECOND MAN

A second participant in the alleged conspiracy was the self-implicated Lloyd Jowers. Jowers was partial owner of Jim's Grill, a café on the ground floor of Brewer's Boarding house. The restaurant was beneath what served as the sniper's nest according to officials. Jowers later attempted to receive immunity to prosecution for his testimony regarding Dr. King's murder.

In his initial story to the Memphis Police, Jowers suggested having no knowledge of the shooting. Jowers claimed hearing a noise in the kitchen of Jim's Grill. In several additional interviews, Jowers' statements change several times. In his initial deception, Lloyd Jowers named Jim Holt as the Assassin of Dr. King.[dclxxiii]

Jowers then stated a man named Frank Liberto approached him. Liberto was an associate of notorious crime boss Carlos Marcello. According to Jowers, the Marcello family offered him one hundred thousand dollars and forgiveness of all debts to aid the conspiracy. Unfortunately, Frank Liberto was already dead and could not be questioned.

In my view, this was disinformation attempting to implicate Mafia connections to a plot. Not all Mafia theories are possible to discount currently. However unless they can be fully substantiated, they distract from the evidence. The Mafia is just the usual suspect, included without thought to the reasons for its existence.

The family oriented social club the Mafia appears to be is the veneer of the organization. Its lifeblood is ambitious men who want power and wealth. Intimidation is the real power of the Mafia. Its use exposes the true objective in most crime, profit. The Mafia gains no advantage for killing Dr. King. This was unlike President Kennedy's assassination which had clearer motives and perceived benefits to the Underworld.

Plans to kill Dr. King allegedly occurred at Jim's Grill beneath the Brewer Boarding house. Lloyd Jowers identified a Memphis Police sharpshooter and three unknown men. Jowers vaguely identifies them as government agents. In later versions, the Jowers' story becomes more plausible.

According to Lloyd Jowers, a sniper fired outside the rear door of Jim's Grill concealed in the heavy bushes. Jowers then dismantles the rifle and destroys the shell casings. He quickly covers and conceals it, an unknown agent picked up the weapon for disposal the next day. Jowers alleged Earl Clark; a Memphis Police Department officer was the sniper. However, this was not the first individual Lloyd Jowers named as Martin Luther King's assassin.[dclxxiv]

# CHAPTER 10

*"Hey, Hey, LBJ! How many kids did you kill today?"*

~Anonymous
1966 United States Anti War Demonstrators slogan

## THE OFFICIALS HAND

Official fears included Dr. King's revolutionary social agenda. King pledged to fight against the Vietnam War and for the national redistribution of wealth. If the Federal powers rankled at Dr. King's past success, any chance that his new ideas could succeed inspired renewed loathing. Martin Luther King's agenda targeted the Vietnam War, and financial business interests.

From the earliest boycotts and support offered to Rosa Parks, Martin Luther King attracted notice. The unexpected success of his methods frightened influential leaders and some media outlets. Each asserted King was a radical leading an organization of "subversive" citizens. It was not merely hateful words; but repeated violence Dr. King is subjected to.

While he spoke before a local gathering, arsonists firebomb King's house during the winter of 1956. In the winter of 1965, a National States Rights Party member attacked Dr. King inside Albert Hotel.[dclxxv] Under violent attack, Dr. King maintained a high-minded style and non-violent protests. These protests began to awaken the long troubled American conscience. They are the most important steps in America legally addressing the injustice of slavery and remaining prejudice.

When Martin Luther King attacked the Vietnam War, he directly endangered the Military-Industrial Complex's profit margin. The Officials Hand had a single goal, to manage the population and discover a way to maintain wartime objectives. The status quo required stopping the boycotts, protests, and maintaining current law and policy. Some modern American Presidents' emulate this flawed governance style.

Dr. King, like Robert Kennedy, was a man of great will and commitment to his causes. The charges of Communist sympathies that consistently followed King are false. Somehow, these lies continue skulking around the fringes of political thought. Similar emotional views animated the malign thoughts in this alleged intrigue. Overreaction and emotion have and will inspire the vilest chapters of history.

Many American leaders created a perpetual fear of Communism in the last century. They acquired power demonizing those with contrary views and conducting wars based on deceptive information. A prior Senator's deception incited public rage of a largely nonexistent Communist conspiracy. Americans faced mental submission or the consequences of unreasoning authority.

Created fears have often blinded Americans to true national threats. Although the United States has been a victim of foreign spies, only in recent history did a large Russian contingent operate actively. When the Red Scare stalked the halls of government, many of those targeted were law-abiding citizens. The large group of affirmed Russian spies arrived decades later. A modern allegedly democratic Russia is responsible for the subterfuge.

Most subversives tried during the Red Scare were not threats. Communism and its farcical ideas are untenable, yet the Constitution of the United States provides freedom to all non-violent political beliefs. No matter how ridiculous they might be. Communists, similar to some American religious groups, have the right to be misguided and fanatic. Ignorance does not relinquish citizen rights and ignorance of law does not excuse illegal actions.

If Americans ignore any non-violent groups' legal rights, they do not merely wound the offending target. It further wounds the American society. The most offensive words are reasonable in proper forum. So long as speech does not overtly incite violence, physical damage, and legal harm, it remains protected by the United States Constitution. All speech is part of the great marketplace of ideas where democracy, republicanism, and the United States Constitution are the enduring bedrock. These principals are the foundations of America.

Other ideas, including detestable ideas, provide distinction revealing what voters could and would not publicly support. Take for instance the United States first registered lobbyist for the Nazi Party.[delxxvi] Any group associated with a former military enemy and genocide should be illegal in my opinion. Yet in America, citizens have the right to follow ridiculous beliefs whether political or religious.

However when authorities use intimidation and violence to enforce beliefs, they become the greatest danger to society. No single man or group can lawfully be judge, jury, and executioner under the American Constitution. Similar unconstitutional measures like the Patriot Act and its ilk attempt to supersede the Bill of Rights. All ought to fear what many have accepted without legal challenge.

Many Americans fail to see the Patriot Act has provisions unsupported by the Unites States Constitution. The Counter Terrorism Fund remains the most financially irresponsible portion of the Act. The fund provides unlimited amounts of money for executive branch use to reimburse itself, pay rewards for capture, and provide for associated costs of terrorist detainees. The word "unlimited" provides an eternal blank check, a debt that weighs down America potentially forever.[delxxvii]

The Patriot Act offers huge financial incentives to continue funding counter terrorism methods. These tactics have not proven superior to full transparent investigations. The published Act and its powers are unknown to a majority of the public. Americans must guard against terrorism and official egotism. For this vanity is the impetus for all political assassination.

Some in government believe an individual, elected or appointed, can decide the fate of American citizens without due process of law. This implies authorities possess a wisdom the American people do not. Some American leaders remain just as ignorant and fallible as the worst of citizens. This is despite press conferences to the contrary. From repeated errors, scandals, and later discoveries, some officials have ever deluded themselves. Some might be dead; but none escapes the judgment of history.

# The Origins of the Civil Rights Act

Many American political leaders declared King's scheduled March on Washington D.C. would provoke chaos. Local and national media organizations reported this would lead to civil unrest. Instead of the mass riots predicted, the enormous crowd was non-violent. Hundreds of thousands peacefully protested. Americans of all cultures and creeds supported the gathering to promote the Civil Rights Movement.

The height of this gathering was Dr. King ending the event with his iconic "I Have a Dream" speech. Hundreds of thousands of Americans vocally demanded societal evolution. Despite all public criticisms, the march was a grand success. It remains a defining moment in American history. A moment obtained with a heavy cost.

Dr. King faced not only public attacks but many throughout his private life as well. Death threats, hate mail, and all manner of intimidation followed King as protester and public speaker. This looming violence and hatred illustrates the extreme position some opposed Americans had. It was a dangerous struggle for King and his contemporaries in religious and political circles.

The modern Civil Rights Movement began in the streets and churches of the Deep South. This movement was a reaction to centuries of black Americans repeatedly subject to illegal arrest, imprisonment, and lynching. Civil Rights Movement leaders inspired many citizens to the streets using non-violent protests and marches. President Eisenhower created the first Civil Rights Acts in 1957, and strengthened it 1960. John and Robert Kennedy had spoken out for continued additional provisions. These further additions to the bill were before the American Congress in 1963.

Despite this memorable display and the many gathered in support, Senator Strom Thurmond and others blocked the Civil Rights bill and it sputtered in congress. When John F. Kennedy died, Lyndon Johnson assumed control of the bill. Vice President Johnson had formerly been a supporter of some defending this political ignorance.

Political groups like the John Birch Society claimed black Americans were attempting to create a separate black Communist society.[dclxxviii] This fantasy displays the depths of paranoia in these men. Similar hatred and absurd rhetoric used against President Kennedy now targets Dr. King. The passage of time has not erased these groups from American politics.

In 2010, the John Birch Society sponsored the Conservative Political Action Committee (CPAC) Convention.[dclxxix] However, the John Birch Society received no invitation to the 2012 CPAC convention. Perhaps these fringe beliefs were not popular during elections. The question is with their history revealed will it matter to their supporters?

The "old" John Birch Society had repeated false accusations of black rioting, separatism, and radical action. All based on ridiculous cultural paranoia. They ignored centuries of violent repression and the social abuse of black Americans. Past events additionally enraged a handful of eminent officials.

The Federal Bureau of Investigation placed Dr. King and his allies under constant surveillance. This was under J. Edgar Hoover's personal instruction. Publicly unseen were deep policy conflicts within the executive branch. Hoover made it his mission to learn other authorities' and varied celebrities' secrets. The Bureau's leader used these secrets for alleged blackmail and smear campaigns.

Hoover's secrets and power as the Federal the Bureau of Investigation's director made him a formidable and dangerous enemy. Most Americans alive at the time feared just displeasing J. Edgar Hoover. Men like Hoover launched subtle political crusades against men they disliked. Hoover despised Martin Luther King. Hoover's disregard for law was a common belief shared with his friend and superior.

Lyndon Johnson presided over a needlessly violent portion of America's history. His presidency began with the death of a greatly renowned president. Johnson had to secure votes just before the coming election. Johnson possibly realized the Civil Rights bill would become the necessary political solution. This was a public tribute to the Kennedy doctrine portraying Johnson as a unifying humanitarian. It also reversed a long history of legal injustice.

However, Lyndon Johnson had quite a way with words. Johnson nominated Thurgood Marshall the first black American Supreme Court nominee. Referring to this he states, "when I appoint a nigger to the bench, I want everybody to know he's a nigger." [dclxxx] Is Johnson graced with new insight, or just a detestable opportunist? Jesse Jackson fondly reflected on Lyndon Johnson in subsequent interviews. I suppose Johnson's ruse worked.

Johnson used the legislation to provide other legal protections for minorities. As these actions gained the support of most Americans, Johnson began to accelerate the Vietnam War. Although his domestic policies bore a resemblance to President Kennedy's, Johnson's foreign policy was a complete reversal. Johnson's election secures a massive deployment of troops, funds, and military hardware for the Vietnam War.

Lyndon Johnson was the consummate political boss. He faced the untenable position of governing in John F. Kennedy's shadow. Kennedy's demise recast him into the role of martyr. National grief and endless questions drowned out former criticisms, and the Johnson administration required certain answers.

The reversal of systemic cultural repression had become central factor in every American's life since Civil Integration proceeded. Johnson's success in congress failed to translate to the executive branch. Johnson was quite aware of the mounting deaths in Vietnam, and that America was spending billions on the deception. Lyndon Johnson wanted a tidy political solution.

Johnson used his considerable influence as former Speaker of the Senate to accomplish his goals. He ensured the passage of the Civil Rights Act to secure a place in history. Some attribute the credit for civil rights legislation to Lyndon Johnson. Johnson merely bowed to public sentiment and political expedience.

Dr. King and his supporters marched in the streets for years. Fighting for civil rights, they lived under constant threat of official harm and worse. Men and women who bleed for a cause deserve the credit for its accomplishments. As Dr. King succeeded, he did not rest and instead attempted to promote more legal change.

Having achieved social protections for minorities Martin Luther King now attempted to have the Voting Rights Act passed. This bill's purpose was to prevent discriminatory practices at polling areas. Despite the members of America's Congress who opposed it, the Voting Rights Act passed. As time and the law supported the Civil Rights Movement, Dr. King later turned his influence against the Vietnam War.

A man of peace, King opposed the war and its supporters. This increased the surveillance on Dr. King and fellow demonstrators in official reports. Publicly unknown was the network of agents and informants surrounding the Civil Rights Movement. One undercover Memphis Police officer is present among related groups at Dr. King's assassination.


## THE MEMPHIS POLICE DEPARTMENT

Unknown parties disrupted the Memphis Sanitation workers march and it became violent. The march was regarded a failure and had to be attempted again. A few authors speculate an undercover Memphis Police officer caused this riot. Subsequently, Martin Luther King quickly returned to Tennessee into the midst of a deadly plot.

Upon his return authorities began to make errors. Memphis Police superiors asserted King's entourage requested no security. This seemed odd to Police Captain Jerry Williams because King usually received a specific group of officers for security. Once the replacement officers arrived, the situation deteriorated.

Memphis Police ignored Dr. King's close associates and failed to provide the usual arranged police escort. Memphis Police replace the usual security group. All previous security officers were black in every prior event Dr. King attended. For this last event, police send a team of all white police officers.

Some might view having all black officers a minor fact despite its significance. Dr. King and his supporters endured lifelong abuse from white police. This brutal violence happened less than ten years before. Imagine pro-segregationist Governor George Wallace appeared in Memphis. Would authorities have given him an all black police security detail?

Police failed to follow security arrangements; the usual police security is changed. The all white replacement group leaves. Memphis Police replacement and removal of security remains unexplained. Replacement detail Inspector Don Smith said he perceived members in the King group were unsure or did not require security.

The two members of Dr. King's party Smith cited were the Reverend James Lawson and Tarlese Matthews. However, the Department of Justice report on the matter quotes Billy Kyles stating Dr. King's group did not want police protection.[dclxxxi] A reasonable standard of conduct is nothing less than direct confirmation prior to leaving your post. Yet by just the word of a few, they abandoned the King party.

Would police just abandon other famous guests on statements from peripheral members of their entourage? Dr. King did not possess basic defense any famous visitor to Memphis received. His long used police security detail this one time was not available. The single time it would matter.

Inspector Don Smith asserted he telephoned Chief of Detectives Houston, who then granted permission to remove the security detail. The House Select Committee on Assassinations heard this allegation from later Memphis Police Chief Henry Lux. He suggested former Police Chief James McDonald authorized Inspector Smith to remove the detail. However, there is a problem.

Under questioning from House Select Committee on Assassinations these claims are disproven. Former Memphis Police Chief McDonald had no memory of Houston's decision to remove the security detail. Houston never requested permission to do so.[dclxxxii] Congressional findings confirm drastic changes to usual security arrangements without approval.

The Memphis Police Chief during these events testified he was not aware of the removal. Fire and Safety Director Frank Holloman additionally reported being unaware of the removal. The Memphis Police removal occurred without official sanction. The House Select Committee on Assassinations reprimands the Memphis Police in their findings.

Congressional authorities found "...it was highly improper for the security detail to have been withdrawn". "Regardless of the attitude of Dr. King and the members of his party toward the security detail...the violence that attended the March 28th demonstration...tensions in Memphis...numerous threats that had been made on Dr. King's life" were unconsidered. The Committee decided it was "...improper for members of the Dr. King's party not to have been informed of the withdrawal of the detail".[dclxxxiii] This confirms the complete failure of police security.

The replacement security detail's assignment and removal is with eminent incompetence officially. Someone may have intended to make Dr. King more vulnerable to attack. Security errors resulted from deficiencies in the Memphis Police chain of command. Perhaps this explains why Memphis Police additionally failed to seal off the Lorraine Motel until five minutes following the assassination.

Memphis Police did not transmit an All Points Bulletin for James Earl Ray's Mustang. They did not set up roadblocks on areas leading out of Memphis.[dclxxxiv] The Memphis Police Department forgot many normal procedures initially. Police attention seemed focused elsewhere. Memphis sanitation worker Maynard Stiles stated police were subsequently concerned with other aspects of the crime scene.

On the morning following King's death, Stiles received a call from Memphis Police Department. Inspector Sam Evans was "requiring assistance clearing the brush and debris from a vacant lot near the site of the assassination." Less than fourteen hours later, the Memphis Police Department's objective was not continued investigation. It was nearby site modification.

The Memphis Police had a duty to secure the crime scene until thorough investigation occurred. Instead, authorities had the bushes located behind Jim's Grill cleared.[dclxxxv] The bushes were present for years; police decided they now required maintenance. Police altered this single area for unexplained reasons.

Southern Christian Leadership Conference member Andrew Young said, "One of the disturbing features about that day for us was that when we were pointing, we were pointing over across the street. There was a building there, but there was also a 6 to 8 foot pile of bushes and some people thought the shot came from the bushes. The Federal Bureau of Investigation said it came from a bathroom window. But when we got up the next morning, those bushes were gone"[dclxxxvi] Eyewitness Ralph Abernathy stated to the Federal Bureau of Investigation he believed the shot came from "directly in front of the door and not from any great distance." This less distant placement of gunfire possibly emerged from within the bushes behind Jim's Grill.[dclxxxvii]

The official sniper's nest was in Bessie Brewer's Boarding house upstairs restroom, and other areas were fair game apparently. These later actions resulted in compromising the scene. They possibly removed the alternative sniper's nest from evidence. These actions might support a following conspiracy.

If just a few of Memphis Police had protected and secured the area around Dr. King, he might have walked out of Memphis. Thousands of Bureau agents pursued James Earl Ray. A few police officers on scene might have prevented the horrible situation from occurring. Criminal investigation appeared secondary to the apprehension of a second lone gunman.

# CHAPTER 11

*"...the greatest purveyor of violence in the world today,"*

~Dr. Martin Luther King Jr.
Riverside Church speech
*Referring to the American government and its conduct of the Vietnam War*

## THE MILITARY INTELLIGENCE HAND

William Pepper alleged military personnel were feasibly involved in the assassination conspiracy of Martin Luther King. Pepper referenced a Senate Subcommittee observing military connections to a plot. The American Senate's (Church) Committee on Intelligence Activities discovered military groups were observing Dr. King. The military had a pointed interest in Dr. King's location.

These reports included details of the city, address, and the layout of the buildings King visited. Conceivably this level of onsite military deployment is either defensive or offensive. Dr. King was not made aware of them, so which are they?[dclxxxviii] The Committee wondered why such information was necessary. No pondered explanation is complimentary.

## THE FEDERAL BUREAU OF INVESTIGATION

In the alleged conspiracy against President Kennedy, the Federal Bureau of Investigation falls within the Officials Arm. The Federal Bureau of

Investigation had previously operated as a flawed enforcement agency regarding the matter. However, the Bureau assumed the role of aggressive intelligence agency in this investigation. Hoover's obsession with hounding Dr. King overtook any professional objectivity.

J. Edgar Hoover conducted meetings to determine methods to hamper ongoing civil reforms. Hoover possessed multiple associations with wealthy oilman Harold Hunt. They allegedly discussed concerns about the growing Civil Rights Movement. Men who had so hated John F. Kennedy were additionally common enemies to Dr. King. They feared King's popularity, and his policies unseating Johnson as President of the United States.

Despite the near impossibility of the claim, these men seemed convinced. Hunt operated in wealthy social circles that were vulnerable to political change. Unlikely events might change government policy and Hunt could have suffered great financial losses. Being a chief supporter of President Lyndon Johnson, Hunt retained financial interest in seeing the status quo maintained.

J. Edgar Hoover might have feared a new president beyond his control would jeopardize his lifetime appointment. "Hoover said he thought a final solution was necessary. Only that action would stop King".[delxxxix] Internal Bureau documents revealed its leaders plotted King's removal from the National stage. Past Bureau actions had successfully ruined the Ku Klux Klan and Communist groups. J. Edgar Hoover decided to utilize a specific method against the Civil Rights Movement.

"COINTELPRO" was among the illegal methods Hoover used to sidestep the jurisdictions of agencies like the Justice Department. It went far beyond information gathering and investigating people to include hundreds of violations of law. Its objective was to destroy an entire organization and the lives of all connected to a targeted leader. COINTELPRO is eventually defined by the House Select Committee on Assassinations as "...never a legitimate FBI function...described in Dr. King's case as an active covert campaign intended to influence "political choices and social values." The Committee additionally states, "It must be concluded that in its COINTELPRO activities, the Bureau grossly abused and exceeded its legal authority".[dexc]

In the unofficial limbo J. Edgar Hoover had constructed no official case existed. Therefore, any individual he did not inform remained unaware of the ongoing actions. Prior Agency concerns were asserted of the Bureau, some feared it could become the American Gestapo. The Bureau once served as government agency and Hoover's personal vendetta group.

J. Edgar Hoover did everything feasible to discredit Martin Luther King. The House Select Committee on Assassinations report confirms the Bureau Director's obsession. Hoover learned nearly every personal detail and habit of Dr. King through his intensive surveillance.[dcxci] This plot against King and his cadre included sending damaging true and false information to spouses, family members, and the media.[dcxcii]

Blind prejudice and hatred motivated Hoover. Hoover secretly attempted to engineer Martin Luther King's personal downfall. Hoover wasted the Bureau's resources while actual crimes were occurring. He tracked Dr. King and monitored his legal activities. The American public funded an official's fixation on punishing a man guilty of no crime for years. Hoover attempted to suppress constitutionally protected rights of speech, expression, and assembly.

J. Edgar Hoover used COINTELPRO in attempts to "neutralize" Dr. King and the Southern Christian Leadership Conference. Hoover decided "no opportunities be overlooked for counterintelligence action." COINTELPRO expanded to forty-four Bureau offices to "prevent the rise of a messiah who could unify and electrify the militant Black Nationalist movement".[dcxciii] According to the contents of a Bureau memo, J. Edgar Hoover had assigned the COINTELPRO agenda in more than a dozen major cities.

The Memphis Federal Bureau of Investigation office joined the list in 1964.[dcxciv] The Bureau Director assigned one or more agents to setting up COINTELPRO operations. Bureau operations in Tennessee were ongoing before the violent disruption of the Memphis Sanitation Worker event. COINTELPRO was active in Memphis years prior to Dr. King's assassination.

Once the Federal Bureau of Investigation had largely dismantled the Ku Klux Klan, it turned its power on alternative organizations. This included peaceful ones like Southern Christian Leadership Conference. The evidence proves American officials were undertaking conspiracies against United States citizens. So how can people dismiss the possibility of the Bureau neglecting to reveal evidence?

Inside a memo to J. Edgar Hoover, the motivations of the Bureau's leadership concerning Dr. King are clear "...to all of us that Martin Luther King must, at some propitious point in the future, be revealed to the people of this country and to his Negro followers as being what he actually is - a fraud, demagogue and scoundrel. When the true facts concerning his activities are presented, such should be enough, if handled properly, to take him off his pedestal and to reduce him completely in influence. When this is done, and it can be and will be done, obviously much confusion will reign, particularly among the Negro people... The Negroes will be left without a national leader of sufficiently compelling personality to steer them in the proper direction."

"This is what could happen, but need not happen if the right kind of a national Negro leader could at this time be gradually developed so as to overshadow Dr. King and be in the position to assume the role of the leadership of the Negro people when King has been completely discredited. For some months I have been thinking about this matter. One day I had an opportunity to explore this from a philosophical and sociological standpoint with an acquaintance whom I have known for some years.... I asked him to give the matter some attention and if he knew any Negro of outstanding intelligence and ability to let me know and we would have a discussion. He has submitted to me the name of the above-captioned person."

"Enclosed with this memorandum is an outline of (the person's) biography which is truly remarkable for a man so young. On scanning this biography, it will be seen that (Samuel Pierce) does have all the qualifications of the kind of a Negro I have in mind to advance to positions of national leadership.... If this thing can be set up properly without the Bureau in any way becoming directly involved, I think it would be not only a great help to the FBI but would be a fine thing for the country at large. While I am not specifying at this moment, there are various ways in which the FBI could give this entire matter the proper direction and development. There are highly placed contacts of the FBI who might be very helpful to further such a step. These can be discussed in detail later when I have probed more fully into the possibilities".[dcxcv]

This memo describes a concerted Bureau effort to denigrate and replace Dr. King with a chosen representative. The Federal Bureau of Investigation leaders were making plans to cause Martin Luther King's public downfall. They attempted to place a loyal agent in the Civil Rights Movement. As the United States Congress has stated these actions were not in the Federal Bureau of Investigation's legal powers.

Bureau member William Sullivan authored a second damning letter. House Select Committee investigators obtained evidence that exposed a related despicable operation. Dr. King received a tape and letter containing threats and lethal instructions. "King, there is only one thing left for you to do. You know what it is. You have just 34 days in which to do (this exact number has been selected for a specific reason, it, has definite practical significance). You are done. There is but one way out for you. You better take it before your filthy fraudulent self is bared to the Nation".[dcxcvi]

The tape contained damaging personal information from Bureau wiretapping efforts. Using this information the Bureau's assets clearly tried to induce Dr. King to kill himself. Some messages were real and others fabricated, each designed to advance COINTELPRO. Past leaders in the Federal Bureau of Investigation wanted Dr. King dead for personal reasons. Keep that fact in mind.

The Federal Bureau of Investigation and Hoover repeatedly subjected Dr. King to constant surveillance, harassing letters, and violent intimidation. Hoover used false stories designed to damage Dr. King in the American media. Ernest Withers a longtime photographer for the SCLC was one of five paid Bureau informants present in Memphis.[dcxcvii] The Bureau investigated and tracked Ralph Abernathy, Andrew Young, and Coretta Scott King as well. This continued beyond Dr. King's assassination.

Suspicions of Dr. King's eminent danger were not paranoia. Why keep such meticulous track of Dr. King if not to protect him? Based on every Federal Bureau of Investigation statement, King was a hated and dangerous enemy. They had already recorded him in private situations. This continued harassment served only nefarious purposes.

All these statements are within the public record. Why do members of the public face contempt for the similar views? Officials reject this horrible truth in general. A majority of Americans might believe the Assassination Conspiracy occurred, but few totally understood events preceding it. Most do not have any notion of the blatant interferences plaguing King's daily life.[dcxcviii]

At what point do repeated actions become standard practice? Can all these official actions be innocent oversights and not sinister intent? Obviously despicable intent guided the entirety of COINTELPRO. According the House Select Committee on Assassinations, "In October 1962, the FBI opened its security investigation of the Southern Christian Leadership Conference and its president Dr. King."

The Bureau does not "formally" target Dr. King until March 1968.[dcxcix] Dr. King is subject to COINTELPRO long before the officially cited date. According to Bureau files, they spied on Dr. King. They sent him suicide messages and intimidated King's friends and family. The Bureau publicly assassinated King's character, and harassed him. Yet they did not "target" him until years later.

COINTELPRO repeatedly attacked organizations the Bureau considered "subversive", including Dr. King's organization. Subversives included whomever J. Edgar Hoover determined was a possible threat to national security. Under the guise of security, J. Edgar Hoover sidestepped the

American justice system. Hoover conducted illegal surveillance against Americans, including multiple United States leaders.

Powerful officials like J. Edgar Hoover violated American law for decades. Security and government policy must never become more important than legally binding guarantees of the American Constitution. How are the sacrificed rights of the individual going to provide reasonable safety? What prevents any modern high official from repeating these actions? How many generations would pass until the American public became aware of such deceptions?

Despite all pieces of supporting evidence, the Bureau ignored them. The Federal Bureau of Investigation declared a lone racist murdered Dr. King. Officially, the shot came from the second floor Boarding house above Jim's Grill. In contrast are the many pieces of evidence and testimony that conflict with this determination.

# CHAPTER 12

*"A shocking crime was committed on the unscrupulous initiative of
few individuals, with the blessing of more, and amid the passive
acquiescence of all."*

~Publius Cornelius Tacitus
Senator of the Roman Empire
*"The Murder of Galba"*

## THE ASSASSINATION CONSPIRACY

The events leading to King's assassination could have begun months or
years prior. Hoover supervised most COINTELPRO operations directly
targeting Dr. King.[dcc] Its use against the Southern Christian Leadership
Conference was ongoing. Many do not realize Dr. King had already been
in Memphis weeks before his assassination.

While there, he organized and participated in the Memphis Sanitation
Workers Strike. This is the first march Dr. King ever sponsored in which
protesters became violent. Some witnesses have alleged it resulted from
Bureau, Agency, or Memphis Police Department provocateurs. Public
suspicion is reasonable.

The failed event disturbed King. It left a doubt upon his many years of
leading successful non-violent protests. The House Select Committee on
Assassinations stated, "Dr. King was upset and deeply depressed by the
bloody march".[dcci] King would not accept this attack on the Civil Rights

Movement. His return to Memphis was easy to predict considering Martin Luther King's dedication.

The background of a particular man who attended Dr. King's events is quite interesting. Undercover Memphis Policeman Marrell McCollough was present infiltrating the Invaders, a militant black group. He was present at the previous failed march and the later assassination. McCollough was prior a military policeman.[dccii]

Someone benefited from this disruption. It facilitated an opportunity for Dr. King's assassination. The Hands of the Conspiracy had contrived a possible scheme and executed plans to kill Dr. King. Unlike other alleged conspiracies, these were not all highly practiced paramilitary groups or the Mafia. Prejudiced criminals allegedly were organizing a murderous plot.

Again, possible guilt does not rest with any whole government agency. Blame lies in the repeated actions of certain authorities. Disclosed are the series of official misdeeds and documented errors. If they would seek King's personal downfall and death, disrupting his peaceful event seems quaint. King returns to Memphis.

Dr. King and his entourage arrived in Memphis under the fear of a reported bomb threat.[dcciii] Officials contend a local newspaper article released possibly influenced King moving to the Lorraine Motel. Feasibly the article was part of ongoing COINTELPRO efforts.[dcciv] Prior to King's arrival, the Federal Bureau of Investigation illegally tapped his phone at the Lorraine Motel. Revealed were conversations in which others urged Dr. King to run for the American Presidency. King and his cadre participated in local events and returned to their rooms at the Lorraine Motel.

April 4, in the late afternoon Conference members began to reemerge. Billy Kyles summoned Dr. King to dinner by knocking on his door. Dr. King and fellow Southern Christian Leadership Conference members began congregating outside to leave. A lone shot rings out.

Marrell McCollough, undercover Memphis Police officer identifies the source of gunfire. He stated the shot came from the Brewer's Boarding house. Others also repeated this as fact. This designation matches subsequent official determinations.[dccv]

A different possible sniper's nest existed within the dense bushes behind Jim's Grill. Vegetation covered this area with bushes six to eight feet tall. A minority of eyewitnesses have alleged the shot originated from this location. These bushes do not appear in many subsequent photographs of the scene. Prior Memphis Police alteration of the bushes near Jim's Grill removed them from consideration in the ongoing inquiry.[dccvi]

Eyewitness Solomon Jones served as Dr. King's driver and was present in the Lorraine Motel courtyard during the assassination. Jones told the House Select Committee he observed movement in the bushes behind Jim's Grill. This would corroborate Lloyd Jowers final statements in court. It could explain the bushes quick removal observed by Andrew Young and others. Unfortunately, Young and three other witnesses stated no law enforcement agency present interviewed them. Eyewitness James Bevel states Memphis Police blocked the Lorraine Motel stairs and threatened to arrest them as some attempted to leave.[dccvii]

The Select Committee disregarded Jones because he failed to identify a person responsible for the movements he observed. Witnesses not supporting the official narrative seem held to greater standards, this ignores repeated official decisions based on circumstantial and inferential evidence. The House Select Committee made definitive claims based upon things that "may have" occurred. [dccviii] In some instances, the Committee resembled the Commission of old.

Officially, James Earl Ray fires the precision shot and packs up to leave. "Despite the presence of so many law enforcement officers, James Earl Ray was able to assassinate Dr. King, gather his belongings, and successfully flee the scene without being observed by a single policeman".[dccix] A dozen police were initially on the scene, not one caught a glimpse of James Earl Ray. Carrying a box with ammunition, a radio, and his rifle, no one views Ray emerge.

No member of King's party observes or reports Ray. He officially becomes invisible to more than forty people while escaping. Does Ray flee when the opportunity comes? No, he chose to waste important time leaving evidence to implicate himself. Again, we encounter the intelligent lone gunman who acted foolish.

Why be weighted down with extra possessions he would soon discard in public? Why leave a box filled with evidence on Main Street for the world to discover? How could a master of escape forget to wipe down the murder weapon? According to authorities, that is exactly what Ray did. Some contend the timing of this event remains highly questionable.

The Canipe Amusement Company was located on Main Street near the Lorraine Motel. The owner told James Earl Ray's former legal counsel Arthur Hanes, a well-dressed man dropped a package in front of the store and fled. One witness contended it all occurred ten minutes prior to Dr. King's murder.[dccx] This statement remains unverified.

While this point is interesting, a single witness cannot determine this assertion. The official timeline has Ray leaving the box at Canipe

Amusement Company following the assassination. One witness states it occurred before the assassination, a majority of testimony states it occurred after. Unless repeated evidence supports the prior claim, the original evidence is more compelling.

Most witnesses in Canipe Amusement Company reported a man in a dark suit dropped the official murder weapon and other evidence just following the assassination. This evidence connected James Earl Ray to Dr. King's assassination. However, witnesses and authorities failed to identify the individual who left it.[dccxi] A man unknown to eyewitnesses was officially determined to be James Earl Ray despite the evidence.

James Earl Ray escapes in his white Mustang. A Citizen's Band (CB) radio transmission simultaneously deceives local police. Memphis Police mistakenly followed the false transmission as it described gunshots and a high-speed chase occurring with a white Mustang. Memphis Police never identify the party responsible for broadcasting the transmission.

What are the chances a random individual chose that exact time to broadcast a false story? This individual secured James Earl Ray's escape by reporting his exact vehicle model and color. The action seems designed to confuse authorities and provide James Earl Ray an opportunity to flee.[dccxii] How lucky for Ray.

In a later stroke of official fortune, an unknown woman identified James Earl Ray's military serial number to the Federal Bureau of Investigation. Her information matches the discarded evidence on Main Street. An unknown woman, of unknown credibility, offered information including the army serial number that identified James Earl Ray as the lone gunman.[dccxiii] How lucky for officials.

## SCIENTIFIC AND LEGAL FINDINGS

At St. Joseph's Hospital, doctors were unable to revive Dr. King. Doctors inform family and local authorities of King's demise. The autopsy occurs at Gaston Hospital. Dr. Jerry T. Francisco the Shelby County medical examiner concluded a "gunshot wound to the chin and neck with a total transaction of the lower cervical and upper thoracic spinal cord and other structures of the neck."[dccxiv] Questions later rose about the conduct of the autopsy and ballistics inconsistencies.

The House Select Committee formed a panel to study the evidence. Official experts later determined Dr. Francisco neglected to conduct portions of relevant scientific inquiry in the autopsy. Many official excuses soon followed. The most ridiculous excuse is, "The panel concluded nevertheless, that the autopsy findings were generally accurate." In a legitimate inquiry, "generally accurate" information is not a reliable standard. How can general accuracy be an acceptable standard for evidence in this important case?

The original autopsy had left the bullet's path undetermined. Congressional retained expert Dr. Joseph Baden explained, "Tracing the bullet track properly at the time of the autopsy would have given additional information for the questions that might arise later."[dccxv] Similar to the Kennedy case, medical professionals again were neglecting to perform complete testing. Questions additionally extend to the possible murder weapons.

Not one but multiple rifles were tested. Strangely, James Earl Ray's fingerprints were not on every rifle attributed to him. Ray's fingerprints were on a single rifle. If Ray wiped down one firearm, it would likely be the incriminating rifle, not every other weapon. Additionally, multiple unknown fingerprints at the scene were unidentified. Officials ignored these inconsistencies. Ray is completing his transformation into the necessary lone gunman.[dccxvi dccxvii dccxviii dccxix]

The Federal Bureau of Investigation had selected the rifle with James Earl Ray's fingerprints. Now we move onto the once undetermined origins of the bullet. Various rifle ammunitions were present. Why take multiple types of rounds if James Earl Ray required a few bullets?

The Bureau insisted the King bullet would be too damaged and beyond recognition. Unofficially the origin was known a day later to the Federal Bureau of Investigation. Why did this information remain concealed for a decade?[dccxx] The bullet was a .30-caliber soft point sporting type of Remington-Peters manufacture. A box contained the ammunition James Earl Ray reportedly used, inside were four military cartridges with full metal-jackets.[dccxxi] Ray must have obtained these recently yet officials do not determine their complete origin.

Despite such meticulous cataloguing of the bullet, mutilation had occurred. The bullet failed to implicate the rifle firing it.[dccxxii] The Select Committee panel concluded the alleged murder weapon "cannot be identified or eliminated as having been fired". The weapon that killed Dr. King remains in question.[dccxxiii] The Bureau did not match the ballistics evidence to James Earl Ray. Undetermined fingerprints remained; the fingerprints and the possible unknown suspects fade away.

The Select Committee asserted of the sniper "Although the scientific evidence did not independently establish the location of the assassin..."

The United States Congress failed to establish the bathroom as the bullet's point of origin. The Committee in official but unsubstantiated style continues, "(the rifle allegedly used by Ray)…was the type that could have fired the bullet that killed Dr. King".[dccxxiv] This is true.

However, a sniper using a rifle positioned behind Jim's Grill could have killed Martin Luther King as well. Unfortunately, again, evidentiary mishandling and incomplete medical findings leave this an open question. Despite official tests, the strength of evidence did not affirm James Earl Ray's conviction. Neither do the unproven declarations of Ray's guilt suffice.

Circumstantial evidence was the majority of what officials possessed. They failed to identify the bullet. They assumed the rifle with Ray's fingerprints was the murder weapon. Anonymous informants and the supposedly drunken eyewitness were the best testimonials they had. One thing allowed James Earl Ray's legal incarceration, his own plea of guilty.

In 1998, attorney William F. Pepper launched a criminal evidentiary hearing for James Earl Ray. Pepper was seeking to retest the ballistics evidence between Ray's gun and the bullet extracted from Dr. King. Presiding Judge Joe Brown allowed the ballistics test to proceed. This could prove if the rifle matched the bullet fired. It would settle the matter scientifically and improve the legal record.

In response, the Memphis District Attorney petitioned the Court of Criminal Appeals to prevent Judge Brown's order. The test never happened. If Memphis civil leaders wanted an accurate and untainted trial, would they seek to exclude crucial evidence? Conceivably a reason to oppose testing was due to the information it could reveal. The official reason stated tests would damage evidence.

The trial ended with the Judge Joe Brown's removal for bias in favor of James Earl Ray. The case never concluded because no replacement judge is available. This seemed a permanent legal conclusion. With the criminal trial halted, the King family started a civil suit to attain justice.

In 1998, a case entered the United States Civil Court system, "King Family vs. Lloyd Jowers and other Unknown Conspirators".[dccxxv] The trial's results prove instrumental in legally asserting a conspiracy did occur. Martin Luther King's family and their attorney William F. Pepper undertook this successful trial.

A small group of the involved parties attended this momentous trial. Its results are unknown to many, yet remain on the legal record. The trial was a civil case in which official agencies subsequently were accused of complicity in the King assassination. Dr. William F. Pepper named the

Federal Bureau of Investigation and United States Military Intelligence as pivotal in the matter. Official agencies had likely ordered and concealed the matter, the court found them guilty of conspiracy. [dccxxvi]

Testimony from Lloyd Jowers supported the feasibility of a plot. Jowers admitted to prior knowledge of police absence at the scene. He testified a decoy would be used, possibly this was James Earl Ray. The Jowers interview appeared before the jury and within the legal record. [dccxxvii] The jury ultimately found Jowers partially responsible, yet it placed the majority of guilt on United States government agents.

The later retested ballistics evidence used in the House Select Committee was inconclusive. The Federal Bureau of Investigation and congressional tests were unable to determine if the designated rifle was responsible. Ultimately, circumstantial evidence placed Ray firing the shot that killed Dr. King. [dccxxviii]

The House Select Committee on Assassinations found James Earl Ray did not act alone. They found a white supremacist group in St. Louis possibly hired him to kill Dr. King. James Earl Ray allegedly receives fifty thousand dollars. The Select Committee established an assassination conspiracy. Although previously reported from major news sources it somehow remains widely unknown. Lone Gunman rumors have overshadowed the official conclusions.

A civil court decision and the American Congressional determination found evidence supporting a conspiracy. [dccxxix] This did not occur until decades later. Many still are unaware of this development. The questions of who exactly ordered and undertook the plot are unknown, but the preponderance of evidence supports its existence.


## THE ASSASSIN

Unlike the assassination of President Kennedy, prejudiced official actions surrounded Dr. King's murder. Although President Kennedy had at least some security initially, Dr. King's security vanishes before the assassination. Compounding these mistakes were the aggressive and illegal actions of the Bureau and Military Intelligence. All these factors with the assassin's intent stole the most influential black leader of the last century from America.

If James Earl Ray were the assassin, reasonably you would consider if he received assistance. Lloyd Jowers and Ray's Contact are feasible choices. If two men or more are involved, a conspiracy occurred. However, these men could not remove the bushes behind Jim's Grill or call off Dr. King's security.

These men could not send the CB transmission that disrupted Memphis Police. Neither Ray nor Jowers could assign undercover agents to observe Dr. King. Accomplices would be required. Conceivably, based on the evidence and legal proceedings, at least two men at scene were involved.

## THE CONTACT:

Jerry Ray, Raul, or an unknown American government asset

## THE POSSIBLE ASSASSIN:

A mercenary sniper, or rogue official sharpshooter were among the possible assassins

## THE OFFICIAL ASSASSIN:

James Earl Ray

# CHAPTER 13

*"Let America be the dream the dreamers dreamed, let it be that great strong land of love, Where never kings connive nor tyrants scheme, that any man be crushed by one above."*

~Langston Hughes
American Poet
*"Let America be America"*

## EXPERTS, WITNESSES, AND POSSIBLE DISINFORMATION

Protest does not exist merely for those who organize national events. It remains the obligation of Americans unfairly denied rights or justice. Despite suffering mistreatment and disdain by commentators and officials, much has resulted from American citizen determination. Authors' efforts combined with the unsung private researcher have allowed more truth to emerge. Some people endure ridicule, intimidation, and violence to see the facts exposed.

The true heir of the Civil Rights Movement was Martin Luther King's best friend, Ralph Abernathy. He shared death threats, police violence, and jail cells with Dr. King in the name of human decency. Abernathy is among the few who endured the suffering experienced by King himself. These original members of the Civil Rights Movement share the credit for major expansions in American citizen freedoms.

Abernathy led the Southern Christian Leadership Conference following Dr. King's death. He continued leading marches conducting himself according to King's doctrine of non-violent protest. He led the Southern Christian Leadership Conference for a decade, and then retired to a life of religious ministering. Abernathy was among those who believed a conspiracy occurred. He once said Dr. King's murderer was "...someone trained or hired by the FBI... under the orders from J. Edgar Hoover".[dccxxx]

Dr. King additionally considered Ambassador Andrew Young a confidant. He was a loyal friend who served in the Civil Rights Movement since 1961. Unlike others who were hot-tempered and vocally dramatic, Young is eloquent and composed in his manner. Young had joined Dr. King's protests in the dangerous Jim Crow South. Andrew Young subsequently forged ahead becoming the Mayor of Atlanta.

Later he served as the United States Ambassador to the United Nations. Representative Young was the first black congressional member from Georgia. He fulfilled achievements only imagined by former generations. His dedication and service spanned the realms of domestic and international human rights. Young is a paragon of the Civil Rights Movement.

Joseph Lowry was the Southern Christian Leadership Conference successor to Ralph Abernathy. Dr. Lowry himself had been the victim of legal and physical attacks. Dr. King chose Lowry to lead the Selma to Montgomery march. He led the Southern Christian Leadership Conference in many following years. Lowry dedicated much of his life to honoring and pursuing Dr. King's goals despite the necessary sacrifices.

Those acting in King's spirit, not claiming power in his name were his successors. They are true leaders of the Civil Rights Movement. Pretenders instead of seeking improved cultural relations, profited from cultural division. What American black leader since Dr. King ever legally accomplished progress of such historic meaning? What other leader has so enriched the lives of so many American minorities?

Martin Luther King laid down his life not for war, but peace. He did not act with pride or hatred and embraced compassion through understanding. He sought respect and a fair day's wage for all. The sacrifices of dedicated men made the path to legal equality possible. Disregarded were any who opposed the predetermined course officials had set.

James McCraw was a taxi driver and associate of Lloyd Jowers. He encountered Charles Stevens an official eyewitness who states the man fleeing "closely resembled" James Earl Ray. Stevens was according to McCraw intoxicated and lying on his bed in the Brewer Boarding house. Memphis Police Captain Tony Smith reported Stevens and his wife were "intoxicated." So how did the official eyewitness Charles Stevens become sober enough to identify James Earl Ray positively? Additionally Stevens' later accounts to investigators vary; he later files a legal claim to attain reward money for his incomplete testimony.[dccxxxi dccxxxii]

Eyewitness Grace Stevens reported she lived with Charles Stevens in the Boarding house. She asserts both of them were drinking. This casts doubt on all testimony each offers. Officials support that Stevens was able to identify a dashing man in the hallway as James Earl Ray. When dashing to the hallway Stevens observes the back of a fleeing man.

Despite allegedly being observed intoxicated by McCraw and Smith, investigators credit Mr. Stevens with a full identification. An unidentified man had reportedly carried a bundled package quickly down the hallway past Charles Stevens. Officials pursue the portions of testimony only implicating Ray. However, a different eyewitness identified someone other than James Earl Ray in the bathroom.

The House Select Committee referred to the Bureau statement of William Anschutz in determining Ray's guilt. Anschutz testified he attempted to use the bathroom from which the official shot emerged, when he found the door locked he returned to his room. He like eyewitnesses Charles Stevens observed a man run down the hallway. However, Anschutz did not identify the man as James Earl Ray.[dccxxxiii] Selective use of official testimony is not isolated to the Kennedy inquiry.

Again, note the similarity of the actions in the possible assassination conspiracies. The assassin was again purported to have been alone. Why are officials again using selected portions of testimony and not the entire record? Until the demise of many concerned the files are sealed, some remain classified.

What purpose other than to conceal uncomfortable facts would justify these repeated actions? Repeated actions usually have a goal, especially when concerning the same type of event. As some critics state, we humans are indeed pattern seeking creatures. However, this does not render all uncomfortable subjects to innocent coincidence. Some patterns emerge from reason, evidence, and fact.

## THE STRANGE BEHAVIOR OF JESSE JACKSON AND BILLY KYLES

The reverend Billy Kyles has claimed a closer relationship with Dr. King than many contemporaries substantiate. If Kyles were a close associate of Dr. King, would he not request police security to ensure Dr. King's safety? At least inform other members new security arrangements were necessary.

Instead, Kyles according to the official record dismissed the police security. The removal disregarded a previous bomb threat issued on Dr. King's arrival.

Prior to the assassination Kyles offered King, Ralph Abernathy, others, and he were inside a Lorraine Motel common room.[dccxxxiv] Dr. King and Ralph Abernathy returned to King's room, and Kyles states he entered this room as well. Memphis Police surveillance reports state Billy Kyles never entered the room. Kyles only knocked on the door to summon Dr. King to dinner and waited outside.[dccxxxv] Kyles was not alone in his mistaken statement. Jesse Jackson affirmed Kyles' statement as well.

Jackson was recently arguing with Dr. King. Eyewitnesses Marshall Frady and Andrew Young affirmed, King and Jackson had an explosive argument the day before the assassination.[dccxxxvi] Regarding Jesse Jackson and Dr. King, Ralph Abernathy stated, "Relations between them had been cool for the past few days". Just before leaving for dinner, Dr. King spoke briefly with those present from the motel balcony. Then a shot rang out.[dccxxxvii]

In a following Associated Press interview of Jesse Jackson, Samuel "Billy" Kyles again supported these recollections. They asserted Kyles spent time in King's hotel room. This contradicts other sources who reported Abernathy and King were in the room. In later interviews, Kyles briefly enters after summoning Dr. King to dinner. What seems the most probable?

Dr. King was speaking with Ralph Abernathy who aided him nationwide for years. Alternatively, King was talking with Abernathy and Billy Kyles who according to official reports never entered the room. Additionally, Jackson and Kyles were more recent and peripheral members of the Conference. The inconsistencies begin to mount as further statements from Jackson and Kyles emerge.

After the shot, Billy Kyles said look "and pointed to the Boarding house." However, remaining evidence indicates the Boarding house determination might have been incorrect. Other statements given seemed to inflate Jesse Jackson's role in historic events. Jackson theoretically could have used King's death to improve his political standing.[dccxxxviii]

In one later interview, Jesse Jackson recounts the identification of the official source of gunfire. Jackson states, "It had come from this direction, it was the only way it could have come from." Again, Jesse Jackson, like Billy Kyles, is not a firearms expert. His recounting is just a personal opinion. Other easily observable alternative points of fire did exist.[dccxxxix] Jesse Jackson later asserted Dr. King was tired and thinking of retiring from the Civil Rights Movement.[dccxl]

Dr. King occasionally had grave doubts and was in danger because of his protests and political agenda. King had lamented and considered retirement before. However, no witness or close friend of Dr. King ever said anything about him seriously considering retirement. He would not abandon the Civil Rights Movement at that critical point. Jackson's comments seem more opinion than history.

Accounts of Jesse Jackson's history and motivations are not complimentary. Under normal circumstances, the reverend title necessitates years of divinity schooling. Jackson allegedly failed out of Chicago Theological Seminary early in his attendance. Jesse Jackson was somehow still ordained two months following Dr. King's murder. "It essentially was a political ordination, he never submitted himself to the authority of the church. He has never had a church himself, and he has been accountable to no one". "When the shots rang out, he (Jesse Jackson) fled and hid behind the swimming pool area".[dccxli]

Jackson feasibly spared little time for mourning Dr. King. Jackson was busy enhancing his place in the Civil Rights Movement on the day King died. Later statements include claims of Jackson being the last to cradle Dr. King as he died.[dccxlii] Jackson and Billie Kyles were standing many feet away from King when he collapsed according to most eyewitnesses present.

Then Jackson's claim shifts to King reaching out toward him. This offers the possible insincerity attributed to Jackson by New York Mayor Ed Koch.[dccxliii] It was actually Ralph Abernathy Dr. King's best friend, who cradled King and spoke reassuringly to him. This displays Jackson's possible manipulation of a horrific event to his advantage.

Jackson had a Southern Christian Leadership Conference publicist booking him on television the day following King's murder. In these interviews, Jesse Jackson initially asserted the bullet striking Dr. King came from the left. Ironically, this indicates a shot from the bushes behind Jim's Grill to the left of King, not the Brewer's Boarding house to the right.[dccxliv] Jesse Jackson might have used a pivotal moment in American history pursuing ambitions to lead the Civil Rights Movement.

In a subsequent interview regarding the aftermath following Dr. King's assassination, Jesse Jackson states, "Yes because he (Dr. King) was lying on the floor of the balcony. I was on the ground level. He was lying there on the balcony, and I remember a Mr. Withers, a photographer, who's still alive, scooped up a jar of blood, said "Take this. This is precious." Jesse Jackson replied, "I can't touch it. It's too morbid." Blood was everywhere by that time".[dccxlv]

Now it could be Jesse Jackson has a horrible memory again. He and Billy Kyles did incorrectly recall multiple events surrounding Martin Luther King's demise. Nearly all other accounts from officials and eyewitnesses are far different. They include Jesse Jackson dipping his hands into Dr. King's blood and smearing it on his sweater. Why was it too morbid then perfectly acceptable to later touch? Perhaps later political use overcame Jackson's initial aversion.[dccxlvi]

Jackson told those present at the crime scene to follow Dr. King to the hospital. He allegedly suggested that fellow members of Dr. King's group should not speak with the media. Once they had left, Jackson began appearing in news reports telling his version of events.[dccxlvii] Jackson reportedly asserted King's entourage was gone and he required a ride from reporters. So does a friend rush with you dying to the hospital or commence speaking to reporters?

The morning following Dr. King's murder, Jackson appeared on television in Chicago, he wore the bloody sweater.[dccxlviii] An NBC press interview with Don Rose implied Jesse Jackson was the heir apparent to Dr. King. This claim relies on Dr. King's support for Jackson in leading the Civil Rights Movement after his death. According to most commenting members of King's inner circle, no one ever considered Jesse Jackson's succession.

Witness Marshall Frady asserted Jackson later used the bloody sweater to convince Chicago Mayor Daley to let him speak at a public memorial service.[dccxlix] If true, this is not a disciple's actions but those of an opportunist. Based on some witnesses Jackson possibly began manipulating events minutes after Dr. King's murder. Former New York Mayor Ed Koch later commented Jackson used Dr. King's death "in a way that was false and to feather his own nest."[dccl]

Jesse Jackson's relationship with Dr. King's coalition ends poorly. Unknown to most was Jesse Jackson's subsequent resignation from the Southern Christian Leadership Conference. Chairman Ralph Abernathy suspended Jackson for administrative impropriety and breaching organizational rules. Jackson subsequently resigned. Some alleged this resulted from Jackson misappropriating funds. Others supported Jackson despite his suspension.

Leaving in protest with Jackson was a young member of the Southern Christian Leadership Conference, Al Sharpton. Occurring less than five years later, Jackson proceeds to create Operation Push. This group eventually became the Rainbow-Push Coalition in following years. Some however remained members of the King coalition.

Jackson then unsuccessfully ran for President of the United States twice. He made claims he was handicapped by Democratic Party rules. In a previous interview with a Washington Post reporter, Jackson acted without the cultural respect he preaches. He formerly called New York City "hymie-town".[dccli] The comment was an excuse for his campaigns failure to attain local Jewish voter support.

Once the public learned of the comment, Jackson ironically claimed Jews were conspiring against him. This was despite Jackson's disbelief of any conspiracy surrounding Dr. King's assassination. His actions display a proficiency in making excuses for his political failings.[dcclii] Jackson later admitted believing the conversation was private and eventually said he was wrong for using the term.

A past description of Jackson and his other younger contemporaries by Andrew Young supports their inherent ambition "...all of them in some way, maybe subconsciously, wishing he was Martin Luther King".[dccliii] Andrew Young and Ralph Abernathy were among King's closest loyal advisers. Mutual respect and friendship were the basis of their support for Dr. King.

The ambitious men who desired to become King might eventually believe Dr. King an impediment to their advancement. A few might realize Dr. King would long control the Southern Christian Leadership Conference. Perhaps they understood King would remain the dominant leader of the Civil Rights Movement. King's murder to a few was not just tragedy but opportunity.

Jesse Jackson's wife suggested, "...we were totally dependent on Dr. King and all of a sudden...the movement was our responsibility. The children now belonged to Reverend Jackson and it was his responsibility to feed them".[dccliv] Although Brown can freely express her interpretation of events, she is wrong in nearly all respects. No one chose Jackson to lead the Civil Rights Movement. He was a feasible pretender, like Johnson before him.

In a more recent interview, Jackson defends and tries to imply Lyndon Johnson's instrumental place in history.[dcclv] Of the men involved in the Civil Rights Movement, no influence is less genuine than Johnson's was. Jackson supports Johnson despite the public knowledge of Hoover's crimes against Dr. King. Praising Johnson instead of his contemporaries is laughable. In my view, it molds Jackson into the pretender he praises.

The Reverend Ralph Abernathy, unlike Jesse Jackson, worked with Dr. King in the violent 1950s. Jackson did not work personally with Dr. King until 1965. He joined King following legal Civil Rights protections in

1964. Abernathy and Jackson's actions subsequent to King's demise might reveal their intentions.

Abernathy did not use King's death to parley advantage. He kept supporting and leading the Civil Rights Movement for legal equality. Abernathy did not ascribe King's success to himself. Jackson then quickly acquired the trappings of religious leader. Jackson for a time controlled some political power of the Civil Rights Movement in the years following Dr. King's death.

Some far exceeded Jesse Jackson in their faithful commitment to human rights. Men like Ralph Abernathy, with a respect and loyalty in keeping with Dr. King's wishes. Andrew Young additionally possessed his contemporaries respect and could have led the Movement just as competently. Jesse Jackson left King's organization, possibly using events to his political advantage. Over the years, Billie Kyles and Jesse Jackson have mixed history with speculation.

# CHAPTER 14

*"All visible objects, man, are but pasteboard masks.*
*But in each event...in the living act, the undoubted deed...there,*
*some unknown but still reasoning thing puts forth the mouldings of*
*its features from behind the unreasoning mask.*
*If man will strike, strike through the mask!"*

~Herman Melville
American Author
*"Moby Dick"*

## FINDINGS AND CONCLUSIONS

So who lurked within the shadows? Which of the Hands' leaders undertook the assassination conspiracy? They had to possess eminent influence within official circles. They required access to resources and criminal agents. These men exhibited constant hatred for Martin Luther King and feared his continued political influence. They would kill to stop the realization of universally protected citizen rights in America.

## THE CONSPIRATORS

Using available facts, the Criminal Hand's leader is undetermined. No full public disclosure of indisputable evidence has occurred. However, the lack of this person's identity does not preclude the assassination conspiracy. The House Select Committee on Assassinations previously determined a conspiracy.

Although this explanation feels deficient, take solace in the later King Family case verdict. In which a judge attributes "Unknown United States Government Agents" as being responsible. This provides continued questions but discloses the feasible origins of a violent intrigue. James Earl Ray by legal judgment and most considered evidence is a dupe. He likely was part of a conspiracy to kill Martin Luther King Jr.

The Contact, Raul might have been a false identity to conceal one of James Earl Ray's brothers. It could explain a deception to protect his family from similar prosecution. The House Select Committee found evidence possibly linking the Ray brothers to a series of bank robberies. These might have partially funded Ray's international escape. However, it could not provide the ability to execute a conspiracy as the lone gunman. If indeed a mysterious Raul existed and still lives, he never answered for his crimes.

## THE LEADERS OF THE ASSASSINATION

### THE CRIMINAL HAND:
Unknown past or present United States government agents

## THE LEADERS OF THE CONSPIRACY

### THE OFFICIALS HAND:
Lyndon Johnson

### THE MILITARY INTELLIGENCE HAND:
J. Edgar Hoover, William Sullivan

## DID THE ASSASSINATION CONSPIRACY OCCUR?

Illegal government operations surrounded Dr. King for years. These plots attempt to inspire King's suicide. This clearly provides the motive, means, and opportunity for past leaders of the Federal Bureau of Investigation. Now consider the repeated Memphis Police failures, American congressional findings, and a civil judgment. Finally consider the second unpracticed lone gunman. All this implies Martin Luther King and the related facts were victims of conspiracy.

Of all the discussed assassination conspiracies, this perhaps might be the most tragic and yet legally supported. Nothing will ever restore those lost to a sniper's bullet. Yet if they are beloved, their death can have meaning and purpose. The Kennedys had more privileged lives, Dr. King had a message and worn shoes to march in.

King had overcome much to attain his place in society. The Kennedys had a historic path to power. This does not diminish the role of the Kennedys; it further distinguishes Martin Luther King based on the adversity he overcame. In death, Dr. King earned accolades and political statements of mourning from many former public enemies. Unfortunately, it required King's demise to elicit these public statements.

Dr. King's murder sparked a huge nationwide revolt in multiple cities across the country. Rioting and looting occurred in Detroit, Chicago, Atlanta, and more than a hundred other cities. In a rare display of cultural unity, Robert Kennedy spoke to a large Indianapolis crowd. The area was not devastated by angered protesters and rioting mobs. The United States Capitol was damaged which prompted Lyndon Johnson to deploy military troops to protect the White House.

While Lyndon Johnson hid in the White House behind armed troops, Robert Kennedy walked among the American people. This is a perfect example of the difference between these men. While Lyndon Johnson called for a Great Society, Robert Kennedy attempted to create it. Kennedy like King was a political crusader, Johnson merely a craven politician.

However, following King's example we must not hate others who are resistant to social change. We ought to attempt respectfully coexisting. The injustice of Martin Luther King's demise and resulting suppression of evidence must end.[dcclvi] We cannot remain silent if true change is to come. Organized non-violent protest remains the cornerstone of political change.

As with the Kennedys, when King was struck down he became something greater. He became a dramatic American martyr for social justice. Despite any of Dr. King's personal errors, his message inspired generations of legal progress. A legal judgment and official findings support Dr. Martin Luther King died from an assassination conspiracy. With the abundance of legally supporting evidence, why do most American officials remain silent?

# RFK

# CHAPTER 15

*"...it is much safer to be feared than loved because ...love is preserved by the link of obligation which, owing to the baseness of men, is broken at every opportunity for their advantage; but fear preserves you by a dread of punishment which never fails."*

~Niccolo Machiavelli
*"The Prince"*

## REASONS FOR THE ASSASSINATION CONSPIRACY

The reasons were many and the alleged Conspirators long in waiting. Robert Kennedy had run a successful presidential campaign while a young man. He was the youngest Attorney General in United States history. Most impressively, Kennedy is an American Senator before he was forty years old. Robert Kennedy for years had attracted the notice of political adversaries.

Kennedy promoted civil rights legislation before it was politically advantageous. His quick wit, strong will, and accomplishments soon made lifelong allies. However, some believed Robert Kennedy was stubborn, intellectually vain, and relentless. This soon made Kennedy eternal foes as well.

From Lyndon Johnson to J. Edgar Hoover, the establishment in Washington D.C. did not appreciate the Kennedy family's prominence. Only John F. Kennedy could have appointed his brother with such ease and tacit public acceptance. Robert Kennedy's successful legal attacks on the

Mafia created enemies. His eventual opposition to Vietnam and later presidential campaign were a danger. A threat in my view conspirators had potentially killed for twice already.

Robert Kennedy had just won the California Primary, and it was likely he would be an unstoppable Democratic candidate. He had unified the large political coalitions that worked for President John F. Kennedy, Martin Luther King, and Labor groups. Robert Kennedy gained wisdom from his experience as Attorney General. He was President Kennedy's confidant and gained insights the executive branch rarely offered.

John F. Kennedy possessed great charm and style, Robert Kennedy was a more thoughtful and ardent individual. Yet his national initiatives helped shape the future of law enforcement. Robert Kennedy was staunchly opposed to the Mafia and their allies in the labor and financial communities. Kennedy might have been the reason Lyndon Johnson did not seek re-election.

Johnson knew the political tide was rising against him. The president viewed the public begin to embrace Robert Kennedy as they once did his brother. Johnson relented instead of facing political loss to a Kennedy campaign amidst the Vietnam War. However, Lyndon Johnson would not step aside gracefully.

Some officials hated and feared Robert Kennedy. Those fears increased when Robert Kennedy opposed the Vietnam War in his public speeches. Kennedy publicly attacked the previous actions of the Central Intelligence Agency and Federal Bureau of Investigation. These groups previously concealed facts surrounding President Kennedy's murder.

Possible Hands of the Conspiracy formed. A handful of men seemingly learned from the previous mistakes of authorities. Without dedicated people seeking evidence, much would have been lost and withheld. The Los Angeles Police Department's actions potentially would remain unknown. Left to their own devices, the Bureau and Agency would allegedly have concealed the evidence again.

The similarities among feasible conspiracies repeat as each unfolds. Once more, local authorities mismanaged and summarily destroyed evidence at the crime scene. Federal and Local government ignored the public outcry for answers. Authorities withheld a number of important documents for many years.

In reviewing the most famous assassinations in modern American history, three exist in which evidence is repeatedly lost and altered. It was twenty or more years until American leaders provided access to remaining evidence. Many surviving files are public knowledge and offer serious questions. Officials do not welcome them.

Congressional committees and legal decisions have found United States government agents or assets were involved in two of three possible conspiracies. Robert Kennedy's murder provided an opportunity for public disclosure of the facts. It could have inspired a resulting boon of citizen loyalty. Perhaps it would have revived some faith in the American government.

Some critics believe these facts and circumstances are just coincidences. They are purported to be unintentional authority errors. This was a third series of important mistakes hampering a third political assassination. Blunders made by some of the same men in just over five years. Official neglect has left many lingering questions.

Unfortunately, the official inquiry was subject to distortion and incompetence. This accompanied the destruction of evidence before Sirhan Sirhan's appeals process was complete. Eyewitnesses claim officials changed their original testimony. The race to locate a final lone gunman had commenced.


## THE HANDS OF THE CONSPIRACY

### THE CRIMINAL HAND:
A possible assassin and their accomplices

### THE OFFICIALS HAND:
Local and national leaders that sought to suppress evidence.

### THE MILITARY INTELLIGENCE HAND:
A possible rogue military trained enemy with murderous intentions.

### THE CONSPIRATORS:
The men who could have planned, funded, and executed the assassination and those who later conspired to conceal the evidence.

# CHAPTER 16

*"Crime must be concealed by crime."*

~Lucius Annaeus Seneca (Seneca the Younger)
Roman Statesman and Philosopher

## THE CRIMINAL HAND

The Criminal Hand comprises possible assassins and disinformation peddlers. This could provide the alleged Conspirators with easily discredited agents. A single criminal faced punishment for Senator Robert Kennedy's assassination, Sirhan Bishara Sirhan. Officials had chosen a final unlikely lone assassin.

Sirhan's family immigrated to America when he was a boy. His father soon left the family and returned to the Middle East. Sirhan later suffered a head trauma during his employment at a horse track. Some allege following his accident Sirhan began to show consistently irrational and suspicious behavior.

Sirhan's initial behavior in police custody was strange. Sirhan requests water. Before he will drink, he asks Sergeant Jordan of the Los Angeles Police Department to taste it first. Does Sirhan have a legitimate fear being of poisoned? Alternatively, was he delusional yet sober as the Los Angeles Police Department claims?

Sergeant Jordan said Sirhan had a "very quick mind".[dcclvii] Circumstantial evidence such as this exists in massive quantity, unlike the important

— 204 —

evidence police destroyed. These evidentiary losses made the matter nearly impossible to solve. Covering actions were possibly underway.

In Sirhan's case, the Defense and Prosecution initially assented to a plea bargain. The bargain would have prevented Sirhan from suffering the death penalty and seemed in all parties' interests. This would have included saving the taxpayers millions and would have prevented most subsequent trial inconsistencies. However, Judge Walker demanded a trial following the Oswald affair. At trial Sirhan's greatest liability was himself.

Sirhan's displayed mental changes, erratic actions, and emotional displays. He fired his attorneys without valid reasoning. Sirhan denied his own insanity plea because he refused to accept his mental deficiency. He then declared his innocence in the years following his confessed guilt.

Sirhan replaced his attorneys so often it wasted significant amounts of time. Every new attorney had to reestablish and learn the immense case file. Sirhan had many legal counsels including, A.L Wirin, Robert Kaiser, Grant Cooper, Russell Parsons, Emile Berman, Godfrey Isaac, Michael McCowan, Lawrence Teeter, and William F. Pepper. However, Grant Cooper allowed the prosecution to dominate the case in trial.

Cooper neglected to use the full evidentiary record available to him as well. The resulting proceedings display glaring official problems. One such problem was the Prosecution's assertion of Sirhan's motive. They in part relied on Robert Kennedy's speech advocating the sale of American jets to Israel. The Los Angeles District Attorney used this reasoning for Sirhan's attack.

Prosecutors connect Sirhan's notebook to the speech and initially it seems reasonable evidence. Until the date of the notebook page cited as May 18. This was two days before the speech appeared in television broadcasts. It was eight days prior to Robert Kennedy giving a notable public speech directly supporting Israel. In this later event, Senator Kennedy supported providing aircraft to the Israelis.[dcclviii] Sirhan could not see in to the future, this renders the official reasoning suspect.

Officials stated Middle East loyalties were the reasoning for Sirhan's attack on Robert Kennedy. Sirhan was not Muslim but Greek Orthodox Christian. Christian missionaries brought Sirhan to America. Sirhan was a young child with no real memories of Jordan. Prosecutors declared he was killing in the name of a homeland Sirhan failed to remember. He had no religious claim in the fight.

Sirhan following a head injury became engrossed in "the occult and metaphysical"[dcclix]; he read books on mind control and developing supernatural powers. Authorities themselves reported Sirhan researching the occult, not being an ardent Islamic militant. He is not a Palestinian supporter who attended meetings, but a Mystical Order of Rosicrucian member. He was a native of Jordan with no actual interest in the country.

No extensive library of pro-Jordanian or Palestinian literature was in Sirhan's house. Sirhan did not belong to any militant group and did not attend a Mosque. Prosecutors implied a Palestinian motive from a few unconfirmed college meetings. Allegedly, Sirhan belonged to an "informal chapter" of the Organization of Arab Students. The Bureau still pursued this lead despite the formal organization announcing there was no local chapter. The Organization of Arab Students affirmed Sirhan was not a member at Pasadena College.[dcclx]

Despite these facts, some continue to classify Sirhan a terrorist or Communist. An individual who formerly employed Sirhan reported he possessed anti-Semitic beliefs. His past employer noted he was "a good worker and honest man." The employer also stated, "But he had a lot of complexities, mainly related to Israel. He resented the State of Israel."

His statement appeared in a news article titled "Suspect Hate for Israel Told." The story quickly emerges the day following Robert Kennedy's demise. Unnamed acquaintances claim Sirhan to be a "virulent anti Semite." In my view, it was premature to make an informed statement. Who are these acquaintances?[dcclxi] Without any clear evidence of loyalties to Arab or Muslim interests, Sirhan undertook the attack on Robert Kennedy. Yet Grant Cooper does not raise these issues in Sirhan's defense.

Cooper's trial behavior was far too passive for a seasoned advocate. When Grant Cooper called witnesses at trial, he missed opportunities to introduce vital evidence. He instead allowed politically motivated advisers to influence his defense. Sirhan's original defense was not political but mental deficiency. Cooper failed to challenge police evidence and concentrated upon harder proven psychological motivations.[dcclxii]

The later trial exposed flaws in Grant Cooper's explanation to the court. Responding to a witness, Cooper offered Sirhan was not psychotic, but a borderline paranoid schizophrenic. Scientific jargon did not aid Sirhan's case or prove mental deficiency claims. [dcclxiii] Cooper's defense tactics had little chance of success.

Cooper's past legal career was more relevant than some imagine. Most attorneys might use courtroom inexperience or lack of education to excuse themselves, Cooper was able to claim neither. Grant Cooper was at one time president and founding member of the American College of Trial Lawyers. Cooper also served as the California State Bar vice president and Chief Deputy District Attorney of Los Angeles County. [dcclxiv]

Cooper is among the most experienced trial attorneys in Los Angeles. So why did he use an unpersuasive defense? Did Grant Cooper intentionally bungle Sirhan's trial? Some did not regard Cooper's own pending judgment for contempt in a separate case. Cooper faced sentencing regarding perjury and receiving stolen grand jury transcripts. If Cooper made Sirhan's trial difficult for prosecutors, prosecutors could make Cooper's sentencing difficult as well.

Why did Cooper later disregard the ballistics analysis expert William Harper offered? Why did he not pursue every avenue to build a defense? Why did Cooper summarily agree to most Prosecution assertions? Grant Cooper rested his client's life on theoretical leniency for unpersuasive arguments.

Cooper allowed defense mental health advisers to meet repeatedly with the prosecution's mental health expert. This made the prosecution aware of many ideas and strategies the defense would later use in Court. It provided information to counter many witness and expert testimonies the defense might use. The Prosecution received certain advantages.

Prosecution witness Dr. Seymour Pollack reversed his stance during the course of these meetings.[dcclxv] Pollack asserted Sirhan was pretending not to remember critical periods during the crime.[dcclxvi] Pollack additionally testified to the Court "I don't believe Sirhan expected to be caught".[dcclxvii] In my view, Dr. Pollack should have considered the facts.

Sirhan was five feet four inches, weighing less than one hundred and thirty pounds. How could Sirhan not be delusional and psychotic if Pollack's assertion was correct? How could Sirhan not have been caught? A huge contingent of Los Angeles Police surrounded the building. Volunteer bodyguards such as Olympian Rafer Johnson and NFL player Roosevelt Grier are in the same room. Dozens of Kennedy campaign staff filled the area.

Kennedy supporters occupied the Ambassador Hotel, so where exactly was Sirhan Sirhan going? Only the greatest of fools could imagine they would escape. He could not overpower a single individual let alone a bodyguard in the Kennedy cadre. If Sirhan had a "quick mind" according to Los Angeles Police following the attack, how could he be so incompetent?

Some conspiracy advocates have speculated regarding possible hypnotism and mental control of Sirhan Sirhan. These ideas are not required to prove a plot. Sirhan for unknown reasons chose belatedly to embrace political motivation. While on the witness stand, Sirhan admitted to nearly whatever the Prosecution had alleged. In one exchange when being asked if he shot

Paul Schrade, Sirhan responded, "If that's what the indictment reads, I must have".[dcclxviii]

Sirhan makes perhaps the most foolish declaration a defendant could. He seemed to embrace his guilt as destiny. The most ridiculous claim Sirhan offered in court was killing "Robert Kennedy willfully, premeditatedly and with 20 years of malice aforethought..." The problem is Sirhan's age. Sirhan was in his early twenties rendering this an impossible statement.

This would mean Sirhan was plotting the murder since he was four. According to Sirhan as a boy in Jordan, he planned and waited decades to assassinate Robert Kennedy. His claim is ridiculous.[dcclxix] It demonstrates his likely incompetence and the judge disallowed Sirhan's impossible claim. This fantasy remains on the record amidst many official errors.

The word impossible is not sufficient. Sirhan could not conspire before he could attend primary school. Sirhan's obviously false claim supports his mental deficiency in accounting for his actual motivations or simple deception. Presently Sirhan claims to be a dupe. Unlike Lee Harvey Oswald, multiple consistent eyewitnesses actually observed Sirhan fire a gun.

Cooper subsequently let "slip" to the Los Angeles District Attorney's office Sirhan had practiced shooting three times.[dcclxx] It led authorities to finding the gun ranges. Eventually authorities collected this ballistics evidence and used the information legally. The practice further implicated Sirhan Sirhan in premeditating Robert Kennedy's murder.

Grant Cooper shared evidence with officials. This friendly attitude was not the policy of the Los Angeles District Attorney's office. Cooper in my view aimed to please. A Federal Bureau of Investigation Airtel message clearly states "...it was stated intention of the DA's Office to refuse to make available to Cooper those items requested". "Deputy Los Angeles County District Attorney John Howard, however, advised that in all probability Superior Court Judge Herbert V. Walker would order those items be made available to Cooper".[dcclxxi] The District Attorney's Office refused to return Cooper's professional courtesy without a court order.

Additionally, officials did not consider Sirhan's firing position feasibly prevents him from the killing shots. His wildly fired shots made wounds inconsistent with most eyewitnesses' testimony. Sirhan could not possess foreknowledge of schedules, security errors, and operate without some aid or direction. The location chosen for the attack on Robert Kennedy fails to support Sirhan's alleged terrorist background.

Why did Sirhan not linger where Senator Kennedy was to meet the news media? He would have a room full of reporters to witness the crime. It would seem the ideal location to publicize the Jordanian cause. This is one of the multiple contradictions in Sirhan's later story. Sirhan did attempt to assassinate the Senator. Yet substantial evidence suggests Sirhan did not fire the shots killing Robert Kennedy.

Sirhan ambushed and shot at Robert Kennedy without a proven motive. From the beginning, various American leaders had determined Sirhan's guilt. They did so without complete evidence. Similar to Lee Harvey Oswald, Sirhan was a man with possible mental and emotional problems. Unlike Oswald and James Earl Ray, Sirhan had no military training.

Some evidence suggests a few leaders and officers of the Los Angeles Police Department had preconceived ideas. When normal dismissive procedures failed, dissenting voices politically were condemned. Critics of conspiracy staunchly affirm the Los Angeles Police Department and Federal agents employed sufficient methods. They do not consider the entire record.

The facts are Sirhan fired his gun, eight shots at maximum. The bullets from the gun struck six victims, some more than once, and were a possible distraction. Allegedly, it allowed the assassination of Robert Kennedy to occur. From audio, forensic and photographic evidence complied with eyewitness testimony; the bullet count may exceed eight.[dcclxxii]

Speculation at trial creates motivation for Sirhan. These were not the extensive public acts of the alleged Communist lone gunman Oswald. Sirhan failed to have the extensive criminal background and intelligence attributed to James Earl Ray. He was just an unsuccessful gambler and practitioner of ridiculous metaphysical ideas.

Political assassination does not explain Sirhan Sirhan's true motivation in the murder of Senator Kennedy. Similar to Lee Harvey Oswald, Sirhan craved attention. Each man seemingly offered himself to serve a conspiracy. Sirhan's foolish beliefs and poor advice from earlier legal advisers condemned him. After his guilty plea, his legal fate was sealed.

Prosecutors were again endeavoring to construct a dangerous criminal and had a poor subject to mold. The improbable official story has always maintained a single mindedness despite the opposing facts. The lone gunman in this case, did not exhibit any notable militant or criminal actions. Sirhan's own legal counsel would later assert doubt.

Grant Cooper post trial is baffled "I never dreamed that anybody else fired a shot".[dcclxxiii] This displays a naïve trust or possible incompetence. It could have been Cooper's intent to ignore the apparent flaws in the Prosecution's case against Sirhan Sirhan. Perhaps he wanted to secure a light judgment for his personal trial.

The professional links among the men in the Courtroom are notable. Grant Cooper had served as Chief Deputy Assistant District Attorney of Los Angeles County. The judge of Sirhan's case, Herbert V. Walker, was a past assistant Los Angeles District Attorney.[dcclxxiv] In a true coincidence, then Governor Earl Warren appointed Walker.[dcclxxv]

However, in Sirhan's case the judge, defense attorney, and prosecuting District Attorney Evelle Younger were present or previous District Attorney's office members. All these men had intimate knowledge of tactics. Cooper had possible former contacts, loyalties, and tried to please officials. Possessing these insights, how did Cooper not perform better for his client? Although this does not prove Cooper intentionally lost the trial, it does reveal possible conflicts of interest.

Unfortunately, Cooper's bungling was akin to the earlier attorneys of James Earl Ray, possible incompetence with intent. How many other trials did he conduct without utilizing the complete evidentiary record and expert testimony? Why could he not dispel the prosecutions obviously deficient claims? Had Grant Cooper defended a client while under a personal litigation at other times in his career?

Cooper had prior represented Maurice Friedman in the Friars Club trial for gambling impropriety. Cooper stated, "He and other defense lawyers would seek acquittal, new trials, and arrest of judgment on the day of sentencing."[dcclxxvi] This commitment to his client is seemingly absent from Sirhan's trial. Some allege Friedman's co-defendant Johnny Roselli possibly planted the evidence that incriminated Grant Cooper. Roselli's professed connections to the Agency could support this idea.

Once Sirhan Sirhan's trial concluded, Cooper faced his pending sentencing for use of illegally obtained documents. He could have faced a harsh financial penalty and time in prison; Cooper instead pays a thousand dollar fine. Although Grant Cooper's reputation was tarnished, Evelle Younger's reputation was gleaming from Sirhan's conviction. Younger became California's Attorney General in 1970.

Before Sirhan's use of legal appeal was complete, Los Angeles Police destroy evidence. Grant Cooper and the Los Angeles District Attorney never used much of this physical evidence at trial. It could have answered remaining substantial questions. Why did the Los Angeles Police attack the evidentiary record?

Sirhan Sirhan remains in prison many decades later. Some people in America have murdered, raped, and perpetrated horrific acts of mayhem. Many of these convicts have served lesser sentences. Although Sirhan's crime was substantial, Americans supposedly are equal under the law. If the United States aspires for equality, no life is of greater importance than others are. No individual ought to be condemned without a fair and accurate trial.

Despite official actions, other evidence supports a possible second gun. A recording by foreign correspondent Stanislav Pruzinsky captured audio of the attack. Pruzinsky who was in the pantry at the Ambassador Hotel inadvertently taped the assassination. Authorities determined the recording to contain eight shots.

Several reviews of the tape revealed striking insights to modern audio professionals. Forensic audio expert Philip Van Praag determined 13 shots occur from the front and back of Robert F. Kennedy.[dcclxxvii] Audio expert Robert Joiling additionally confirmed hearing more than eight shots on the Pruzinsky tape.[dcclxxviii] The possible extra shots themselves would implicate a second gun present. Additionally, double shots occurred nearly simultaneously. These shots could have been imperceptible on older equipment used in the tape's initial review.

The original tape was lost, however a later copied version survived. Unlike the Zapruder film, this copy had always remained in official hands. Until 2004, it rested in the California State Archives. Researchers found the recording and had a full review conducted by experts. The tape has been determined authentic.[dcclxxix]

Some experts state more shots occurred than Sirhan's gun could fire. A majority of witnesses additionally place Sirhan at three feet or more from Robert Kennedy. Sirhan according to most witnesses is located in front of Robert Kennedy. The scientific evidence places the assassin behind Robert Kennedy. This requires a second assassin and weapon.

The ballistics and surviving physical evidence form a conclusion unlike subsequent official claims. A majority of eyewitness testimony fails to support the findings of the United States government. Sirhan Sirhan did fire a majority of the shots in the Ambassador Hotel pantry. Yet evidentiary reviews and experts found they were not the shots killing Robert Kennedy.

Sirhan was possibly a mentally unstable man used as a dupe. He later accepted notoriety and his behavior changed to suit. Sirhan might not be guilty of murder despite the protest of critics. Sirhan is guilty of multiple counts of attempted murder. Yet he may be innocent of the crime that earned him infamy.

## POLKA DOTS, DISINFORMATION, AND THE OTHER GUN

Here again the case becomes a distractive mess. Conspiracy advocates and critics have debated the Girl in the Polka dot dress since the murder of Senator Kennedy. The American government contends it was Valerie Schulte. Alternatively, was she a girl with dark hair in a white dress with dark polka dots? Witnesses viewed her standing near Sirhan Sirhan allegedly. According to the account of witness Sandra Serrano, the girl escaped declaring, "we shot him!" Serrano testified to the story, recanted, and then reaffirmed her original statement.

Thankfully, it is unnecessary to untangle this mystery to solve the case. Like the matter of Sirhan Sirhan's possible mental programming, this debate shifts focus from the facts as they stand. Any Polka Dot dressed woman does not prove a conspiracy. Other strange and identified participants support nefarious possibilities. Among the figures seen near the crime scene was Eugene "Jim" Brading.

The Los Angeles Police Department question Brading regarding his presence near Robert Kennedy's assassination. Brading was additionally in the Daltex building around the time of the John F Kennedy's murder. Now he appears in Los Angles the night of Robert Kennedy's assassination. This possible disinformation agent might have provided his services for two operations.

A few have alleged Jimmy Hoffa ordered the death of Robert Kennedy. The Select Committee found Hoffa and one Teamster subordinate did "…discuss the planning of an assassination conspiracy against President Kennedy's brother, Attorney General Robert Kennedy, in July or August of 1962". [dcclxxx] Yet Hoffa's weakened power failed to prevent his jailing in 1968. Why undertake a dangerous mission employed by an incarcerated man of reduced influence? Perhaps authorities had made additional mistakes.

During Robert Kennedy's assassination, more than seventy people were crammed in the kitchen pantry of the Ambassador Hotel. After flashes and sounds of gunfire fill the air, trapped witnesses panic. Some were scrambling to and from the scene. This chaotic tableau has fueled many possible theories. Some accuse previous suspects from other Assassination Conspiracies.

Unconsidered for years by authorities was security guard Thane Cesar. Ace Security business records list him as a temporary employee. Investigators affirmed Cesar did not perform an assignment for Ace Security for "months and months…" He replaced a different guard at the last minute. In Mexico, Cesar was imprisoned repeated times according to private investigator Alex Bottus and author David Schiem. Cesar also might have possessed links to the Mafia.[dcclxxxi]

According to the official record, Sirhan Sirhan was armed and fired eight times. A single other man was seen with a gun drawn. He was the only security presence in the room during the attack. Two armed men were in the Pantry according to witnesses and officials. These men were Sirhan Sirhan and Thane Eugene Cesar.

# CHAPTER 17

*"The thing which amazes me is that I know perfectly well, as a
historian, that there is corruption in any government...there's
always corruption..."*

~Michel Brunet
Canadian Historian.

## THE OFFICIALS HAND

The hatred between Robert Kennedy and Lyndon Johnson had begun years
earlier. It was born when Robert Kennedy first spent private time with him.
Kennedy went to Lyndon Johnson's Texas ranch to weigh Johnson's political
intentions in 1959. It was the first of many following mutual deceptions.

At the meeting, Lyndon Johnson made three verbal agreements to Robert
Kennedy. The first was a promise he would not seek the Democratic
nomination in 1960. Johnson offered no interference in Kennedy attempts
for the American Presidency. Finally, he would stop the repeated nomination
of Adlai Stevenson. Johnson eventually broke all these promises.

While staying at the ranch, Johnson insisted Robert Kennedy and he go
hunting. While they hunted, the recoil from a gun threw Robert Kennedy to
the ground. Johnson commented, "Son, you've got to learn to handle a gun
like a man".[dcclxxxii] Unspoken rivalry and shared dislike slowly developed
into apparent hatred. Contemptuous disregard between the men increased
as their political futures entwined.

Many earlier Johnson camp accusations regarding the Kennedys were utter lies. A Johnson aide proposed one such claim to journalist Theodore White: "I think you should know that John and Bobby Kennedy are fags." "We have pictures of John Kennedy and Bobby Kennedy in women's dresses at Las Vegas this spring at a big fag party. This should be made public."[dcclxxxiii] Despite the Johnson worker's report, no pictures emerge. The entire story was a fabrication.

John Kennedy's wife and feasible girlfriends[dcclxxxiv] and Robert Kennedy's eleven children disprove this claim. These were attempts at using rumors to influence policy. Similar rumors had previously weakened the candidacy of Adlai Stevenson. Yet similar allegations regarding Johnson's Special Assistant Walter Jenkins were not mere innuendo.[dcclxxxv] The Kennedys however gave Johnson several reasons to dislike them. Such an instance occurred when Johnson accepted the Vice Presidency, at the Democratic Convention in 1960.

When the Kennedy brothers added Johnson to their political slate, internal tensions worsened. Speculation about this decision asserts that J. Edgar Hoover provided damaging information to Johnson and his benefactor Clint Murchison. Despite these unproven claims, the Kennedys required Johnson to carry the South and his power to influence delegates.[dcclxxxvi] Johnson seemed the perfect candidate in theory to complement the Kennedy campaign.

Both camps would soon regret their political choices. The Kennedys observed the chaos on the convention floor resulting from the Johnson selection. Kennedy and Johnson supporters felt betrayed by their respective candidate's decision. This resulted in near physical altercations in the roaring Democratic crowd. The Kennedys faltered in the choice and began to reconsider.

It was then John and Robert Kennedy decided, "The problem was, if it wasn't a good idea, how you'd get him (Johnson) out of it. Secondly if you did get him out of it, how bitter would he be?"[dcclxxxvii] What followed were meetings, phone calls, and hand wringing tension. Each side grew hostile as the continued meetings and non-committal statements occurred. Time began to run out for them.

Finally, as their supporters began to revolt for the decision, Johnson and the Kennedys in desperation settled on political compromise. Emerging as a united coalition, they joined seemingly bitter rivals in a single ticket. This was just the beginning of the long poisoned relationship between Lyndon Johnson and Robert Kennedy. As time passed, it grew more strained from continued loathing.

"Bobby, you don't like me." "Your brother likes me. Your sister in law likes me. Your daddy likes me. But you don't like me. Now, why?" Lyndon Johnson asked and Robert Kennedy gave no reply.[dcclxxxviii] The Kennedys kept Johnson politically leashed and denied his attempts to strengthen vice presidential powers. Allegedly, the Kennedys might have taken credit for the support Johnson had produced to win the election.

Robert Kennedy took no pains to avoid privately criticizing and demeaning Johnson to others. His own friends had presented him with a Lyndon Johnson voodoo doll.[dcclxxxix] Johnson sought to serve elsewhere and began an international vice presidential touring campaign. When John F. Kennedy died, the feud became more personal between Robert Kennedy and Lyndon Johnson.

Robert Kennedy had a serious dislike for Lyndon Johnson. This extended the rift between the two men. Continued years of enmity only deepened the hatred they shared. President Kennedy's death forever altered the Attorney General.

Bobby Kennedy was a ruthless campaign manager, and Ivy League attorney who supported the Central Intelligence Agency. Tragedy starkly influenced him. From grief, he emerged a high-minded senator, embracing the poor and disadvantaged with Martin Luther King. Robert Kennedy spoke out against the ever-accelerating and unpopular Vietnam War.

Kennedy redoubles his support for additional civil reforms in the United States Senate. Robert Kennedy supported minority wage increases and increased safety measures for immigrant labor. Kennedy became the established political order's most eminent outspoken enemy. He was a threat, just as his brother John F. Kennedy had been.

Some however rightly feared for Robert Kennedy's life when he became a presidential candidate, among them was Jacqueline Kennedy Onassis. She said to biographer Arthur Schlesinger Jr. she feared, "the same thing that happened to Jack" would happen to his brother. Jacqueline observed, "There is so much hatred in this country, and more people hate Bobby than hated Jack".[dccxc] Yet President Johnson's concerns were not for, but about Robert Kennedy. Official reports subsequently questioned if Robert Kennedy ordered a Justice Department Investigation of a Johnson retainer.

Bobby Baker was a close Johnson political connection; an inquiry focusing on him could expose unpleasant secrets. However, conflicting subsequent reports on this matter emerged. Johnson Attorney General Ramsey Clark said he could find no evidence Robert Kennedy had the investigation launched. Hoover and the Federal Bureau of Investigation informed President Johnson that Robert Kennedy "was behind the Baker investigation".[dccxci]

Hoover marked Robert Kennedy as Johnson's most dangerous enemy with this assigned guilt. Johnson as president then investigated the former attorney general's actions raising continued questions. The later investigation required a district judge's involvement. The judge ordered the Bureau to produce raw files concerning the matter. The information revealed is shocking.

"What is surprising is this is the first time in history the Justice Department has ever seen an FBI raw file. It is an amazing document, containing all sorts of innuendo, rumor, and undigested fact." The Federal Bureau of Investigation was apparently as secretive as the Central Intelligence Agency with its files. This policy included coworkers, and their superiors in the Department of Justice. "...the fact that Justice Department officials had never before seen a raw FBI file gives some indication of the power accumulated by the FBI...The power to inform, the power to eavesdrop, and the power to operate without having funds double-checked by any other government agency can become dangerous".[dccxcii]

Attorney General Ramsey Clark requested J. Edgar Hoover to provide a list of all cases using illegally acquired evidence. In response J. Edgar Hoover, Clark's subordinate employee, refused this order. Hoover never personally maintained the legal standards he required of citizens.[dccxciii] His self-righteous image seemed eternal, while Robert Kennedy evolved from the painful events in his life.

A previous Bureau leak offered inconclusive derogatory information about Paul Corbin, a former Kennedy adviser during the 1960 presidential election. The allegations sought to mark Corbin as a Communist and damage Robert Kennedy's future political aspirations. Historian Arthur Schlesinger commented, "Hoover hated Robert Kennedy and Johnson was delighted to get the information."[dccxciv]

When Robert Kennedy subsequently left the Johnson administration, the pretense of Democratic unity was shattered. This longtime rivalry and bitterness strained Democratic Party morale. Robert Kennedy then became senator of New York, and spoke of not pursuing the American Presidency. However, in 1967 his anti-war position directly opposed Johnson administration policies.

Robert Kennedy's policies about Vietnam and economic equality, took on greater meaning with Martin Luther King's death. Robert Kennedy as Attorney General allowed the Federal Bureau of Investigation to monitor Dr. King. Despite this action, Robert Kennedy was unaware of J. Edgar

Hoover's long-standing illegal tactics and prejudice. Consider Kennedy himself was a target of similar plots. The demise of his brother spurred internal change and the assassination of Dr. King completed it.

Some critics stated Robert Kennedy's actions were political opportunism; yet no famous critic joined Kennedy amidst the hostile crowds. No critic sought to speak for the disenfranchisement of many Americans. Men of wealth and position do not often act counter to personal interest. Robert Kennedy became the last powerful Democratic political voice of his generation. Few influential political voices spoke for a peaceful solution to Vietnam.

Kennedy embraced the Anti-War Movement. This initiated two reactions, the end of Lyndon Johnson's political career and enabled additional support for the Anti-War movement. The feud between President Johnson and Senator Kennedy lasted beyond Robert's demise. The Kennedy family requested the Senator receive a grave next to his brother's within Arlington National Cemetery. Then something happened, the Johnson administration ignored affirming the honor.

It was not until Richard Nixon's administration this request was granted. Despite Robert Kennedy's murder, although Johnson remained the president, Big Lyndon could never relent against a personal enemy.[dccxcv] President Johnson was not the only highly placed enemy Robert Kennedy had. The man who knew Johnson's secrets again posed a serious threat.


## CONCEALED MOTIVES

The Federal Bureau of Investigation publicly asserted it had no opinion and was not investigating Robert Kennedy's murder. Thousands of files regarding KENSALT a Bureau codename for the investigation prove otherwise. Los Angeles Police consulted the Bureau to obtain independent ballistics testing. This might have prevented many later questions plaguing Robert Kennedy's assassination.

Referring to standing policies the Bureau responded, "Advise appropriate authorities that the Bureau will not re-examine the KENSALT firearms evidence." Hoover failed to aid investigators with a technologically advanced and well-funded laboratory.[dccxcvi] Why did they not assist the Los Angeles Police? What purpose did it serve?

The Bureau had aided the Los Angeles Police Department before in the case. Hoover allowed the use of the Bureau laboratory to analyze documents and handwriting with connections to Sirhan Sirhan. A former

letter appears supportive and agreeable, which is the opposite of Bureau's actions concerning later evidence. The Bureau had foreshadowed its motives in a document sent to District Attorney Younger.

The memo states: "Please be assured of our desire to be of assistance to you in all matters of mutual interest".[dccxcvii] The Bureau aided the Los Angeles Police in some respects. It just would not study what remained of ballistics evidence once Police Criminologist DeWayne Wolfer had "examined" it. Hoover might be aware of Wolfer's sloppy reputation.

It was not of "mutual interest" to aid the Los Angeles Police Department in this area so the Bureau did not study ballistics evidence.[dccxcviii] Consider the gaffes of the previous Oswald case. These errors publicly and permanently damaged Hoover and the Bureau's reputation. However, the professed non-involvement of the Bureau was an illusion in most cases.

Privately the Bureau and J. Edgar Hoover were quite interested in other facets of the case including the autopsy. They had requested advanced reports and every photograph taken of Robert Kennedy's corpse. This included pictures not used in the official report. Despite the possible implications, Hoover's unhealthy Kennedy obsession continued.

Commander Charles J Stahl "…and two other doctors were sent from Washington D.C. to assist in the Robert F. Kennedy matter." These men were part of the armed forces subject to orders from President Lyndon B. Johnson. However, Commander Stahl displayed rare courage and integrity. He attempted to deny the Bureau every autopsy photograph. Commander Stahl feasibly might have realized a few circumstances.

For what purpose was additional nonmedical inquiry necessary? If the Bureau desired multiple copies of these photographs, it might have been for unofficial and illegal use. Conceivably, by Hoover or his subordinates. Stahl is a doctor protecting the interests and medical information of his patient.

Stahl was "…informed that the order still stood as originally given, that the FBI desired six copies of all the photographs taken at the time of the autopsy".[dccxcix] The key word is order. Someone in the chain of command forced American troops to provide the Bureau and Hoover with private information they had no right to. Where is the past official regard for the Kennedy family's rights to privacy?

The Federal Bureau of Investigation was deceiving the public and conducting an investigation. If the Bureau failed to aid the Los Angeles Police in ballistics inquiries, why did it want to examine wounds shown in the autopsy? What other purpose would this morbid evidence serve? Why did J. Edgar Hoover demand to review any information if not to help solve the investigation?

Perhaps if superior investigators with modern scientific equipment studied the evidence, it would lead to disturbing questions. In the months following Sirhan's incarceration, unknown people kept sending incriminating "Communist" messages and threats. These plausibly served no purpose than to add more disinformation. They fed the already unfounded Communist scenario some American leaders sought to prove.

However, the evidence would many years later support a plot. The Federal Bureau of Investigation originally acquired a tape recording of the attack. Having reviewed the tape, the Bureau laboratory officials determined "it does not appear that anything pertinent to this investigation is contained on the recording." It might be the Bureau was just a victim of the age, we are fortunate modern technology has allowed further review.[dccc]

## CONFLICTED INTERESTS

J. Edgar Hoover, who initiated countless draconian actions, had produced copious files on the private activities of many famous and influential people. An unnamed Bureau official viewing them called these sensitive files "Twelve drawers full of political cancer".[dccci] Hoover's dislike of the Kennedys is legendary. Yet he possessed considerable hatred for Robert Kennedy himself.

The relationship began with a man thirty years younger tasking Hoover with assignments. Director Hoover enjoyed a relatively free reign for decades and several American Presidential administrations. While Hoover had constructed the Federal Bureau of Investigation, Robert Kennedy attended school. When Hoover launched secret investigations, Robert Kennedy studied at college.

Conceivably the age difference was insurmountable between the men. Instead of attempting to reason and deal with his new boss, Hoover continued his secret actions heedless to the law. Hoover demanded increasing surveillance on Robert Kennedy. These orders did not serve a security purpose and were for personal reasons.

Attorney General, Robert Kennedy attempted to curb J. Edgar Hoover's abuses of power and control him. A definite mistrust soon followed. Hoover's most loyal disciple hated Robert Kennedy as well. His right hand was Assistant Director of the Federal Bureau of Investigation Clyde Tolson. Tolson allegedly referenced Senator Kennedy stating, "I hope that someone shoots and kills the son of a bitch..."[dcccii] Tolson mirrored J. Edgar Hoover's attitude regarding the Kennedys and everything in general.

Tolson was Hoover's ultimate supporter. He acted blindly while aiding illegal endeavors. Programs like COINTELPRO served Hoover's agenda but violated citizen rights granted by the American Constitution. Bureau agents constructed a list of eminent Mafia leaders in previous years. The list in Hoover's opinion was "baloney".[dccciii] The list reemerged to members of the Kennedy Justice Department. Robert Kennedy began focusing on the Mafia in earnest.

Robert Kennedy's actions to reform the Justice Department began the war on organized crime. This war threatened J. Edgar Hoover's interests.[dccciv] Kennedy had quick success in fighting a criminal group Hoover maintained did not exist. These actions diminished Hoover's stranglehold on criminal prosecutions and repeatedly exposed the Bureau's incompetence.

Hoover's long denial of the Organized Crime cartels harmed the Bureau's public creditability. Hoover over decades enriched the Federal Bureau of Investigation with immense political influence and funding. Robert Kennedy was able to endow the Justice Department with extra staff and funding immediately. Justice Department investigators became the prominent force combating the Mafia. The mutual disrespect grew with each passing year and successful prosecution.

J. Edgar Hoover and Clyde Tolson used any opportunity to track the Kennedy administration. When Robert Kennedy grew in public eminence, Hoover received added reports from Bureau agents. One report detailed Robert Kennedy's vacation habits. It also listed his guests on vacation, and details why they attended.

Hoover followed the Attorney General's movements nationwide. Kennedy's detailed travels appear in miscellaneous information reports. Agents sent these reports from various cities across the nation. The reports carried details on Robert Kennedy's future private arrangements.[dcccv] One Bureau agent at the scene mentioned Robert Kennedy is misusing the Forestry Service. The agent reported Kennedy was using government employees for personal reasons at their department's expense.

This criticism was interesting because Hoover sent out paid Bureau agents to spy on the Attorney General. These were not the alleged mistakes of previous conspiracies. It was calculated, patient, allegedly illegal surveillance. This establishes Hoover's private disregard for the law when it suited his purposes.[dcccvi]

The Federal Bureau of Investigation additionally reviewed most articles concerning Robert Kennedy from major news sources. Bureau informants were sending Hoover private American congressional subcommittee reports. In one instance, Hoover's interest concerned a legal provision that might have affected Bureau appropriations. Hoover spoke of law and order while continually manipulating other government leaders.[dcccvii]

Many repeated actions demonstrate Hoover's paranoia concerning Robert Kennedy. A detailed report of a television interview with Robert Kennedy was among the memos received. It states the interview was "monitored by a Special Agent of the Crime Research Section." Again, Hoover used the Federal government's resources in his personal vendetta. For someone who claimed no Mafia existed, Hoover knew its tactics well.

The most interesting line in the memo read "There was no mention whatsoever of the Director or the FBI".[dcccviii] Some might state it is ridiculous to suggest Hoover had the Attorney General unofficially stalked. However, the facts dispute such claims. The listed reports are not regular observation. These documents are intrusive and paranoid regarding any criticism of the Bureau's director.

Hoover's job was not to divine the reasons for Attorney General Kennedy's appearances or trips.[dcccix] These memos contained repeated statements like "shook hands with each person present", "made complementary remark about..." and "nothing unusual brought up". J. Edgar Hoover wanted every detail; his obsession with Robert Kennedy was limitless. Hoover's obsession included using Kennedy's political enemies.

Among Hoover's political allies in the American legislature was Congressman Louis C Wyman. Congressman Wyman was reported to have stated having the utmost respect toward the "the Boss" (Hoover). Wyman goes on to gush the Bureau could depend on his support on any matter on which it might call on him. "He (Wyman) indicated a strong dislike and distrust of former Attorney General Robert Kennedy"[dcccx]

The stalking continued as Hoover received private information that catalogued Robert Kennedy's staff members. The Bureau used five informants "closely acquainted with or have furnished current information" about Robert Kennedy. The information regarded a person in Robert Kennedy's employ with possible Communist links.[dcccxi] Hoover subsequently did not hesitate to interfere following Robert Kennedy's death.

Following the ambush, the Federal Bureau of Investigation was immediately on the scene. Officials transport Robert Kennedy to a medical facility located across from the Los Angeles FBI office. Los Angeles Police informed the Bureau within minutes of the attack. Bureau files state,

"Mr. De Loach advised that under no circumstances should we give the impression that we are investigating this matter"[dcccxii]

Attorney General Ramsey Clark insists on direct Bureau inclusion during interviews. Assistant Director of the Federal Bureau of Investigation, Cartha De Loach, explained "…that Attorney General Ramsey Clark has communicated with him numerous times since 4:00 A.M." So contrary to official statements of non-involvement, Bureau employees arrive just following the shooting. The Bureau presence was officially to protect against "allegations being made against the Los Angeles Police Department in regard to civil rights violations". This provided Hoover opportunities to influence the case.[dcccxiii]

Anonymous informants and unnamed "accomplices" further guided the Bureau's actions. One such Bureau informant claimed Sirhan had planted a bomb in his girlfriend's car. The informant said he could submit the location of a woman who could substantiate these claims. They would possess no real credibility without proof, unless sufficient people had affirmed this claim.

No credible evidence emerged from this lead. Perhaps unknown interests used disinformation and sought to mold Sirhan into a radical. Sirhan was unaware of how to construct a bomb. He was too busy studying the occult, gambling, and not attending Communist rallies. For a bombing Sirhan would require assistance.[dcccxiv]

An unnamed Bureau informant reported having a conversation with (name withheld) about the upcoming election season. The informant said "…if Kennedy wins the election, a couple of guys would (repeated word) kill him. Subject also stated he knew four guys in the Vets. (Veterans) Hostp. (Hospital), Ex GI's (General Infantry) who was going to kill Kennedy." Being unproven it faded away with other leads. These stories display the wide range of possible disinformation pouring into government agents.[dcccxv]

A separate unknown informant contacted the Bureau regarding the assassination of Senator Kennedy. The memo states the informant called long distance and wanted to discuss a plot to kill Senator Kennedy. Fifteen minutes later, the unidentified informant called back. He wished to speak with special agent (name omitted) and wanted full amnesty for his actions.

The convict explained he would call again later. He called the Bureau thirty minutes later and states a person involved in the conspiracy was an attorney. He stated this attorney lived in Miami Florida. The telephone number is unavailable. The informant said he would call back the next day.[dcccxvi] No additional information is given.

Charlie Hostetter reported an unnamed person in a complaint to Federal Bureau of Investigation. He confirmed his wife Lenora saw Sirhan the morning of June 4, 1968. Lenora Hostetter noted observing Sirhan with a "bushy haired" companion during her shift at a local restaurant. According to Hostetter, they were discussing what resembled a blueprint to her. Was this a blueprint or drawing of the Ambassador Hotel?[dcccxvii]

In officially redacted accounts begins the tired link of Sirhan and known "Communists." It sounds familiar because this is a classic mantra of critics about the assassination of John F. Kennedy. Like the butler, some authorities ever believe the Communists did it. This implication has no substantial evidence to support it.[dcccxviii]

One Federal Bureau of Investigation memo from an unnamed agent and informant has Sirhan making prior claims to kill Robert Kennedy. A different prison informant asserted he might have seen Sirhan Bishara at pro-Arab and Nazi rallies. A separate inmate asserted Sirhan Sirhan was at a Communist rally in Mexico. He heard Sirhan was planning to kill someone.[dcccxix] Again, these claims are similar to Oswald's unproven Mexican appearances and Communist ties.

People do not tell inmates of their conspiratorial plans. These are feasibly imprisoned men seeking infamy belatedly. The Bureau was in my estimation designing ragged implied correlations between Sirhan Sirhan and subversives. It disregarded any notion of a subtle professional assassination conspiracy.

The most unrealistic assertion came from a local restaurant in Raywood, Texas. A dining patron claimed, "I am going to California. My life isn't worth two cents. I'm going to the campaign meeting in California and straighten that ---- (shit) out. I am going to turn California upside down. I am going to kill them sons of ------ (bitches)." The informant claimed the unknown male's reasoning was "Because they are killing the Communists. I want to make it good for the Communist." He never actually claimed to be a Communist, assassin yes, but he was not a Communist.[dcccxx]

First, let us address the references to "the Communists". He did not state "us Communists" or describe himself as "a Communist supporter". He just wanted to make things better. This speech seems a bit direct for cunning typical Communist. Would a Communist assassin brag to someone about secret intentions? Would he endanger his later success to impress a restaurant employee? Yet the speculations continued.

An unnamed woman claims she rented a small house out to a young man named Sirhan. She asserted he moved out suddenly just before or following Senator Kennedy's wounding. She noted he received a great deal of mail from Arabia.[dcccxxi] This is similar to Lee Harvey Oswald's alternate living arrangements. However, no evidence of any kind proves this claim.

If Sirhan moved out suddenly just before the attack, he could not have been at the Ambassador Hotel in time. Not to mention the fact all his possessions in that house would have been in the car. Traveling light, more than a neat array of incriminating evidence would fill Sirhan's car. Sirhan in reality had left the Ambassador Hotel in police custody. However, a named possible accomplice is stranger.

Khaibar Khan was an alleged Iranian foreign intelligence agent who brought Sirhan to join the Kennedy volunteers. He accompanied Sirhan or someone resembling him at the Kennedy Los Angeles headquarters according to eyewitnesses. Kennedy workers notified the Federal Bureau of Investigation, a brief questioning of Khan followed. Khan and six asserted family members volunteered to work for Senator Kennedy's campaign headquarters during June 1968.

This could explain the repeated appearance of Sirhan Sirhan in Khan's company.[dcccxxii] No verified proof exists Khan was not acting of his own accord. His alleged manipulations of Sirhan just add further possible circumstantial influences. Some officials conducting the investigation disregard him.

Witness Ethel Crehan affirmed viewing Sirhan with other men at the Kennedy Campaign headquarters May 30, 1968. She observed Sirhan Sirhan and others made an inquiry about a future public appearance by Robert Kennedy.[dcccxxiii] In pivotal moments of the official review, some observe Sirhan with companions. Sirhan is noted with others attending Kennedy appearances prior to the assassination.

These sightings begin weeks before the Los Angeles Police captured Sirhan. Discounted were all other feasible accomplices. Authorities ignored contrary facts and plausible evidence. The Bureau, the Agency, and the Justice Department could not determine a single accomplice. Covering actions might have begun one final time.


## THE LOS ANGELES POLICE DEPARTMENT

The Los Angeles Police Department was responsible for destroying thousands of pieces of evidence in the assassination of Robert Kennedy.[dcccxxiv] The destruction began subsequent to Sirhan's initial trial. Police did not consider pending legal petitions regarding disclosure. They obliterated relevant evidence with abandon prior to the completion of Sirhan's legal appeals.[dcccxxv]

Destroyed evidence included ceiling tiles, woodwork, and thousands of crime scene photographs and reports. Consider the explanations they offered for destroying portions of the evidentiary record. Police leaders claimed it occurred because the evidence "proved nothing".[dcccxxvi] Authorities destroy physical evidence because it "would not fit in a filing cabinet".[dcccxxvii]

These pieces of evidence never presented to a judge might have refuted portions of the official case. However, authorities instead maintained useless evidence. A polka dot dress with no proven significance is for display, but they destroyed feasibly crucial evidence.[dcccxxviii] The Los Angeles Police seemed concerned with suppression rather than protection of evidence.

The United States government's stance on this case has always remained Sirhan Sirhan was the lone gunman. However, some officials do not agree with the Los Angeles Police assessments. Prior Federal Bureau of Investigation agent William Bailey was present at the crime scene. Bailey noted two additional bullet holes in the hotel kitchen wall.

Bailey's statement does not appear in the later official report.[dcccxxix] Once police and Bureau reports concluded Bailey explained, "I have serious reservations about whether Bobby was hit by bullets from Sirhan's gun".[dcccxxx] As a trained former member of the Bureau, he was qualified to make such judgments. Bailey's words corroborate similar witness claims.

Retired police Sergeant Paul Sharaga affirmed his Los Angeles Police interview "contains false and deliberately misleading statements." Archivist John Burns stated official polygraph examiner Enrique Hernandez intimidated witnesses to alter testimony.[dcccxxxi] These allegations during the course of inquiry find support from multiple sources.


## WOLFER

Los Angeles Police Criminologist DeWayne Wolfer disrupted, misread, and allegedly concealed relevant facts. Modern critics speak of him being the official authority. Many conspiracy advocates regard Wolfer officially incompetent. Subsequently, Wolfer's investigation faced criticism from authorities and experts alike.

Questions regarding the murder weapon arose when a trial exhibit serial number did not match Sirhan's gun from official reports. Wolfer asserted it was a clerical error. The Los Angeles Police Department received a following subpoena to produce evidence analysis reports. The Los Angeles Police Department produced a single summary progress report. DeWayne Wolfer offered summaries of his personal daily log covering activities from June 5 until June 19, 1968. This was definitely not a majority of the evidence.

Later before a panel of court ordered ballistics experts, Wolfer said, "…he could not recall…" if he marked the evidence bullets from the crime scene. Wolfer suggested too many people handled the ballistics evidence. Damage could have occurred to the exhibits. Wolfer then produced evidence years later in 1975. Wolfer furnished photographs he forgot to introduce at Sirhan's trial in 1968.

The photographs in Wolfer's possession had no chain of evidence. Are we now to trust DeWayne Wolfer's competence? The man waited years to introduce relevant evidence.[dcccxxxii] Are these repeated blunders legitimate? Perhaps Wolfer's intentions are more insidious.

People and scientific reviews began vanishing from Wolfer's memory. Among the many tests he failed to recall was examination of the official murder weapon, bullets, ceiling panel x-rays, and microscopic studies. Wolfer forgot his later ballistics studies of the "Kennedy" bullet. He failed to recollect examining the gun's cylinder. He could not remember which bullets he used for comparison testing at trial.[dcccxxxiii]

Wolfer is hazy about meeting Coroner Thomas Noguchi and constructing devices to conduct muzzle tests. He failed to mention later studies with Noguchi at the Los Angeles Police Academy testing muzzle distance. Wolfer overlooked the chemical tests he performed with Robert Kennedy's jacket. He disregarded reproduction of maps, photography, and evidence studies. Wolfer forgot venturing to a gun shop listed and dated in his log.[dcccxxxiv]

It slipped Wolfer's mind about his later visits to the Ambassador Hotel. Ballistics testing, the destroyed x-rays of the divider, and vanishing photographs, all escaped him. Wolfer did not know significant details and important events. All this unrecalled legitimate testing further discredits him in my view. DeWayne Wolfer cannot accurately remember the most important evidentiary procedures he conducted.

"The apparent lack of reports, both written and photographic, either made by Wolfer or destroyed, or never in existence, raised serious doubts as to the substance and credibility of the ballistics evidence presented in the original Sirhan trial." Los Angeles District attorney Thomas Kranz commented the subsequent inquiry "…might be the first through examination of bullet evidence in the case"[dcccxxxv] Despite Wolfer's meticulous listing in the single presented file, evidence and specific actions were officially insufficient. The file was called "…sketchy at most, and did not provide very thorough information concerning the types of tests conducted, or analyzed evidence reports." Wolfer had kept excellent proof detailing his failure to maintain an evidentiary record.[dcccxxxvi]

Within the Federal Bureau of Investigation report detailing the events, some understated facts appear. "The actual bullet which killed the Senator (People's Exhibit #48) was so badly damaged upon its entry and fragmentation in the brain of the Senator that this particular bullet could never be positively identified, either by Wolfer in his 1968 analysis, or during the 1975 ballistics reexamination. It should be emphasized that the actual murder of Robert Kennedy by the firing of the particular People's 48 was by inferential and circumstantial evidence including eye witness testimony, and matching the characteristics of several other bullets to the fragments of People's 48". [dcccxxxvii]

Official conclusions used select portions of testimony and a minority of eyewitnesses. Ironically, authors offering circumstantial evidence face criticism. They face attack for utilizing any inferential testimony. Critics of conspiracy forget the government's case utilized these exact methods.

Without further credible review, Americans would have believed the original determinations. Why reasonably doubt them? Without public interest, laws such as the Freedom of Information Act would not exist. Some authors, critics, and concerned experts revealed a wealth of new information. However, a slight minority of civil authorities have attempted to redress public grievances.

Los Angeles County Supervisor Baxter Ward gathered what evidence he believed relevant and announced a public hearing. The hearing addressed recurring questions about Robert Kennedy's murder. It scrutinized ballistics issues and portions of the Los Angeles Police Department's investigation. The Board of Supervisors consulted analysis, testimony, and evidence to make its determinations.

William Harper was a noted expert in criminal ballistics and physics. Harper swore an affidavit in 1970 reporting his scientific observations. The statement appeared in evidence before the Board of Supervisors. His findings establish the same gun could not have fired two bullets in evidence. [dcccxxxviii]

William Harper labeled six distinct grooves to identify the Kennedy bullet. Using photographs, Harper compared this bullet to a separate victim bullet and their characteristics did not match. These findings support two separate guns fired the bullets striking victims in the Ambassador Hotel.[dcccxxxix] If

Harper's studies and affirmations are correct, they are scientific proof of a second gun.

Herbert Mac Donell, former Laboratory of Forensic Science Director also provided his affidavit before the Los Angeles County Board of Supervisors. Utilizing photographs of the bullets, Mac Donell inspected them and observed two bullets did not match. He studied the Robert Kennedy neck bullet and a bullet from a separate victim. These reviewed bullets possessed different properties according to Mac Donell.[dcccxl] This would additionally corroborate two separate guns firing.

Mac Donell reported discrepancies with the official firearm angles, trajectory analysis, and condition of the bullets' physical attributes. Federal leaders dismissed the scientific inquiry Mac Donell and William Harper presented. However, the Board of Supervisors did not ignore expert analysis.[dcccxli] These experts kept meticulous notes to support their scientific affirmations.

DeWayne Wolfer in response offered having "no record or written notes to determine the rifling pitch. Markings of scars or indentations concerning the lands and grooves of the barrel, or the projection and pitch of the bullet from the barrel were not recorded. Wolfer stated he could not tell if the barrel revolver itself was in the same condition in September 1975 as it was in 1968."[dcccxlii] Wolfer had conducted a thorough inspection he failed to remember.

American leaders themselves called Wolfer negligent "in permitting such reports and documents to be destroyed".[dcccxliii] The official response for many ballistics inconsistencies was to deny Sirhan being face to face with Senator Kennedy. Authorities stated during previous investigation and Grand Jury testimony Senator Kennedy is glancing slightly to the left. This does not answer the ballistics problems, and fails to account for Sirhan's position. Let us take a moment and define "slightly". Senator Kennedy, according to official reports, was responding to a question and barely turning to his left. Critical authors believe this slight turn explains bullets striking Kennedy at upward angles.

At no time did evidence and witness testimony support Kennedy turning halfway or completely around. DeWayne Wolfer's findings corroborated direct shots from the rear, subsequently affirmed by the Los Angeles Coroner's office. This fails to provide a firing line for Sirhan Sirhan. If you accept the official excuses about the line of fire, critics still have forgotten something. This explanation has never accounted for the powder burn. The final shot left a powder burn, directly behind Senator Kennedy's ear.

Sirhan was never close enough to fire the required two or less inches at Robert Kennedy. The gun had to nearly press against the Senator's head. From the original and most official modern accounts, Sirhan's gun could not reach. Even if Kennedy's head was slightly turned, Sirhan's weapon is out of range. Despite Sirhan's thrashing, no one ever originally witnessed his weapon two inches from Robert Kennedy.

Attempts to rebut this fact resemble the makings of a new Single Bullet Theory. All scientific testing has proved this powder burn. All initial witnesses' statements place this shot beyond Sirhan Sirhan's reach. Logically it requires a second individual to fire the killing shots. An individual located in the correct firing position behind Senator Kennedy.

# CHAPTER 18

*"Even the walls, the only sharers of secrets, were feared."*

~Ammianis Marcellinus
Roman Soldier and Scholar

## THE MILITARY INTELLIGENCE HAND

This portion of the Assassination Conspiracy includes a few possible members. Possible connections lead to someone associated with the Central Intelligence Agency. It is the Agency's policy to neither confirm nor deny information about possible assets past or present. Unless it serves Agency's plans to do so.

The Agency can expose agents or attribute membership to malign a critic. This ploy confounds and dissuades efforts to investigate the Agency's operations. The Agency undertook many unsanctioned actions to hide its wide reaching agendas. These agendas were not always legal.

A minority of Agency operations violated American laws repeatedly. Findings of the President's (Rockefeller) Commission offered multiple examples.[dcccxliv] In several official inquires the Agency was exposed for manipulating government policy and ignoring oversight. These schemes occurred in America and other countries.

Ron Rickenbach, a former United States Agency for International Development official affirmed: "Early on, I think that we all believed that what we were doing was in the best interest of America. That we were in fact perhaps involved in some not so desirable aspects of the drug traffic…" Rickenbach had served the Agency in secret military operations in the Southeastern Asian country of Laos.[dcccxlv] A series of counter allegation and denials follow many statements given by former Agency officers and assets.

Multiple Agency operatives confirm the previous allegation. Central Intelligence Agency former assets Tony Poe, Victor Marchetti, and Fred Platt stated illegal activities occurred. These included drug smuggling and laundering programs in the plain sight of Agency commanders. Joe Nellis, former counsel of the House Select Committee on Narcotics, possessed the rare ability to view the files concerning the Agency's operations.

Nellis confirmed, "People in the CIA certainly knew it, and at that time Dick Helms I think was head of the office, and I'm sure he must have reported it to Nixon".[dcccxlvi] Helms had previously tried to destroy evidence of illegal human trials the Agency had conducted.[dcccxlvii] Director Richard Helms in response asserted he had no idea regarding such activities. He further claimed these actions were not the policy of the Agency.

Nellis confirmed the opium trade funded Central Intelligence Agency confederates in Laos. Allies would financially reciprocate and fund unsanctioned Agency programs. The secret war in Laos was undertaken using local tribes and selling drugs. This cost sixty million dollars more than budgeted by the United States government. Despite official condemnation of most drugs, some Agency leaders shared no such belief.[dcccxlviii]

Subsequent plans funded illicit operations around the Vietnam War. The Agency's lucrative illegal financial arrangements were a result of extended conflict in Laos and Vietnam. These operations continued despite repeated congressional intervention and heightened oversight.[dcccxlix] Eventually the Central Intelligence Agency would repeat similar errors in the future.

Some in the Agency created international plots to see Communist enemies abroad reduced to oblivion. What could they do to a perceived domestic threat? Is it so improbable to ponder someone manipulated the events around Robert Kennedy's demise? One man and his case file are not beyond the influence of rogue agents.

This would necessitate a man in the Los Angeles Police Department. Emmanuel Pena was a veteran Los Angeles Police Department homicide officer serving at the time of Robert Kennedy's murder. In March 1968, Pena retired from the Los Angeles Police Department. Pena received a position at the Agency for International Development.[dcccl]

Pena's new employer has additional unseen connections. According to former members, the Central Intelligence Agency had direct ties with the Agency for International Development. Some members called it a front to support illegal operations.[dccclii] Former Director of Central Intelligence William Colby subsequently testified the Agency performed repeated illicit operations.

From 1968 to 1971, Colby had run many intelligence operations. Secret plots occurred under the guise of the Agency for International Development.[dccclii] William Colby served as Agency Station Chief in Saigon during the most violent years of the Vietnam War. He was the only Director to offer an internal view of the Central Intelligence Agency's history of failed policies.

One secret program was responsible for over twenty thousand Vietnamese deaths. He testified to the American Congress among these deaths was "illegal killing."[dcccliii] Director Colby additionally exposed unsanctioned Central Intelligence Agency spying practices on Americans. Agency officers labeled Colby a traitor.

Colby destroyed his official reputation by admitting the truth.[dcccliv] Yet he confirmed the Agency for International Development was masking a classified agenda. Based on Colby's statements, former Agency employees, and the congressional record, this organization was a front.[dccclv] It was a hidden extension of the Central Intelligence Agency. Emmanuel Pena aided this possible front organization in Latin American with counterintelligence activities.

Pena soon returned to the Los Angeles Police, three months before Robert Kennedy's death.[dccclvi] All leading officers would have foreknowledge of security regarding Senator Kennedy's visit. This information offers Los Angeles Police would not be inside the Ambassador Hotel. Police would be aware that Ace Security Company provided the only armed men inside the event.

Los Angeles Police would have been aware only volunteers would surround Robert Kennedy. Most had little or no security training and all were unarmed. Police leaders were aware of those coming and going positioned around the hotel for external security. The hotel staff and members of the public would have known media and campaign event schedules.

The information is available long before the event. The security layout and nearly all major preparation details were at Emmanuel Pena's disposal. A few in the Central Intelligence Agency possibly knew of these arrangements. Lieutenant Pena could have shared these details with them, possibly as a mere formality. Perhaps he just passed along information about a critic.

Former Los Angeles Police Department officer Paul Schraga was among the police responding to the Ambassador Hotel. He explained then

Lieutenant Emmanuel Pena and Sergeant Enrique Hernandez arrived quickly at the scene. Just minutes following the shooting police launch a command and control center in the Ambassador Hotel.[dcccvii] Subsequently the Los Angeles Police Department forms Special Unit Senator.

Police Chief Houghton created the task force to investigate the assassination of Robert Kennedy. The insular group's surviving files did not emerge until the late 1980s. A few lead members among the compartmentalized force guided the investigation's ultimate determinations. Captain Hugh Brown led Special Unit Senator. Brown eventually increased the unit to include sixty-one members. Three Lieutenants appointed to command the Unit aided Brown.

The Day Commander appointed to lead operations was veteran officer Emmanuel Pena.[dcccviii] The other man some claim possessed intelligence connections was Sergeant Enrique Hernandez. The Los Angeles Police sent Hernandez to the Justice Department for training South American forces in mob control.[dcccix] Hernandez additionally was an overzealous supporter of the official story.

Hernandez later served as polygraph operator reviewing all witnesses involved who underwent lie detector examination. Allegedly, Pena and Hernandez had "…literally terrorized all witnesses in Robert Kennedy Assassination who saw or heard evidence conflicting with the thesis of Sirhan's sole guilt. Mr. Hernandez instructed people to change their testimony or suffer dire consequences".[dcccx] From statements on surviving audio tapes, Hernandez displays a less than neutral disposition regarding witness testimony.[dcccxi]

Emmanuel Pena could approve or dismiss evidence. Hernandez feasibly could filter nonconforming statements. Working in tandem, they could essentially influence the major determinations of witnesses and physical evidence. Officers with strong political agendas controlled the investigation. However, Pena was the only verified Los Angeles Police Department officer with intelligence associations in control.

Emmanuel Pena is conceivably the intelligence lynchpin as Day Commander of Special Unit Senator. Pena could exercise direct oversight of operations and evidence gathering. This review found no confirmed evidence Pena or Hernandez knew of a conspiracy. However, Los Angeles Police Department officers acted zealously to defend the official story. They did so despite all contrary evidence.

# Corporate Intelligence

The Lockheed Aircraft Corporation was a long-term supplier and partner with the Central Intelligence Agency. They had a similar arrangement with the American military. Clarence Johnson was a talented aircraft engineer who eventually became a Lockheed Board of Directors member in 1964. His contributions won many awards including the Central Intelligence Agency Distinguished Intelligence Medal and the National Security Medal.[dccclxii]

Among Johnson's accomplishments are his design and aid in the creation of several aircraft. Lockheed specifically constructed some aircraft for Central Intelligence Agency use. One significant example is the U-2 Spy plane. The U-2 Spy plane program served the Central Intelligence Agency from 1954 and 1974.[dccclxiii]

The association was just one of many Agency vehicle programs. Someone in the Agency could have easily planted assets within Lockheed Aircraft to track operations and potential threats.[dccclxiv] Agency operatives utilized this tactic repeatedly to monitor and influence corporate policy toward its goals. A former Agency member details this practice of domestic spying, manipulation, and disregard for citizen rights.[dccclxv]

It explains why corporations working closely with the American government prosper despite immensely exceeding funding limits. Costs could reach double the approved funding. These budgets never felt the heat of public scrutiny until decades later. Similar practices continue today within recent American government legislation. The final cost is a worry only for the taxpayers.

Modern controversies surrounding large military suppliers like Halliburton and others still endure.[dccclxvi] Some corporations have allegedly overcharged the United States government for services. Some businesses have faced little serious government review. However, useful civilian projects endure public scrutiny to obtain a fraction of the same government funding.

Former Agency member testimonies confirm schemes including assassinations, propaganda, and unsanctioned military operations. Some programs resulted in "illegal deaths." The entire Central Intelligence Agency was not directly responsible for the death of Robert Kennedy. However, proof exists of certain Agency operatives committing verified murders. Others undertook the infiltration of businesses, such as media corporations.

Perhaps an Agency employee had infiltrated Lockheed Aircraft, and was acting under commands from a rogue superior. The possible connection might prove important. The night of the Senator Kennedy's assassination, a Lockheed Aircraft employee was present at the scene. He had given several assorted stories regarding his presence and background. Officials without immediate review cleared this man of any involvement. A man named Cesar.

# CHAPTER 19

*"But is it coincidence? Are there not subtle forces at work*
*of which we know little?"*

~Sir Arthur Conan Doyle
English Author
*"The Casebook of Sherlock Holmes"*

## THE ASSASSINATION CONSPIRACY

Robert Kennedy's earlier political manipulations and divisive actions created no shortage of detractors. From Carlos Marcello to J. Edgar Hoover, Jimmy Hoffa to Lyndon Johnson, Kennedy made powerful enemies in his political tenure. Each man possessed deep personal grievances and for most homicide was routine business. A powerful group might have subsequently targeted Robert Kennedy.

Robert Kennedy if elected could possibly erase generations of Central Intelligence Agency and Federal Bureau of Investigation enrichment. When the Agency and Bureau grew in influence and funding, so did their near self-determination. The Central Intelligence Agency performed actions without American Congressional or Presidential consent. Hoover's repeated illegal actions under COINTELPRO ignored the required consultation with superiors.

Robert Kennedy would not be a passive civil servant. Kennedy's crusading nature would not accept illegal covert operations and continued military intervention abroad without oversight. Kennedy had previously attempted to oversee intelligence activities. Robert Kennedy eventually opposed Vietnam, and other military actions. This undermined the Central Intelligence Agency's ongoing agendas.

Yet evidence and witness testimony rarely displayed overt attacks until the Senator's assassination. Additionally less known reported violence appears within the record. Related threats to Senator Kennedy began in May 1968, while he was in transit. Van Nuys Police report a shower of rocks hit Senator Kennedy from an overpass in his open convertible.

The report exposes obvious holes in Senator Kennedy's security. Authorities believed several youthful persons were responsible. This was subsequent to police receiving a not so youthful anonymous death threat against Kennedy.[dcclxvii] Campaign worker John Ahrndt asserted viewing Sirhan at Kennedy campaign headquarters. This occurred weeks before the attack on Senator Kennedy.[dcclxviii]

This substantiates the similar testimony of other eyewitnesses. This may indicate Sirhan and others began stalking the Senator long before most investigators were aware. These possible sightings offer additional circumstantial evidence.

Following a Democratic Party primary event at the Benson Hotel, a separate incident occurred. Someone was theoretically practicing the future attack. Senator Kennedy's bodyguard Ronald R. Huntley had initially asserted he encountered Sirhan Sirhan and an unnamed accomplice.[dcclxix] Huntley's original report contains a statement declaring Huntley was "certain" Sirhan Sirhan is the more slender of the two men.

In the second report filed, the Federal Bureau of Investigation changes this statement to a wholly different individual. The man is now three inches taller, nearly thirty pounds heavier, and of a separate cultural background than Sirhan.[dcclxx] Robert Kennedy's local security was certain he witnessed Sirhan Sirhan and his accomplice feasibly practicing the later assassination. Eyewitnesses frequently declare alterations to their statements occurred.

Margret Mary Venables observed two "young Mexicans", "…prowling around the department and requested of her or one of the employees…they furnish these individuals mess jackets so they could pose as waiters to get into the "Kennedy quarters." Hans Korthoff, an Assistant Manager at the Ambassador Hotel, submitted this statement.[dcclxxi] Venables' additional statement contained a description of the two men.

The taller man was dressed in a sport shirt with a large Kennedy button. He had black curly hair, long sideburns and was medium height and weight. The smaller man which some have alleged was Sirhan had tan wash trousers and straight hair combed back, and a white short sleeved t-shirt with a Kennedy button as well.[dccclxxii] Neither of these individuals caught in the linen room was Sirhan. However, they were asking about Senator Kennedy's location in the Ambassador Hotel. They were trying to obtain hotel staff uniforms for an unknown purpose.

The official Bureau report lists the "taller" intruder as five feet five inches. Julio, whose last name was unlisted, was the Ambassador employee bringing these two intruders to hotel security. No added measures were taken to prevent these individuals from reappearing the following night. They like so many unidentified persons were free to come and go.

The Kennedy Staff is unaware of these intruders. A few hotel employees and security assigned the night before knew of them. These two were among the many unidentified people lurking around with unknown motivations. Many were requesting details about Senator Kennedy's plans and location. Sirhan Sirhan was allegedly breaching security prior to his attack on Robert Kennedy.

The night of June 4 campaign workers force Sirhan and one companion to leave the ballroom for not having credentials. Kennedy campaign worker Judy Royer ejected Sirhan and his companion "an hour or two" before Robert Kennedy's speech. Kitchen personnel then later observed Sirhan Sirhan in the pantry.[dccclxxiii] Security failed to keep the area clear of non-invited guests like Sirhan Sirhan. Who is Sirhan's newest companion?

Other unknown men were additionally seeking to breach hotel security. Boston Herald reporter William McCarthy gave observations from the Colonial Room. A man requested McCarthy's media credentials. McCarthy confirmed the man was early twenties, five feet six inches, with dark curly hair, Mediterranean type skin, and had a normal voice. He wore a velour pullover and short sleeve shirt beneath. McCarthy stated "….this man bore a striking resemblance to the photograph of Sirhan but did not believe they were identical".[dccclxxiv]

Senator Kennedy was later giving his victory speech before a huge crowd. Simultaneously, a man of broadly similar appearance to Sirhan Sirhan is asking Boston Globe reporter Robert Healey questions. The unknown stranger's questions included if Healey would give him personal media credentials to enter the Colonial Room. The young man repeatedly inquired about obtaining media credentials.

Healey described a nineteen-year-old man. He was five feet eight, dark brown, curly hair, long sideburns, and had a dark complexion possibly of Mexican extraction. The unknown man had no accent, wore several badges including a Kennedy badge. He had some resemblance to Sirhan Sirhan.[dcccxxv]

Robert Healey states, "...he was amazed that this man had evidently gained entry into the Colonial Room despite the fact that security men were positioned at the room's door". [dcccxxvi] Other witnesses observed the man resembling Sirhan in locations Sirhan never was. Healey and McCarthy's testimony were only an inch from the exact height of someone in the pantry with Senator Kennedy. One witness affirmed his exact age and the other was two years off. Each said he had black curly hair, was swarthy, and acting strangely. He wore a shirt and dark pullover with badges, including a large Kennedy badge.

The description feasibly describes Michael Wayne, five feet seven, who ran to exit the pantry when shots fired. He and Sirhan appear vaguely similar according to various witnesses throughout the pantry. Wayne had a pull over, political buttons, badges, and a poster case. Yet Healey noted that security men were checking press credentials at the doorway.

Did Michael Wayne gain entry despite Thane Cesar posted at the doorway? Gerald Robert Amster told the Federal Bureau of Investigation following 11 pm he "...had no difficulty whatsoever in entering any of the ballrooms and no one stopped him or asked for identification."[dcccxxvii] So where was Thane Cesar and hotel security?

Before the shooting Thane Cesar attested, he was checking media identification at the Colonial Room. Cesar then abandoned his post; this allows intruders entry into the room. Cesar asserted superiors instructed him to walk beside Robert Kennedy. He reportedly left his post at the Colonial Room to do so. Cesar's every statement is wrong.

William Gardner, the Ambassador Hotel Chief of Security reported to the Bureau he assigned no guard to Kennedy. Gardner had forbidden security officers to go near Senator Kennedy with a weapon. [dcccxxviii] Cesar without orders, in fact armed in defiance of them, tracks down Kennedy. Security failures elsewhere provided access to the pantry for Michael Wayne and Sirhan.

Sirhan's position reveals some people knew of the pantry's later use. Kennedy Campaign Worker David Mark Esquith spoke with fellow campaign worker Jim Lowe. Esquith learned Robert Kennedy was going to leave through Ambassador Hotel kitchen. This requires using the pantry. Lowe had to learn the information from someone as well before the attack. The question becomes who and how many knew of this route? [dcccxxix]

Someone in the area must have told Sirhan where to encounter Robert Kennedy. According to the Federal Bureau of Investigation, witness Jesus

Perez indicated to the media "that subject Sirhan Bishara Sirhan asked him three or four times if Kennedy would pass through the narrow passageway where Sirhan was standing just prior to the shooting."[dccclxxx] Someone nearby must have confirmed this fact. Sirhan knows where Kennedy is to appear, verifying the earlier route change.

Cesar reappears at Senator Kennedy's side as he exits the stage. Karl Euker guides Robert Kennedy in front at the left wrist. Thane Cesar grasps Robert Kennedy's back right elbow. Robert Kennedy enters the pantry. Kennedy shook hands with supporters and autographed Michael Wayne's memorabilia. Senator Kennedy completed shaking his last hand and Karl Euker gives a pull forward.

This according to some witnesses is when Kennedy turned his head forward to continue walking.[dccclxxxi] A wide-eyed Sirhan Sirhan advances; he yells and commences to fire his gun. While Sirhan fired nearly the entire room was charging, pushing, and screaming. The room became utter insanity as people reacted.

In the moments between the first shot and end of the second, Michael Wayne dashes. Some authors focus on the possibility of Michael Wayne using a firearm to help assassinate Robert Kennedy. This weapon theory is speculation; more interesting was his reported motivation for running. Wayne claimed he was seeking a phone.

Having witnessed a chaotic shooting do you help those wounded around you? Perhaps you might seek shelter or a security officer until it was over? Wayne chose instead to run while knocking people aside to make a phone call. Witnesses believing him feasibly connected with Sirhan grabbed him.

Witness statements prove Wayne distracted others present. He sought media passes to allow him access to restricted areas. This illustrates Wayne desperately wanted to be present. Wayne knocks his way toward the exit distracting people around him, causing some witnesses to yell, "Stop him!" To avoid injury, many push as the gathered crowd surges. Some believe fireworks are going off or balloons were popping.

It all occurs as Sirhan's gun fires eight shots. Remember Sirhan Sirhan was not the only individual crouching and conceivably firing. Thane Eugene Cesar affirmed having drawn his gun. He fell down and rose from a crouch. According to Cesar, his gun is out before and following this moment depending on the interview.

Cesar's placement allows him the opportunity to fire the killing shots.[dccclxxxii] The Los Angeles Police, Federal Bureau of Investigation, and the Los Angeles District Attorney's Office later questioned Thane Cesar. Nearly all Cesar's public statements have conflicting details.

Cesar expounded, "The only way the gun would've gone off is if I pulled the trigger".[dcccxxxiii]

Cesar's firing position behind Robert Kennedy is consistent with forensic evidence gathered to explain Kennedy's wounds. Los Angeles Coroner Thomas Noguchi located a gunpowder burn directly behind the right ear in the official autopsy. Powder burns result from close physical contact with a firearm. The gun firing the killing shot had to be two inches or less from Robert Kennedy's head.

The former mentioned Agency review of political assassination states, "The Pistol…In all cases the subject should be hit solidly three times for complete reliability".[dcccxxxiv] Kennedy received three wounds; a fourth shot verified from Sirhan's gun damaged his suit. Additionally three bullets struck his back and head. From a steep upward angle, the killing shots come from behind Robert Kennedy.

The lunging Sirhan according to witness statements was nearly facing Senator Kennedy. Kennedy's hands rise up protectively as Sirhan fires two shots. Sirhan fires many times after this point but not direct shots. Sirhan had two clear shots at the Senator according to most original and modern witness statements.

Maître d Karl Euker and others grapple Sirhan, Cesar allegedly falls or crouches. Cesar draws his gun as he rises; no one is directly looking at him. Eyewitness Evan Freed observed someone behind Robert Kennedy drawing a gun and firing it.[dcccxxxv] Directly behind Senator Kennedy is the single other gun.

Several nearly simultaneous shots occur in the barrage of gunfire, according to witnesses and experts reviewing Pruzinsky's audio tape. Thane Cesar during this time has drawn a gun behind Senator Kennedy. Cesar has always denied using his weapon.[dcccxxxvi] Could Thane Cesar have fired the shots?

The previously mentioned Pruzinsky tape exhibits at least two occurrences of double shots in the Ambassador Hotel pantry. These shots occur nearly simultaneously and reveal a problem, the firing speed. Sirhan's gun was a .22-caliber Ira Johnson Cadet revolver that fired and recycled too slowly.

Two shots fired occurred with impossible speed. This requires a second gun.[dcccxxxvii dcccxxxviii] No .22-caliber revolver manufactured in 1968 could fire so quickly. Scientific findings additionally support the shots were from a position Sirhan Sirhan was never in.

Substantial official evidence support a second gun allegedly was fired. After reviewing audio evidence, multiple experts have independently supported nine to fourteen shots occurred. This exceeds the eight-bullet capacity of Sirhan's .22-caliber pistol. Much scientific evidence supports two possible gunmen.

The autopsy report identified shots to the back and head came from the rear of Robert Kennedy at close range.[dccclxxxix] The gunman would have to be located behind Senator Kennedy. In the autopsy summary is a description of the bullet paths "slightly to the front…back to front, upward…back to front, upward".[dcccxc] Someone behind Kennedy could fire a small caliber gun that crowd noise and Sirhan's repeated fire would conceal.

"If the assassin is to escape…If such concealment is desirable the operation will be called "secret…". " While if the assassination requires publicity to be effective it will be termed "terroristic".[dcccxci] This assassination conspiracy in my estimation involved each aspect. Sirhan Sirhan was the terroristic element. The second assassin is potentially a "secret" one.

Once the shooting commences, the crowd erupts. When the chaos has begun to subside, Senator Kennedy has suffered critical wounds and five others had serious and extreme injuries. Each lost minute limited Robert Kennedy's chances of survival. Officials transported Kennedy first to Central Receiving Hospital at 12:30 a.m. wasting precious time.

Senator Kennedy does not receive full medical attention at his initial destination. Unlike its title, Central Receiving was not a functional hospital. It was a glorified first aid center without surgery capability.[dcccxcii] This medical center in all but name was located across the street, from the fully functioning Good Samaritan hospital. Instead of Robert Kennedy going to surgery directly, at least an hour passes.

The wounds appeared to be mortal and Senator Kennedy's life still might have been lost. Yet this delay ensured it. This was the crowning incompetence or the greatest malign action of leading authorities. Those commanding Kennedy's transportation obviously should have chosen the fully equipped hospital. Many, including then local government representatives share justified anger.

The Los Angeles City Council determined responsible authorities had contributed to Robert Kennedy's demise. The Council believed those authorities who made the fatal choice bypassed rational procedure.[dcccxciii] The matter was a news story in the Los Angeles Times featuring additional City Council demands. The Council ordered a full investigation of Central Receiving Hospital.

Councilman Thomas Bradley listed the lack of resources Central Receiving offered "… it is obvious that the hospital did not have a full complement of equipment and services such as X-ray, blood transfusion equipment, experienced surgeons and the like".[dcccxciv] Councilman Bradley noted the transfer resulted in a one-hour delay or more. Precious time was lost as Robert Kennedy lay dying; a frail opportunity for survival is wasted. Again, critical errors occur at vital moments. Taken as single events each mistake theoretically could have just been repeated incompetence. However, this final mistake defies all reason.

Robert Kennedy's security at political events fails. Unreported are men at repeated events were allegedly stalking him. Unknown campaign volunteers, official death threats, attacks on Kennedy himself. Officials manipulate the case, destroy evidence, and squander Kennedy's lone chance for survival. All these actions support the possibility of a conspiracy. One man could not be responsible for everything.

Delayed medical treatment sealed the fate of Senator Robert Kennedy. An overwhelming series of these errors render the official findings to shambles. Were some authorities involved fools or villains? American leaders still have not decided which the suitable answer will be. Perhaps a few were both.


## THE CONFLICTING MR. CESAR

Thane Cesar has given many varying statements following the possible assassination conspiracy. Cesar said he worked at the Ace Guard Service consistently for six months, this was proven to be weeks. He claimed to have guarded the Ambassador Hotel previous times. Cesar's first time ever working at the Ambassador Hotel was the night of Robert Kennedy's assassination.

Cesar is one of two armed men present. He exits the scene without his gun logged in evidence. This provides Cesar with opportunities, such as to switch weapons allowing him to fire one and later carry a second. This feasibly could have occurred prior to later inspection.

Thane Cesar subsequently produced his .38-caliber security handgun for authorities. However, Cesar personally owned a .22-caliber pistol. William Harper and Herbert Mac Donnell's findings conclude two separate .22-caliber weapons had fired. Thane Cesar later asserted he sold this .22 caliber pistol prior to Robert Kennedy's murder. Similar to many other claims Cesar made, this was incorrect.[dcccxcv]

Following Robert Kennedy's murder, Cesar sold his personal firearm according to a signed receipt. Jim Yoder who associated with Cesar purchased the gun. Listed on the receipt is a .22-caliber, nine shot pistol.

Lawrence Teeter, Sirhan Sirhan's previous attorney, affirmed Yoder stated Thane Cesar advised him to "be careful with this weapon it was used in a police shooting."

Thane Cesar told Los Angeles Police he previously sold the weapon. According to Jim Yoder's signed receipt, Cesar sold the gun three months subsequent to Robert Kennedy's death.[dcccxcvi] An unknown party steals the pistol from Yoder and it resurfaced much later.[dcccxcvii] This evidence is perplexing and Cesar's statements are repeatedly contradictory. These words allegedly betray Cesar despite his insistence of ignorance.

During an interview following the attack, Cesar states, "I definitely would not have voted for Bobby Kennedy, because he had the same ideas John had. He sold this country down the road; he gave it to the Commies and definitely the minorities, and one of these days at the rate their going there will be a civil war in this country between whites and blacks and blacks will never win".[dcccxcviii]

Cesar has a deep resentment of Robert Kennedy and the Civil Rights Movement. In the minutes following the attack on Senator Kennedy, John Marshall interviews Thane Cesar. Marshall asks, "…Officer, can you confirm that the senator was shot?" Thane Cesar responds "Yes, I was there holding his arm when they shot him." Who are they? Cesar must have misspoken.

However, this does prove Cesar was holding onto Senator Kennedy. Accordingly, Kennedy's back was facing Cesar during the shooting. Marshall continues, "Was it just one man?" Cesar answered "No. Yeah, one man", Marshal then asks "…And what sort of wound did the senator receive?" At this point Cesar displays a medical accuracy rarely seen in the average security guard.

"Well, from where I could see it looked like he was shot in the head and the chest and the shoulder".[dcccxcix] Cesar's response expertly placed all three shots, reaffirming he was directly behind Robert Kennedy. Cesar knew these facts long before later investigating medical staff corroborate his perceptive amateur findings. Cesar listed wounds his vantage point offered.

If Cesar was on the floor jostled by the crowd, how did he accurately observe wounds and events? He was not an acrobat, and could not just flip back to his feet. If he observed the wounds, Thane Cesar should have observed a hidden assassin. He could not accurately observe wounds and events while on the floor jostled by the crowd.

Thane Cesar identified the wounds origin, so he was looking directly at Robert Kennedy. Cesar accurately describes shots fired behind Senator

Kennedy's position. Three forward and upward shots occur possibly from a crouch. The final killing shot to the head is two inches or less from behind Kennedy.

Cesar previously claims he fell down, scrambled to his feet, and drew his gun. Supposedly, Cesar was attempting to regain his balance and because of the large crowd, he then holstered his gun.[cm] According to Cesar, he moved to avoid injury from the panicked crowd. Nevertheless, he remained behind Robert Kennedy.

How could he fail to see a gun two inches or less from Robert Kennedy's head? Cesar asserts drawing his gun at the beginning of the shots, in other reports Cesar drew his gun on the floor. Cesar had various answers to fit the necessary occasion.[cmi] Once time passed, Cesar began to adjust his statements attempting to improve prior discrepancies.

In some accounts, he speaks about gunpowder in his eyes from Sirhan's weapon. The problem is Cesar was not close enough to have this occur from Sirhan's gun. Ballistics expert William Harper noted powder discharge could only emerge from Caesar's weapon.[cmii] Cesar was speaking of something only possible if he fired.

Thane Cesar volunteered for questioning because he was "...ignored during the chaos following the shooting of Senator Kennedy".[cmiii] Cesar restated having later given his .38-caliber guard pistol to Los Angeles Police for inspection. Police visually examine the gun but do not scientifically test it. Cesar had a long duration to feasibly prepare a story and hide evidence.

Years following Senator Kennedy's murder, Thane Cesar underwent multiple polygraph tests. These tests were one critical author's basis for exonerating Thane Cesar.[cmiv] Los Angeles Police and other authorities relied on these scientifically unconfirmed methods in their determinations of fact. A separate use occurs on daytime television shows to determine relationship fidelity. You might hear them given during radio shows to comedic ends.

The American legal system rarely admits polygraph (lie detector) tests because of variable standards and proven inaccurate readings. Polygraphs are not legally reliable in determining someone's credibility because they can be defeated. The stress test Thane Cesar underwent for reporter Ted Charach is also untenable. Again, it was not a scientific way to discover innocence and guilt. Like the "lie detector," it remains highly speculative to assume stress readings can accurately reveal the truth.[cmv cmvi cmvii]

However, Charach's actions generated interest among some federal agencies. This included the Federal Bureau of Investigation. A Bureau memo discussing Charach states Los Angeles District Attorney "...Howard is of the opinion that Charach's conduct might possibly jeopardize prosecution's opposition to Sirhan's appeal". How could verified evidence be dangerous to the truth? [cmviii]

Subsequently the district attorney's office becomes "...interested in obtaining information on Thane Caesar (Cesar)" It took bureaucrats until September 29, 1970 to follow the Cesar lead. Over two years following the death of Robert Kennedy authorities finally decided to investigate the other armed individual present. Unfortunately, Sirhan Sirhan was already serving a life sentence. [cmix]


## VANISHING EVIDENCE AND AUTHORITY ERROR

Coroner Thomas Noguchi conducted the Autopsy of Robert Kennedy. It remains the standing official document concerning related medical findings. During the investigation, Noguchi marked a bullet TN 31 and Los Angeles Police secured it. The recovered bullet was from Senator Kennedy's body. It then was stored in an envelope and given to Sergeant W. Jordan of the Los Angeles Police Department. [cmx]

The bullet is among the many pieces of evidence to vanish. Officials never account for the bullet last held by the Los Angeles Police and DeWayne Wolfer. Coroner Noguchi's report stands apart from the many errors cluttering the official case. After later analyzing the autopsy, military doctors found no scientific inaccuracies within Noguchi's report.

This vanishing evidence includes the endless mistakes of DeWayne Wolfer. The remains of Wolfer's original report do not corroborate the current official story. "Wolfer was unable to positively identify the bullet that actually killed Senator Kennedy, People's 48, as having been fired from the Sirhan gun due to the fragmentation of the bullet." His report of the bullet trajectories found "a. The first bullet entered Senator Kennedy's head behind the right ear and was later recovered from the victim's head..."

Wolfer affirmed "d. The fourth bullet entered Senator Kennedy's right rear back approximately 1" (inch) to the right of bullet #3. This bullet traveled upward and forward and exited the victim's in the right front chest". [cmxi] Wolfer's original determinations essentially matched the findings of Coroner Noguchi, William Harper, and Herbert Mac Donnell.

The official conclusions normally would support Sirhan Sirhan as the lone assassin. How can shots from the rear occur if Sirhan is facing Kennedy? All witnesses originally said Sirhan was in front of him. No photographic and audio evidence placed Sirhan behind Robert Kennedy. Magical bullets do not exist.

These are not speculative ramblings but the original conclusions of the Los Angeles Police Department. The findings receive affirmation from the report of the Los Angeles Coroner's Office and United States military review. Evidence appears on many legal documents regarding the subject. They are the scientific facts of the matter.

Despite the lower caliber of the weapon, the Agency's Study of Assassination states "...Less powerful rounds can suffice but are less reliable."[cmxii] However, two guns at close range are lethal if simultaneously fired in two directions. Sirhan's gun was feet away; the only known second gun was mere inches behind Senator Kennedy.

Sirhan's handgun contained eight rounds fully loaded. Seven bullets had struck the victims. One bullet was determined to have gone into the ceiling and was lost. With all eight bullets explained, we can examine other possible bullet holes. Authorities did not consider them relevant and dismissed them as "peripheral gouges and ricochet marks". Contrary evidence again went ignored.

A prior Federal Bureau Investigation agent on the scene initially asserted other bullet holes. In one example, photographers displayed two officers trying apparently to extract a bullet from the center pantry divider. Once the media reported these activities, official sources later deny them. Attempts to explain away other bullet holes included ricochet's accounting for two ceiling tile holes.

Multiple possible bullets holes were among the officially removed evidence. Los Angeles Police destroyed most evidence that might corroborate the photographs. Some authorities initialed the possible bullet holes marking them as evidence. After the trial of Sirhan Sirhan, paint and repair had covered these marks.

Independent witnesses viewing other possible bullet holes included carpenter Dale Poore. Poore in his interview with the Los Angeles Police Department explained "...he had been requested by two police officers to remove the wooden facing...he had noticed two apparent bullet holes on the east portion..." Wesley Harrington, a different carpenter who built portions of the woodwork "...had noted "two apparent bullet holes" in the facing of the east portion (pantry side) or the center post."[cmxiii]

Two alleged bullet holes in the pantry's wooden divider produce no bullets. Authorities later discovered two fired bullets in Sirhan's car. If these bullets were vital enough to retain, why did Sirhan leave them on the front seat? The fired bullets were further evidence used to legitimize Sirhan's guilt.

Until these bullets were found to contain traces of wood. How could they have wood traces present on them if not from recent extraction? "Additionally, Special Counsel Kranz was never able to find to his satisfaction an explanation as to why there were two bullets with traces of wood that were found on the front seat of Sirhan's car".[cmxiv] Perhaps it was a coincidence.

These two bullets could have been among the other bullets retrieved from the Ambassador Hotel pantry. Why did authorities fail to compare traces on the bullets against the woodwork from the pantry? Could they have matched? This documented lack of considering evidence possibly became standard procedure for some authorities.

Police destroyed thousands of pictures, ceiling tiles; Ambassador Pantry related woodwork, and original scientific analysis.[cmxv] Police rendered confirmation of this evidence impossible. Overall, repeated official deception and destruction of evidence was rampant. DeWayne Wolfer made repeated errors some believe currently as fact. Disregarded evidence for decades reasonably substantiates official incompetence. Supporting evidence and official implications of conspiracy are publicly verifiable.

Wolfer and the Los Angeles Police could have fully proven their later claims if they had not destroyed evidence. Instead "Wolfer and the L.A.P.D. had no records to substantiate whether these door jambs and wooden frames were still in existence, or had been destroyed along with the ceiling panels and x-ray analysis in 1969".[cmxvi] Testifying before the Los Angeles City Council, Assistant Chief of Police Daryl Gates stated the ceiling panels no longer existed. Destruction was reportedly to have occurred in 1969, shortly following Sirhan's first trial.

The destruction of the ceiling panels and other items seemed to conclude the matter. However, in 1971, "interdepartmental correspondence to Chief Davis apparently made reference to the ceiling tiles".[cmxvii] Federal Bureau of Investigation records confirmed that Chief Davis and officers of the Los Angeles Police allegedly concealed this evidence. What other reason could exist for this action besides protecting the integrity of their investigation?

The report states the possibility of verifying these discrepancies "is not certain at this time".[cmxviii] Unfortunately, it remains officially uncertain. Police were unable to determine if they destroyed or concealed evidence. The ceiling tiles were just the beginning; many other exhibits followed them into bureaucratic oblivion.

Other interesting comments of later Los Angeles Police Chief Daryl Gates include "…Our investigation from the beginning was very, very, intense, very complete".[cmxix] Chief Gates is quite wrong. Outside spectators compromised the crime scene and outside agencies influenced events. Among those never fully questioned was Thane Cesar. This was neither an intense nor a complete investigation. Some authorities occupied themselves with policing any mention of a conspiracy after Robert Kennedy's demise.

Connected officials did not want the public discussing the matter. Lieutenant Manuel Pena "requested any information concerning potential publications with respect to the Kennedy assassination. Pena was particularly concerned about any attempts to write stories regarding the assassination which might tend to suggest a conspiratorial aspect".[cmxx] The Los Angeles Police Department wanted help. The Federal Bureau of Investigation aided them in monitoring any mention of conspiracy.

The Los Angeles Police claimed they were requesting information to pursue all leads to exhaustion. If that were true, police would not have destroyed evidence in the first place. They would not seek to attack critical public views if they contained legitimate evidence. Various official agency practices deterred inspection and the Los Angeles County Grand Jury verdict condemned these official actions.

The Grand Jury found non-compliance with official procedure and care of exhibits. The Los Angeles County Clerk's office according to the Grand Jury, suffered from gross mismanagement. "It is the feeling of this Grand Jury that such management, if allowed to continue, can only weaken the integrity and structure of County Government in general". They found it would "...decrease the efficiency and effectiveness of other County Agencies who rely on the services of the County Clerk Office".[cmxxi] Authorities responsible for securing evidence used by the Los Angeles Police had "grossly mismanaged" the Kennedy exhibits.

The question is how many people can be lying? How large is the supposed conspiracy among experts, authors, witnesses, and legal proceedings to determine the truth? Would most advocates offer their own money and toil simply to endure arguments and derision? The claims of some instead emerge from seeking justice and greater understanding.

Most disbelieving the official story are not deluded. Many authors, speakers, and conspiracy proponents are not greedy fame seekers. Those laughs in contempt at the Lone Gunman theories are patriotic. Reviewing the facts and official documents reveals deep flaws in the American government's conclusions.

## DISTRACTION AND ASSASSINS

The scale of this alleged conspiracy was compact. It was possibly a few men aided by the incompetence and deception of some authorities. Two men according to evidence and witness testimony were feasibly acting to assassinate Senator Kennedy. Wayne's unexplained sprinting distracted witnesses. The convicted assassin who shot the coat of Robert Kennedy and all other victims, and the other armed man, positioned directly behind the Senator.

## THE DISTRACTION
Michael Wayne

## THE CONVICTED ASSASSIN
Sirhan Bishara Sirhan

## THE POSSIBLE ASSASSIN
Thane Eugene Cesar

Sirhan Sirhan will likely die in custody based on a crime he might not have committed. Sirhan might die without impartial justice and having spent his adult life in prison. How can justice prevail if most ignore it? With Sirhan Sirhan's death, a portion of the truth will vanish.

# CHAPTER 20

*"...the price we pay in our own innermost lives,*
*and in the spirit of this country"*

~Robert F. Kennedy
Speech regarding the costs of American involvement in Vietnam.

## EXPERTS, WITNESSES, AND POSSIBLE DISINFORMATION

Thomas Noguchi served in the Los Angeles County Coroner's office and performed Robert Kennedy's autopsy. His findings confirm rear direct shots killed Senator Kennedy. Noguchi withstood public derision, official review, and efforts professionally to discredit him. Among Noguchi's detractors was the Federal Bureau of Investigation. The Bureau subsequently attempted to obtain Noguchi's autopsy report.

The Los Angeles Bureau office reported Noguchi is "well aware that the previously imposed court instruction with respect to release of information in this investigation does not apply to the FBI." Hoover was not pleased.[cmxxii] Noguchi explained his superiors attempted to prevent any discussion regarding the case. Noguchi refused. Officials suspend him on allegations of "drug use, abuse of employees, poor administration of his office, and a desire for tragedy that would bring him personal fame".[cmxxiii]

Attorney Godfrey Isaac later represented Dr. Noguchi. While Isaac was questioning Noguchi before a judge, authorities warned Isaac if he continued he would cause an international incident. Prosecutors indicated added questioning would cast doubt on government findings. Isaac's statements also exposed official hypocrisy in utilizing Noguchi's autopsy results. Authorities used them to attack Noguchi despite the medical record supporting him.

Dr. Noguchi eventually was fully cleared and reinstated. Thomas Noguchi subsequently became Los Angeles County Coroner. As Coroner, he performed the autopsy and scientific evaluation for many important citizens of Los Angeles. Noguchi respectably served the public despite political attacks and threats to his professional capacity.

The ballistics expert officially critical of DeWayne Wolfer's ineptness was William Harper. His testimony later appeared in most official reviews of Robert Kennedy's assassination. Harper aided in the establishment of the Pasadena Police Department Crime Lab, and the Wisconsin State Police Crime Laboratory. He additionally consulted for varied criminal laboratories across the United States.

Harper operated a business offering expertise in firearms and scientific testing. He reviewed hundreds of cases and the Los Angeles Police ignored his findings. Harper also attempted to provide Sirhan's attorney Grant Cooper with information regarding DeWayne Wolfer. His warning included examples of Wolfer's unscientific practices and faulty conclusions. He referred to DeWayne Wolfer as someone happy to provide authorities with the desired results.[cmxxiv]

Unfortunately, Grant Cooper rejected Harper's advice. Ballistics questions went unasked in Sirhan's initial defense. William Harper authored scientific texts and was the first expert to stand against the unscientific practices of authorities. Despite continued mischaracterization of Harper's expertise by detractors, his contributions are valuable additions to the record.

Inventor of a widely used fingerprint device and blood spatter analysis expert, Herbert Mac Donell conducted forensic investigations for decades. He offered his expertise to official reviews concerning the Robert Kennedy's assassination. Mac Donell is a notable member of the scientific community who disputed the lone guilt of Sirhan Sirhan. He additionally served as the Laboratory of Forensic Science's director.

Attorney Bernard Fensterwald worked in the United States State Department, and served during wartime in the Navy. A Harvard law graduate, Fensterwald exposed internal government corruption and illegal practices. This includes unsanctioned wiretaps by government agencies and abuse of citizen rights. He obtained important evidence in the Kennedy investigations and the King inquiry. Fensterwald was instrumental in obtaining repeated classified exhibits for public review.

These experts utilized relevant evidence to guide them. Most witness testimony supports a possible conspiracy. Many instances of suspicious behavior and people surrounded Robert Kennedy's murder. Sirhan Sirhan made several appearances with unnamed persons. Never contemplated, pursued, or apprehended were possible accomplices.

The Ambassador Hotel parking attendant previously witnessed four possible suspects in a white Chevrolet between 11 and 11:30 p.m. Fallah Ben-Jabor states the men were inquiring about the Kennedy entourage. One spoke with a foreign accent and stated, "...he wanted to shake hands with Senator Kennedy." These men do not appear in further Bureau's files.

This does resemble three other men seen with Sirhan in a green mustang June 2, 1968. This was two days before the Senator's assassination.[cmxxv] These are among the uninvestigated figures observed prior to the attack. Authorities believing Sirhan the lone gunman disregard some witness testimony.

Eyewitness Don Schulman observed he saw Robert Kennedy hit with gunfire multiple times. "I saw the security guards draw their weapons".[cmxxvi] Could Thane Cesar have fired? Other witnesses would additionally suggest Cesar fired. The caliber of Cesar's weapon initially following the attack is unknown.

Schulman observing two security guards with guns in the pantry is true; however, other guards arrived following the sounds of gunfire. A single guard, Thane Cesar, had drawn a gun during the attack. The other guard was Jack Merritt who arrived once the shooting ceased according to officials.[cmxxvii] Schulman's testimony affirms Cesar's statement of having a gun out during the events. "The guard did fire..." Schulman asserted fifteen minutes later.[cmxxviii]

Karl Euker is an eyewitness and assisted in subduing Sirhan Sirhan. He restrained Sirhan preventing the necessary firing position. Euker affirmed that following the second gunshot he forced the weapon away from Kennedy. Euker confirmed subsequent to shaking hands with a kitchen helper, Kennedy turned forward again looking at him and they began to advance.

Subsequent witnesses affirmed this detail about Robert Kennedy's position. Kennedy perhaps was not slightly facing to the side as some government sources assert. Euker testified Kennedy was looking forward as eyewitnesses affirm and independent ballistics evidence supports.[cmxxix] Unfortunately, for authorities, evidence and nearly all testimony leave the killing shots beyond Sirhan's reach.

Multiple witnesses affirm Robert Kennedy was indeed looking forward to advance with Karl Euker. Karl Euker remarked about his direct position between Sirhan and Senator Kennedy, "...Sirhan never came that close to Kennedy". Euker continued "It was completely impossible (for Sirhan to fire the shots) because Sirhan was in front of me".[cmxxx]

Euker was among the handful of witnesses who place Sirhan under three feet from Kennedy. Despite this closer distance, it remains impossible for Sirhan to have made the direct rear shots. Four or more men eventually seized Sirhan's body and pinned him. Sirhan could not fire three rear shots from his position.

How can it be possible Senator Kennedy has three rear wounds if Sirhan only had two clear shots in the front? Euker confirmed having Sirhan in a side headlock prevented additional direct shots. The wild shots Sirhan was firing could have easily struck other victims and created random bullet holes. Bullets were lost in the ragged firing pattern of Sirhan Sirhan and evidence mishandling. Can it be so improbable other bullets were lost as well? Supporting Euker's statements is the testimony from the man directly behind him, Eddie Minasaun.

Grand Jury testimony indicates Minasaun noted Sirhan's gun barrel was "three feet" from Senator Kennedy. Although officials have attempted to explain away the head wound, it still leaves two rear wounds to account for. Three wounds occurred from the rear according to the autopsy report. Several well-placed eyewitnesses testified Sirhan could not have fired one, not to mention three rear shots.[cmxxxi] Many closely located eyewitnesses would confirm Kennedy's position and be dismissed. Witnesses spoke of other inconsistencies as well.

A witness who allegedly heard more shots than officially counted is Roger Katz. Katz heard the initial two Sirhan shots then heard a quick-fire series of shots "too rapid to be one person".[cmxxxii] Katz's statement corroborates other witnesses who heard additional shots in the Ambassador Hotel pantry. This supports prior expert assertions of double shots.

Hotel worker Juan Romero observed "He (Robert Kennedy) was shaking my hand and had just turned away".[cmxxxiii] The statement reinforces the testimony of Karl Euker and exhibits Sirhan's inability to fire the shots contained in the autopsy report. Romero explained Sirhan Sirhan's gun was a yard away from Robert Kennedy.[cmxxxiv]

Peter Hamill told the Federal Bureau of Investigation "after Kennedy shook hands he turned and continued to walk straight ahead".[cmxxxv] These eyewitnesses independently have stated Senator Kennedy had a forward position. That would create additional contradictions in the evidentiary record. The contradiction would refute official arguments.

Witness Evan Freed stated Kennedy took a couple steps forward and the shooting began. Freed affirmed five feet separated Sirhan and Robert Kennedy. This again supports Karl Euker and Juan Romero's testimony of too great a distance. Freed testified in an affidavit he witnessed a different gunman shoot Kennedy from behind.[cmxxxvi] Freed saw a man running who he believed might have been an accomplice, Michael Wayne.

Boris Yaro stood three feet from Senator Kennedy as the shooting began. Yaro states "…the gunman started firing at point blank range" not he had the gun pressed to the Senator's head as officially implied. Point blank range is generally three feet or less. Sirhan Sirhan was three feet or less from Robert Kennedy according to Yaro.

Yaro continues, "Kennedy backed up against the freezers as the gunman fired. He cringed and threw his hands up over his face." This would mean Senator Kennedy might have been farther from Sirhan than legally determined.[cmxxxvii] Witnesses and experts suggest Robert Kennedy was facing Sirhan Sirhan. An individual does not cringe at something in their peripheral sight.

Why would the Senator throw his arms up over his face away from the gun? You cannot realize to protect your face, unless the danger is visible in front of you. Although some might attempt to dismiss this as but a minor detail, it renders the fact no less valid. Robert Kennedy reacted to Sirhan because witnesses affirm he was facing him.

Vincent Di Pierro initially affirmed Sirhan Sirhan was not more than eight feet from Robert Kennedy. Di Pierro now recalls a new set of circumstances. However, new recollections do not supersede dozens of other eyewitnesses and his original statements. Was it more likely his recent memory was incorrect or most original witnesses are wrong? In Sirhan's trial testimony, DiPierro noted "two feet to eight foot".[cmxxxviii]

Paul Schrade was a friend of Robert Kennedy and critically wounded in the deadly gunfire. Schrade has reviewed Senator Kennedy's assassination and worked with various authors for years. He affirmed from his later investigations the Los Angeles Police Department had "badgered and browbeat witness to get them to change their story".[cmxxxix] Schrade is just one of the many eyewitnesses that do not support official determinations.

Eyewitnesses have variable recollections of the distance between Sirhan's weapon and Senator Kennedy. Valerie Schulte affirmed six feet and Frank Burns asserted a foot and a half to two feet. Thane Cesar and Richard Lubic state two feet, Martin Patrusky stated three feet, and Juan Romero recalls a yard (three feet). Edward Minasaun said three feet was between the gun and the Senator, and Pete Hamill states "about two feet from the Senator". Sirhan was never observably close enough, nor in the right position to have fired the deadly shots. An outspoken eyewitness prior renewed her public calls for reinvestigation.[cmxl]

In late April 2012, Nina Rhodes-Hughes affirmed to the American media she heard two guns firing during the attack on Robert Kennedy. Placed only feet from Senator Kennedy, she stated "...there was another shooter to my right..." Prosecutors contend Rhodes-Hughes heard no more than eight shots. They argue she was among several witnesses reporting eight shots fired.[cmxli]

Rhodes-Hughes counters she originally said twelve to fourteen shots. She commented Robert Kennedy had straightened his head and continued walking forward. Accordingly, he was facing Sirhan Sirhan. Many have noted the official failure to match Sirhan's position with the ballistics evidence.

Some witnesses did not have direct eye contact with Senator Kennedy in the cramped hotel pantry. They instead heard the attack. Among those in the room was Jesse Unruh, Speaker of the California Assembly. Unruh noted hearing the Los Angeles Police Department hearing between "five and ten shots."[cmxlii]

Witness Booker Griffin, having just entered the pantry's eastern doorway, affirmed hearing two shots followed with "...10 or 12" further shots. Witness Estelyn LaHive was located just outside the west pantry entrance. LaHive heard "...at least 10 shots", this is reported to the Los Angeles Police and seemingly ignored. Nina Rhodes-Hughes states she heard "much more rapid fire" than initially distinguished.[cmxliii]

Many witnesses nearest to Kennedy corroborate the later scientific analysis of forensic audio specialist Philip Van Praag. Van Praag states locating more shots on the Pruzinsky tape than Sirhan's gun alone could fire.[cmxliv] Attorney and former President of the American Academy of Forensic Sciences Robert Joiling affirmed hearing too many shots as well. Forensic audio analyst Wes Dooley affirms both prior expert statements.[cmxlv]

This affirms the rapid-fire descriptions of Jesse Unruh, Booker Griffin, Estelyn LaHive, Nina Rhodes-Hughes, and Roger Katz. Rhodes-Hughes was among those never before called to testify. Authorities have reviewed and disputed her statements. Rhodes-Hughes was the first witness to emerge in nearly a decade.

Responding to Rhodes-Hughes' most recent statements the California Attorney General disagreed. Despite acknowledging the alleged presence of a second gunman at the scene, authorities insist Sirhan remains guilty. Despite the admitted possible existence of other parties involved, Sirhan remains the rallying point for critics and authorities.[cmxlvi]

Sirhan's current attorney, William F. Pepper, explained Rhodes-Hughes identified fifteen errors in her Bureau statement. Errors included altering the number of shots Rhodes-Hughes reported to investigators. Although official "covering actions" might continue, their claims have become untenable. Transformed assertions have become increasingly obvious to the public. Some nearby witnesses observed and heard too many shots for a single assassin. This testimony implies a possible assassination conspiracy.

Two guns were feasibly present in the pantry according to many witnesses, some experts, and scientific evidence. One gun could only fire eight shots, the ballistics tests and official statements prove this. A single man was possibly in the necessary position defined by medical and scientific experts to fire killing shots. This was not the man prosecuted and imprisoned for the crime.

# CHAPTER 21

*"People of the same trade seldom meet together, even for merriment and diversion, but the conversation ends in a conspiracy against the public, or in some contrivance to raise prices."*

~Adam Smith
Scottish Economist and Philosopher

## FINDINGS AND CONCLUSIONS

Robert Kennedy had proven highly placed enemies who repeatedly defied the law seeking to end his political career. He had massive conflicts with military commanders, the Mafia, intelligence leaders, and President Johnson himself. These highly placed enemies based on repeated actions were capable of nearly any action to achieve their chosen agenda. These men may have overseen a concealment of the facts.

## THE CONSPIRATORS

So who were the men behind it all? Which of the Hands leaders had the most understanding of the assassination and conspiracy? They must possess great influence within American society with access to untraceable wealth and agents. A second possible Kennedy presidency again threatened a few individuals' financial and political futures.

# The Leaders of the Assassination

## The Criminal Hand:
Possible Rogue Central Intelligence Agency member or Mafia contact to Thane Cesar

## The Leaders of the Conspiracy
Those men who conceivably based upon their actions and statements oversaw the alleged official suppression of events.

## The Officials Hand:
Lyndon Johnson, J. Edgar Hoover

## The Military Intelligence Hand:
Central Intelligence Agency contact to Manuel Pena


# Did the Assassination Conspiracy Occur?

The overwhelming majority of original scientific evidence, witness statements, and official attacks on the record suggest a feasible plot. Verified evidence and circumstances regarding the ambush suggest Robert F. Kennedy was the victim of a deadly conspiracy. Witnesses continue to emerge with familiar assertions of government obstruction. The record does not speak well for the United States government's case if Sirhan Sirhan obtains retrial.

This marked a third American political assassination in just more than five years. Robert Kennedy's murder created a significant rift among those who believed officials and those supporting conspiracy. American culture was no longer the seemingly idealistic place many believed. Destroyed was the long American belief that its own politics were somehow immune to unconscionable tactics used abroad.

Lost forever were the innocence and trust of generations. In death, Robert Kennedy was the final American political martyr. His murder echoed throughout the United States, it was a final theft of American democracy visible to all. Unfortunately, Robert Kennedy's demise failed to receive a proper investigation.

Although John F. Kennedy and Martin Luther King's assassinations' have undergone repeated later Congressional inspection, this last death never did. While the years passed, much fell to the American public to piece together. The aid from international experts, technological developments, and the release of documents has brought more focus to what once seemed impossible to discern.

Author Ted Charach released information in a press conference in 1993. Charach stated having found Cesar's personal .22-caliber pistol. The gun reportedly emerged from a pond in Arkansas. It possessed the matching serial numbers to the receipt kept by Jim Yoder long ago.[cmxlvii] Since 1998, no conclusive information on the weapon has been forthcoming.

However, legally documented past malfeasance by the Federal Bureau of Investigation's leadership is verified. Central Intelligence Agency leaders that ignored United States law ought to trouble every American. Many authorities neglected a huge segment of witnesses and exhibits they did not wish published, for whatever reason. With investigation and verification, some reasonable facts and evidence is readily available.

Despite the invalidation of important claims in the official reviews and providing contending primary evidence, some will never accept feasible conspiracy. Some will never believe anything in any book with contrary evidence. Some will likely also seek to malign any individual connected to it. Ignore the speculation and remember the full truth is a mixture of the evidence and facts in many texts. Facts not opinions must eventually prevail.

No text on any subject is a standalone work. You must pursue all reasonable evidence to find some truth. This book hopefully will offer new insights and generate conversations. No single book will ever be the final word. No author enjoys the final word despite various claims.

It remains the curse of historic assassination conspiracies. Similar to Julius Caesar's demise, the perpetrators are ever sought out for revulsion and loathing. In a thousand years conceivably, stage dramas might include a tale of three American tragedies. Yet these events and their effect on America remain critically important. Political ambitions began long ago have transformed into dangerous realities.

Each public murder quickened the eventual corruption of a once functioning democratic process. Things have not improved. The United States political system is drowning in endless allegations. Proof of mismanagement and manipulation exists in abundance. In my estimation, some current laws exist solely on unfounded precepts. These past events and those developments are connected.

# CHAPTER 22

*"I don't give a shit about the law"*

~Richard M. Nixon
President of the United States

## UNCONSTITUTIONAL POWERS

The assassinations of John F. Kennedy, Martin Luther King, and Robert Kennedy are symbolic. Each leader's death permanently affected the American Republic. These men of diplomacy and peace died. Men of propaganda and war have long ruled in their place. Some who replace great leaders often seek greater unconstitutional power as well. The American Executive's powers have increased with the expansion of military and industrial operations.

The unconstitutional expansion of executive branch power has continued in modern American history. Some American President's subordinates when convenient disregard their own legal system. Central Intelligence Agency employee Sam Halpern told the Senate (Church) Committee, the Agency had the power to conceal any information it considered important. He claimed the Agency had the ability to do so eternally if this suited their goals.[cmxlviii]

Like the President's (Warren) Commission, various official inquiries were subject to Central Intelligence Agency machinations. Congressional leaders, including the Senate (Church) Committee were all partially deceived. This is a brazen example of nefarious actions undertaken by the

Agency. These actions occurred against elected congress members and their lawful investigations.

The American public demanded accountability from the Central Intelligence Agency for repeated unsanctioned programs. The United States President's (Rockefeller) Commission on Central Intelligence Agency Activities was undertaken. President Gerald Ford's executive order created the group. This Commission reviewed the Agency's repeated unsanctioned practices. The President's (Rockefeller) Commission was convinced, "the great majority of the Central Intelligence Agency's domestic activities comply with its statutory authority". However, it also found "...the CIA has engaged in some activities that should be criticized and not permitted to happen again—both in light of the limits imposed on the Agency by law and as a matter of public policy".[cmxlix]

The Commissioners addressed the inherent oversight flaws occurring because of "ambiguities." Unfortunately, like the President's (Warren) Commission, this report was full of recommendations. The Commission ought to have created new standards for congressional review and implementation. However, this Commission did at least suggest President Ford "should by Executive Order prohibit the collection of information about the domestic activities of United States citizens (whether by overt or covert means)".[cml]

The Report of the President's (Rockefeller) Commission confirmed, "For a period of over 20 years, however, an agreement existed between the Department of Justice and the CIA." The agreement allowed the Agency "...to investigate allegations of crimes by CIA employees or agents which involved Government money or property or might involve operational security." Therefore, the Department of Justice failed to fully monitor and hold the Agency employees responsible for their actions.[cmli] The Department of Justice plausibly allowed the Agency to run amok for decades.

The Commission Report additionally stated, "Some improvement in the congressional oversight system would be helpful." This need for additional oversight and improvement has remained for decades.[cmlii] In some cases, the Agency confirmed its negligence. However, executive branch organizations consistently failed to share information with the American Congress in a timely manner.

The Senate Select (Church) Committee Report states, "Prior to the 1947 National Security Act, Congress did not seek to expressly authorize or regulate foreign intelligence activity by statute. Congress' decision not to act however, did not reduce or eliminate its constitutional power to do so in the future".[cmliii] Yet, the Senate Report did verify the Agency consulted with congressional leaders in some operations.

Congressional advisement occurred in roughly a quarter of all operations.[cmliv] These were enduring Agency practices, to act with authority neither it nor any American President ever possessed. Some CIA officials sought approval only when they felt it was necessary. These oversights and illicit actions still affect modern diplomacy.

Central Intelligence Agency operations had unexpected future prices. These shortsighted victories eventually caused many long-term dangers for America. Agency foreign tactics, instead of being subtly applied, involved heinous actions. Weak societies the Agency influenced created additional unintended consequences.

"In some cases covert support has encouraged a debilitating dependence on the United States. In one Western nation, the Agency's covert investment...controlled local politics. According to a former CIA station chief in that country: Any aspiring politician almost automatically would come to CIA to see if we could help him get elected...They were the wards of the United States, and that whatever happened to them good or bad was the fault of the United States".[cmlv] However, the American public remained unaware of these actions until years later.

This secretive attitude toward fellow government entities caused dire American intelligence failures. The Central Intelligence Agency has performed these actions repeatedly under several executives with similar intent. Many American Presidents have manipulated the purpose and scope of their powers using the Agency. The Chief Executive might be the highest lawful authority in America. Yet some failed to protect the rights of fellow citizens.

Now consider overreaching executive power concerning American Congressional War authority. Congress has used its own war powers less than fifteen times in United States history when a war actually began. American Presidents have sent troops into combat operations abroad hundreds of times.[cmlvi] The Executive Branch allegedly continues to use powers beyond those provided in America's Constitution.[cmlvii]

During the Reagan administration, government employees raised a lawsuit against forced secrecy contracts. The United States Congress had already banned two former documents that executive agency employees refused to sign. These federal employees argued secrecy requirements breached the previous legal ban. What followed was a glaring move of egotistic overreaching. The Reagan administration declared the standing ban unconstitutionally curbed executive powers. They suggested the American President had "sovereign rights" to control national security information.

The executive branch was asserting powers it never had. The sovereign rights the Reagan administration claimed do not exist. However, a judge ruled in their favor. It was a simple case of judicial activism in my view. However, those now decrying judicial activism were silent. Some who decry activist judges seem to hail possibly illegitimate legal decisions that support their political agenda.

The presiding judge confirms in his ruling "neither political branch (Congressional and Executive) is expressly charged by the Constitution with regulation, accumulation of, or access to, national security information."[cmlviii] The Constitution must prevail despite what some agency, executive, or lower court judge believes. Unfortunately, this does not prevent misinterpretation with disastrous effects. Congressional action could have stopped these executive power seizures.

The Supreme Court should have already perused and dismissed these ridiculous claims of power. American Presidents have used foreign policy to defend assumed war powers. Previously the Senate Select (Church) Committee report discussed the Constitution's grant of "concurrent jurisdiction to the Congress in foreign affairs and Congress' exclusive constitutional authority to declare war. There is little to support such an extravagant claim of Presidential power in peacetime."[cmlix]

False information was the basis for multiple disastrous American executive declared military engagements. Flawed intelligence gathering led to the Gulf of Tonkin deception, failing to anticipate the Tet Offensive, the latest Iraq War, and the Afghanistan quagmire. America repeatedly enters into protracted foreign wars on unreliable information or impossible goals. Why does it keep happening and who benefits from the rise of dominant military, industrial, and political groups?

The United States must conclude simultaneous presidential wars that continue to drain the economy. Politicians without true fiscal principals perpetually increase the current United States national debt. Trillions of American public dollars have funded open-ended military operations.[cmlx] American military commanders and political leaders ignore the reality on the ground. The leading United States commander in Afghanistan ensures troops will be present for years to come.[cmlxi]

Repeatedly endured are the forgotten lessons of Vietnam. There are no painless solutions. United States leaders have painted its citizens in a military ideological corner, again. American soldiers endure the Afghanistan campaign and return to "advise" in Iraq, as previous soldiers advised in Vietnam. The United States is again responsible for other countries because of executive ambitions.

These expansive modern wars, clandestine operations, and failed policies are the costs of executive power unchecked. The murder of important men in American society had dire consequences. It accelerated the rise of dangerous, increasingly oppressive official and corporate power. This legacy has left America with enduring problems that will plague its people for generations.

A "Compassionate-Conservative" president started unnecessary wars and presided over the greatest period of citizen monetary loss since the Great Depression. His "Liberal-Socialist" successor provided a financial windfall to some benefiting from America's economic implosion. Instead of liberal policies, citizen rights continue to diminish and campaign promises remain unfulfilled. So long as Guantanamo Bay is operational, no honest American claims moral superiority. Until American soldiers are home from unnecessary wars and given proper care, America's officials have failed. The truth remains for those who do not turn from it.

These are the heavy costs of repeated policy errors, as one American branch of government seizes the legal powers granted to a second. Possible executive branch corruption is additionally observable in modern Secret Service controversies. This indicates corruption has long existed within the executive branch. Secret Service agents faced greater than sixty cases of past misconduct in less than a decade. These prior charges do not include the Colombian prostitution scandal, which is a different matter entirely.

Most Secret Service agents have taken up an important official position and provide worthy civil service. However, many prior misconduct allegations and current accusations do imply something. Some elite agents felt a sense of entitlement, which has increased over the years. Power corrupts all people to some degree, including those who serve as the American President's final line of security.

In President Kennedy's time, Secret Service partied the night before the assassination. Modern times have allowed for added disregard of government policy and law.[cmlxii] This vanity has not receded but grown in other positions of government. A minority in various United States agencies view the Constitution as a barrier to pierce, instead of honored text and final legal authority.

Over generations, the national security business has increased and continued to enforce unconstitutional executive mandates. Officials financed their errors at the public expense, all in the vague name of security. If the American public continues to ignore these problems, they will continue to worsen. If government ambitions prevail over freedom and citizen rights, America shall no longer be a Republic, but an Empire.


## THE CONSEQUENCES OF UNCONSTITUTIONAL AMBITION

Former associations of the executive branch in time have transformed American military operations into a perpetual war machine. The machine President Eisenhower warned us of long ago. Many have spoken of this militaristic nightmare. For many Americans mistrust and apathy have replaced patriotism.

Unsustainable economic policies have resulted in the devastation of small businesses and the middle class. Political corruption and societal discord have increased with overbearing unnecessary government expansion. Using deceptive titles some leaders have declared powers that ignore constitutional rights. They are powers because to call them laws would imply legitimacy.

Within the Patriot Act, the United States military can be used to "Enforce Prohibition in Certain Emergencies". This implies American troops could enforce Federal mandates regarding any prohibition they contrive.[cmlxiii] It allows the Federal government to use the American military as a blunt object. All to enforce mandates against the will of United States citizens. A quiet threat of Martial Law for any reason, without due process, ought to offend you.

This section of the Patriot Act violates United States constitutional laws in my view. These military deployments to "prohibit" Americans do not allow them peaceable assembly nor "to petition for redress of grievances".[cmlxiv] It does not offer the legal protections including "a speedy and public trial, by an impartial jury…" only military enforcement of law.[cmlxv] It additionally violates the American public's right to "be secure in their persons, houses, papers, and effects".[cmlxvi]

A military occupation would deny these constitutional rights. Prohibitive actions for reasoning determined by unelected leaders are possible. This is not what America's Founders had in mind. These claims are powers that no American Executive does or ought to possess. Many politicians in each dominant political party supported these powers.

Congressional Republicans and Democrats have gained great power in the American political system. These parties have ground the wheels of progress to a near halt. If American leaders will not reason with each other to serve the country, whom instead are they serving? Forgotten are the endless promises of accountability.

Yet a few members of the American judiciary have stood with the Constitution and law. For its use of warrantless email and telephone data seizure, the Federal Bureau of Investigation faced legal reprimand. United States District Court Judge Victor Marrero found authorities had exceeded their authority and the American Constitution's limits. Government secrecy provisions according to Judge Marrero are "the legislative equivalent of breaking and entering, with an ominous free pass to the hijacking of constitutional values".[cmlxvii]

United States District Judge Ann Aiken of Oregon stated the Patriot Act awarded the American government too much surveillance power of suspected criminals. In 2008, the Bush administration appealed this ruling in a different state. American executives display little regard for jurisdiction and constitutional law. The American government will not protect the Constitution if citizens do not legally compel it to.

The executive branch has never claimed such unconstitutional power without massive legal repercussion. The House and Senate have never been more dysfunctional since the Civil War. The Republic shudders, the People call out for relief, and this immense array of injustices remain unanswered. American citizens suffer and authorities dismiss mentions of valid legal grievance.

## POSSIBLE ANSWERS

The President's (Rockefeller) Commission investigated and confirmed previous government illegality. The Commission included a statement current American leaders ought to review, "Government Must Obey the Law, The individual liberties of American citizens depend on government observance of the law. Under our form of government, authority can be exercised only if it has been properly delegated to a particular department or agency by the Constitution or Congress".[cmlxviii]

However, it is not solely the fault of the current executive branch. Varying past ambitious officials also should bear the blame. American Presidents unconnected to these ambitions later suffered political blowback. These reprisals stemmed from actions their executive predecessors committed. Iran, Iraq, Cuba, Venezuela, and Afghanistan for instance. Modern America pays the cost of failed past operations and allies who become enemies.

Current practices resemble forgotten mistakes. Are modern counterterrorism surveillance methods different from the illegal wiretapping programs of J. Edgar Hoover? In recent history, the executive branch prior claimed domestic threats might face assassination without due process. Legally, American citizens with full constitutional rights are not subject to summary execution if their president alone determines them a "threat". For how could this decision be justly determined?

What flawed standards could imagine this action was just? What mood will accompany your one-man judge, jury, and executioner? Any individual who imagines they deserve the power of life and death over American citizens without trial is a shallow egotist. Ideally, Americans would not elect them in the first place.[cmlxix][cmlxx] These are not American principals but tyranny.

Liberty is the most precious gift we possess. Centuries of blood and conflict have raged to gain current American rights. What value are these past sacrifices if Americans easily give away their liberty? American citizen rights must prevail in a lawful court and with legal protest, no matter the cost.

Just because the American government declares it can suspend the Constitution, does not give them power to do so. If the government succeeds, it remains illegal. This is a tyrannical claim of power that deserves contempt in a nation of laws. If the document investing the American government with its authority is suspended, then so too is the power it provides. No United States government is greater than the American Constitution or its citizens, no matter the context.

The essence of the United States Constitution legally prevents the denial of due process to citizens in the name of security. American due process always includes a judge and jury of your peers, despite the prior opinions of political leaders. The less care and attention given to America's political system, the further it will observably wither. American citizen loyalty is the reason law and order thrives. Unconstitutional laws damage the people and the government.

The United States National Security Agency "Prism" surveillance program was more recently unmasked. The program represents confirmation of the worst suspected abuses of government. Millions of American taxpayer dollars fund the expanded digital net over Internet users. Despite official assurances theses invasive practices violated the American Constitution in some instances.[cmlxxi][cmlxxii] Therefore, past fears of government ambition are now a reality. Some judges have additionally ruled these programs unconstitutional as well.

Despite the mounting costs to America and its citizens, its government now seeks additional military quagmires. Multiple foreign wars linger on the horizon. The United Nations should resolve current disputes. It is not the responsibility of America to fix every international tragedy. Instead of creating new international problems, the American government should focus on domestic responsibilities.

Apathy, silence, and tacit consent will not prevent a democratic republic's fall. Executive ambitions have continued during praised administrations. Their political reaching exceeds their legal grasp. Yet many legal authorities are silent. If American citizens allow increasing domestic repressions of freedom, they will continue to observe the Military-Industrial Complex prosper.

With all executive power increases, a loss of democratic protections has occurred. History attests once rights are forfeit they never return without great sacrifice. Security is far less important than individual freedom. So long as the United States Constitution is the ultimate authority, government remains shackled with responsibility to the American people. Citizen liberty and government service is essential in a free society.

American Presidents have been constrained by term limits. Term limitations are necessary for the American Congress as well. This would prevent lifelong politicians who occupy positions heedless of modern innovation and social change. American officials could use time more productively realizing they have a set duration. With no time to build a fortune and legacy, they might consider rebuilding the American infrastructure.

Will democratic republicanism and limited yet independent Federalism guide the course? Shall the United States Congress reclaim the War and other legal powers it has largely ceded to the executive branch? Shall false and unconstitutional powers stand? If the United States government acts so freely with citizen rights, how long shall citizens possess them? There is no simple solution to these problems and official suppression solves nothing. It merely insults the intelligence of America's citizenry and the character of its republic.

# GLOSSARY

**Arm of the Conspiracy:**
A group comprised of members serving possible Conspirators.

**Arms of the Conspiracy:**
This represents the entire association of people. Some acted alone and in concert to perform the assassination and conceal a conspiracy.

**American Gestapo:**
The term represents the worst possible abuses of the Central Intelligence Agency and Federal Bureau of Investigation under the wrong leadership.

**Assassination Conspiracy:**
A form of political murder to accomplish set illegal goals that often destabilizes national governments. This includes subsequent unlawful attempts to suppress the truth. Large nations have used it to control smaller countries. Governments have used it repeatedly throughout history from the murder of Julius Caesar to the murder of Abraham Lincoln.

**Big Lyndon's Boys:**
A mixture of political, criminal, and government officials who served the interests of local, state, and national office holder Lyndon Johnson.

**Grand Conspiracy Theory:**
The impossible claim that 50, 100, or more people acted in tandem to accomplish a large conspiracy. Often this idea is a rallying cry that all possible domestic conspiracy is impossible despite the evidence.

**Hand of the Conspiracy:**
A small group comprised of members serving possible Conspirators.

**Military-Industrial Complex:**
A diverse group of corporations that maintains influence and success based upon continuous military operations.

**Sniper A:**
The alleged person located in Dealey Plaza that fired the killing shots at President John F. Kennedy.

**Sniper B:**
The alleged person located at the Texas School Book Depository who fired the shots that struck an eyewitness, President John F. Kennedy, and Governor John Connally.

**The Conspirators:**
The few associated people who shared murderous intent that possibly designed and ordered assassination conspiracies. Each possessed motive, means, and opportunity.

**The Criminal Commission:**
The Mafia leaders who preside over all national Mafia operations.

**The False Oswald Imposter:**
A mixture of deception and evidence the Central Intelligence Agency offered to officials and the public.

**The Lone Gunman Theory:**
This idea contends a single assassin in multiple political murders despite the substantial contending evidence. This idea appeared in American culture with positive and negative associations.

# CHAPTER QUOTATIONS

1.  Niccolo Machiavelli, "The Discourses of Livy", Ninian Hill Thomson, Digireads.com Publishing, January 2008, p. 55

2.  John Webster, "The Duchess of Malfi", Act Four, Scene Two, 1623

3.  Sam and Chuck Giancana, "Double Cross: The Explosive, Inside Story of the Mobster Who Controlled America." Warner Books, 1992, p. 215

4.  Antony Jay, "The Oxford Dictionary of Political Quotations", Oxford University Press, 2001, Satires by Juvenal, p. 195

5.  Alison Jones, Stephanie Pickering, Megan Thomson, "Dictionary of Quotations", Chambers Publishing, September 17, 1997, anonymous bus passenger, p. 23

6.  Simon Wiesenthal, excerpt of the "The Sunflower: on the Possibility of Forgiveness", wiesenthal.com

7.  Henry David Thoreau, "Walden", 1854, p. 276

8.  "I have been to the Mountaintop speech", Dr. Martin Luther King Jr. in Memphis, Tennessee, April 3, 1968

9.  Niccolo Machiavelli, "The Prince", Oxford University Press, New York, 1984, p. 65

10. A. Jones, S. Pickering, M. Thomson, "Dictionary of Quotations", p. 25

11. "Riverside Church Speech", M.L. King referring to the US Government and its conduct of the Vietnam War, April 4, 1967

12. Cornelius Tacitus, "The Histories, section 28, The Murder of Galba", circa 69 to 96 ACE

13. Langston Hughes, "The Collected Poems of Langston Hughes", Alfred A. Knopf, Inc. 1994, p. 130

14. Herman Melville, "Moby Dick", Chapter Thirty Six, Planet EBook, 1851, p. 258

15. N. Machiavelli, " The Prince", p. 56

16. Lucius Annaeus Seneca (Seneca the Younger), "Phaedra" an adaption of Euripides "Hippolytus"

17. A. Jones, S. Pickering, M. Thomson, "Dictionary of Quotations", p. 163

18. A. Jones, S. Pickering, M. Thomson, "Dictionary of Quotations", p. 15

19. Sir Arthur Conan Doyle and Kyle Freeman, "The Casebook of Sherlock Holmes", "The Complete Sherlock Holmes", Spark Educational Publishing, 2003.

20. "Speaking of the costs to American society in Vietnam", Robert F. Kennedy, Kansas State University on March 18, 1968, RFK American Experience, www.pbs.org

21. Adam Smith, "An Inquiry into the Nature and Causes of the Wealth of Nations", Book One, Chapter Ten, Part Two, 1776

22. Peter Kunhardt, "Nixon by Nixon: In His Own Words", HBO Documentary Films, 2014

# INDEX

**Dealey** Plaza (Scene of the JFK Assassination) 38, 47, 72, 102, 112, 134, 135, 141, 142, 152

**de Mohrenschildt**, George (Oswald associate) 97-98, 144, 150, 151

**Di Pierro**, Vincent (Eyewitness) 256

**Directorio** Revolucionario Estudiantil (DRE), (Anti-Castro group funded by the CIA) 28, 91, 93

**Dulles**, Allen (CIA Director) 55, 60, 61, 74-75, 76, 77, 78, 79, 81, 82, 152

**Ebersole**, John (Bethesda Doctor) 122-123, 126

**Edwards**, Sheffield (CIA and US Military Officer) 55, 76, 78, 82

**Edwards**, Robert (Eyewitness) 138-139

**Eisenhower**, Dwight D. (President and General) 18, 26, 55, 79, 168, 267

**Elkins**, Harold (Eyewitness and Deputy Sheriff) 140

**Estes**, Billy Sol (Johnson Associate) 52

**Euker**, Karl (Eyewitness) 241, 242, 254-255, 256

**Federal** Bureau of Investigation (FBI, the Bureau) 20, 21, 22, 25, 28, 32, 37, 40-45, 47, 50, 53, 54, 57, 60-61, 62, 63, 68, 71, 72, 75, 76, 77, 83, 91, 93, 97, 98, 99, 100, 101, 105, 106, 107, 108, 109, 110, 112, 116, 123, 124, 126, 129, 131, 133, 138, 144, 145, 146, 151, 153, 157, 162, 169, 173, 174, 175, 176, 177, 178, 179, 180, 181, 183, 184, 186, 190, 197, 202, 206, 208, 216, 217, 218, 219, 220-224, 225, 226, 228, 237, 238, 239, 240, 241, 246, 248, 249, 250, 252, 254, 255, 258, 261, 268

**Fensterwald**, Bernard (State Department Official) 253

**Ferrell**, Mary (Law Secretary and Researcher) 137

**Ferrie**, David (Previous alleged suspect) 26, 44, 45, 91, 92, 147

**Files**, James (Asserted gunman) 145-146, 147, 148

**Finck**, Pierre (Forensic Pathologist) 116-117, 118, 121, 124, 126, 127

**Ford**, Gerald (Congressman and President) 57, 59, 61, 62, 87, 132, 139

**Ford**, Declan (Marina Oswald's representative and CIA asset) 144

**Foreman**, Percy (Early trial attorney of James Earl Ray) 163

**Frady**, Marshall (Eyewitness) 191, 193

**Frazier**, Buell (Witness) 107, 139

**Frazier**, Robert (FBI expert) 72

**Frente** Revolucionario Demicratico (FRD) (Anti-Castro group funded by the CIA) 90-91

**Freed**, Evan (Eyewitness) 242, 256

**Gardner**, William (Ambassador Hotel Security Chief) 240

**Garrison**, Jim (Prosecutor and Judge) 44, 46, 121, 136-137, 147, 148

**Giancana**, Sam (Mafia Leader) 24, 26-27, 28

**Grassy** Knoll (Possible second origin point of shots in Dealey Plaza) 39, 48, 104, 111, 112, 131, 134, 137-141, 142, 144, 145

**Gregory**, Charles (Parkland Doctor) 115

**Griffin**, Booker (Dr. King's Driver) 257

**Griffin**, Burt (President's Commission attorney) 33

**Gunn**, T. Jeremy (ARRB Chief Counsel) 97, 117, 120, 121, 122, 123, 124

**Haldeman**, H.R. (Nixon Chief of Staff) 66, 76

**Hamill**, Peter (Eyewitness) 255, 257

**Hanes** Sr., Arthur (Lawyer for James Earl Ray) 162-163

**Harper**, William (Forensic Expert) 207, 228-229, 244, 246, 247, 253

**Hartmann**, Melbourne (CIA Research Staff Agent) 89

**Harvey**, William (CIA Officer and former FBI Agent) 75-76, 83, 152

**Healey**, Robert (Witness) 239-240

**Helms**, Richard (CIA Director) 65, 75, 76, 77, 81-82, 83, 84, 148, 152, 153, 232

**Hernandez**, Carlos (Anti-Castro Cuban militant) 92-93

**Hernandez**, Enrique (LAPD) 226, 234

**Hickey**, George (Secret Service Agent) 39

**Holloman**, Frank (Memphis Director of Fire and Safety) 172

**Hoover**, J. Edgar (FBI Director) 18, 31, 32, 40-41, 43, 44, 45, 46, 53, 54, 60, 63, 64, 68, 75, 77, 83, 101, 106, 116, 123, 124, 131, 142, 152, 153, 163, 169, 175, 176, 178, 179, 180, 189, 197, 201, 215, 216, 217, 218, 219, 220, 221, 222, 223, 237, 252, 260, 269

**Hosty**, James (FBI Agent) 41, 42, 100

**Humes**, James (Bethesda Lead Doctor) 116, 117-120, 122, 125, 126, 127

**Hunt**, Everett Howard (CIA Agent) 64, 65, 72

**Hunt**, Lafayette Harold (Influential Political Donor) 33, 34, 72, 175

**Huntley**, Ronald R. (Kennedy Security) 238

**Hutton**, Pat (Parkland Nurse) 114

**Jackson**, Jessie (SCLC Member) 169, 190-195

**Jenkins**, James (Bethesda Staff) 125, 126

**Jenkins**, Marion (Parkland Doctor) 114

**Jenkins**, Walter (Assistant to President Johnson) 215

**Jim's** Grill (Near the possible origin of the shot killing MLK) 161, 163, 164, 172, 173, 179, 181, 182, 185, 187, 192

**John** Birch Society (Political Organization) 69, 70, 72, 73, 168-169

**Johnson**, Lyndon (President and Senator) 28, 35, 36, 40, 43, 44, 45, 48-51, 52, 53, 54, 55, 56, 57, 58, 59, 61, 64, 66, 68, 69, 72, 75, 84, 116, 127, 129, 130, 132, 133, 142, 152, 157, 158, 168, 169-170, 175, 194, 197, 198, 201, 202, 207, 214, 215, 216, 217, 218, 219, 235, 237, 242, 259, 260

**Joiling**, Robert (Audio Expert) 211, 257

**Jones**, Ronald (Parkland Doctor) 113, 115

**Jones**, Solomon (Eyewitness) 182

**Jowers**, Lloyd (Possible Accomplice) 163, 164, 182, 185, 186, 187, 189

**Katz**, Roger (Eyewitness) 255, 257

**Katzenback**, Nicholas (Attorney General) 53, 54, 55, 57, 58, 63, 64, 130, 132

**Kennedy**, John F. (Senator and President) 17, 18, 19, 21, 22, 24, 25, 26, 27, 29, 32, 35, 36, 37, 38, 41, 44, 50, 51, 52, 54, 55, 56, 64, 67, 68, 69, 70, 72, 73, 74, 76, 77, 79, 80, 81, 83, 90, 92, 96, 101, 102, 103, 105, 106, 108, 111, 112, 113, 116, 117, 126, 130, 131, 133, 134, 135, 139, 142, 144, 145, 150, 152, 153, 157, 159, 160, 161, 168, 174, 175, 186, 215, 260, 262

**Kennedy**, Robert F. (Attorney General and Senator) 17, 24, 25, 28, 48, 49, 55, 57, 58, 86, 127, 166, 168, 198, 201, 202, 205, 206, 208, 209, 211, 212, 214, 215, 216, 217, 218, 220, 221, 222, 223, 224, 225, 228, 229, 230, 233, 234, 235, 237, 238, 239, 240, 241, 242, 243, 244, 245, 246, 247, 248, 250, 251, 252, 254, 255, 256, 257, 260, 262

**Kennedy**-Onassis, Jacqueline (First Lady) 116, 216

**King**, Joseph Caldwell (CIA Officer) 55, 77, 96, 152

**King** Jr., Martin Luther (Civil Rights Leader) 17, 69, 157, 158-159, 160, 161, 162, 164, 165, 166, 168, 169, 170, 171, 172, 173, 174, 175, 176, 177, 178, 180, 181, 182, 183, 184, 185, 186, 187, 188, 189, 190, 191, 192, 193, 194, 196, 197, 198, 202, 216, 217, 218, 262

**Kyles**, Billy (SCLC Member) 171, 181, 190, 191, 192, 193, 195

**LaHive**, Estelyn (Witness) 257

**Lane**, Mark (Author and Attorney) 46

**Lansky**, Meyer (Mafia leader) 26, 28, 30, 31, 152

**Larson**, William (CIA Chief of Information Staff) 88-89

**Lemnitzer**, Lyman (General) 67-68

**Los** Angeles Police Department (LAPD) 202, 204, 207, 209, 210, 212, 218, 219, 222, 223, 225, 226, 227, 228, 232, 233, 234, 241, 245, 246, 247, 248-250, 253, 256, 257

**Lovelady**, Billy (Eyewitness) 140

**Lubic**, Richard (Eyewitness) 256

**Lux**, Henry (Chief of Memphis Police) 171

**Mac Donell**, Herbert (Forensic Expert and Former President of the Academy of Forensic Sciences) 229, 253

**Ray**, James Earl (Official Assassin) 158, 161-163, 173, 182, 183, 184, 185, 186, 187, 189, 190, 197, 209, 210

**Reilly**, Frank (Witness) 140

**Riebe**, Floyd (Bethesda medical staff) 125, 126

**Roberts**, Emory (Secret Service) 38

**Rhodes-Hughes**, Nina (Eyewitness) 257, 258

**Romero**, Juan (Eyewitness) 255, 256

**Roselli**, Johnny (Mafia and Cuban exile contact for Castro Plots) 29-30, 31, 75, 76, 78, 150, 151, 152, 210

**Rowley**, James J. (Secret Service Chief Agent) 37

**Royer**, Judy (Witness) 239

**Ruby**, Jack (Assassin) 32-34, 46, 103, 107, 131, 147, 149

**Russell** Jr., Richard (Senator) 50, 56, 57, 59, 60, 62, 86, 87, 133

**Rybka**, Henry (Secret Service) 38

**Scelso** (Whitten), John (CIA Agent) 76, 77, 83, 95, 99

**Shanklin**, J. Gordon (FBI Officer) 42, 43

**Sharaga**, Paul (LAPD) 226

**Schrade**, Paul (Eyewitness) 208, 256

**Schulman**, Don (Witness) 254

**Secret** Service (Presidential security) 37-39

**Shaw**, Clay (Garrison Suspect) 121, 137, 147

**Shaw**, Robert (Parkland Doctor) 115

**Siebert**, James (FBI Agent) 124, 126

**Simons**, James (Eyewitness) 140

**Sirhan**, Sirhan (Official Assassin) 203-209, 210, 211, 212, 213, 218, 223, 224, 225, 226, 229, 230, 238, 239, 240, 241, 242, 243, 247, 248, 251, 253, 254, 255, 256, 257, 258, 260

**Smith**, Don (Memphis Police) 171

**Smith**, Edgar (Witness) 139

**Smith**, Joe M. (DPD) 141

**Smith**, Sergio Arcacha (CRC Delegate) 44, 45, 91

**Smith**, Tony (Memphis Police) 189, 190

**Sorrels**, Forrest (Secret Service) 39, 141

**Southern** Christian Leadership Conference (SCLC) 172, 176, 178, 180, 181, 188, 189, 192, 193, 194

**Specter**, Arlen (President's Commission Staff) 117, 119, 124

# NOTES

ABBREVIATIONS:

SA ............. Special Agent

SAC ........... Special Agent in Charge

(n.d.) .......... No listed date

Pres. ........... President's

Com. .......... Commission

Comm. ....... Committee

sub. ............ subject

subs. .......... Subsection

HSCA ......... House Select Committee on Assassinations

## JFK

i ................. Antony Jay, "The Oxford Dictionary of Political Quotations", Oxford University Press, 2001: Dwight D. Eisenhower Presidential Farewell Address p. 123

ii ................ John F. Kennedy, speech to the Greater Houston ministerial Association during the Presidential campaign, 1960

iii ............... United States Select Committee on Assassinations of the U.S. House of Representatives (House Select Committee on Assassinations, HSCA), Segregated Central Intelligence Agency File, Incident Report Re: John E. Donovan Acquaintance with Lee Harvey Oswald, Box 41, December 1, 1963, Mary Ferrell Foundation (MFF), maryferrell.org

iv ............... Hearings of the President's Commission on the Assassination of President Kennedy (President's Commission, Warren Commission, Pres. Com.), Volume VIII, John Donovan, pp. 291-293

v ................ House Select Committee on Assassinations, Segregated Central Intelligence Agency File, Microfilm reel 8, Golitsyn-Hernandez, Personal Information Data, Grigoriy Golub, (n.d.)

vi ............... Report of the Select Committee on Assassinations, President's Commission Memorandum from William Coleman and W. D. Slawson, Report of Oswald's Foreign Activities, (n.d.), p.55

vii ............. Report of the President's Commission on the Assassination of President John F. Kennedy, Washington, DC (Report of the

President's Commission on the Assassination of JFK, The Warren Commission) Appendix XV, Transactions between Lee Harvey Oswald and Marina Oswald, and the U.S. Department of State and the Immigration and Naturalization Service of the U.S. Department of Justice, pp. 761-769

viii ............Central Intelligence Agency File, Oswald 201 File, Vol. 24 Bulky, Oswald Chronology, Part 2, Name Trace Appendix Draft, Summary of 24 May 1962

ix ...............Report of the Pres. Com., The Loan from the State Department, pp. 770, 771

x ................David Fanning, "Who was Lee Harvey Oswald?", PBS, November 16, 1993, pbs.org

xi ...............President's Commission Document 10, Report of FBI Agent John W. Fain, August 30, 1962, pp. 1-3

xii ..............Housewife Reveals Role as F.B.I. Agent, (December 11, 1964), Archives Section, the New York Times, nytimes.com

xiii ............Chuck Goudie, (November 22, 2007), 44 Years after JFK's death, New Assassination Plot Revealed, ABC News/WLS-TV, abcnews.go.com

xiv ............M.G. Hollo, David Osterlund, "The JFK Conspiracy", Witness Productions Inc., 1978

xv ..............David E. Kaiser, "The Road to Dallas: The Assassination of John F. Kennedy", Harvard University Press, 2008, pp. 94, 95

xvi ............HSCA Report, Section I. Part C, subsection 4, p. 169

xvii ...........HSCA Report, Appendix X, Section XII, David Ferrie, pp. 105, 110-113

xviii ..........Department of Justice Memo, Dave Ferrie - In connection with United States v. Marcello, Conspiracy, New Orleans, March 29, 1967, Harold Weisberg Archives (HWA), Hood College, jfk.hood.edu

xix ............Ibid

xx ..............HSCA Report, Appendix IX, Section IV, p. 107-108, 110-115

xxi ............HSCA, Segregated CIA File, Banister's alleged involvement with Cuban exile activities, November 21, 1967, p. 1

xxii ...........HSCA, FBI Subject File, David William Ferrie, October 30, 1961, p. 3

xxiii ..........Executive Session Summary of the House Select Committee on Assassinations, Untitled Document, Testimony of Carlos Marcello before the Select Committee, January 11, 1978, pp. 2-4

xxiv .......... HSCA Report, Sec. I, Pt. C, subs. 4, James R. Hoffa, p. 176

xxv ........... H. Bradford Westerfield, Richard M Bissell (n.d.), Reflections of A Cold Warrior review – From Yalta to the Bay of Pigs, cia.gov

xxvi .......... United States Senate Select Committee to Study Governmental Operations with Respect to Intelligence Activities (Senate Select Comm., Church Committee), Interim Report: Alleged Assassination Plots involving foreign leaders, Part III, Section B, The Assassination Plots, 1975, pp. 71-90, Assassination Archives and Research Center, aarclibrary.org

xxvii ......... HSCA, FBI Subject file, Report of SA James Flynn, La Causa (sic) Nostra Anti-Racketeering-Conspiracy, January 31, 1963

xxviii ........ Jack Anderson, "American Exposé - Who killed JFK?", Saban Production, 1988

xxix .......... HSCA, Segregated CIA File, Staff Notes, Staff Report on the evolution and implications of the CIA sponsored assassination conspiracies against Castro, (n.d.), pp. 62, 63

xxx ........... HSCA, Segregated CIA File, Memo: Salvatore Giancana and Richard Cain, Microfilm Reel 48: defectors, 201 files, ci/sig, ig reports..., January 10, 1974, pp. 1-4

xxxi .......... HSCA, Segregated CIA File, Memo: Richard S. Cain 272 141, Box 8, October 09, 1967, pp. 1-4

xxxii ......... HSCA, Segregated CIA File, Office of Security-Tile (sic) on Cain, Richard S, Information concerning Directorio Estutandil, Box 40, (n.d.)

xxxiii ........ HSCA, FBI Subject File, C-D, Richard Cain, No Title, Search of Gerald Tomaszek residence, October 3, 1963

xxxiv ........ HSCA, Segregated CIA File, Box 8, Cain, p. 1

xxxv .......... Ibid

xxxvi ........ Ben Joravsky, (April 12, 2001), Backstabbers, Chicago Reader, chicagoreader.com

xxxvii ....... HSCA, Segregated CIA File, Office of Security-Tile (sic) on Cain, Richard S. Recent newspaper publicity Re Assassination of President Kennedy, Box 40, December 12, 1967

xxxviii ...... HSCA, Segregated CIA File, Staff Notes, File 180-10145-10205, (n.d.), p.15

xxxix ........ Santo Trafficante, Reputed Mafia Chief, Dies at 72, (March 19, 1987), New York Times Archives, nytimes.com

**xl** ...............Report of the House Select Committee on Assassinations, Section I. Part C, subs. 4, Santos Trafficante, p. 173

**xli** ..............HSCA, Exec. Session transcript, Immunized Testimony, (n.d.)

**xlii** ............HSCA, Immunized Testimony of Santos Trafficante, November 14, 1977, pp. 8-16

**xliii**............Ibid, pp.45-47,75,79,80

**xliv** ............HSCA Report, Appendix Vol. X, pp. 166-169

**xlv** .............Ibid, p. 171

**xlvi** ............HSCA, Segregated CIA File, Staff Notes, File 180-10145-10205, (n.d.), p.16

**xlvii** ...........HSCA Report Appendix X, pp. 178-180

**xlviii** ..........Senate Select Comm., Book 5, Appendix C, pp. 99, 100

**xlix** .............Rudy Maxa, (September 12, 1976), The Calculated Rise and abrupt Descent of Johnny Roselli, The Washington Post, pp. L1, L4

**l** ..................Jack Anderson with Les Whitten, (October 9, 1976), Washington Merry-go-round, HWA

**li** .................Senate Select Comm., Interim Report, Part 3, Section B. Did President Kennedy learn anything about assassination plots as a result of the FBI Investigation of Giancana and Roselli?, pp. 129-31

**lii** ...............HSCA Segregated CIA File, Memo on Galvatore (sic) Giancana, Johnny Roselli, and Santos Trafficante Agen, Subject: Johnny Roselli, Box 48, August 9, 1976

**liii** ..............HSCA, Segregated CIA File, Plots to Assassinate Castro, Gambling Syndicate, Box 9, October 17, 1978

**liv** ..............HSCA, CIA Segregated File, Staff Notes, Staff Report on the evolution and implication of the CIA sponsored as, March, 1979

**lv** ...............HSCA, Federal Bureau of Investigation Subject files, G-H, Sam Giancana, May 5, 1961, pp. 50-51

**lvi** ..............HSCA, FBI Subject File, A-B, Gus Alex, No Title, Report of SA William F. Roemer, pp. 1-4

**lvii** ............HSCA, FBI Subject File, S-T, Santo Trafficante, No Title, Airtel to Hoover from SAC Chicago, October 20, 1964

**lviii** ...........HSCA, FBI Subject File, A-B, Gus Alex, No Title, Anti-Racketeering report of SA Roemer, May 24, 1973, p. 3

**lix** ..............HSCA, FBI Subject File, A-B, Gus Alex, No Title, Informant Contact Report on Gus Alex, April 20, 1973

lx .............. Peter Moruzzi, Havana before Castro: when Cuba was a tropical playground, Gibbs Smith, 2008, pp. 172-200

lxi ............. T. J. English, Havana Nocturne: How the Mob owned Cuba…and then lost it to the Revolution, MJF Books, 2007, pp. 13, 15-17, 19-20

lxii ............ Ibid, pp. 22-25

lxiii ............ Ibid, p. 32

lxiv ........... Christopher Lehmann-Haupt, (October 17, 1991), Books of The Times, A Life of Meyer Lanksy says he died Hard Up, New York Times Archives, nytimes.com

lxv ............ M.G. Hollo, D. Osterlund, "The JFK Conspiracy"

lxvi ........... HSCA, Segregated Central Intelligence Agency File, Staff Notes, 180-10144-10027, (n.d.), p. 10

lxvii .......... HSCA, Segregated CIA File, Memo Re An Article in the New York Times of a Bahama Gambling Group that link Resorts International, Inc., Box 8, August 18, 1976

lxviii .......... Ibid, p. 2

lxix ........... Jason Cohn, "J. Edgar Hoover's Secrets", History's Conspiracies, Season 1, Episode 5, National Geographic Channel, August 12, 2007

lxx ............ HSCA Report, Appendix Volume IV, testimony of Dallas Police Captain Jack Revill, p. 572

lxxi ........... Report of the Pres. Com., Chapter 6, Possible conspiracy involving Jack Ruby, p. 343

lxxii .......... Report of the Pres. Com., Appendix 16: A Biography of Jack Ruby, Underworld Ties, pp. 800, 801, the United States National Archives and Records Administration (NARA), archives.gov

lxxiii ......... Hearings of the Pres. Com., Vol. XXII, Exhibit 1300, Statement of Paul Jones, December 17, 1963, p. 478

lxxiv ......... Hearings of the President's Com., Vol. V, Testimony of Jack Ruby, p. 189

lxxv .......... HSCA Report, App. Vol. IX, Section V, Possible Associations between Jack Ruby and Organized Crime, Part D, pp. 188-196

lxxvi ......... FBI Memo, Special Agent in Charge of Houston to Director and SAC Dallas, JR. Interviews Negative, NARA ID: 124-10070-10354, November 26, 1963

lxxvii ........ HSCA, Segregated CIA File, Jack Ruby as a FBI Informant, Box 2, (n.d.), p. 1-2 lxxviii ........FBI, Headquarters File 105-82555, Oswald HQ File, Section 106, Revised statement of Director Hoover, March 3, 1964

lxxix .........FBI File 105-82555, Oswald HQ File, Section 94, p. 4

lxxx ..........HSCA Report, App. IX, The Shooting of Lee Harvey Oswald, Relationship with the Dallas Police, Part A, p. 129

lxxxi .........Pres. Com. Key Persons File, Patrick T. Dean, Memo to Counsel Rankin concerning Off the Record Conversation with P.T. Dean and Burt Griffin, March 31, 1964, pp. 1-4

lxxxii .........HSCA, Segregated CIA File, Jack Ruby as a FBI informant, Box 2, (n.d.), p. 1

lxxxiii ........HSCA, Vol. IX, Sec. V, Pt. D, pp. 166, 167, 173

lxxxiv ........HSCA, FBI Subject File, Joe Campisi, May 22, 1959, p. 5

lxxxv .........HSCA, FBI Subject File, J. Campisi, March 25, 1969, p. 21

lxxxvi ........HSCA, FBI Subject File, J. Campisi, May 22, 1961, p. 3

lxxxvii .......HSCA, FBI Subject File, J. Campisi, September 24, 1970

lxxxviii ......HSCA, FBI Subject File, No Title, Joe Campisi: Joseph Campisi, September 29, 1967, p. 1-2

lxxxix ........National Security Action Memo Number 271, John F. Kennedy Presidential Library, November 12, 1963, jfklibrary.org

xc .............National Security Action Memo 263, John F. Kennedy Presidential Library, October 11, 1963, jfklibrary.org

xci .............Thomas W. Lippman (July 7, 2009), Defense Secretary, Architect of U.S. Involvement in Vietnam Robert McNamara Dies, washingtonpost.com

xcii ............"Conspiracy Files – JFK Assassination, The Mob Connection", Discovery Channel, 2006

xciii ..........Final Report of the Assassination Records Review Board (ARRB), Chapter 8: Federal Agency Compliance with the JFK Act, Part B, Section 3: The Secret Service, September, 1988, p. 149

xciv ..........C. Goudie, 44 Years after JFK's death, New Assassination Plot Revealed

xcv ..........HSCA, Segregated CIA File, Memo Re: Richard S. Cain 272 141, Box 8, October 9, 1967, p. 1

xcvi ..........C. Goudie, 44 Years after JFK's death

xcvii .........J. Anderson, "American Exposé"

xcviii ......... Hearings of the Pres. Com., Vol. XVIII, Ex. 1019, United States Secret Service memo to General Counsel Rankin of President's Commission, May 5, 1964, p. 666

xcix .......... Hearings of the Pres. Com, Volume V, Testimony of James J. Rowley and Robert Carswell, June 18, 1964, pp. 451, 454, 458, 459

c ............... Ibid, p. 459

ci .............. President's Commission Document 3, Volume 1, Report of the United States Secret Service on the Assassination of President Kennedy, December 18, 1963, Washington D.C., p. 12

cii ............. Bruce Halford, "Jfk: Day the Nation Cried", View Video, August 1, 1996

ciii ............ HSCA Report, Section 1, Part D, pp. 228-237

civ ............ University of California Santa Barbara, "The American Presidency Project -Lyndon B Johnson, Number 604-Remarks to the Secret Service and Presentation of an Award to James J. Rowley", November 23,1968, www.presidency.uscsb.edu

cv .............. Hearings of the Pres. Com., Vol. XVIII, Ex. 1024, Treasury Department Memo to J. Rankin, Statements of the Secret Service personnel, pp. 722-94

cvi ............ Pres. Com. Doc. 3, Vol. 1, Report of the United States Secret Service on the Assassination of President Kennedy, p. 10

cvii ........... Pres. Com. Doc. 3, Vol. 1, Report of the United States Secret Service on the Assassination of President Kennedy, P. 33

cviii .......... Letter from to Attorney General Robert Jackson from Congressman G.W. Norris, Re: Alleged FBI illegality, February 22, 1940

cix ............. "Our Lawless G-Men", (March 2, 1940), the Nation, pp. 296-297

cx .............. "Investigate the American Ogpu", (March 11, 1940), the New Republic, pp. 330-332, 345

cxi ............ "Congress Should Investigate", (March 25, 1940), the New Republic pp. 393-394

cxii ........... Alison Jones, Stephanie Pickering, Megan Thomson, "Dictionary of Quotations", Chambers Publishing, September 17, 1997, Anonymous FBI Agent, p. 25

cxiii........... John M Crewdson, "Censored Version of Secret Hoover File on Official's Misconduct", New York Times, November 24, 1976, nytimes.com

cxiv ............Orr Kelley with Ted Gest and Joeseph P. Shapiro, "The Secret Files of J. Edgar Hoover", U.S. News and World Report, December 19, 1983, pp. 45-50, HWA

cxv ............J. Crewdson, "Files from Hoover's Backers Reported", New York Times, February 2, 1974, nytimes.com

cxvi ...........Anthony Summers, "Official and Confidential- The Secret Life of J. Edgar Hoover", Open Road Media, January 17, 2012, Chapter 33 quotation

cxvii ..........Hearings of the Pres. Com, Vol. XVII, Ex. 833, Memo from Hoover to J. Lee Rankin, pp. 1-9

cxviii .........Senate Select Comm., Bk. 5, Appendix A, p. 90

cxix ...........HSCA, Segregated CIA File, Report of Lee Harvey Oswald about his background, connection with Fai, Box 7, November 7, 1963, p. 3

cxx .............Senate Select Comm., Bk. 5, Appendix A, p. 91

cxxi ...........HSCA, Segregated CIA File, Report of Lee Harvey Oswald about his background, connection with Fai, SA Kaack Report, Box 7, November 7, 1963, p. 4

cxxii ..........HSCA, FBI Subject File, Miscellaneous File: 6 document items, No Title, p. 8

cxxiii .........HSCA, Segregated CIA File, Report of Lee Harvey Oswald about his background, connection with Fai, SA Kaack Report, p. 2

cxxiv ..........Ibid, p. 3

cxxv ...........FBI File, Statement of Nannie Lee Fenner, Dallas, Texas, September 2, 1975, p. 1-3

cxxvi ..........Paul Vitello (June 19, 2011), James P. Hosty, Investigated Oswald, Dies at 86, nytimes.com

cxxvii .........Senate Select Comm., Bk. 5, Appendix B, pp. 96, 97

cxxviii .......P. Vitello, James P. Hosty, Investigated Oswald Dies at 86

cxxix ..........Senate Select Comm., Bk.5, Appendix B, p. 97

cxxx ...........HSCA Administrative Folder P-8, Lee Harvey Oswald, Volume III, Internal Security, January 25, 1964

cxxxi ..........Pres. Com. Document 8, Report of FBI Agent Fain, July 3, 1961, pp. 2-10

cxxxii .........Pres. Com, Doc. 9, Report of FBI Agent Fain, July 10, 1961, pp. 2-12

cxxxiii .......Pres. Com. Doc. 10, Report of FBI Agent Fain, August 30, 1961, pp. 2-7 cxxxiv ....... Pres. Com. Doc. 11, Report of FBI Agent Hosty, September 10, 1963, pp. 1-3

cxxxv ........ Pres. Com. Doc. 12, Report of FBI Agent Kaack, October 31, 1963, pp. 3-5, 11,12,13-15

cxxxvi ....... HSCA, Segregated CIA File, Report on Lee Harvey Oswald about his arrest, affiliation with Fair Pla, Box 7, November 8, 1963

cxxxvii ...... Report of the Pres. Com., Chap. 4, the Assassin, Oswald's Palm print on the Rifle Barrel, p. 123

cxxxviii ..... FBI Warren Commission Liaison File 62-109090, Section 7 "Letter from J. Lee Rankin to J. Edgar Hoover", March 16, 1964, p. 1

cxxxix ....... Phone Conversation between FBI Director J. Edgar Hoover and President Lyndon Johnson in the Whitehouse, (n.d.), p. 2, History Matters, history-matters.com, November, 1963

cxl ............. HSCA, Segregated CIA File, Memo from New Orleans Office Re Garrison Investigation, Box 37, May 23, 1967

cxli ........... HSCA, Segregated CIA File, Memo No. 8: Garrison and Kennedy Assassination (Identifies 30 Persons), Box 37, January 12, 1968

cxlii ........... HSCA Report, App. X, pp. 126-127

cxliii .......... HSCA, Segregated CIA File, Staff Notes, Anti-Castro Activities and Organizations And LHO in New Orleans, March, 1967, p. 10

cxliv .......... Senate Select Comm., Bk. 5, Intelligence Agencies, Part III Summary and Findings, p. 32

cxlv ............ Ibid

cxlvi .......... HSCA Administrative Folder- L8, Lee Harvey Oswald (New File), CIA Activities and the Warren Commission Investigation, March 24, 1976

cxlvii ......... Senate Select Comm., Bk. 5, Appendix A, p. 87

cxlviii ........ Senate Select Comm., Bk. 5, Part IV, Summary and Findings, p. 55

cxlix .......... Senate Select Comm., Bk. 5, Part I, p. 5

cl ............... City of Dallas Municipal Archives, Office of the Secretary, The JFK Collection, Affidavit of Deputy Seymour Weitzman, Box 2, Folder 1, Document 8, jfk.tx.us

cli ............. Hearings of the Pres. Com., Vol. XXIV, Ex. 2169, Press Conference of District Attorney Wade in Assembly Room, pp. 829-31

clii ............ HSCA, Administrative Folder Q-6, Ticklers Volume II, Small Arms of the World, Mannlicher Carcano Rifle, (n.d.)

cliii ...........Mark Lane, "Two Men in Dallas", Tapeworm Video Distributors, 1976

cliv ............Garrison Investigation File, Lead Files No. 3, Memorandum from Mark Lane to Jim Garrison, United States National Archives and Records Administration, November 3, 1967, media.nara.gov

clv..............Hearings of the Pres. Com., Vol. III, Testimony of Eugene Boone, pp. 294-295

clvi.............Hearings of the Pres. Com., Vol. IV, Testimony of Jesse Curry, p. 181

clvii ...........Hearing of the President's Commission, Vol. VII, Testimony of Seymour Weitzman, pp. 107-109

clviii ..........Jay Watson, Bert Schipp, Tom Alyea, Texas Schoolbook Depository internal footage and interview transcripts, WFAA, November 22, 1963

clix.............Report of the Pres. Com., Chapter 3, Expert Examination of the Rifle, Cartridge Cases and Bullet Fragments, p.79

clx .............HSCA, Segregated CIA File, Lee Harvey Oswald, Also known as, Lee Harry Oswald; Alex Hidell; Harvey, Box 26, November 25, 1963, p. 2

clxi ............FBI File 105-82555, Oswald HQ File, Section 71, Assassination Weapon–Alleged background, pp. 39-41

clxii ...........Dallas Police Department Arrest Report, Suspect: Harold Doyle, Arresting Officer: W. E. Chambers, November 22, 1963

clxiii ..........Dallas Police Department Arrest Report, Suspect: John Gedney, Arresting Officer: W. E. Chambers, November 22, 1963

clxiv ..........Dallas Police Department Arrest Report, Suspect: Gus Abrams, Arresting Officer: W. E. Chambers, November 22, 1963

clxv ...........Report of the Pres. Com., Chapter 4, The Assassin, The killing of patrolman J.D. Tippit, p. 157

clxvi ..........Hearings of the Pres. Com., Vol. VI, Testimony of Domingo Benavides, pp. 447-449

clxvii .........Affidavit of Sam Guinyard, John F. Kennedy- Dallas Police Department Collection, County of Dallas, Texas, November 22, 1963

clxviii ........Affidavit of Virginia Davis, John F. Kennedy-D.P. D. Collection, November 22, 1963

clxix ..........Hearings of the Pres. Com., Vol. XXIV, Commission Exhibit Number 2003,Affidavit of T.F. Bowley, p. 202

clxx ...........Report of the Pres. Com., App. XII, Speculations and Rumors, The Murder of J.D. Tippit, p. 651

**clxxi** .......... J.D. Tippit Supplementary Offense Report, City of Dallas Police, November 22, 1963,texashistory.unt.edu

**clxxii** ......... CIA File, Oswald 201 File, Vol. 25, Part 2, Statement of Elbert Austin, January 22, 1964

**clxxiii** ........ HSCA Report, App. Volume VII, Findings and conclusions of Firearms Panel concerning the Kennedy Assassination, Tippit Murder, p. 377

**clxxiv** ........ Peter Dale Scott, interview with Jesse Curry former Dallas Police Chief "The Fifth Estate", Canadian Broadcasting Network, 1977

**clxxv** ......... Jeffery Shesol, "Mutual Contempt: Lyndon Johnson, Robert Kennedy, and the Feud That Shaped a Decade", W.W. Norton and Company, October 1997, p. 33

**clxxvi** ........ J. Shesol, "Mutual Contempt..." p. 34, 35

**clxxvii** ....... Seymour Hersh, "The Dark Side of Camelot", Back Bay Books, September 1, 1998, p. 406-407, 446-447

**clxxviii** ...... National Security Action Memo No. 273, Office of the Historian, U.S. Department of State, November 12, 1963, history.state.gov

**clxxix** ........ Wilkes, Donald E. Jr., "JFK Killer Not Alone, UGA Professor Says", (1994), Popular Media, Paper 117, University of Georgia Law, digitalcommons.law.uga

**clxxx** ......... Telephone Conversation between President Johnson and Republican leader Charles Halleck, Number 163, November 29, 1963, transition.lbjlibrary.org

**clxxxi** ........ Hollo, Osterlund, "The JFK Conspiracy"

**clxxxii** ....... Federal Bureau of Investigation Memorandum, Letter from Cartha DeLoach to Clyde Tolson, April 4, 1967, HWA

**clxxxiii** ...... Hanson Baldwin, "The McNamara Monarchy", Saturday Evening Post, Volume 236, Issue 9, p. 8

**clxxxiv** ...... Kenneth P. O' Donnell and David E. Powers "Johnny, We Hardly Knew Ye: Memories of John Fitzgerald Kennedy", Little Brown and Co, September, 1972, p. 16

**clxxxv** ....... James K. Gailbraith, (September 1, 2003), Exit Strategy: In 1963, JFK ordered complete withdrawal from Vietnam, Boston Review, bostonreview.net

**clxxxvi** ...... Antony Jay, "The Oxford Dictionary of Political Quotations", Oxford University Press, 2001: Robert McNamara p. 237

**clxxxvii** ..... Jack Anderson and Les Whitten, (October 27,1975), Washington Post, HWA

**clxxxviii** ....Ibid

**clxxxix** .......Department of Justice Memo, Tentative Outline of Report Summarizing Investigation of the Assassination of the President, Section J. Federal Jurisdiction, November 27, 1963 p. 5

**cxc** .............White House telephone transcript, Conversation between the President and Mr. Joe Alsop, November 25, 1963, Lyndon Baines Johnson Presidential Library, p. 1, 5

**cxci** ...........White House telephone transcript, Conversation between the President and Director Hoover, Nov. 25, 1963

**cxcii** ...........FBI Memo from Office of the Director, Re: conversation with Nicholas Katzenbach about not forming a Presidential Commission, November 25, 1963, HWA

**cxciii** .........Report of the Pres. Com., Chap. 4, the Assassin, the Rifle in the Building, conclusion, p. 137

**cxciv** ..........White House Press Secretary Release, Letters between President Kennedy and Director of Intelligence Allen Dulles, November 28-29, 1961, John F. Kennedy Presidential Library and Museum, jfklibrary.org

**cxcv** ...........HSCA Report, App. Vol. XI, Operations and Procedures, p. 6

**cxcvi** .........HSCA, Segregated CIA File, Roselli, John, Box 1, February 15, 1972

**cxcvii** ........HSCA, Segregated CIA File, Discussion with Allen W Dulles on Oswald Case, Box 5, April 13, 1964

**cxcviii** ........Hollo, Osterlund, "The JFK Conspiracy"

**cxcix** ..........William C. Sullivan, "The Bureau: My Thirty Years in the Federal Bureau of Investigation", W.W. Norton & Company, 1979, p. 53

**cc** ..............James Hohmann, (June 9, 2010), Great Profanity in History, Politico Magazine, politico.com

**cci** .............Garrick Utley, John J. McCloy and the Splendid Reconciliation (n.d.), U.S. Diplomatic Mission to Germany, usembassy.de

**ccii** ............Hollo, Osterlund, "The JFK Conspiracy"

**cciii** ...........The New Georgia Encyclopedia, Richard B Russell Jr., georgiaencyclopedia.org

**cciv** ............Pres Com. Document, First Commission Staff Conference Summary of Melvin A. Eisenberg, February 17,1964, HWA

**ccv** .............President's Commission Executive Session, December 5, 1963, p. 14

**ccvi** ...........Pres. Com. Exec. Session, December 16, 1963, p. 39

**ccvii** ..........Pres. Com. Exec. Session, December 16, 1963, p. 50

ccviii ........ Report of the Pres. Com., App. III, Public Law 88-202, p. 473

ccix ............ Pres. Com. Exec. Session, January 21, 1964, p. 20

ccx ............. Ibid

ccxi ........... Pres. Com. Exec. Session, January 22, 1964, p. 6

ccxii .......... HSCA, Inquiry Concerning Page 696 of the FBI Report of December 23, 1963 by Special Agent Robert P. Gemberling, December 7, 1977

ccxiii ......... Transcript of J. Edgar Hoover's statements for President Johnson prepared by aide Walter Jenkins, November 24, 1963

ccxiv ......... Pres. Com. Exec. Session, January 27, 1964, p. 144

ccxv .......... Pres. Com. Exec. Session, January 22, 1964 p. 12

ccxvi ........ Pres. Com. Exec. Session, January 22, pp. 12-13

ccxvii ........ Pres Com. Exec. Session, January 27, 1964 p. 163

ccxviii ....... Pres. Com. Exec. Session, January 27, pp. 185, 186

ccxix ......... Gerald Ford, "A Presidential Legacy and the Warren Commission", Flat Signed Press, 2007, Preface

ccxx .......... G. Ford, "A Presidential Legacy and the Warren Commission", p. 40

ccxxi ......... Senate Select Comm., Bk. 5, Part IV Intelligence Agencies, p. 55

ccxxii ........ HSCA, Security Classified Testimony of J. Lee Rankin, August 17, 1978, p. 27

ccxxiii ....... Live television Broadcast with Walter Cronkite, CBS News, November 22, 1963

ccxxiv ....... United States House of Representatives Letter, Representative Earle Cabell to Attorney General Nicholas Katzenbach, September 13, 1965, p.1, History Matters Archive, history-matters.com

ccxxv ......... HSCA, Secuirty Classified Testimony of Everett Howard Hunt, November 3, 1978, p. 29

ccxxvi ....... David Frost Interviews Richard Nixon, David Paradine Productions, 1977

ccxxvii ...... Andrew Glass, (February 2, 1973), James Schlesinger becomes the CIA's ninth Director, www.politico.com

ccxxviii ..... Tim Weiner, "Legacy of Ashes - The History of the CIA", Doubleday Broadway Publishing, 2007, p. 325

ccxxix ....... Ibid

ccxxx ......... David Ruppe, (May 2001), U.S. Military Wanted to Provoke War with Cuba, abcnews.go.com

ccxxxi ........Memo for the Secretary of Defense from Lyman Lemnitzer, Chairman of the Joint Chiefs of Staff, March 13, 1962, National Security Archives, George Washington University, gwu.edu

ccxxxii .......D. Ruppe, U.S. Military Wanted to Provoke War with Cuba

ccxxxiii ......Daniel Trotta, (March 14, 2013), Iraq war costs U.S. more than $2 trillion: study, Reuters, reuters.com

ccxxxiv ......Matt Potter, (January 5, 2011), Oil in Politics in La Jolla, sandiegoreader.com

ccxxxv .......M. Potter, (January 12, 2011), The Big Rich, Part Two, sandieoreader.com

ccxxxvi ......HSCA Numbered File, No Title, NARA ID: 180-10090-10220, November 9, 1963, pp. 4-6

ccxxxvii .....HSCA Report, Sec. I, Pt. D, Significant Threats in 1963, pp.232-233

ccxxxviii ....Rachel Maddow Show transcript, (December 23, 2009), msn.com

ccxxxix ......Ibid

ccxl ...........HSCA, FBI Subject File, A-B, John Birch Society, No Title, Subjects JBS, Aca…, February 18, 1964, p. 1, 2

ccxli ..........Armed Forces: I Must be Free…, (November 10, 1961), Time Magazine, www.time.com

ccxlii .........Steven E. Atkins, "Encyclopedia of Right Wing Extremism in Modern American History", ABC-CLIO, 2011, pp. 182-88

ccxliii .........Claude Sitton, (October 2, 1962), "3000 Troops Put Down Mississippi Rioting And Seize 200 as Negro Attends Classes; Ex-Gen. Walker is Held for Insurrection, Shots Quell Mob, Enrolling of Meredith Ends Segregation in States Schools", partners.nytimes.com

ccxliv .........National Indignation Convention Footage , Dallas, Texas, December 13, 1961

ccxlv...........Report of the Pres. Com., Chapter 4, The Assassin, The Attempt on the Life of Maj. General Edwin A. Walker, p. 183

ccxlvi .........FBI, Files on Edwin Walker, Cross References 7, Witness Statement of Robert A. Surrey, June 4, 1964

ccxlvii ........FBI, Files on Edwin Walker, Cross References 7, Witness Statement of Walter K. Coleman, June 4, 1964

ccxlviii .......Pres. Com Doc. 79, Secret Service Interviews with Marina Oswald 30 Dec 1963, ATSAIC Gopadze Interview, December 10, 1963

ccxlix .........Report of the Pres. Com., Chap 4, pp. 187-188

ccl .............HSCA Report, App. Vol. XI, p. 126

**ccli** ........... Pres. Com. Doc. 430, FBI Report of 25 February 1964 re: Marina Oswald, February 24, 1964

**cclii** ........... Pres. Com., Exec. Session, January 27, 1964, p. 195

**ccliii** .......... FBI File 62-10906, JFK HQ File, Section 36, Latent Print Examination, December 5, 1963

**ccliv** .......... FBI, Files on Edwin Walker, Cross References 7, Interview of Marina Oswald, December 4, 1963

**cclv** ........... Brian Yamashita and Mike French, "Latent Print Development", Chapter 7 , National Criminal Justice Reference Service, United States Department of Justice, ncjrs.gov

**cclvi** .......... CIA, Oswald 201 File, Volume 37 b, German Press and extensive factual and editorial on killing of Oswald, November 28, 1963, p. 1

**cclvii** ......... FBI File 105-82555, Oswald HQ File, Section 201, Memo to Rankin, August 11, 1964, pp.1-2

**cclviii** ........ FBI, Files on Edwin Walker, File 116-165494, Section 1, The Victory Purge pamphlet, September, 1961

**cclix** .......... FBI, Files on Edwin Walker, Cross References 8, Desegregation of the University of Mississippi-Racial Matters, November 9, 1962

**cclx** ........... HSCA, Administrative Folder I-11, Outgoing Field Reports, Volume II, Lee Harvey Oswald-Internal Security-Russia, February 14, 1964

**cclxi** .......... CIA File, Oswald 201 File, Volume 44, Investigation concerning attempted assassination of General Edwi, June 1, 1964

**cclxii** ......... Report of the Pres. Com., Chapter 4, The Attempt on the Life of Maj. General Edwin A. Walker, p. 186

**cclxiii** ........ FBI File 105-82555, Oswald HQ File, Section 108, Memo from Jevons to Conrad, March 27, 1964

**cclxiv** ........ Report of the Pres. Com., Appendix X, Expert Testimony, The Walker Bullet, p. 562

**cclxv** ......... HSCA Report, App. Vol. X, Section IV, Cuban Revolutionary Council: A Concise History, pp. 57-59

**cclxvi** ........ David Miller, "The JFK Conspiracy", Universe, 2002, pp. 24-27

**cclxvii** ....... Pres. Com. Exec. Session, January 27, p. 199

**cclxviii** ...... T. Weiner, "Legacy of Ashes" pp. 81-90

**cclxix** ........ The Agency and the Hill, Part 2, Chapter 5, Legislation Center for the Study of Intelligence, cia.gov

**cclxx** ......... HSCA, Segregated CIA File, Notes in Draft Re Project ZRRIFLE, Box 5, (n.d.), pp. 1-9

**cclxxi** .........HSCA, Segregated CIA File, Extension of Authorization of ZRRIFLE Agent Activities, Box 56, March 3, 1963

**cclxxii** ........HSCA, Segregated CIA File, Briefing of the DDCI on "Johnny" Developments, Box 1, May 18, 1966

**cclxxiii** .......HSCA, Segregated CIA File, Johnny Roselli - Request For Favor, Box 1, July 26, 1968, p. 2

**cclxxiv** .......HSCA, Segregated CIA File, Report by William King Harvey On Johnny Roselli, Box 1, March 21, 1968

**cclxxv** ........ HSCA, Segregated CIA File, Johnny Roselli, Box 48, May 8, 1967, pp. 1-3

**cclxxvi** .......HSCA, Segregated CIA File, Meeting between William K. Harvey and Mr. Sam Papich FBI Liaison (RE Johnny Roselli), November 8, 1967

**cclxxvii** ......HSCA, Segregated CIA File, Report of Meeting between Colonel Sheffield Edwards and "Johnny" Rosel, Box 8, May 18, 1966 pp. 1-4

**cclxxviii** .....HSCA, Segregated CIA File, Misc Security memos on John Roselli, Memos on telephone conversations, Box 48, (n.d.)

**cclxxix** .......HSCA, Segregated CIA File, Officer of Security Answers to SSCI Request on Robert A. Maheu, Johnny Roselli and Sam Giancana, Box 48, May 22, 1975

**cclxxx** ........H.R. Haldeman and Joseph Dimona, "The Ends of Power", Dell, 1978, p. 69

**cclxxxi** .......HSCA, Security Classified Testimony of James Angleton, October 5, 1978, p. 88

**cclxxxii** ......Ibid, p. 89-90

**cclxxxiii** .....HSCA, Security Classified Testimony of Agent John Scelso, May 16, 1978, pp. 71, 113,114

**cclxxxiv** .....Ibid, pp. 73, 74

**cclxxxv** ......Ibid, pp. 168-169

**cclxxxvi** .....HSCA, Segregated CIA File, Memo – Subj: Possible Questionable Activities, Box 40, July 1, 1975

**cclxxxvii** ....HSCA, Testimony of John Scelso, pp. 136, 137, 167

**cclxxxviii** ...HSCA, Segregated CIA File, Recollections of Thomas B Casasin about Oswald's unusual behavior in USSR, Box 8, November 25, 1963

**cclxxxix** .....Ibid

**ccxc** .......... HSCA, Segregated CIA File, Roselli, Johnny; Summary of Activities In Cuba, December 9, 1970, p. 1

**ccxci** .......... T. Wiener, "Legacy of Ashes" pp. 26, 27, 32-33, 54, 55, 58, 59, 64-70, 95-104,109,114,115,136-140, 142, 143

**ccxcii** .......... H. Westerfield, (n.d.), Reflections of A Cold Warrior review, cia.gov

**ccxciii** ........ HSCA Report, Appendix Vol. X, p. 179, 180

**ccxciv** ........ CIA OK's MK-ULTRA Mind Control Tests- This Day in Tech (April 13, 1953), wired.com

**ccxcv** .......... Tim Weiner, (March 10, 1999), Sidney Gottlieb, 80, Dies; Took LSD to C.I.A., nytimes.com

**ccxcvi** ........ CIA Guatemala 1954 Documents, "A Study of Assassination" and transcript, National Security Archive Electronic Briefing Book No. 4, George Washington University, georgewashington.edu, pp. 2-14

**ccxcvii** ....... Ibid

**ccxcviii** ...... HSCA Document, Classified Testimony of James Wilcott, March 22, 1978

**ccxcix** ........ Ibid

**ccc** ............. Ibid

**ccci** ............ Ibid

**cccii** .......... HSCA, Classified Testimony of Richard McGarrah Helms, August 9, 1978, p. 26,27

**ccciii** .......... Senate Select Comm., Bk. 5, Part V, Summary and Findings p. 77

**ccciv** .......... Senate Select Comm., Bk. 5, Part IV, p. 70

**cccv** ........... Ibid

**cccvi** .......... HSCA Exec. Session, Classified Testimony of John Scelso, p. 146

**cccvii** ......... Ibid

**cccviii** ........ Ibid, pp. 148, 149, 150

**cccix** .......... Ibid, p. 113-114

**cccx** ........... HSCA, Segregated CIA File, Report on Lee Harvey Oswald About His Arrest, Affiliation with Fair Play, Box 7, November 8, 1963, p. 1-7

**cccxi** .......... CIA Document, #1035-960, Re: Concerning criticism of the Warren Report

**cccxii** ......... HSCA, Testimony of John Scelso, pp. 11,49,125,127,128

cccxiii ........HSCA, Security Classified Testimony of William F. Larson, June 27,1978, p. 22,27-29,59,60,61

cccxiv ........HSCA, Segregated CIA File, Summary of Oswald 201 File, Box 18, January 13, 1961 (sic), pp. 1-3

cccxv .........HSCA, Segregated CIA File, Documents Available in Oswald's 201, Box 7, February 20, 1964

cccxvi ........HSCA, Testimony of William Larson, p. 26

cccxvii .......Ibid, pp. 35, 53-54, 65

cccxviii ......HSCA, Security Classified Testimony of Bernard Hugh Tovar, p. 34

cccxix ........HSCA, Security Classified Testimony of Melbourne Paul Hartmann, October 10, 1978, p. 21,51,54

cccxx .........HSCA, Segregated CIA File, Interception of Letters between members of Oswald's Family, Box 5, September 14, 1964

cccxxi ........Senate Select Comm., Bk.5, Part IV, p. 58

cccxxii .......Ibid, Bk.5, Part I, Performance of the Intelligence Agencies, Summary and Findings, p. 6

cccxxiii ...... English, Havana Nocturne, pp. 118-119

cccxxiv ...... HSCA, Segregated CIA File, Cuban Democratic Revolutionary Front, Box 1, March 7, 1968

cccxxv ....... HSCA, Segregated CIA File, Box 1, Additional Information on Sergio Arcacha Smith, p. 2

cccxxvi ......HSCA Report, Appendix Vol., X, p. 110

cccxxvii .....HSCA, Anti-Castro Activities and Organizations and LHO in New Orleans, Staff Notes, March, 1979

cccxxviii ....FBI File 105-82555, Oswald HQ File, Section 198, Internal Security-Russia-Cuba Report, Re Carlos Bringuier, p. 18

cccxxix ......HSCA, Segregated CIA File, Additional Info on Carlos Bringuier, Box 1, p. 2

cccxxx .......HSCA, Segregated CIA File, Dade County Request for Agency Assistance Regarding Death of Johnny Roselli, Box 1, October 8, 1976, p. 3-4

cccxxxi ......Report of the House Select Comm., Appendix Vol. X, p. 158

cccxxxii .....HSCA, Segregated CIA File, Microfilm Reel 19: MFR: AMWHIP/ 1 Meeting, New York City, Thursday, 14 November 1963

cccxxxiii ....HSCA, Segregated CIA File, Espinosa Allegations, Box 7, October 15, 1965, pp. 1-4

**cccxxxiv** .... HSCA, Segregated CIA File, Debriefing on Training and Demolitions given to Anti-Castro Cuban Exiles, Box 1, January 17, 1977, p. 1

**cccxxxv** ...... HSCA, Segregated CIA File, Dade County Request for Agency assistance regarding the death of Johnny Roselli, Box 8, October 8, 1976, p. 3

**cccxxxvi** .... HSCA, Immunized testimony of Carlos Eduardo Hernandez Sanchez, April 30, 1978

**cccxxxvii** ... Senate Select Comm., Bk.5, Part I, p. 7

**cccxxxviii** .. HSCA Staff Report, Report on Lee Harvey Oswald's Trip to Mexico City, p. 117

**cccxxxix** .... Hearings of the Pres. Com. Vol. XVI, Ex. 237, Photograph of unidentified man, p.638

**cccxl** .......... Hearings of the Pres. Com., Vol. XI, Affidavit of Bardwell Odum, James R. Malley, and Richard Helms pp. 468-470

**cccxli** ......... CIA File, Classified Message MEXI 6453, October 8, 1963

**cccxlii** ........ CIA File, Classified Message MEXI 7025, November 23, 1963

**cccxliii** ...... HSCA Staff Report, Report on Lee Harvey Oswald's Trip to Mexico City, pp. 138-142

**cccxliv** ....... Ibid, p. 115

**cccxlv** ........ Ibid., p. 63

**cccxlvi** ....... Ibid, p. 119

**cccxlvii** ...... HSCA, Melbourne Hartmann, Security Classified Testimony, p. 33

**cccxlviii** .... HSCA, Report on LHO Oswald's Trip to Mexico City, p. 118

**cccxlix** ....... CIA File, President's Commission Report on the Trip to Mexico City by W. David Slawson, April 22, 1964, p. 16

**cccl** ............ HSCA, Security Classified Testimony of Agent John Scelso, pp. 89

**cccli** ........... Ibid, p. 40, 160, 161

**ccclii** .......... Ibid, p. 31

**cccliii** ........ CIA File, Chronology of Mexico City, date unknown, NARA ID: 104-10086-10001

**cccliv** ......... CIA File, Information disseminated to the Secret Service..., March 24, 1964, NARA ID: 1993.06.23.07:52:25:650700

**ccclv** .......... CIA File, Memorandum: Summary of Relevant Information on Lee Harvey Oswald, Russ Holmes Work File, November 24, 1963, NARA ID: 104-10400-10296

ccclvi .........CIA File, Memorandum: Complete Recheck Photos All Visitors to Cuban EMB Aug thru first half Nov against good press photos shows no evidence Oswald visit, November 23, NARA ID: 104-10015-10336

ccclvii ........HSCA, Segregated CIA File, Review of Agency Holdings Re: Photo of Unidentified Individual in Mexico, May 2, 1975, p. 5

ccclviii .......HSCA, Security Classified Testimony of David Atlee Phillips, April 25, 1978, pp. 37-38, 50, 64-65

ccclix .........CIA File, CIA Dissemination of information on Lee Harvey Oswald, March 24, 1964

ccclx ..........CIA File, Cable- Oswald Ordered Rifle of the same type used to kill the President from Klein's mail order house in Chicago, November 24, 1963

ccclxi .........CIA File, Memorandum: Lee Harvey Oswald, September 25, 1964, p. 1-3

ccclxii ........CIA File, Cable: CIA Director to Mexico City station Our present plan in passing information to the Warren Commission..., Russ Holmes Work File, December 20, 1963

ccclxiii .......CIA File, Dispatch from Mexico City Chief of Station to Western Hemisphere Division, November 22, 1963

ccclxiv .......HSCA, Classified Testimony of John Scelso, p. 100

ccclxv ........HSCA, Staff Report, Lee Harvey Oswald's Trip to Mexico City, p. 116

ccclxvi .......HSCA, Segregated CIA File, Review of (Official Deletion) Files at the (Official Deletion) Record's Center, Box 7, May 2, 1977

ccclxvii ......HSCA, Segregated CIA File, Review of Agency Holdings Re Photo of Unidentified individual in Mexic, Box 7, May 2, 1975, p.1, 34

ccclxviii .....CIA File, Meeting with Ann Goodpasture, OLC 78-3136, November 24, 1978

ccclxix .......ARRB Transcripts, Deposition of Anne Goodpasture, Testimony of Central Intelligence Agency employees, December 15, 1995, p. 152, maryferrell.org

ccclxx ........HSCA., Lee Harvey Oswald's Trip to Mexico City, p. 123

ccclxxi .......HSCA, Segregated CIA Files, Staff Notes, Summary of CI soft file on the Unidentified Man photographs, March 15, 1978, p. 11

ccclxxii ......HSCA, Segregated CIA File, House Select Committee on Assass. Request, OLC 78-0070/33, Box 8, March 30, 1978, pp. 2-3

ccclxxiii .... HSCA, Segregated CIA File, Security clearance for George De Mohrenschildt, Box 34, August 13, 1958

ccclxxiv ...... ARRB, CIA Document, Memo from Helms to Rankin, George and Jeanne De Mohrenschildt, June 3, 1964, p. 1-3

ccclxxv ....... Pres. Com. Document 734, FBI Wood Report 28 February 1964 re: George De Mohrenschildt, Internal Security, p. 16

ccclxxvi ...... HSCA, Segregated CIA File, Microfilm Reel 5: Conte - de Mohrenschildt, George de Mohrenschildt, December 10, 1964

ccclxxvii .... Hearings of the Pres. Com., Vol. IX, p. 235

ccclxxviii .. HSCA Staff Report, Vol. XII, G. De Mohrenschildt, Staff Report, p. 53

ccclxxix ..... D. Fanning, "Who was Lee Harvey Oswald?"

ccclxxx ...... Report of the Pres. Com., Chap. IV, the Assassin, Oswald's Marine Training, p. 191

ccclxxxi ..... Hearings of the Pres. Com., Vol. VIII, J. Donovan, p. 296

ccclxxxii .... Report of the Pres. Com., App. 13, Biography of Lee Harvey Oswald, Early Years, p. 684

ccclxxxiii .. Bill Rockwood, (November 19, 2013),Who was Lee Harvey Oswald? - Twenty Four Years Chronology, PBS, pbs.com

ccclxxxiv ... HSCA, Testimony of John Scelso, p. 109

ccclxxxv .... HSCA, Segregated CIA File, Internal CIA Request from Papich for Info. On Ex-Marine Recently Defect, Box 7, November 2, 1959

ccclxxxvi ... Fanning, Who was Lee Harvey Oswald?

ccclxxxvii .. HSCA, Security Classified Testimony of Bernard Hugh Tovar, pp. 5,7, 20

ccclxxxviii HSCA, Security Classified Testimony of John Scelso, pp. 8, 10

ccclxxxix ... Report of the Pres. Com., App. 15, the Loan from the State Department, pp. 770-73

cccxc ......... Report of the Pres. Com., Chapter VIII, Intelligence functions relating to presidential protection at the time of the Dallas trip, p. 436

cccxci ........ HSCA, Segregated CIA File, Report on Lee Harvey Oswald about his background connection with Fai, SA Kaack Report, Box 7, November 7, 1963, p. 7

cccxcii ....... Report of the Pres. Com., Chapter IV, Purchase of the Rifle by Oswald, p. 122

cccxciii ......Report of the Pres. Com., Chapter VII, Defection to the Soviet Union, p. 393

cccxciv ......Ibid, 393-394

cccxcv .......Hearings of the Pres. Com., Vol. XVII, Ex. 833, United States Department of Justice, Federal Bureau of Investigation Memo from Hoover to Rankin, April 6, 1964

cccxcvi ......HSCA Administration Folder- Q10, Federal Bureau of Investigation File, Airtel to Director from SAC WFO, November 19, 1963

cccxcvii .....FBI File 105-82555, Oswald HQ File, Section 85, Allegation that Lee Harvey Oswald was an FBI informant, February 12, 1964

cccxcviii ....CIA File, Russ Holmes Work File, Transcript of Warren Commission discussion about Hudkins and story that Oswald was an FBI or CIA Agent, (n.d.), p. 207

cccxcix ......Report of the Pres. Com., Chapter IV, the Assassin, Oswald's rifle Practice Outside the Marines, p. 192

cd ...............Ibid, Ownership and Possession of Assassination Weapon, p. 125

cdi ............Hearings of the Pres. Com. Vol. X, Testimony of Homer Wood, pp. 388-390

cdii ...........Hearings of the Pres. Com. Vol. X, Testimony of Sterling Wood, pp. 392, 393

cdiii ..........Report of the Pres. Com., Chapter IV, the Assassin, Oswald's Marine Training, p. 191

cdiv ..........Report of the Pres. Com., Chapter IV, Oswald's Rifle Practice Outside the Marines, p. 192

cdv ............Hearings of the Pres. Com., Vol. V, Testimony of Mrs. Lee Oswald, pp. 405-406

cdvi ..........Report of the Pres. Com., Chap. IV, pp. 121, 128

cdvii .........Hearings of the Pres. Com., Vol. V, p. 398

cdviii ........Report of the Pres. Com., Chapter VI, Background of Lee Harvey Oswald, pp. 318-320

cdix ..........Ericsson K. Anders, Ralf Th. Krampe, and Clemens Tesch Romer, (July, 1993), The Role of Deliberate Practice in the Acquisition of Expert Performance, Psychological Review Vol. 100, No. 3, The American Psychological Association, apa.org

cdx..............Report of the Pres. Com., Chap. VI, Oswald's presence in the Depository Building, p. 246

cdxi ..........Report of the Pres. Com, Chap. II, The Motorcade Route, pp. 31-32

**cdxii** .......... HSCA, Segregated CIA File, Review at HQ, Oswald Chronology, Volume II, Box 50, (n.d.), pp. 145-146

**cdxiii** ......... Report of the Pres. Com., Chap. III, At the Triple Underpass, p. 76

**cdxiv** ......... HSCA Report, App. VI, Section IV Conspiracy Questions, Part IV, p. 109

**cdxv** .......... FBI, File 105-82555, Oswald HQ File, Section 177, Memo to Rankin from Hoover, June 22, 1964, pp. 1-2

**cdxvi** ......... Report of the Pres. Com., Chapter 4, Oswald at the Window, pp.155, 156

**cdxvii** ........ Live television Broadcast with Walter Cronkite, CBS News, November 22, 1963

**cdxviii** ....... Report of the Pres. Com., Chap. 4, Oswald's Actions in the Building After the Assassination, p. 149-56

**cdxix** ......... Report of the Pres. Com., Chap. 4, Oswald's Movements After Leaving the Depository pp. 157, 161, 165

**cdxx** .......... Report of the Pres. Com., Chap. 4, Oswald's Movements, Oswald's Arrest, pp. 176, 178, 179

**cdxxi** ......... HSCA Report, Appendix Vol.3, Testimony of James R. Malley, November 24, 1963, p. 471

**cdxxii** ........ Hearings of the Pres. Com., Vol. XII, Testimony of Captain W. B. Frazier, March 25, 1964, p. 55

**cdxxiii** ....... Hearings of the Pres. Com., Vol. II, Testimony of Buell Frazier, p. 226

**cdxxiv** ....... CIA, Oswald 201 File, Vol. 8, FBI Statement of Buell Wesley Frazier, December 2, 1963

**cdxxv** ........ FBI, File 62-109090, Warren Commission HQ File, Section 7, Commission Memo to Hoover, March 23, 1964

**cdxxvi** ....... Frank de Haas and Dr. Wayne van Zwoll , "Bolt Action Rifles- 4th Edition", Krause Publications, 2003, p.66

**cdxxvii** ...... Lp Brezny, The Gun Digest Book of Long-Range Shooting, Gun Digest Books, June 4, 2007, p. 51, 53

**cdxxviii** ..... Hearings of the Pres. Com. Vol. III, Testimony of Ronald Simmons, pp. 450-451

**cdxxix** ....... Report of the Pres Com., Chapter IV, p. 157

**cdxxx** ........ Report of the Pres. Com., Chapter III, The Trajectory, p.97

**cdxxxi** ....... Ibid, p.105, 107

**cdxxxii** ......Ibid, p. 109

**cdxxxiii** .....Hearings of the Pres. Com., Vol. XXIV, Rifle Bullet C1, p. 412

**cdxxxiv** .....Report of the Pres. Com., Chap. IV, The Assassin, Oswald's Palm print on the Rifle Barrel, p. 123

**cdxxxv** .......CIA, "A Study of Assassination"

**cdxxxvi** .....Ibid

**cdxxxvii** ....Ibid

**cdxxxviii** ...Ibid

**cdxxxix** .....Ibid

**cdxl** ...........Ibid

**cdxli** ..........Ibid

**cdxlii** .........Ibid

**cdxliii** ........Department of Justice Memo, Herbert J. Miller Jr. response to letter from J. Edgar Hoover regarding John F. Kennedy Miscellaneous Information, August 3, 1964, HWA

**cdxliv** ........HSCA Report, Sec. I, Pt. B, Summary of Evidence, p. 93

**cdxlv** .........Ibid, p. 70

**cdxlvi** ........Report of the Pres. Com., Chap. IV, The Assassin, Eyewitness Identification of the Assassin, pp. 146, 147

**cdxlvii** .......HSCA, Volume VI, Recovered bullet during JFK autopsy, p. 304

**cdxlviii** ......Hearings of the Pres. Com., Vol.VI, Testimony of Dr. Charles Carrico, p. 3

**cdxlix** ........Hearings of the Pres. Com., Vol.VI, Dr. Paul Peters, p. 71

**cdl** .............Hearings of the Pres. Com., Vol. VI, Dr. Robert Nelson McClelland, p. 33

**cdli** ...........Hearings of the Pres. Com., Vol. VI, Dr. Malcolm Oliver Perry, p. 9

**cdlii** ..........Hearings of the Pres. Com., Vol. VI, Dr. Ronald Coy Jones, p. 53

**cdliii** .........HSCA Report, App. Vol. VI, Pt. VII, pp. 302-05

**cdliv** .........Report of the Pres. Com., App. 8, statement of Administrator Mr. C.J. Price, p. 530

**cdlv** ...........Hearings of the Pres. Com. Vol. VI, Dr. C. Carrico, p. 3

**cdlvi** ..........Hearings of the Pres. Com. Vol. VI, Dr. William Kemp Clark, p. 20

**cdlvii** .........Report of the Pres. Com., App. 8, Parkland Memorial Hospital Admission Notes Dr. Malcolm Perry, p. 521** This citation was unavailable in the National Archives transcription, see: The Warren Commission Report, Report of the President's Commission on the Assassination of President John F. Kennedy (Official Complete and Unabridged), Washington, D.C, Barnes and Noble Books, 2003

**cdlviii** ........ Hearings of the Pres. Com. Vol. VI, Dr. Don Teel Curtis, p. 60

**cdlix** .......... Hearings of the Pres. Com. Vol. VI, Dr. P. Peters, p. 71

**cdlx** ........... Hearings of the Pres. Com. Vol. VI, Dr. Gene Coleman Akin, p. 65

**cdlxi** .......... Hearings of the Pres. Com. Vol. VI, Dr. Kenneth Everett Salyer, p. 81

**cdlxii** ......... Hearings of the Pres. Com. Vol. VI, Dr. Charles Rufus Baxter, p. 41

**cdlxiii** ........ Hearings of the Pres. Com. Vol. VI, Dr. R. Jones, p. 56

**cdlxiv** ........ ARRB, Meeting Report with Nurse Audrey Bell, April 14, 1997

**cdlxv** ......... Hearings of the Pres. Com., Vol. IV, Testimony of Dr. Robert Roeder Shaw, p. 109

**cdlxvi** ........ Hearings of the Pres. Com, Vol. IV, Testimony of Dr. Charles Francis Gregory, pp. 127

**cdlxvii** ....... FBI, Headquarters File 105-82555, Oswald HQ File, Section 234, Assassination of President Kennedy, June 29, 1967, p. 2

**cdlxviii** ...... FBI Memo, FBI HQ File 62-109060, Author William Manchester appointment and interview with J. Edgar Hoover, June 4, 1964, HWA

**cdlxix** ........ State of Louisiana v. Clay Shaw Transcripts, Testimony of Dr. Finck, February 24, 1969, pp. 51, 52

**cdlxx** ......... Assassination Records Review Board, Testimony of Dr. Pierre Finck, May 24, 1996, p. 78

**cdlxxi** ........ Ibid

**cdlxxii** ....... State of Louisiana v. Clay Shaw Transcripts, February 24, 1969, pp. 48, 49

**cdlxxiii** ...... Ibid, p. 50

**cdlxxiv** ...... ARRB, Testimony of Dr. Pierre Finck, May 24, 1996, p. 42

**cdlxxv** ....... Ibid, pp. 49-67

**cdlxxvi** ...... Ibid, p. 68

**cdlxxvii** ..... Ibid, p. 96

**cdlxxviii** .... Hearings of the Pres. Com., Vol. II, Testimony of Dr. Pierre Finck, p. 382

**cdlxxix** ...... ARRB, Testimony of Dr. James Joseph Humes, February 13, 1996, pp. 136, 137

**cdlxxx** .......Ibid

**cdlxxxi** ......Ibid, p. 132

**cdlxxxii** .....Ibid, pp. 137, 138

**cdlxxxiii** ....State of Louisiana v. Clay Shaw Transcripts, P. Finck, February 24, 1969, p. 46

**cdlxxxiv** ....ARRB, Medical Exhibit Number 5, Handwritten Notes of Phone call between Dr. James Humes and Dr. Malcolm Perry, November 23, 1963

**cdlxxxv** .....ARRB, Dr. James Humes, February 13, 1996, p. 52

**cdlxxxvi** ....Vincent Bugliosi, "Reclaiming History: The Assassination of John F. Kennedy, W.W. Norton and Company, May 17, 2007, p. 386

**cdlxxxvii** ...ARRB, Testimony of Dr. J Humes, February 13, 1996, p. 81

**cdlxxxviii** ..Ibid, pp. 83, 84

**cdlxxxix** ....Ibid, p. 102

**cdxc** ...........Ibid, pp. 106, 107

**cdxci** ..........Ibid, p. 223

**cdxcii** .........Ibid, p. 144

**cdxciii** .......ARRB, Medical Exhibit Number 3, Autopsy Protocol of John F. Kennedy, Dr. James Humes, Dr. Pierre Finck, Dr. J Thorton Boswell, (n.d.), p. 2

**cdxciv** ........ARRB, Medical Exhibit Number 75, Department of the Navy Memorandum, Letter of non- disclosure from Commanding Officer, J.M. Stover Jr. to Commander James Joseph Humes, United States Naval Medical School, November 26, 1963

**cdxcv** .........Hearings of the Pres. Com., Vol. II, Testimony of Dr. James Humes, pp. 374, 375

**cdxcvi** ........Ibid

**cdxcvii** .......ARRB, Testimony of Dr. J. Thornton Boswell, February 26, 1996, pp. 23, 24

**cdxcviii** .....Ibid

**cdxcix** ........Ibid, p. 33

**d** ...............Ibid, p. 54

**di** ..............Ibid, p. 108

**dii** .............Ibid, p. 170

**diii** ............Ibid, p. 176, 180, 199

**div** ............ Ibid, p. 209

**dv** ............. Ibid, p. 210, 211

**dvi** ............ ARRB, Medical Exhibit Number 76, Department of the Navy Memorandum, Letter of non-disclosure from Commanding Officer, J.M. Stover Jr. to Commander J. Thorton Boswell, United States Naval Medical School, November 26, 1963

**dvii** ........... ARRB, Deposition of John T. Stringer, July 16, 1996, p. 125

**dviii** .......... Ibid, p. 137, 139

**dix** ............ ARRB Medical Exhibit Number 4, Review of Autopsy Materials by Dr. Humes, Dr. Boswell, and Dr. Ebersole, January 26, 1967, p. 2

**dx** ............. ARRB, John T. Stringer, July 16, 1996, p. 155

**dxi** ............ Ibid, p. 184

**dxii** ........... Ibid, pp. 215-218

**dxiii** .......... ARRB, Medical Exhibit Number 81, Department of the Navy Memorandum, Letter of non- disclosure from Commanding Officer, J.M. Stover Jr. to Mr. John Stringer, United States Naval Medical School, November 26, 1963

**dxiv** .......... ARRB, Medical Document 60, Ebersole HSCA Medical Panel Testimony, March 11, 1978, p. 3

**dxv** ........... Ibid, p. 5

**dxvi** .......... Ibid, pp. 6, 11

**dxvii** ......... ARRB, Testimony of Francis X. O'Neill Jr., September 12, 1997, p. 24

**dxviii** ........ Ibid, p. 69, 70

**dxix** .......... Ibid, pp. 158, 159

**dxx** ........... Ibid, pp. 164-166

**dxxi** .......... ARRB, Testimony of James W. Siebert, September 11, 1997, pp. 64-67

**dxxii** ......... Ibid, pp. 126, 127

**dxxiii** ........ Ibid, p.137

**dxxiv** ........ ARRB, Deposition of Floyd Albert Riebe, May 7, 1997, pp. 44, 45, 55

**dxxv** ......... ARRB, Medical Exhibits Number 138, Department of the Navy Memorandum, Letter of non-disclosure from Commanding Officer, J.M. Stover Jr. to Floyd Albert Riebe, United States Naval Medical School, November 26, 1963

**dxxvi** .........ARRB, Med. Ex. No. 177, ARRB Call Report Summarizing 2/14/97 Telephone Interview of Dennis David, February 19, 1997

**dxxvii** ........ARRB, Med. Ex. No. 65, Jenkins-Purdy HSCA Interview (8/29/77), p. 12

**dxxviii** .......ARRB, Deposition of Saundra Kay Spencer, June 5, 1997, p. 44-46

**dxxix** .........Ibid, p. 38-58

**dxxx** ..........ARRB, Med. Ex. 19, House Select Committee interview by Mr. Purdy of Rear Admiral George Burkley, (n.d.), p. 6

**dxxxi** .........ARRB, Med. Ex. 68, President Johnson's notes on conversation with Acting Attorney General Ramsey Clark, 6:29 pm, January 26, 1967

**dxxxii** ........HSCA Report, App. VII, Section III, Part I, Chain of Custody of the Materials Acquired during the Autopsy, p. 23

**dxxxiii** .......ARRB, Medical Exhibit 235, Meeting Report of Carl Belcher, October 7, 1996

**dxxxiv** .......HSCA Report, App. Vol. VII, Sec.III, Part I. p. 4

**dxxxv** ........Memo from Doug Horne, Supervisory Analyst, sub: Unanswered questions Raised by the HSCA's Analysis and Conclusions Regarding the Camera Identified by the Navy and the Department of Defense as the Camera Used at President Kennedy's Autopsy, Staff Memo, August 27, 1998, p. 4

**dxxxvi** .......Ibid, pp. 5-7

**dxxxvii** ......CIA File, Letter to Jeffrey P. Hoyle, August 17,1979, p. 1-2

**dxxxviii** .....HSCA, Segregated CIA File, HSCA Request, Box 9, June 27, 1978, p. 2

**dxxxix** .......CIA, "A Study of Assassination"

**dxl** .............FBI Memo, J. Edgar Hoover to FBI Officers regarding call to Katzenbach, November 26, 1963

**dxli** ............HSCA, Seg. CIA file, Staff Notes, 180-10142-10036, November 28, 1963, p. 61

**dxlii** ...........Senate Select Comm., Bk.5, Part III, Summary and Findings p. 23

**dxliii** ..........T. Weiner, "Legacy of Ashes" p. 227

**dxliv** ..........FBI Memo to J. Edgar Hoover to Officers..., November 25, 1963

**dxlv** ..........Senate Select Comm., Bk.5, Part IV, Intelligence Agencies, Summary and Findings, p. 45

**dxlvi** ..........Ibid, Part III, p. 23

**dxlvii** .........Ibid

**dxlviii** ....... Ibid

**dxlix** .......... Senate Select Comm., Bk.5, Part III, p. 25

**dl** .............. CIA File, Information developed by CIA on the activities of Lee
Harvey Oswald in Mexico City, September 28 to October 3, 1963

**dli** ............. CIA File, Russ Holmes Work File (RHWF), Memorandum: Lee
Harvey Oswald, September 25, 1964, p. 1-3

**dlii** ............ CIA, RHWF, Cable: Refs Obviously Crossed. If station view dangers
Para A, p.1

**dliii** .......... Senate Select Comm., Bk. 5, Part III, p. 77

**dliv** ............ Ibid, Part I, p. 2

**dlv** ............ Pres Com. Exec. Session, June 4, 1964, p. 6655

**dlvi** ............ Ibid, pp. 6655, 6656

**dlvii** .......... Ibid, p. 6658

**dlviii** ......... Pres. Com. Exec. Session, January 27, p.171

**dlix** ........... Justice Department Letter from Fred Vinson to George R. Brown,
July 12, 1968

**dlx** ............ Justice Department Letter from Frank M. Wozencraft to Senator B.
Everett Jordan, December 28, 1968

**dlxi** ........... United States Congressional Letter, Congressman Graham Purcell to
Attorney General Ramsey Clark, December 19, 1967

**dlxii** .......... Justice Department Letter, Martin F. Richman to Congressman Tom
Railsback, February 19,1968

**dlxiii** ......... Justice Department Letter, Frank M. Wozencraft to Congressman
John W. Byrnes, March 8, 1968

**dlxiv** .......... Justice Department Letter, Frank M. Wozencraft to Congressman
Richard Hanna, December 15, 1968

**dlxv** .......... Justice Department Letter, Frank M. Wozencraft to Senator Vance
Hartke, December 11, 1968

**dlxvi** ......... Justice Department Letter, Fred Vinson to Congressman Frank
Horton, December 1968

**dlxvii** ........ Justice Department Letter, Frank M. Wozencraft to Congressman Jack
Brooks, December 6, 1968

**dlxviii** ....... Justice Department Letter, Fred Vinson to Congressman Edward J.
Gurney, November 24, 1967

**dlxix** ......... Justice Department Letter, Martin F. Richman to Congressman Alton
Lennon, February 29, 1968

dlxx ..........Justice Department Letter, Fred Vinson to Congresswoman Margaret Hechler (sic) (Heckler), March 1, 1968

dlxxi .........Justice Department Letter, Frank M. Wozencraft to Congressman L. C. Arends, March 7, 1968

dlxxii ........Justice Department Letter, Martin F. Richman to Senator Robert Casey Sr., March 4, 1968

dlxxiii ........Justice Department Letter, Frank M. Wozencraft to Senator Joseph Montoya, March 1968

dlxxiv ........Justice Department Letter, Martin F. Richman to Senator Lister Hill, March 4, 1968

dlxxv .........Justice Department Letter, Fred Vinson to Congressman James C. Corman, February 2, 1968

dlxxvi ........Justice Department Letter, Fred Vinson to Congressman Clarence Miller, February 20, 1968

dlxxvii .......Justice Department Letter, Martin F. Richman to Senator Joseph Clark, March 1, 1968

dlxxviii ......Justice Department Letter, Martin F. Richman to Congressman Odin Langen, March 1, 1968

dlxxix ........Justice Department Letter, Frank M. Wozencraft to Senator Mike Mansfield, February 14, 1968

dlxxx .........Justice Department Letter, Fred M Vinson Jr. to Congressman George Murphy, January 2, 1968

dlxxxi ........CBS News, Walter Cronkite, November 22, 1963

dlxxxii .......Department of Justice Routing Slip, Grant Lee Oliver to Mr. Yeardley (sic) (Eardley), (n.d.), Hood College, HWA

dlxxxiii ......Jefferson Morley, (November 21, 2007), "What Conspiracy Bashers Get Wrong", huffingtonpost.com

dlxxxiv ......Stewart Galanor (n.d.), "The Art and Science of Misrepresenting Evidence", history-matters.com

dlxxxv .......Report of the Pres. Com., Chap. IV, Oswald at the Window, Eyewitness Identification of the Assassin, pp. 143-46

dlxxxvi ......Ibid

dlxxxvii .....Hearings of the Pres. Com., Vol. III, Testimony of Howard Brennan, pp. 144-145, 161

dlxxxviii ....Ibid, Vol. VI, Testimony of Domingo Benavides, pp. 450-451

dlxxxix........Affidavit of Sam Guinyard, John F. Kennedy - Dallas Police Department Collection, Country of Dallas, Texas, November 22, 1963

dxc ........... Affidavit of Virginia Davis, John F. Kennedy-D.P. D. Collection, November 22, 1963

dxci .......... Hearings of the Pres. Com., Vol. XXIV, Commission Exhibit Number 2003, Affidavit of T.F. Bowley, p. 202

dxcii ......... J.D. Tippit Supplementary Offense Report, City of Dallas Police Department Form OPS-GF-355A, November 22, 1963, texashistory.unt.edu

dxciii ........ Report of the Pres. Com., Appendix XII. Speculations and Rumors, The Murder of J.D. Tippit, p. 651

dxciv ........ Hearings of the Pres. Com., Volume XIX, Statement of Philip Hathaway, p. 477

dxcv .......... Report of the Pres. Com., Chapter IV, Oswald at the Window, p. 146

dxcvi ......... Ibid, p. 147

dxcvii ........ CIA, Oswald 201 File, Vol. 3, Folder 9A, Part 2, p. 164

dxcviii ....... Unit Chief Douglass W. Deedrick, FBI Laboratory Services, Forensic Science Communications, Hair, Fibers, Crime, and Evidence Part 2: Fiber Evidence, fbi.gov

dxcix ......... Hearings of Pres. Com., Vol. XIX, Statement of Robert E. Edwards, November 22, 1963, p. 647

dc ............. Ibid, Statement of John Stevens Rutter Lawrence, p. 482

dci ........... Hearings of the Pres. Com., Vol. II, Testimony of Buell Frazier, p. 234

dcii .......... Hearings of the Pres. Com., Vol. XIX, Statement of William Newman, p. 490

dciii ......... Hearings of the Pres. Com, Vol. XXII, Statement of Orchus Campbell, p. 638

dciv .......... Hearings of the Pres. Com, Vol. III, Testimony of Roy Truly, p. 227

dcv ........... Hearings of the Pres. Com. Vol. XIX, Dallas County Sheriff's Department supplementary report of Harry Weatherford, p.502

dcvi .......... Ibid, Dallas County Sheriff's Department supplementary report of Austin Miller, p. 485

dcvii ......... Hearings of the Pres. Com. Vol. VII, Testimony of Edgar L. Smith Jr., p. 568

dcviii ........ Hearings of the Pres. Com., Vol. VI, Testimony of Frank Reilly, p. 230

dcix .......... Hearings of the Pres. Com., Vol. VI, Vol. XIX, Sherriff's Report of Harold Elkins, p. 540

**dcx** .............Mark Lane, "Rush to Judgment", Judgment Films Corporation, 1966

**dcxi** ...........Report of the Pres. Com., p. 76

**dcxii** ..........M. Lane, "Rush to Judgment"

**dcxiii** .........Ibid

**dcxiv** .........S. Galanor, "The Art and Science of Misrepresenting Evidence"

**dcxv** ...........Hearings of the Pres. Com, Vol. VI, Testimony of Danny Arce, p.365

**dcxvi** .........Hearings of the Pres. Com., Vol. VI, Testimony of Billy Nolan Lovelady, p.338

**dcxvii** ........Hearings of the Pres. Com., Vol. III, Testimony of Sheriff Luke Mooney, p. 283

**dcxviii** .......Hearings of the Pres. Com., Vol. III, Testimony of Sheriff Eugene Boone, p. 292

**dcxix** .........Hearings of the Pres. Com., Vol. VII, Testimony of Ms. Donald (Virginia) Baker, p. 510

**dcxx** ...........Hearings of the Pres. Com, Vol. VI, Testimony of Ronald Fischer, p.195

**dcxxi** .........Hearings of the Pres. Com, Vol. XXII, Deposition of Dorothy Ann Garner, p. 648

**dcxxii** ........M. Lane, "Rush to Judgment"

**dcxxiii** .......Pres. Com. Doc. 205, FBI Gemberling Report, Statement of Mrs. Roberta Parker, December 16, 1963

**dcxxiv** .......Hearings of the Pres. Com., Vol. XXII, Statement of J.M. Smith, July 14, 1964, p. 600

**dcxxv** .........Hearings of the Pres. Com., Vol. VII, Com., Statement of Forrest Sorrels, p. 346

**dcxxvi** .......Hearings of the Pres. Com., Vol. VII, Com., Testimony of James Tague, p. 557

**dcxxvii** ......Hearings of the Pres. Com., Vol. XXII, Statement of Steven Wilson, p. 685

**dcxxviii** .....HSCA, Segregated CIA File, Box 47, Ruth Paine (Individual taking care of widow of Lee Harvey Oswald), December 5, 1963

**dcxxix** .......CIA File, Oswald 201 File, Vol. 6, CD6, Part 2, Statement of Mrs. Emmet Diamond, December 2, 1963

**dcxxx** .........HSCA, Segregated CIA File, Security File on Sylvia Hyde Hoke, Box 43, (n.d.)

dcxxxi ....... FBI File, Ruth and Michael Paine Files, No Title, Report of SA North, March 20, 1964

dcxxxii ...... Report of the Pres. Com. Chapter VI, Oswald's Presence in the Depository Building, p. 246

dcxxxiii. .... HSCA, FBI Subject File, E-F, Declan Ford, No Title, Security Investigation Data, November 10, 1966

dcxxxiv ..... HSCA, FBI Subject File, E-F, Declan Ford, No Title, Civil Service Commission Investigation request, March 3, 1965

dcxxxv ...... CBS News Live Report, Walter Cronkite, November 22, 1963

dcxxxvi ..... Ibid

dcxxxvii .... CIA, Oswald 201 File, Volume 56 b, Information furnished to the Commission by Henry M. Wade, February 10, 1964, p. 1-3

dcxxxviii ... Senate Select Comm., Boxed Files, Memo from Dwyer to Wallach, Scheduled Interview of Alonso Hudkins, November 19, 1975

dcxxxix ..... Bob Vernon, "The Murder of JFK Confession of an Assassin", MPI Home Video September 10, 1996

dcxl ........... Ibid

dcxli .......... Hearings of the Pres. Com., Vol. XXII, Yarborough Seating Pondered article, Dallas Morning News, November 19, 1963, p. 615

dcxlii ......... Jim Lehrer, "Yarborough Gets JFK Table Spot", Dallas Times Herald, November 21, 1963, p. 1, 13

dcxliii ........ Doug McCash, (October 21, 2013), "Lee Harvey Oswald's purported mistress's tour draws conspiracy devotees", nola.com

dcxliv ........ Ibid

dcxlv ......... Report of the Pres. Com., Appendix 13, pp. 698, 699

dcxlvi ........ Pres. Com. Doc. 321, CIA Helms Memo, Oswald's Diary Summary – 1 May 1961, January 25, 1964

dcxlvii ....... HSCA, Administrative Folder I-11, FBI Outgoing Field Reports, Volume II, Lee Harvey Oswald, March 13, 1964

dcxlviii ...... Judyth Vary Baker, "Ten Years of Battle" – Biography, (n.d.), judythbaker.blogspot.com

dcxlix ........ HSCA, Segregated CIA File, Garrison and the Kennedy Assassination Gordon Dwayne Novel, Box 1, p. 1-9

dcl ............. Ibid

dcli ............ HSCA Report, Sec. I, Pt. B, subs. 6, p. 93

dclii .......... HSCA Report, Sec. I, Pt. D, subs. 3, the FBI, p. 242

dcliii .........HSCA Report, Sec. I, Pt. D, subs. 5, The Warren Commission, p. 256

dcliv ..........HSCA, Segregated CIA Collection, Staff Notes, 180-10141-10406, Inspector General's Report; Anti-Castro Activities, January 10, 1978, pp. 7-9

dclv ...........HSCA Staff Report., Vol. XII, George De Mohrenschildt, March, 1979

dclvi ..........J. Anderson, "American Exposé"

dclvii .........HSCA, Segregated Central Intelligence Agency File, Dade Co. Police Request for Investigation of Roselli Murder, Box 1, June 15, 1977, p. 1-4

dclviii ........HSCA, Segregated CIA File, 180-10128-10002, Briefing Books, CIA Witness List, Crimaldi, Charles, (n.d.), p. 7

## MLK

dclix ..........Steve Hendrix, (August 2011), Bayard Rustin: Organizer of the March on Washington was crucial to the movement, Washington Post, washingtonpost.com

dclx ...........HSCA, Segregated CIA File, Bio Summary of Bayard Rustin, Box 10, November 5, 1967, pp. 1-2

dclxi ..........William Bradford Huie, "He Slew the Dreamer", Delacorte Press, New York, 1968, Chapter 9, pp. 114,115

dclxii .........Soledad O' Brien, "Eyewitness to Murder: The King Assassination" and transcript, CNN News, cnn.com

dclxiii ........W.B. Huie, "He Slew the Dreamer", pp. 129-31

dclxiv ........Nick B. Williams, "Who Paid for the Bullet?", the Los Angeles Times, June 16, 1968, p. G-4

dclxv .........Phillip Melanson, "The Murkin Conspiracy", New York: Praeger, 1989, pp. 150-53

dclxvi ........Fred P. Graham, "Suspect of Assassination of Dr. King is Seized in London", the New York Times, June 8, 1968, p. 1-A

dclxvii .......Dividing Line: The Mysteries of James Earl Ray (February 17, 1997), Time Magazine, time.com

dclxviii ......A Very Important Prisoner, (June 26, 1968), Time Magazine, time.com

dclxix ........James Earl Ray, Plaintiff-appellant, v. Percy Foreman, William Bradford Huie, and Arthur J. Hanes Sr., Defendants... United States Court of Appeals, Sixth Circuit-Volume 441 F.2d 1266 April 29, 1971, law.justia.com

**dclxx** ......... Ibid

**dclxxi** ........ Ibid

**dclxxii** ....... HSCA Report, Sec. II, Pt. A, subs. 7, James Earl Ray Knowingly, Intelligently, and Voluntarily Pleaded Guilty to the First Degree Murder of Dr. Martin Luther King, Jr. p. 315, MFF

**dclxxiii** ...... Dr. William F. Pepper, "MLK: an Act of State: The Execution of Martin Luther King" London, January 2003, pp. 20-29

**dclxxiv** ...... MLK Truth LLC, "The 13th Juror - The Official Transcript of the Martin Luther King Assassination Conspiracy Trial" p. 186

**dclxxv** ....... FBI Memo, Washington D.C. Office to the Director of Memphis, Birmingham and Dallas Offices Re: MURKIN, April 9, 1968, HWA

**dclxxvi** ...... Maureen O'Connor, (April 16, 2012), An interview with America's first Neo Nazi Lobbyist, Gawker, gawker.com

**dclxxvii** ..... Public Law 107-56 (USA PATRIOT ACT of 2001) Title I. Section 101, Counter Terrorism Fund, Financial Crimes Enforcement Network, United States Department of the Treasury, October 26, 2001, fincen.gov

**dclxxviii** .... Rachel Maddow Show, December 2009

**dclxxix** ...... Matt K. Lewis, (July 29, 2011), GO Proud and Birchers ousted as CPAC co-sponsors (David Horowitz survives vote), The Daily Caller, thedailycaller.com

**dclxxx** ....... Charles J. Ogletree, "All Deliberate Speed: Reflections on the First Half Century of Brown V. Board of Education", W.W. Norton & Company, 2004, p. 184

**dclxxxi** ...... W. Pepper, "MLK: an Act of State" pp. 289-99

**dclxxxii** ..... HSCA Report, Sec. II, Pt. D, subs. 2, Memphis Police Department, pp. 417, 418

**dclxxxiii** .... Ibid, p. 418

**dclxxxiv** .... Ibid, p. 426

**dclxxxv** ..... MLK Truth LLC, "The 13th Juror", pp. 109,110,144

**dclxxxvi** .... Madison Grey, (Monday March 31, 2008), Martin Luther King: An Assassination Remembered - The Witnesses, Time Magazine, time.com

**dclxxxvii** ... FBI Case File, Re: UNSUB Eric Starvo Galt, Harvey Lowmeyer, John Williard, Victim: Martin Luther King Jr., April 17, 1968, p.49

**dclxxxviii** .. W. Pepper, "MLK: an Act of State", p. 76

**dclxxxix** .... Dr. William F. Pepper, "Orders to Kill", Carrol and Graf, 1996, p. 464

**dcxc** ..........HSCA Report, Sec. II, Pt. E, Department of Justice, and the FBI, p. 432

**dcxci** .........Justice Department Memo, Review of FBI files on King Murder, Assistant Attorney General J. Stanley Pottinger to Robert A. Murphy, March 31, 1975

**dcxcii** ........Senate Select Comm., Bk. 3, Pt. D, Disseminating Derogatory Information to Family, Friends, and Associates p. 50

**dcxciii** .......HSCA Report, Sec. II, Pt. D, subs. 1, the FBI p. 409

**dcxciv** ........Senate Select Comm., Vol. 6: FBI, Memo to the Special Agent in Charge (SAC) of the Atlanta FBI office from Director Hoover Exhibit 14, p. 378

**dcxcv** .........A. Summers, "Official and Confidential...", pp. 423, 424

**dcxcvi** ........HSCA Report., Sec. II, Pt. E, Electronic Surveillance of Dr. King, p. 436-37

**dcxcvii** .......Marc Perrusquia, (December 19,2010), Memphis FBI agent led cadre of informants that included Ernest Withers, the Commercial Appeal, commercialappeal.com

**dcxcviii** .....HSCA Report., Sec. II, Pt. E, Manipulation of the Media, p. 437

**dcxcix** ........HSCA Report, Sec. II, Pt. D, subs. 1, the FBI, p. 408

**dcc** .............Senate Select Comm., Bk. 3, Supplementary Staff Report on Intelligence Activities and the Rights of Americans, pp. 4-12

**dcci** ...........HSCA Report., Sec. II, Findings, the Road to Memphis, p. 280

**dccii** ..........FBI Central Headquarters File, King Assassination, Section 7, Memphis Office to Director, Summary of Investigation, April 13, 1968, pp. 4-5

**dcciii** .........HSCA Report, Sec. II, Findings, p. 281

**dcciv** ..........Justice Department Memo, Review of FBI files on King Murder

**dccv** ...........HSCA Report, Sec. II, Pt. A, James Earl Ray fired one shot at Dr. Martin Luther King, the shot that killed Dr. King, subs. 1, p. 292

**dccvi** ..........M. Gray, The Witnesses

**dccvii**..........M. Gray, The Witnesses

**dccviii** .......HSCA Report, Sec. II, Pt. A, p. 292

**dccix** ..........HSCA Report, Sec. II, Pt. D, Memphis Police Department, p. 425

**dccx** ...........MLK Truth LLC, "The 13th Juror", p. 210

**dccxi** ..........HSCA Report, Sec. II, Pt. A, subs. 3b, p. 295

dccxii ........ HSCA Report, Sec. II, Pt. C, Conspiracy Allegations: Memphis, p. 383

dccxiii ....... FBI Central Headquarters File, Sec 2, To Special Agent in Charge Indianapolis, St. Louis, From: Director FBI, Anonymous Caller, April 9, 1968

dccxiv ....... HSCA Report, Sec. II, Pt. A, subs. 1, Dr. King was killed by one shot fired in front of him, p. 289

dccxv ........ HSCA Report, Sec. II, Part A, subs. 1, pp. 289, 290

dccxvi ....... FBI Central Headquarters File, Sec. 2, Latent Print Examination, April 8, 1968

dccxvii ...... Ibid, SAC Memphis to SAC New Orleans, MURKIN, April 7, 1968

dccxviii ..... Ibid, Director to SAC New Orleans, April 7, 1968

dccxix ....... Ibid, Director to SAC Memphis, April 7, 1968, pp. 1-2

dccxx ........ Ibid, Teletype to Director to SAC Memphis, Ballistics Evidence Report, April 5, 1968

dccxxi ....... Ibid

dccxxii ...... Ibid, Director to SAC Memphis, Unsub, April 5, 1968, pp. 1-2

dccxxiii ..... HSCA Report, Sec. II, Pt. A, subs. 3b, pp. 295, 296

dccxxiv ..... Ibid, p. 293

dccxxv ...... MLK Truth LLC, "The 13th Juror", p. 227

dccxxvi ..... "The 13th Juror", pp. 731,732

dccxxvii .... "The 13th Juror", p. 192

dccxxviii ... James Earl Ray Dead at 70, (February 11, 2009), CBC News, cbs.com

dccxxix ..... Ibid

dccxxx ...... Anthony Summers, "Official and Confidential"

dccxxxi ...... United States Department of Justice, Civil Rights Division, Report on the Assassination of Martin Luther King, Criminal Section, Footnotes, justice.gov

dccxxxii .... P. Melanson, "The Murkin Conspiracy", pp. 93-97

dccxxxiii ... HSCA Report, Sec. II, Part A, subs. 2, p. 291

dccxxxiv ... M. Gray, The Witnesses

dccxxxv .... "The 13th Juror", p. 357

dccxxxvi ... Will Lyman, "The Pilgrimage of Jesse Jackson", April 30, 1996

**dccxxxvii** ...Ralph David Abernathy, "And The Walls Came Tumbling Down", Harper & Row Publishers Inc, 1989, p. 440

**dccxxxviii** .W. Lyman, "The Pilgrimage of Jessie Jackson"

**dccxxxix** ...."The Assassination of Martin Luther King Jr., Jesse Jackson Aftermath of the King Assassination", the History Channel, 2012, history.com

**dccxl** .........M. Gray, The Witnesses

**dccxli** ........Geoff Metcalf interviews author Ken Timmerman, (March 31, 2002), Unmasking Jesse Jackson, wnd.com

**dccxlii** .......Joyce Purnick, (April 18th, 1988), Koch Says Jackson Lied About Actions After Dr. King Was Slain, New York Times, nytimes.com

**dccxliii** ......Ibid

**dccxliv** .......W. Lyman, "The Pilgrimage of Jessie Jackson"

**dccxlv** ........Amy Goodman, (January 15, 2007 ), Reverend Jesse Jackson on Witnessing the Assassination of Dr. King, democracynow.org

**dccxlvi** .......W. Lyman, "The Pilgrimage of Jessie Jackson"

**dccxlvii** .....G. Metcalfe interviews K. Timmerman, Unmasking Jesse Jackson

**dccxlviii** ....J. Purnick, Koch Says Jackson Lied About Actions After Dr. King Was Slain

**dccxlix** .......W. Lyman, "The Pilgrimage of Jessie Jackson"

**dccl** ...........J. Purnick, Koch Says Jackson Lied About Actions After Dr. King Was Slain

**dccli** ..........Larry J. Sabato's, "Feeding Frenzy", (July 1998), washingtonpost.com

**dcclii** .........Ibid

**dccliii** ........W. Lyman, "The Pilgrimage of Jessie Jackson"

**dccliv** .........Ibid

**dcclv** ..........Mark Mardell (September 28, 2011), Jesse Jackson's love for often derided Lyndon Johnson, BBC News, bbc.co.uk

**dcclvi** ........."American Experience- Citizen King" program and transcript, PBS, pbs.org

## RFK

**dcclvii** .......Federal Bureau of Investigation, Robert F. Kennedy Assassination Summary Files (Codenamed: KENSALT), part A, Report of the Special Counsel to the Los Angeles County District Attorney's Office, p. 7

dcclviii ...... William Klaber and Philip H. Melanson, "Shadow Play", St. Martin's Press, 1997, p. 159

dcclix ........ FBI, RFK Assassination Summary Files, part A, Report of the Special Counsel to the Los Angeles County District Attorney's Office, Evidence Presented at Trial, p. 11

dcclx ......... Federal Bureau of Investigation, Memo to SAC New York, SAC Los Angeles, Subject: KENSALT, Investigation of Organization of Arab Students, July 3, 1968

dcclxi ........ Jerry Cohen, (June 6, 1968), Suspect's Hate for Israel Told p. I-19, latimes.com

dcclxii ....... W. Klaber and P. Melanson, "Shadow Play", p. 68

dcclxiii ...... FBI, Office of the Los Angeles District Attorney News Release, Weekly Summary of the Sirhan Sirhan trial no. 40, March 12, 1969, p. 16

dcclxiv ...... Myrna Oliver, (May 9, 1990), Grant B. Cooper, 87; Defended Sirhan Sirhan, Los Angeles Times, latimes.com

dcclxv ....... W. Klaber and P. Melanson, "Shadow Play", p. 166

dcclxvi ...... FBI, L.A. D.A. News Release, Weekly Summary of S. Sirhan trial 44

dcclxvii ..... FBI, Wk. Summary 44

dcclxviii .... FBI, Wk. Summary 40

dcclxix ....... FBI, Wk. Summary 39

dcclxx ....... FBI, Court Appearance of Sirhan Bishara Sirhan, Re: Corona Police Department Shooting Range, June 1, 1968

dcclxxi ...... FBI, Airtel message to Director, SAC Los Angeles, Sub: KENSALT, Grant Cooper and L.A. District Attorney Office, December 24, 1968

dcclxxii ..... Shane O' Sullivan, "Who Killed Bobby? The Unsolved Murder of Robert F. Kennedy", Union Square Press, 2008, pp. 376-79

dcclxxiii .... S. O' Sullivan, "Who Killed Bobby?", p. 205

dcclxxiv .... Associated Press, "Los Angeles Judge To Preside at Trial", the Southeast Missourian, September 18, 1968, p. 2

dcclxxv ..... A.P., "Tough, Veteran Judge Assigned Sirhan Trail", Kentucky New Era, September 21, 1968, p. 14

dcclxxvi .... A.P., (December 3, 1968), "Five Convicted for Cheating", The Toledo Blade, p. 24

dcclxxvii ... United States District Court for the Central District Court for the Central District of California, Sirhan Bishara Sirhan v. George Galaza, Warden, et al, CV-00- 5868-CAS (AJW) Petitioner's

Objections to Magistrate Judge's Proposed Report and Recommendation; Memorandum of points and Authorities, submitted by Attorneys for the Petitioner William F. Pepper and Laurie D. Dusek, March 28, 2013.

**dcclxxviii** ..Adrian Finighan, "RFK Assassination Looking back 40 years later", CNN International, April 16, 2008

**dcclxxix** .....Ibid

**dcclxxx** ......HSCA Report., Sec. I, Pt. C, subs. 4, James R. Hoffa, p. 176

**dcclxxxi** .....Michael Newton, "The Encyclopedia of Unsolved Crimes" Second Edition, InfoBase Publishing, 2010, p. 204

**dcclxxxii** ....J. Shesol, "Mutual Contempt...", p.10

**dcclxxxiii** ..J. Shesol, "Mutual Contempt...", p. 37

**dcclxxxiv** ...Cynthia R. Fagen, (February 5, 2012), JFK's teen mistress addresses relationship in memoir, New York Post, nypost.com

**dcclxxxv** ....United States Department of Justice Memorandum, FBI Security Investigation of Walter Jenkins, October 22, 1964, HWA

**dcclxxxvi** ...U.S. News Staff, (July 2, 2009), Historic Whispers: Kennedy Chooses Johnson as Presidential Running Mate, US News, usnews.com

**dcclxxxvii** .J. Shesol, "Mutual Contempt..." p. 52

**dcclxxxviii** ...David M. Oshinsky, (October 26, 1997), Fear and Loathing in the White House: Why couldn't L.B.J. and Bobby Kennedy just get along?, nytimes.com

**dcclxxxix** ...Ibid

**dccxc** .........Thurston Clarke, Henry Holt and Company, "The Last Good Campaign: Robert F. Kennedy and 82 Days That Inspired America", May 27, 2008, p. 3, 4

**dccxci** ........FBI, portion of the Washington Merry Go Round "Who's Telling the Truth on RFK Feud?" by Drew Pearson and Jack Anderson, the Washington Times Herald, Section C, February 15, 1968, p. 15

**dccxcii** .......Ibid

**dccxciii** ......Ibid

**dccxciv** ......Patrick Jasperse, "Documents trace smear of Kennedy aide to FBI", the Milwaukee Journal, February 17, 1991, Page A-4

**dccxcv** .......D. Oshinsky, (October 26, 1997), "Fear and Loathing in the White House...", nytimes.com

**dccxcvi** ......FBI, Airtel message to SAC L.A., Director, Sub: KENSALT, Denial of reexamination of firearms evidence, January 16, 1969 dccxcvii ....FBI, Letter to D.A. Evelle J. Younger, SAC Wesley G. Grapp, statement to aid in LAPD Investigation, June 7, 1968

dccxcviii ...FBI, Memo to SAC Los Angeles, S.A. (name withheld), Sub: KENSALT, Re: Autopsy Photos of Robert F. Kennedy, June 7, 1968

dccxcix .....Ibid

dccc ...........FBI, Airtel message Director, FBI, SAC Los Angeles, FBI, Re: KENSALT, Re: Stus Pruzinsky

dccci .........A. Jones, S. Pickering, M. Thomson, "Dictionary of Quotations", Chambers Publishing, Anonymous FBI Agent, p. 25

dcccii ........T. Clark, H. Holt and Company, "The Last Good Campaign...", p. 25

dccciii .......John H. Davis, "The Kennedys: Dynasty and Disaster", SP Books, 1993, pp. 375-77

dccciv .......Ibid

dcccv .........FBI, U.S. Department of Justice, Communications Section, Tele type marked URGENT, Special Agent in Charge of San Francisco Office, August 6, 1962

dcccvi .......FBI, Visit of the Attorney General to Seattle and the Northwest memo, August 7, 1962

dcccvii ......FBI, L.A. File, RFK Associated Documents, Vol. 14-15, US Gov. memo To: Mr. De Loach, From: T.E. Bishop, S. 917; Omnibus Crime Control and Safe Streets Act of 1967, November 22, 1967

dcccviii .....FBI, M. A. Jones, Appearance of the Attorney General on the Tennessee Ernie Ford Show WMAL-TV, American Broadcasting Company Network, 11 a.m., August 17, 1962

dcccix .......FBI, Regarding Attorney General Robert F. Kennedy, Visit to Houston, Texas", February 6, 1963

dcccx .........FBI, Memo to Mr. De Loach, R.E. Wick Congressman Louis C. Wyman Republican– New Hampshire, January 19, 1967

dcccxi .......FBI, Re: Bureau letter to Chicago dated November 7th, 1967

dcccxii ......FBI, Memo to SAC L.A., Sup. William John Nolan, Sub: Robert F. Kennedy, June 5, 1968

dcccxiii .....FBI, Memo to SAC Los Angeles, ASAC Richard D. Rogge, Sub: UNSUB, aka Robert Gene Gendroz, Attempted Assassination of Senator Robert. F. Kennedy, L.A. California, June 5, 1968

dcccxiv .....FBI, Memo to SAC of L.A., SA (name omitted), Sub: KENSALT, Leads, June 8, 1968 dcccxv .......FBI, Unnamed Complainant (Assassination of Robert F. Kennedy), 08:12 a.m., June 5, 1968

dcccxvi ......FBI, Memo to SAC L.A., Supervisor (name omitted), Sub: KENSALT, Unnamed Informant 2:15 pm, June 5, 1968

dcccxvii .....FBI, KENSALT, Charlie Hostetter, Alhambra, California, 9:23 a.m., June 6, 1968

dcccxviii ....FBI, Memo to SAC L.A., Supervisor (name omitted), Sub: KENSALT, Unnamed Informant 2:15 pm, June 5, 1968

dcccxix ......FBI, Memo to FBI Director, Sub: KENSALT, Wisconsin State Reformatory, Unnamed inmate, June 7, 1968

dcccxx .......FBI, Dept. of Justice, Unknown Subject; aka John, Threat against Presidential Candidate, Houston, Texas, June 6, 1968

dcccxxi ......FBI, Memo to SAC L.A., S.A. (name withheld), Sub: KENSALT, statement of unnamed female informant, June 13, 1968

dcccxxii .....FBI, Additional Information Concerning Khaibar Khan, Formerly known as Khaibar Goodarzian, and family, (nd) or location included

dcccxxiii ....FBI, SAC L.A., S.A. Amedee O. Richards, Jr., Sub: KENSALT, statement of Ethel Crehan, July 8, 1968

dcccxxiv ....State Release of Files Shows RFK Evidence Destroyed (April 19, 1988), Los Angeles Times, latimes.com

dcccxxv .....FBI, L.A. District Attorney Robert F. Kennedy Assassination Summary files, Hearings before Judge Wenke, Wolfer Examination, September 1975, pp. 45, 46

dcccxxvi ....FBI, RFK Assassination Summary files Pt. B, Cross Examination of Wolfer, pp. 22-24

dcccxxvii ...Bill Kurtis, "Investigative Reports: The Robert Kennedy Assassination", A&E Network in assoc w/ Channel 4, Exposed Films, 1982

dcccxxviii ..State Release of Files Shows RFK Evidence Destroyed

dcccxxix ....Andrea Ford, (April 4, 1992), Investigation Urged in LAPD's Handling of Kennedy Slaying: Assassination: Former aide and retired law enforcement officials call for a grand jury probe, saying police deliberately suppressed evidence and coerced witnesses, L.A. Times, latimes.com

dcccxxx .....Shane O' Sullivan, "RFK Must Die", Dokument Films, November 20, 2007

dcccxxxi ....A. Ford, Investigation Urged in LAPD's Handling of Kennedy Slaying

**dcccxxxii** .. FBI, RFK Assassination Summary files Pt. A, Wolfer Examination, Sept. 1975, pp. 51, 52

**dcccxxxiii** . Ibid

**dcccxxxiv** . FBI, RFK Assassination Summary files Pt. A, Subpoena Ducus Tecum- Items Produced Wolfer's Daily Log, p. 52-53

**dcccxxxv** ... FBI, RFK Assassination Summary files Pt. A, Wolfer Examination, pp. 51, 52

**dcccxxxvi** . FBI, RFK Assassination Summary files Pt. A, Wolfer's Daily Log, pp. 52, 53

**dcccxxxvii** FBI, RFK Assassination Summary files Pt. A, Wolfer's Lab Progress Report, pp. 53, 54

**dcccxxxviii** FBI, RFK Assassination Summary files Pt. A, Affidavit of William Harper Read into the Record, pp. 33, 34

**dcccxxxix** . Ted Charach and Gerard Alcon, "The Second Gun, Documentary Film, American Films Ltd, October 7, 1973

**dcccxl** ....... FBI, RFK Assassination Summary files Pt. A, 1974 Hearings conducted by Supervisor Baxter Ward, Mac Donell Affidavit, p. 31, 32

**dcccxli** ...... FBI, RFK Assassination Summary files Pt. A, Hearings conducted by Supervisor Baxter Ward, pp. 31-33

**dcccxlii** ..... FBI, RFK Assassination Summary files Pt. B, Trajectory Analysis, p. 57

**dcccxliii** .... FBI, RFK Assassination Summary files Pt. B, Cross Examination of Wolfer, pp. 22-24

**dcccxliv** .... Report of the United States President's Commission on Central Intelligence Agency Activities in the Unites States, Part One (President's Commission on CIA Activities, The Rockefeller Commission), Chapter 3, Findings and Conclusions, June, 1975, Findings and Conclusions

**dcccxlv** ..... Andrew and Leslie Cockburn, "Frontline-Guns, Drugs, and the CIA", Episode 613 (w/transcript), PBS, May 17, 1988

**dcccxlvi** .... Ibid

**dcccxlvii** ... CIA, OK's MK-ULTRA Mind Control Tests, wired.com

**dcccxlviii** .. A. and L. Cockburn, "Frontline-Guns, Drugs, and the CIA", Ep. 613

**dcccxlix** .... Ibid

**dcccl** ......... B. Kurtis, "Investigative Reports: The Robert Kennedy Assassination" dcccli .........A. and L. Cockburn, "Frontline-Guns, Drugs, and the CIA"

dccclii ........Tim Weiner, ( May 7, 1996), William E. Colby, 76, Head of the C.I.A. in a time of Upheaval, nytimes.com

dcccliii .......Ibid

dcccliv .......Ibid

dccclv ........Ibid

dccclvi .......A. and L. Cockburn, "Frontline-Guns, Drugs, and the CIA"

dccclvii ......B. Kurtis, "Investigative Reports: The Robert Kennedy Assassination"

dccclviii .....Inventory of the Los Angeles Police Department records of the Robert F. Kennedy Assassination Investigation, 1968-1978, Online Archive of California, oac.cdlib.org

dccclix .......James Flanigan, (April 18, 1999), Confidence and Innovation build a global firm, latimes.com

dccclx ........Ralph Schoenman, (May 28, 1995), "RFK's assassination: The beat goes on", baltimoresun.com

dccclxi .......Report of Special Prosecutor Thomas F. Kranz, Section 2, Exhibit 69, Polygraph Interview of Sandra Serrano, Tape No. 29255, p.1,8, 10-15, 17-35

dccclxii ......Lockheed's Aviation Genius, Center for the Study of Intelligence, CSI Publications, Books and Monographs, A-12, cia.gov

dccclxiii .....The CIA and the U-2 Program, CSIL, CSI Publications, cia.gov

dccclxiv .....HSCA Exec. Session, Classified testimony of William F. Larson, p. 33

dccclxv ......Angus Mackenzie, "Secrets: The CIA's War at Home", Selected Readings, University of California Press, September 16, 1997, pp. 30, 42-45, 63-65

dccclxvi......Halliburton: $61M Overcharge (December 5, 2007), cbsnews.com

dccclxvii ....FBI, Copy of News Article by the Los Angeles Herald Examiner, Death Threat to Kennedy, June 13, 1968

dccclxviii ...FBI, Memo to SAC Los Angeles, S.A. (name withheld), statement of John H. Ahrndt, June 25, 1968

dccclxix .....FBI, Memo to SAC of L.A., S.A. (name omitted), Sub: Attempted Assassination of Senator Robert F. Kennedy, Ronald Huntley June 5, 1968

dccclxx .......FBI, Expanded statement of Ronald Huntley, Special Agent (name withheld), Hillsboro, Oregon, June 12, 1968

dccclxxi .... FBI, Memo to SAC, S.A.(unidentified), KENSALT, statements and Lead, Hans Korthoff and Margaret Mary Venables, June 11, 1968

dccclxxii ... FBI, Memo to SAC L.A., S.A.(name withheld), Sub: KENSALT, statement of Margret Venables, June 24, 1968

dccclxxiii .. FBI, RFK Assassination Summary, Pt. A, Evidence Presented at Trial p. 4, 8

dccclxxiv .. FBI, Statement of William McCarthy, Special Agent (name withheld), June 19, 1968

dccclxxv ... FBI, Statement of Robert Healey, by Special Agent (name withheld), June 25, 1968

dccclxxvi .. Ibid

dccclxxvii . FBI, Statement of Gerald Robert Amster, S.A. (name withheld), New York, New York, July 9, 1968

dccclxxviii Matthew Smith, "Conspiracy- the Plot to Stop the Kennedy's", Citadel Press, Kensington Publishing Corp, 2005, p. 186

dccclxxix .. FBI, S.A (name withheld), Sub: KENSALT, Statement of David Mark Esquith, June 8, 1968

dccclxxx ... FBI, Airtel Message to SAC Los Angeles, FBI Director , KENSALT, News release of statements by Jesus Perez and Paul Grieco, June 11, 1968

dccclxxxi .. T. Charach and G. Alcon, "The Second Gun"

dccclxxxii . Michael Martinez and Brad Johnson, (March 12, 2012), "Attorney for RFK convicted killer Sirhan push "second gunman" argument, CNN News, cnn.com

dccclxxxiii T. Charach and G. Alcon, "The Second Gun"

dccclxxxiv CIA file, "A Study of Assassination"

dccclxxxv . Petition for Writ of Habeas Corpus filed by Lawrence Teeter, Attorney for Sirhan Sirhan to the Supreme Court of California, Court Criminal No.14026, 6-28-07, Section VII, Due Process Was Violated by the Destruction and Suppression of Evidence That More Than One Gun Was Fired in the Hotel Pantry, Exhibit 88, Affidavit of Evan Freed, 1992

dccclxxxvi M. Martinez and B. Johnson, "Attorney for RFK convicted killer Sirhan push 'second gunman' argument"

dccclxxxvii Robert Beemer and Matt Liston, "Conspiracy Test: the RFK Assassination", the Discovery Channel, June 6, 2007

dccclxxxviii M Martinez and B. Johnson, "Attorney for RFK convicted killer Sirhan push 'second gunman' argument"

dccclxxxix .FBI, RFK Assassination Summary files, Pt. A, Report of the Special
Counsel to the L.A. County D.A 's Office, p. 7

dcccxc .......Files of the United States President's Commission on Central
Intelligence Agency Activities in the Unites States (Rockefeller
Commission Files), Report of the Medico-Legal Investigation of
Senator Robert F. Kennedy, Final Summary, pp. 1-4

dcccxci ......CIA file, "A Study of Assassination"

dcccxcii .....Cecilia Rasmussen, (October 2, 2005), A Pioneering Public Hospital
Checks Out, Los Angeles Times, latimes.com

dcccxciii ....Ibid

dcccxciv ....FBI, Copy of news article, "Bradley Demands Council Probe of
Receiving Hospital" by Nick B Williams, Los Angeles Times,
KENSALT, June 14, 1968, p. I-3

dcccxcv .....S. O' Sullivan, "Who Killed Bobby? The Unsolved Murder of Robert
F. Kennedy", p. 205

dcccxcvi ....M. Smith, "Conspiracy- the Plot to Stop the Kennedy's", p.186

dcccxcvii ...W. Klaber and P. Melanson, "Shadow Play", p. 119

dcccxcviii ..T. Charach and G. Alcon, "The Second Gun"

dcccxcix ....John Marshall, (12:30 a.m., June 5, 1968), "Interview of Thane
Cesar", KFWB, Los Angeles, California

cm .............FBI, RFK Assassination Summary files, Pt. B, Second Section,
Conspiracy Theories, Interviews and Investigation, Thane Eugene
Cesar, Don Schulman, Ted Charach, p.6

cmi ............T. Charach and G. Alcon, "The Second Gun"

cmii ...........Ibid

cmiii ..........FBI, RFK Assassination Summary files, Pt. B, T. Cesar, D. Schulman,
T. Charach, p. 6

cmiv ..........R. Beemer and M. Liston, "Conspiracy Test: the RFK Assassination"

cmv ...........The Truth About Lie Detectors aka Polygraph Tests, (August 5,
2004), The American Psychological Association, apa.org

cmvi ..........National Research Council, The Polygraph and Lie Detection,
Washington, DC: The National Academies Press, 2003, pp. 13-16, 18-
19, 21, 30, 32, 35, 47-48, 51, 56- 58, 67-69, 70, 72, 82, 85, 86-91, 118

cmvii .........Ibid, pp. 120, 123, 132, 133, 212, 218

cmviii ........FBI, SAC L.A., Memo regarding Ted Charach, September 29, 1970

cmix ..........Ibid

cmx ........... Files of the U.S. Pres. Com. on CIA, Report of the Medico-Legal Investigation of Senator Robert F. Kennedy, Reports of X-Ray studies, p. 24

cmxi .......... FBI file, L.A. D.A. Report, Evidence presented at trial, p. 8

cmxii ......... CIA file, "A Study of Assassination"

cmxiii ........ The Federal Bureau of Investigation, "Robert F. Kennedy Assassination: The FBI FILES", Filiquarian Publishing LLC, December 31, 2007,pp. 42-46

cmxiv ........ Ibid

cmxv ......... FBI, RFK Assassination Summary files, Pt. A, Admission by the L.A.P.D. of Ceiling Panel Destruction, p. 50

cmxvi ........ FBI, "Robert F. Kennedy Assassination: The FBI FILES", p. 44

cmxvii ....... "Robert F. Kennedy Assassination: The FBI FILES", p. 46

cmxviii ...... Ibid

cmxix ........ R. Beemer and M. Liston, "Conspiracy Test: the RFK Assassination"

cmxx ......... FBI, Airtel message to FBI Director, Sub: KENSALT, Request of Manuel Pena, August 1, 1968

cmxxi ........ FBI, County of Los Angeles, 1971 Grand Jury letter of findings to the Los Angeles Board of Supervisors, Findings, August 24, 1971, p. 5

cmxxii ....... FBI, Airtel message to Director, Re: Autopsy Report Senator Robert F Kennedy, September 4, 1968

cmxxiii ...... FBI, Office of the Los Angeles District Attorney News Release, Wk. Summary of S. Sirhan trial 52, June 4, 1969

cmxxiv ...... W. Klaber and P. Melanson, "Shadow Play", pp. 79, 80

cmxxv ....... FBI, Memo from Supervisor (name withheld), Sub: KENSALT, re: Fallah Ben-Jabor, June 6, 1968

cmxxvi ...... FBI, RFK Assassination Summary files, Pt. B, T. Cesar, D. Schulman, T. Charach, p. 5

cmxxvii ..... FBI, RFK Assassination Summary files, Pt. B, T. Cesar, D. Schulman, T. Charach, p. 6

cmxxviii .... T. Charach and G. Alcon, "The Second Gun"

cmxxix ...... Ibid

cmxxx ....... Ibid

cmxxxi ...... Report of Special Prosecutor T.F. Kranz, Sec. 2, Exhibit 4, Selected Corrections of the Report by Special Counsel (Allard K. Lowenstein and Gregory F. Stone), Subsection II, Eyewitness Accounts, number 16, p.6

cmxxxii .....B. Kurtis, "Investigative Reports: The Robert Kennedy Assassination"

cmxxxiii ....T. Charach and G. Alcon, "The Second Gun"

cmxxxiv ....Los Angeles Grand Jury Exhibits Request, Section 4, "selected Corrections of the Report by Special Counsel" (Allard K. Lowenstien and Gregory F. Stone), Part II. Eyewitness Accounts, p.6

cmxxxv .....T. Charach and G. Alcon, "The Second Gun"

cmxxxvi ....Petition for Writ of Habeas Corpus, L. Teeter, Sec. VII, Exhibit 88, affidavit of Evan Freed, p. 128

cmxxxvii ...FBI file, LAFO, Sub H, Volume 1, Boris Yaro article in LA Times, June 6, 1968

cmxxxviii ..People of the State of California vs Sirhan Bishara Sirhan, Volume XI., Direct Examination of Vincent DiPierro, Supreme Court of the State of California, p. 3216

cmxxxix ....B. Kurtis, "Investigative Reports: The Robert Kennedy Assassination"

cmxl ..........L.A. Grand Jury Exhibits Request

cmxli .........Michael Martinez and Brad Johnson (April 28, 2012), RFK assassination witness tells CNN: There was a second shooter, CNN News, cnn.com

cmxlii ........Brad Johnson and Michael Martinez (July 9, 2012), RFK assassination witness willing to testify for Sirhan Sirhan lawyers, CNN News, cnn.com

cmxliii .......Ibid

cmxliv .......A. Finighan, "RFK Assassination Looking back 40 years later"

cmxlv ........B. Johnson and M. Martinez, RFK assassination witness willing to testify for Sirhan Sirhan lawyers

cmxlvi .......M. Martinez and B. Johnson, RFK assassination witness tells CNN: There was a second shooter

cmxlvii ......M. Newton, "The Encyclopedia of Unsolved Crimes", p. 205

cmxlviii .....D. Kaiser, "The Road to Dallas: The Assassination of John F. Kennedy", p. 54

cmxlix .......Report of the Pres. Com. on CIA Activities, Pt. B, Summary of the Investigation, Chap. 3, Summary of Findings, Conclusions, and Recommendations, p. 10

cml ............ Report of the Pres. Com. on CIA Activities, Pt. B, Chap. 3, pp. 12, 13

cmli ........... Report of the Pres. Com. on CIA Activities, Pt. B, Chap. 3, p. 14

cmlii .......... Ibid

cmliii ......... Senate Select Comm., Bk. I, Pt. III, The Constitutional Framework for Intelligence Activates, p. 38

cmliv ......... Senate Select Comm., Bk. I, Pt. III, pp. 150, 151

cmlv .......... Senate Select Comm., Bk. I, Pt. VIII. Covert Action, the Impact of covert action, p. 155

cmlvi ......... Instances of Use of United States Armed Forces Abroad 1798-2004, Richard F. Grimmett, Specialist in National Defense, Foreign Affairs, Defense and Trade Division, Washington DC, Congressional Research Service, Library of Congress, October 5, 2004, au.af.mil

cmlvii ........ John Yoo, "The Continuation of Politics by Other Means: The Original Understanding of War Powers", California Law Review, 1996, p. 177

cmlviii ....... A. MacKenzie, "Secrets: The CIA's War at Home", p. 168

cmlix ......... Senate Select Comm., Bk. I, Pt. III, p. 36

cmlx .......... Ian S. Livingston and Michael O'Hanlon, (August 22, 2012), Afghanistan Index also including selected data on Pakistan, Brookings Institute, brookings.edu

cmlxi ......... Phil Stewart, (February 14, 2013), Key U.S. General backs keeping Afghan forces at peak strength, Reuters, rueters.com

cmlxii ........ U.S. Secret Service received 64 complaints of misconduct, (May 23, 2012), BBC News, bbc.co.uk

cmlxiii ....... Public Law 107-56 (USA PATRIOT ACT of 2001), Title I, Sec. 104, Requests for Military Assistance to Enforce Prohibition in Certain Emergencies

cmlxiv ....... The Constitution of the United States of America (and selected writings of the Founding Fathers), Barnes and Noble Inc, New York, 2012, Appendix: Amendments to the Constitution of the United States of America, Amendment I, p. 816

cmlxv ........ Ibid.

cmlxvi ....... Amendment VI, the Constitution of the United States of America, pp. 816, 817

cmlxvii ...... Dan Eggen, (Friday, September 7, 2007), Judge Invalidates Patriot Act Provisions, Washington Post, washingtonpost.com

**cmlxviii** .....Report of the Pres. Com on CIA Activities, Part 1: Summary of the Investigation, Chapter 1: the Fundamental Issues, part B, p. 4, 5

**cmlxix** .......Obama's Kill List: Silence is not an option (June 6, 2012), The Nation Magazine, thenation.com

**cmlxx** ........Public Law 107-56 (USA PATRIOT ACT of 2001), Title I, Sec. 106 Presidential Authority, USA Patriot Act

**cmlxxi** .......Kevin Johnson and Richard Wolf, (December 16, 2013), Federal judge rules against NSA spying, USA Today, usatoday.com

**cmlxxii** ......Ewen MacAskill, (August 22, 2013), NSA paid millions to cover Prism compliance costs for tech companies, The Guardian, theguardian.com

63195218R00198

Made in the USA
Columbia, SC
09 July 2019